T0328423

Markets in history

Markets in history

Economic studies of the past

Edited by

DAVID W. GALENSON
University of Chicago

CAMBRIDGE
UNIVERSITY PRESS

CAMBRIDGE UNIVERSITY PRESS
Cambridge, New York, Melbourne, Madrid, Cape Town, Singapore, São Paulo, Delhi

Cambridge University Press
The Edinburgh Building, Cambridge CB2 8RU, UK

Published in the United States of America by Cambridge University Press, New York

www.cambridge.org
Information on this title: www.cambridge.org/9780521359870

First published 1989
Reprinted 1993, 1994
Re-issued in this digitally printed version 2009

A catalogue record for this publication is available from the British Library

ISBN 978-0-521-35200-0 hardback
ISBN 978-0-521-35987-0 paperback

Contents

Preface   *page* vii

Introduction   The economics of historical economics   1
Theodore W. Schultz

**1   The open fields of England: rent, risk, and the rate
of interest, 1300–1815**   5
Donald N. McCloskey

**2   Labor market behavior in colonial America: servitude,
slavery, and free labor**   52
David W. Galenson

**3   Productivity in American whaling: the New Bedford
fleet in the nineteenth century**   97
Lance E. Davis, Robert E. Gallman, and
Teresa D. Hutchins

**4   Households on the American frontier: the distribution
of income and wealth in Utah, 1850–1900**   148
Clayne L. Pope

**5   Businessmen, the raj, and the pattern of government
expenditures: the British Empire, 1860–1912**   190
Lance E. Davis and Robert A. Huttenback

**6   The impact of the economy and the state on the economic
status of blacks: a study of South Carolina**   231
Richard J. Butler, James J. Heckman, and Brook Payner

Contributors   347
Index   349

Preface

This volume originated in a conference session held in New Orleans in December 1986 under the joint sponsorship of the American Economic Association and the Econometric Society. The title of the session was "In Search of Historical Economies: Market Behavior in Past Times." Its purpose was to acquaint economists with the results of recent research in some important areas of economic history. Favorable reactions to that session led to the decision to present its papers in published form. This book consists of those papers, with two additional studies and a shorter contribution by Theodore Schultz, who acted as a discussant at the session.

This volume is in no way intended as a survey of research in economic history, or even as a comprehensive survey of recent research in the field. Rather it is a collection of studies of selected topics in economic history. Yet the contributors believe that these studies share a number of features that are characteristic of research in economic history and that there may consequently be gains from presenting them as a collection.

Each of the studies in this volume summarizes a major research project that has treated a problem central to economics as well as to economic history. The authors were invited to present a critical discussion of the state of research on the subject, including a summary of their own contribution, and to suggest the likely direction of future research on the topic. Although each essay contains some new results that have not been previously published, these essays are not intended to substitute for more detailed presentation of research in scholarly journals and monographs. It was intended, rather, that the essays in this volume could be read by a general audience of economists who might not normally read specialized publications in economic history, and that these readers could not only learn what is currently known about the subjects covered but also derive some sense of the procedures and evidence from which these conclusions were drawn.

Donald McCloskey's paper takes up a question that has long puzzled historians: why most English farmers from medieval times through the eighteenth century held their land in a series of small plots scattered around their villages rather than in a single, consolidated holding. He demonstrates that the answer lies in the economics of risk, and shows that by scattering their plots the farmers were in effect buying insurance. The cost of the insurance was the reduction in expected output that resulted from the inefficiency of working a dozen or more small plots instead of one large field. Its benefit, obtained through spatial diversification of landholdings, was a substantial reduction in the probability that the farmer's output would fall below a level that would sustain him and his family. The widespread use of scattered plots was therefore an early example of households accepting a reduction in expected income in return for a reduction in the variance of that income over time, a result that has been extensively analyzed by economists interested in the theory of portfolio choice. McCloskey further argues that the disappearance of scattering was also an understandable economic response to a series of technological innovations and market improvements that reduced both the riskiness of farming and the cost of alternative forms of insurance. McCloskey's work demonstrates clearly that it was not any irrational attitudes or inexplicable desires of farmers that hampered economic growth in the Middle Ages, but rather the constraints imposed by technology on an agricultural economy whose population was not far above subsistence levels of consumption.

My own paper examines two transatlantic trades in bound labor – for indentured servants and slaves – that were key determinants of labor supply to the economy of colonial America. Recent quantitative investigations have revealed that both of these trades operated with an efficiency that had not previously been appreciated. British indentured servants willing to travel to the West Indies received higher implicit wages than those migrants alike in other respects who traveled to the North American mainland. This premium was a compensating differential for the willingness to serve in the West Indies, where the mortality regime was more severe, the work more rigorous, and the economic prospects for former servants less attractive than on the mainland. The servants' bargains furthermore demonstrate the existence of upward-sloping age–earnings profiles, with steeper profiles for skilled than for unskilled workers, just as economists have found for labor markets in more recent periods. The infamous transatlantic slave trade has long been characterized by abolitionists and historians as not only immoral but economically inefficient. Recent studies have done nothing to lessen the force of the moral indictment, but they have revealed reasoned actions by slave traders aimed at economic efficiency. These studies show, for example, that the selection of slaves in Africa by age and gender responded to both current conditions in American slave markets and changing costs of transatlantic shipping. The research on these transatlantic trades has considerable implications for our understanding of the economic accomplishments of colonial America, for it indicates that the colonial economy benefited from access to highly competitive markets for both European and African labor.

Lance Davis, Robert Gallman, and Teresa Hutchins investigate the determinants of changes in the productivity of whaling voyages over the course of the nineteenth century, using detailed accounts of the individual ventures that sailed from New Bedford, Massachusetts, between 1820 and 1896. They find that technological variables, including changes in the size and design of whaling vessels, had a substantial impact over time on the success of voyages, and that these changes were introduced and employed efficiently by the agents who sent out the voyages, in response to changing conditions in their economic environment. Interestingly, however, Davis, Gallman, and Hutchins find that the most important forces leading to productivity changes in whaling were unrelated to technology. A deterioration over time in the quality of crews, brought about by increasing competition for labor from other industries and perhaps also by the unattractiveness of the increasing length of whaling voyages, was a major factor reducing productivity. Another important influence on productivity was a series of shifts over time in the geographic locus of whaling voyages, from the Atlantic Ocean early in the century, to increasing concentration on the Indian and Pacific oceans in the century's middle decades, and to some activity in the western Arctic after the mid-century. Overall, the authors find the nineteenth-century whaling trade to have been a highly competitive industry operated by economic agents who responded quickly and effectively both to changes in the demand for their products and to changes in the conditions that affected their ability to catch whales.

Clayne Pope's essay explores the changing distribution of income and wealth in Utah during the second half of the nineteenth century. First settled during the 1840s, Utah had very egalitarian distributions of income and wealth in 1850, but the distributions of both variables appear to have become increasingly unequal during the following five decades. To determine why frontier Utah did not long remain a land of equality, Pope uses an extraordinarily rich micro-level data set, constructed by linking manuscript federal census returns to church records and genealogies, to analyze the correlates of income and wealth over this period. He finds that although high rates of occupational and geographic mobility acted as forces tending to lessen the inequality of the income and wealth distributions in early Utah, a number of other factors became established as forces contributing to inequality, and the latter gained in power over time. Among these were increasing investments in human capital (occupational training as well as formal education), a rising importance of foreign-born immigrants who out-performed native-born Americans economically, and increasing econo-mic rewards for migrants' early arrival in Utah as population growth disproportionately increased the locational rents of the land chosen by early settlers as well as raising the value of the experience these settlers had gained in the local economy. Pope also finds that even on this newly settled frontier, where the economic influences of family connec-tions might have been expected to be minimal, family background remained a powerful force underlying the trend toward greater in-equality of economic rewards. Pope concludes that although Utah's experience of the nineteenth century supports the view of many histo-rians of the frontier as a place of considerable economic opportunity, it contravenes the belief that newly settled regions long continued to be places of economic equality.

Lance Davis and Robert Huttenback's essay treats a series of basic questions about the political economy of late-nineteenth-century Brit-ish imperialism. One of these, long debated by politicians as well as historians and economists, concerns the profitability of investments in the empire. Davis and Huttenback find that the returns of British firms that operated in the empire tended to be higher than those of British firms active either within England or in foreign countries between 1860 and 1880, but that from the early 1880s through 1912 this advantage disappeared. They suggest that the higher profitability of imperial investments prior to 1880 may have been the rewards to monopolies gained by early entrants into imperial markets, and that the subse-quent decline might have been the result of the elimination of these monopolies as new entrants into these markets competed for the de-monstrated profit opportunities. Davis and Huttenback then go on to examine the nature of the rent seeking that occurred within the empire. Tracing the channels through which political decisions are influenced to benefit private economic and financial interests is always difficult, for those involved normally wish to obscure their roles from public view. The obstacles to drawing connections between public expenditures and private gains within the British empire prove no exception to this rule, and Davis and Huttenback liken their situation to that of a prosecutor in a murder case who lacks the evidence conclusively to connect a suspect with the crime. Their indirect evi-dence is suggestive, however, and they conclude with a cautious but provocative finding, that both British and local businessmen might have benefited significantly from the government expenditures that were made within British colonies during the late nineteenth century.

Richard Butler, James Heckman, and Brook Payner consider a topic that is central to our understanding of the effectiveness of government action in reducing racial discrimination in labor markets. They critically examine a series of hypotheses that have been advanced to explain the dramatic increase that occurred in the employment of blacks in South Carolina's textile industry during the 1960s. Some scholars have attributed the economic progress of southern blacks during the 1960s to government intervention in labor markets following the passage of the Civil Rights Act of 1964. Others have denied the primary importance of the government's action, and suggested a number of alternative explanations. Some have argued instead that black gains in manufacturing were the result of increases in the productivity of black workers that stemmed from improvements in education; some have attributed the increase in black industrial employment to a decline in southern agriculture that increased the supply of black labor to manufacturing enterprises; and some have argued that the growth of black industrial employment during the 1960s resulted from a general increase in the demand for labor in southern markets. Based on the analysis of detailed evidence on employment and wages in southern labor markets, Butler, Heckman, and Payner conclude that the gains of southern blacks in manufacturing during the 1960s were due neither to the decline of agriculture nor to improvements in the quality and quantity of southern black education. They furthermore argue that the hypothesis of a general increase in the demand for labor cannot fully account for the southern black employment gains of the 1960s, and conclude that these gains were in large measure the result of the insistence of the federal government on equal employment opportunities for blacks.

Although the essays presented here obviously do not cover all the major areas of research in economic history, they do represent a number of the concerns that have been central to the field during the past several decades, and their conclusions hold lessons for economists at a number of levels. These go beyond their many detailed examinations of the behavior of groups of individuals in particular market settings, and even beyond their more general conclusions – often implicit – about the power of economic approaches to the analysis of human behavior in the wide and diverse range of periods and places covered by the studies. For all of the essays in this volume serve to illustrate what has been one of the greatest strengths of much recent research in economic history, the blending of the economist's insistence on logical consistency with the historian's careful attention to reconstructing the past by using many different kinds of evidence, qualitative as well as quantitative.

Because economic historians are often engaged in attempts to explain phenomena involving market settings and institutions that are obviously very different from those that exist today, they are acutely conscious of the need to use any evidence they can find in order to construct the most complete models possible of the market they wish to study. Their response to the obstacles posed by these distances in time and structure often results in substantial gains, for the use of a variety of evidence frequently leads to improved specifications of economic relationships, and consequently to better interpretations of those relations than might be the case if the investigator relied on any single kind of evidence. Ironically, therefore, historical studies of markets often result in more thorough and balanced conclusions than studies of contemporary markets, precisely because economic historians realize they must always be aware of the need for extra efforts aimed at proper specification, estimation, and interpretation of market outcomes, with constant attention to the need for checks of consistency and robustness. As Theodore Schultz stresses in his contribution to this volume, historical investigations into the behavior of otherwise neglected variables can also serve to challenge economic theory, and may consequently lead to extensions of existing theoretical economics.

The essays in this volume serve to illustrate the diversity of sources drawn on by economic historians and the richness of the resulting models of the markets involved. To establish patterns of land ownership and crop yields in medieval England, Donald McCloskey uses such sources as the records of manorial courts and the business accounts of church lands, as well as descriptions of agriculture written by contemporary observers. My research on the transatlantic labor trades of the American colonial period relies on quantifiable evidence drawn from the English legal records of indentured-servant contracts and the business accounts of slave traders, as well as contemporary discussions of these trades in both private letters and published debates. Lance Davis, Robert Gallman, and Teresa Hutchins combine the evidence from a number of manuscript sources based on ships' logs and port records to obtain detailed descriptions of the whaling voyages that sailed from New Bedford in the nineteenth century. Clayne Pope uses a data set constructed by linking the manuscript federal census records of individual households to Mormon church tithing accounts and genealogies to create economic profiles of the lives of thousands of residents of nineteenth-century Utah. Lance Davis and Robert Huttenback use the records of revenues and expenditures of scores of national and colonial governments to trace the aggregate economic redistribution produced by nineteenth-century British imperialism, and then use the business records of hundreds of firms, and the portfolios of thousands of investors, to observe the disaggregated effects of that redistribution. Richard Butler, James Heckman, and Brook Payner show the ambiguities of interpreting aggregate time-series evidence on employment and wages, and demonstrate the value of supplementing these data with evidence disaggregated by location and type of activity in identifying the causes of increased black employment in southern manufacturing during the 1960s.

The study of economic history experienced a renaissance in the late 1950s and early 1960s as the reunification of economic theory with history produced a burst of interest from economists concerned with problems of economic growth and development. This earlier surge has been fueled in the past two decades by several new factors. An increasing concern with micro-level investigations has been aided by the dramatic technological advances in computing that have radically reduced the cost of data retrieval and analysis, making possible detailed reconstruction of many aspects of the behavior of large historical populations that would have been prohibitively expensive twenty years ago. At the same time economic history has undergone an expansion of its research interests into areas like political economy and demography that parallels the expansion that has occurred within the discipline of economics in general. As a result economic history today remains an exciting field, with a greater variety of research topics and a greater richness of approach to many of these than has ever been true in the past. The authors represented in this volume include some of the leading current contributors to research in economic history, but they are very far from constituting a complete gathering of that group. We hope that many readers of this volume will find its essays a lively and interesting introduction to some of the important work that is currently being carried out in economic history, but no more than an introduction, for if successful this volume will stimulate its readers to continue on to examine many of the other valuable economic studies of the past that could equally have been included here.

I am grateful to the contributors to this book for their cooperation and for the care they took in preparing their papers. Their enthusiasm for the project and their professionalism in carrying it out helped make both our original conference session and the preparation of this volume interesting and enjoyable experiences. Stanley Engerman provided his usual wise counsel. And Frank Smith and Colin Day both offered encouragement for the project from its inception and generously afforded the benefits of their extraordinary editorial expertise.

David W. Galenson

Introduction

The economics of historical economics

Theodore W. Schultz

I am strongly committed to McCloskey's solution to the scattered-plots puzzle, to Galenson's labor market analysis of the value of time of slaves and also of indentured servants, and to Butler, Heckman, and Payner's approach to the complex institutional and governmental changes that contribute to lessening of racial discrimination. I feel less qualified to assess Davis and Huttenback's study – not that I am uncomfortable with the results, having been much influenced by Viner on this issue.

I could elaborate on the merits of these essays, but to do so would be to forgo the opportunity afforded by the session that gave rise to this book to examine, however briefly, the decline of this part of economics in faculty appointments and graduate instruction. It is an important issue that entails changes in both the demand and supply of talent to work in this part of economics. In featuring my approach to this issue I am calling it "The Economics of Historical Economics."

It follows that the phrase "In Search of Historical Economics" in the title of the session pleases me. The expression "historical economics" has advantages. Unlike the label "economic history," it does not connote that it is economics to edify scholars of history. To call our specialization "historical economics" denotes cogently and clearly that it is a part of economics, as are international economics, producer or consumer economics, labor or agricultural economics, and for that matter theoretical economics. Work in each of the many parts of economics entails analysis that implies that analysis is not the private property of those who specialize in theoretical economics. On the contrary, analysis is what all parts of economics have in common. There is no license for loose thinking in the analytical work of economics, no matter what part of it is being pursued. Theoretical economics occasionally has a grand analytical moment; so do other parts, including historical economics.

If most professional economists were as comprehensive in their knowledge of historical economics as Simon Kuznets, Joseph Schum-

1

peter, or Adam Smith, my story about the decline in the demand for historical economics would be pointless. If a competent young individual who like Smith had been concentrating on philosophy and moral issues, or if he or she were someone like Kuznets concerned about concepts that could be measured, I doubt that the peer group in our major graduate departments of economics would appoint him or her. A brilliant young Schumpeter would probably fare better.

Why is historical economics being left out of doctoral instruction in economics? Surely there would be agreement on the fact that what is required to make an economist changes over time. Traditional inputs become obsolete as new and better inputs become available. Such is the price of progress. In the United States, foreign languages are no longer necessary, because English has become the international language of economics. Philosophy is too exotic or soft. With some exceptions politics is out. In the United States, general history has long been deemed to be too soft for graduate instruction. The new time-intensive requirement is to learn the mathematical language of those economists who either specialize in producing models or in devising econometric techniques.

At the high table at which appointments are decided, the results of empirical work are generally held in low esteem because such results are deemed to be ever so transitory. Those at the table hold fast to the belief that the permanent component of economics is in its models, techniques, and theory. Accordingly, they do not appoint a candidate to do historical economics who is not first and foremost qualified to do the permanent stuff. By this test both the demand and supply of candidates dwindle. Those who are bent on doing the right stuff are neither motivated nor qualified to do historical economics. Those who have a yen to do historical economics find the so-called permanent component of economics to be far from adequate, for example, in analyzing modern economic growth. They take comfort from a remark by John Hicks in the preface of *Capital and Growth* where he states, "I do not think that there is such a theory. I much doubt if there can be. The phenomena that are presented by a developing (changing) economy are immensely complex; any theory about them is bound to simplify. . . . There is no known approach which is not based on omissions, omissions that can easily prove to be of critical importance."

For reasons of such omissions, appointments and research agendas that satisfy the existing theoretical economics can be the death of creativity in historical economics. The main task of historical economics is to discover important economic events and behavior that theory omits. To bring such discoveries to term as a rule requires strong evidence and logical rigor.

2

An exception to this rule was that of Ernst Engel, a low-keyed statistician, who examined family budgets and discovered that the proportion of a consumer's budget spent on food declines as the consumer's income goes up. We now call it Engel's Law! That the income elasticity of demand for food is less than one was not a hypothesis derived from theory. As an observable regularity, it is one of the truly important empirical entities in analyzing modern economic growth.

In her studies of farm families, Margaret Reid discovered what is now known as the permanent and transitory income components. Milton Friedman is most generous in his consumption function book, stating that "she pressed me to write up the underlying theory . . . . This book is the result." Dorothy Brady's "unrivaled knowledge of the empirical evidence from the family budget data" is also gratefully acknowledged. In his Nobel lecture, Franco Modigliani notes that he too built a basic part of his analysis on the discovery of Margaret Reid.

In the search to account for the unexplained "Residual," Human Capital was discovered.

Contrary to the implications of Ricardo's land-rent theory as population growth occurs, we have discovered that the share of national income accounted for by agricultural land rent declines as modern economic growth occurs.

In the economics of fertility, it has been discovered that quality is substituted for quantity in having children as the family income and the value of the time of mothers increase. Becker and Lewis have made the necessary extension of theory.

To what extent can economics explain the decline of the extended family? Dorothy Brady's evidence on the undoubling of U.S. families would seem to be a strong clue.

Going beyond Schumpeter's innovating entrepreneurs, in view of strong evidence that disequilibria are inevitable as modern economic growth occurs, to what extent can economics identify and explain the equilibrating function of entrepreneurs?

In my part of the Hoselitz festschrift I stated,

The endeavor of adding to the stock of economic knowledge is beset by unsettled issues. Standard theory tends to confine economists to what is essentially a closed analytical system, whereas societies are open-ended both now and in times past. What this statement implies is that useful contributions to economics are not necessarily confined to testing the implications of received theory against historical evidence. To develop useful extensions of theory may appropriately be the ultimate goal, but it frequently is not the objective that motivates creative thinking.

3

Theodore W. Schultz

It could be that the first three brief chapters of *The Wealth of Nations* on the division of labor limited by the extent of the market are the most fruitful historical economics on record.

1

The open fields of England: rent, risk, and the rate of interest, 1300–1815

Donald N. McCloskey

What needs to be explained: the scattering of strips

The peculiar feature of farming in England until the nineteenth century was the scattering of strips. Instead of holding his twenty-four acres of land in a neat little farm, a tenant at Laxton, Nottinghamshire, in 1635 such as John Chapell held it in twenty-three separate strips, here and there, down toward the Westwood Common, in close to the village, over by the mill. So did his neighbors. The fields of Laxton were fragmented into thousands of strips, a chaotic quilt of holdings.

It is difficult to count the average number of strips nationwide, but an estimate is worth venturing, to bring definition to the chaos:

The essay is a reshaping of work done since 1972, and looks toward a fuller version, in a book forthcoming from Princeton University Press. The list of people who have contributed to my thinking would fill a telephone book. But even here I must single out my collaborator and friend John Nash and my adversary and friend Stefano Fenoaltea. The pieces drawn on include "The Enclosure of Open Fields: Preface to a Study of Its Impact on the Efficiency of English Agriculture in the Eighteenth Century," *Journal of Economic History* 32 (March 1972): 15–35; "Persistence of English Common Fields," in E. L. Jones and William Parker, eds., *European Peasants and Their Markets: Essays in Agrarian Economic History* (Princeton, N.J.: Princeton University Press, 1975), pp. 73–119; "The Economics of Enclosure: A Market Analysis," in Jones and Parker, eds., pp. 123–60; "English Open Fields as Behavior towards Risk," *Research in Economic History* 1 (Fall 1976): 124–70; "Risk and Open Fields: A Reply to Fenoaltea," *Explorations in Economic History* 14 (October 1977): 402–404; "Explaining Open Fields: An Exchange of Letters with Charles Wilson," *Journal of European Economic History* 8 (Spring 1979): 203–207; "Another Way of Observing Open Fields: A Reply to A. R. H. Baker," *Journal of Historical Geography* 5 (October 1979): 426–29; "Theses on Enclosure," in *Agricultural History: Papers Presented to the Economic History Society Conference at Canterbury, April 1983* (Agricultural History Society), pp. 56–72; [with John Nash] "Corn at Interest: The Cost and Extent of Grain Storage in Medieval England," *American Economic Review* 74 (March 1984): 174–87; "Scattering and Open Fields: A Comment on Michael Mazur's Article," *Journal of European Economic History* 9 (Spring 1980): 209–14; "Open Field System," in *The New Palgrave: A Dictionary of Economic Thought and Doctrine* (London: Macmillan, 1988).

5

Donald N. McCloskey

BOSWELL: Sir Alexander Dick tells me, that he remembers having a thousand people in a year to dine at his house. . . .
JOHNSON: That, Sir, is about three a day.
BOSWELL: How your statement lessens the idea.
JOHNSON: That, Sir, is the good of counting. It brings every thing to a certainty, which before floated in the mind indefinitely.

Any account will have features of a fairy tale, but the best tales go something like this. Most people in England before the nineteenth century were villagers, living in roughly 8,500 clusters around a church. The typical village before the nineteenth century was two square miles or so, 1,300 acres, say, of which about 900 acres, the area of Central Park, would constitute the plowed land subject to scattering. The plowed land was divided into three (sometimes two) great fields subject to a communal rotation, called open fields because none of the holdings within them were enclosed by fences. Each great field had a different crop in the rotation wheat–barley–fallow. Not all villages scattered their strips in the open fields, and not all indeed had open fields, but in the Middle Ages the heavily populated lowlands away from the spine of west Britain, and the valleys even of the West, did have them and did scatter their strips.

Consider first the average acreage held. Perhaps eighty families lived in the village, some two or three hundred souls. The majority of the souls at the height of the system were tenants of the lord (such tenancies made them serfs, officially speaking), though freeholding was not rare. According to M. M. Postan's survey of 104 thirteenth- and late-twelfth-century manors, 45 percent of the holdings were minute, averaging 3 acres or so, on which a family could not have subsisted.[1] (The smallholders worked for larger landholders; half the adult population had no land at all: England had a rural proletariat well before modern times.) The smallholders occupied only 11 percent of the land of the village – a point about smallholders worth bearing in mind for later use. For present purposes the smallholders can be ignored. The share of the land they held was so small that they had little voice in the layout of the fields.

The bulk of the plowed land was held in virgates or half-virgates, traditional measures of land, plowable four or five times a year by a full team or by a half-team. Full virgaters (at 27 acres, say, on average;

---

[1] M. M. Postan, "Medieval Agrarian Society in Its Prime: England," in M. M. Postan, ed., *The Cambridge Economic History of Europe*, vol. 1, 2d ed. (Cambridge: Cambridge University Press, 1966), p. 619; cf. E. A. Kosminsky, *Studies in the Agrarian History of England in the Thirteenth Century*, trans. R. Kisch, ed. R. H. Hilton (Oxford: Blackwell Publisher, 1956; published in Russian 1935 and 1947), p. 216.

Kosminsky suggests 30 acres) were 22 percent of the tenants in Postan's survey, and half-virgaters (at 13.5 acres on average) were 33 percent of the tenants. (Kosminsky's calculations from a royal survey of twenty-two thousand holdings in 1279 give similar results: The virgates of serfs and freemen were 22 percent, half-virgates 31 percent.) The average size of a tenancy above subsistence was therefore about 19 acres. This is the figure sought: The typical medieval tenant relying on his land for his bread would hold roughly 19 acres.[2]

Consider next the average number of strips per acre, to estimate how many strips the 19-acre average holding contained. The records are voluminous. In his pioneering work *English Field Systems*, for example, H. L. Gray extracted evidence from surveys of manors, church ("glebe") holdings, and grants of land from six hundred villages from the twelfth to the nineteenth century.[3] He extracted it to detect crop rotations (the two-, three-, or *N*-field system). But a fifth of his evidence mentions the number of strips. For instance, at Claydon St. Botolph, Buckinghamshire, in the reign of Henry VIII an account of a $26\frac{1}{2}$-acre holding mentions that in the three fields of the village the land was arranged into 15, 11, and 15 legal strips.[4] Trimming away the cases outside the chief scattered-strip areas and the cases later than the seventeenth century gives ninety-six cases averaging 1.42 strips per acre. So: There were perhaps 1.4 strips per acre on 19 acres, or 27 strips on the average holding.

Consider finally the effective strips per legal strip. Chapell's twenty-three strips at Laxton tended to cluster together, at one place separated from each other by a single neighboring strip twenty yards broad, at another place laid end-to-end across a road. It went this way in the open fields. Christian Coxe in Llancadle, Glamorgan, in 1622 held 39 acres in twenty-seven nominal strips – that is, twenty-seven strips recorded in the field book.[5] When only one foreign half-acre strip separated three of Coxe's, however, the three counted for farming purposes as one, though legally three. If the three strips had been different enough to warrant the bother, Coxe and his neighbor could have traded land to eliminate it. That they did not suggests the difference was small.

The adjustment for effective strips must be to some extent arbitrary.

[2] Kosminsky, *Studies*, pp. 35, 216, 223.
[3] (Cambridge: Harvard University Press, 1915), pp. 23, 140, 307n, 309, 373, 389, 423–29, 549, and Appendix II.
[4] Ibid., p. 455.
[5] M. Davies, "Field Systems of South Wales," in A. H. R. Baker and R. A. Butlin, eds., *Studies of Field Systems in the British Isles* (Cambridge: Cambridge University Press, 1973), pp. 504–505.

Table 1.1. *Effective plots per legal plot at Laxton, 1635*

Holder	Acres of field	Legal no. of strips	Effective/legal
Thomas Tailer, Sr.	48	78	0.62
Thomas Hassard	34	73	0.60
Edward Kelsterne	28	45	0.73
Hugh Tailer	25	44	0.70
John Chapell	24	23	0.83
Robert Rosse	14	23	0.61
Average			0.68

Note: The acres exclude closes (big pieces of land outside the system) and town land for house, barn, and garden.
Source: C. S. Orwin and C. S. Orwin, *The Open Fields* (Oxford: Clarendon Press, 1938), pp. 137–42 and Part III (Survey and Maps).

If one takes a cluster of legal strips to be a single effective one so long as no more than a single foreign strip separated the cluster and no part was outside a radius of, say, 150 yards of the center, then Coxe's twenty-seven legal reduce to twelve or so effective strips. Applying the same criterion to the holdings of six men of Laxton suggests that the effective number was about two-thirds of the legal number (see Table 1.1).

So: The average holding of about 19 acres of plowland would contain $19 \times 1.42 = 27$ legal strips, or $19 \times 1.42 \times 0.68 = 18.4$ effective strips. That is to say, the number of effective strips was about the same as the number of acres, that same 19. Therefore in each of the three great fields the typical tenant would hold six or so effective strips, scattered about the field. Keep the six in mind, for the scale: In each of three open fields the six strips on average were scattered over 300 acres, a half square mile, a six-by-six assemblage of Midwestern city blocks, the area of Central Park below the Metropolitan Museum of Art. Each effective strip was about three city blocks from its nearest neighbor in the holding.

The scattering survived for a long time. The earliest origins of the system are obscure, but during the high Middle Ages it prevailed in lowland and Saxon Britain; even in the higher and Celtic lands to the west and north "runrig" was similar and common. Yet the open-field system was not simply a survival of custom lost in primeval mist. Joan Thirsk has noted that in Germany "it is possible to observe the gradual parcelling of rectangular fields into strips as late as the seventeenth and even the eighteenth centuries," and the same may be said of Russia.[6] The English evidence is similar, though new scattering ends earlier. In the thirteenth century the county of Kent and its neighbor Sussex had loose open-field systems. By the sixteenth century, however, Kent was entirely enclosed, with no scattering; yet parts of Sussex had developed a rigid and elaborate system of scattering.

Enclosure was going on in England from the fifteenth century, with or without official sanction. Even at the height of the system a village would have a ring of closes around its open fields. A German case of early enclosure occurred on lands owned by the Abbey of Kempton in Bavaria, on which consolidation, initiated by the peasants themselves, began in the sixteenth century, three centuries before it began in neighboring places.[7] It is not reasonable, in other words, to view the open fields in the way Gonner did seventy-five years ago, as remnants of ancient racial patterns, bound by rules "consecrated by immemorial usage . . . [that] made conscious change well nigh impossible."[8] On the contrary, conscious change was easily possible, away or toward a system of scattering.

The prevalence of scattering may be judged by what remained in England in 1700 – commercial and progressive England, at the dawn of the industrial age. Much is made of enclosure by act of Parliament, concentrated in a few great waves from 1760 to 1820; and indeed six million acres out of England's twenty-four million or so acres useful for agriculture were enclosed this way. The six-million figure may be high, because within a nominally "open" village, as was just noted, much land was "anciently" enclosed, though normally the ancient enclosures would not be recorded in the enclosure act.

On another and more important count, however, the six-million figure is too low, because it does not include land enclosed without parliamentary sanction. Gilbert Slater guessed in 1912 that during the eighteenth century some eight million acres beyond the six million had been enclosed by nonparliamentary agreement, and Michael Turner recently guessed seven million.[9] J. D. Chambers reckoned on the basis

---

[6] Joan Thirsk, "The Common Fields," *Past and Present* no. 29 (1964): 3–25, p. 3.

[7] Alan Mayhew, *Rural Settlement and Farming in Germany* (New York: Barnes & Noble, 1973), p. 187.

[8] E. C. K. Gonner, *Common Land and Inclosure* (London: Macmillan, 1912), p. 35.

[9] Gilbert Slater, *The English Peasantry and the Enclosure of Common Fields* (London: Constable, 1907), pp. 63–65; Michael Turner, *Enclosures in Britain, 1750–1830* (London: Macmillan, 1984), p. 33.

of local evidence that in eighteenth-century Nottinghamshire fully 41 percent of the land was enclosed by private agreement as against only 25 percent by parliamentary act.[10] A figure for all of England would have to come from a random sample of villages studied in similar detail. What looms through the statistical haze is that something over half of the agricultural land of England still needed enclosure in 1700: Out of the twenty-four million total, six million acres were enclosed after 1700 by parliamentary act and perhaps an equal acreage by agreement. The share of land is in any case an underestimate of the more relevant figure, the share of employment, or still better of farming output, because the places of surviving open fields were cultivated rather than grazed. By any measure, much of England remained to be enclosed in 1700. The open fields had survived for centuries.

Enclosure was not so simple as sheep eating men. A hardy fable supposes that the sixteenth century was the great age of enclosure, grazing land absorbing plowlands. The timing in the tale is wrong. Grazing land in the sixteenth century was falling, not rising, since population was rising swiftly and new mouths demanded to be fed. Edwin Gay used official inquiries into the matter to show that under 3 percent of the cultivated land of England was enclosed from the middle of the fifteenth to the end of the sixteenth century; one could accept a higher figure and still forsake the old fable.[11] In the eighty years since he wrote, no persuasive evidence has been offered to the contrary. Enclosures by agreement went on apace, it seems, in the late fourteenth and early fifteenth centuries, then again in the seventeenth century. Far from being the great age of enclosure, the sixteenth century was a lull. To repeat, there was much left to be done by the eighteenth century. English open fields survived into modern times.

The scattering survived in other parts of Europe still later. The classic open field had dominated Northern Europe in a swath from the middle of England across northern France and Germany, with a northern extension into Scandinavia and through the north Slavic lands to the Urals. The breadth of its hold suggests that the peasants approved. Since the English example of the eighteenth century, followed shortly by Sweden and France, one government after another in Northern

[10] J. D. Chambers, *Nottinghamshire in the Eighteenth Century* (London: P. S. King, 1932), p. 149; cf. R. I. Hodgson estimates, quoted in Turner, *Enclosures*, p. 35, that 56 percent of enclosure in County Durham was voluntary.

[11] E. F. Gay, "Inclosures in England in the Sixteenth Century," *Quarterly Journal of Economics* 17 (1902–1903): 576–97.

Europe passed laws designed to eliminate scattering by force, persuasion, or subsidy. Yet its end was achieved painfully slowly. The Dutch were still passing acts in the 1920s and 1930s making consolidation compulsory if favored by a majority in a village and offering large subsidies (all the costs incurred in the attempt, for example, if the consolidation was not voted and achieved).[12] Nonetheless in the 1950s Dutch consolidation was not complete. France was still consolidating villages in the 1930s and 1950s. The first of many general consolidation acts in Germany was passed in Hannover in 1848 – the date can stand as an emblem for the association of consolidation with progressive politics – yet to this day the farms in many parts of Germany are scattered, if no longer subject to the medieval correlates of scattering.[13] In Poland, too, the land is still scattered, because not collectivized. And the Stolypin Reforms in Russia before the Revolution did not eliminate scattering there.

Scattering of some sort has not been confined in modern times to the regular open-field areas of northern Europe. In the early 1960s Folke Dovring estimated that "at least one-third, and probably over half, of the agricultural land in Europe would need re-allocation or consolidation in order to do away with the technical disadvantages of bad layout, including among these the constraint to conform with neighbours in farming operations."[14] In 1969 the OECD delivered a similar judgment, observing that during the early 1960s in Spain the average number of separate plots per farm was 14 and in Germany 10, both countries having roughly a third of their farms with 10 plots or more.[15] The median number of plots on Czechoslovakian farms in 1938 was 30, and on Portuguese farms in 1940 it was 26.[16] Around 1950 in parts of Greece the farms had 50 to 100 (official) plots per farm, and ten years

[12] Philine R. Vanderpol, "Reallocation of Land in the Netherlands," in Kenneth H. Parsons, R. J. Penn, and P. M. Raup, eds., *Land Tenure: Proceedings of the International Conference on Land Tenure and Related Problems in World Agriculture Held at Madison, Wisconsin, 1951* (Madison: University of Wisconsin Press, 1956), pp. 548–54.

[13] Mayhew, *Rural Settlement*, pp. 178–99.

[14] "The Transformation of European Agriculture," in H. J. Habakkuk and M. Postan, eds., *The Cambridge Economic History of Europe*, vol. 6 (Cambridge: Cambridge University Press, 1965), pp. 630ff.

[15] Organization for Economic Cooperation and Development, *Agricultural Development in Southern Europe*, Agricultural Policy Reports (Paris: OECD, 1969), pp. 18, 83.

[16] Folke Dovring, *Land and Labor in Europe in the 20th Century*, 3d ed. (The Hague: M. Nijhoff, 1965), p. 20, with twenty other cases.

11

later not much had changed.[17] In a backward part of Ireland in the 1960s the typical holding consisted of 60 scattered plots.[18]

Scattering occurs widely outside Europe, too. Among the farmers of east central Tanzania in the late 1960s "the ideal pattern is to hold a number of scattered fields planted with several crops."[19] A similar system can be found elsewhere in Africa and in Latin America. It is common in Asia. Indian concern with scattering, embodied at the state level in a series of consolidation acts, is sixty years old; but the problem (for so it is viewed by planners) remains.[20] A 1969 survey team of the Asian Development Bank, noting the prevalence of scattering in Japan, Korea, Taiwan, Indonesia, Thailand, Pakistan, and India, argued that "the basic cause of operational inefficiency on small farms is the poor farm layout. . . . A farm of one hectare may be divided into more than a dozen small fields."[21] Scattering is not a merely English and medieval phenomenon.

Why it is a puzzle: the inefficiency of scattering

If scattering were not so obviously hurtful to average output it would not be puzzling for the economic point of view. Farmers put designs on their barns and use Mail Pouch tobacco, and no economist objects. It is only when the farmers commence throwing away a big share of output that the economist becomes alarmed.

The question that must be answered is the extent to which scattering threw away output. The best way to answer it would be to look at output before and after enclosure. Unhappily one cannot get such statistics on output, or at least one cannot for a large enough range of farms to make an estimate believable. The English statistics on output during enclosures are poor because there was little reason for a farmer to keep records. (By contrast, in the Middle Ages the statistics of yields are excellent, at least on the lord's farm, because strict account-

---

[17] Euthymios Papageorgiou, "Fragmentation of Land Holdings and Measures for Consolidation in Greece," in Parsons et al., eds., *Land Tenure*, pp. 543–48; Kenneth Thompson, *Farm Fragmentation in Greece: The Problem and Its Setting*, Research Monograph Series, no. 5 (Athens: Center of Economic Research, 1963).

[18] John C. Messenger, *Inis Beag: Isle of Ireland* (New York: Holt, Rinehart & Winston, 1969), p. 27.

[19] T. O. Beidelman, *The Karugu: A Matrilineal People of East Africa* (New York: Holt, Rinehart & Winston, 1971), p. 18.

[20] S. K. Agarwal, *Economics of Land Consolidation in India* (Delhi: Chand, 1971).

[21] OECD, 1969, p. 645; cf. Setsuro Hyodo, "Aspects of Land Consolidation in Japan," in Parsons et al., eds., *Land Tenure*, pp. 558–59.

ing was needed to check stealing by agents of the lord.) Yields per acre do seem to have risen somewhat in the eighteenth century, during parliamentary enclosure (and in the seventeenth century during voluntary enclosure), but other and more important things were happening as well, especially the introduction of Dutch methods and New World crops. The statistics on yields are uncertain and uncontrolled. For the little they are worth, the estimates of rising yields from all causes range from a mere 10 percent per acre over the eighteenth century (and the new agriculture cost *more* in labor) up to 61 percent.

The way around the obstacle is the theory of rent. The value of the increased output, if any, had to accrue to someone as income. If an enclosure was productive it would raise the rewards to inputs of labor, capital, and land. Labor and capital, however, could move between the enclosing village and the rest of the world. Their mobility prevented the enclosure from increasing their prices. More labor and capital would be hired in a more productive village, but merely at the going prices of labor and capital. Land, however, cannot move. Its price would be increased by enclosure. In fact, all the increased productivity of the village, net of the opportunity cost of the labor and capital brought in, would be earned by the landlord.[22]

Happily, the change in rent does the job better than the more obvious and less obtainable measures of increased output. It reflects only the net improvement, not the higher output from a mere piling up of labor and capital. And it reflects as it should the farmers' expectations, not their achievements. A little economic theory goes a long way here, valorizing evidence otherwise merely ornamental. The theory was familiar of course to Ricardo and other observers of English agriculture during the enclosure movement. It was after all the basis for their dismal prediction that the land would pay the taxes imposed on agriculture but would also collect the improvements.

The evidence on rents is ample. It can best be catalogued by source, proceeding from journalistic assertion to the records of actual holdings. The journalistic assertions can be ranged from earliest to latest, giving a (misleading) impression of chronological depth. The 1534 edition of Fitzherbert's *Book of Husbandry*, for instance, asserted that "by the assent of the lords and the tenants every neighbor may exchange lands with [an]other. And then shall his farm be twice so good in profit to the tenant as it was before."[23] The tenant would then be

---

[22] A more formal argument appears in McCloskey, *The Applied Theory of Price* (New York: Macmillan, 1985), pp. 488f.

[23] Master Fitzherbert, *The Book of Husbandry* (1534), ed. W. W. Skeat (London: English Dialect Society, 1882), p. 77 (I have modernized the spelling).

willing to pay twice as much in rent, too, unless "profit" means exactly "net of rent." Norden's *Surveiors Dialogue, Very Profitable for All Men To Peruse, But Especially for Gentlemen . . . Willing To Buy, Hire, or Sell Lands* reckoned enclosed land at 50 percent greater than open. Half a century later Samuel Fortrey put it at three times greater.[24]

The precision and the variation are misleading. The figures are always rounded and undocumented, and their definitions are now uncertain. *The City and Country Purchaser and Builder* said about 1667 that "enclosed lands in many places doth yield half as much, or as much more, as lands in common fields."[25] But is "yield" the yield of rent (a sense that the *Oxford English Dictionary* last records in 1582) or a yield of grain (a secondary but growing sense in the seventeenth century, two centuries before it reassumed its monetary garb as the yield on bonds)? In the latter and more probable case the sum left over for the residual claimant, the landlord, would be larger still. But no matter. These are mere rough guesses, the statistical equivalents of saying, "Enclosure increases rent mightily – more than conservatives might suppose."

Similar figures in the next century might be drawn from the pamphlet literature, though the pamphlets are of course biased. The pamphlets were written against enclosure or in favor of it, and the ones that mention the improved rents are in favor. When Henry Homer, a commissioner in charge of enclosures and an enthusiast for the practice, sets "the general improvement of the field" from the landlord's point of view at a doubling, one cannot give the assessment much weight.[26] One can give more weight to observers later in the century, after the propaganda war in favor of parliamentary enclosure had been won. It is worth quoting at length, for instance, the advice William Marshall, a respected writer on agricultural subjects, gave to landlords in 1804 ("inclosure" means at bottom fencing, "privatization" in the modern jargon):

Among the circumstances which influence the marketable value of lands . . . their state with respect to inclosure is a matter of great consideration. Open

---

[24] Norden 1607 and Fortrey 1663 (*Interest*) are quoted in E. M. Leonard, "The Inclosure of Common Fields in the Seventeenth Century" (1905), in E. M. Carus-Wilson, ed., *Essays in Economic History*, vol. 2 (London: Arnold, 1962), p. 236.

[25] Quoted in Joan Thirsk and J. P. Cooper, eds., *Seventeenth Century Economic Documents* (Oxford: Clarendon Press, 1972), p. 288.

[26] Henry S. Homer, *An Essay on the Nature and Methods of Ascertaining Specifick Shares of Proprietors upon the Inclosure of Common Fields*, 2d ed. (Oxford, 1769), p. 64.

14

lands, though wholly appropriated, and lying well together, are of much less value, except for a sheep walk or a rabbit warren, than the same land would be in a state of suitable inclosure. If they are disjointed and intermixt in a state of common field, or common meadow, their value may be reduced one third. If the common fields or meadows are what is termed Lammas land, and becomes common as soon as the crops are off, *the depression of value may be set down at one half what they would be worth, in well fenced inclosure, and unencumbered with that ancient custom.*[27]

One can also give weight to the generally sober, though still pro-enclosure, productions of the Board of Agriculture, a semiofficial group of agronomists who produced quarto drafts (1793–94) and octavo final editions (1796–1814) of *A General View of the County of X* for each British county. Many of the statistics are undocumented opinions, but the opinions nonetheless of qualified observers. Clark's quarto report on Herefordshire asserted, for example, that "no sooner is land inclosed, than it lets for nearly double the rent than it did when it was in common fields."[28] Pitt's octavo *Staffordshire* reckoned that "in all cases . . . common-field land is improved at least five shillings per acre by enclosure," the rent being from 10 to 30 shillings an acre after enclosure and after some inflation of grain prices.[29] Holt's quarto *Lancashire* reckoned a doubling or "in many instances" a trebling of rents immediately on enclosure, though this is probably enclosure from wasteland, not from land under the plow.[30] Unfortunately these were regions to the north and west of the main swath of open fields surviving. Only 4.3 percent of the area of Herefordshire and 3.3 percent of Staffordshire was arable enclosed by act of Parliament, as against 40 or 50 percent further east and south.[31] But the opinions further east and south are similar. In his 1813 final report on Oxfordshire, for example, Arthur Young quotes a Mr. Davis of Boxham (unfortunately for present purposes, still another commissioner of enclosure): "In general, rents have been increased by the enclosures in Oxfordshire, reckoned at the first letting, nearly double; and much more after ten or twelve years."[32] The first letting would be attributable to the promise of enclosure alone, the rises later perhaps to further improvements, or more probably to the rise in the price of grain.

[27] *On the Landed Property of England* (London, 1804), pp. 13–14 (italics deleted; mine added).

[28] John Clark, *Herefordshire* (1794), p. 74; cf. p. 70n.

[29] W. Pitt, *Staffordshire* (1796), pp. 26, 40.

[30] John Holt, *Lancashire* (1794), p. 51.

[31] Michael E. Turner, *English Parliamentary Enclosure* (Folkestone: Dawson; Hamden, Conn.: Archon, 1980), pp. 180–81.

[32] Arthur Young, *Oxfordshire* (1813), p. 94.

Not all testified to doubling on average. Davis in his quarto *Wiltshire* remarks that "the difference of rent and produce is not so great as in many counties," setting it at a third or a half.[33] In his quarto *Warwickshire* Wedge reports that in the forty years before his report the south and east of the county had been enclosed, producing "an improvement of nearly [that is, only] one-third of the rents, after allowing for expenses."[34] The expenses he puts at 45 shillings an acre (a reasonable figure) "when frugally managed; which, in many instances, was not the case," though there can be some doubt that it is appropriate to resubtract the costs from the increase in rents (which reflect net gain, after costs). Adopting his accounting, if rents before enclosure were about 10 shillings an acre and the interest in perpetuity to pay back the expenses of 45 shillings an acre were 6 percent, the implied rise in rents would be about 60 percent.

Other testimony from the *General Views* deals with particular enclosures, not with opinions "in general" or "in all cases" (see Table 1.2).

Late in the enclosure movement the doubling was the figure used for conventional purposes. For instance, the leading student of the enclosure movement, Michael Turner, cites a letter by John Fellows, commissioner for an unsuccessful attempt to enclose Quainton, Buckinghamshire, as using the doubling convention.[35] John R. Ellis quotes the parties involved in the enclosure of Aldbourne, Wiltshire, in 1805–1809 as using it.[36] In the General Enclosure Act of 1801 Parliament had shown it was well aware of the big capital gains to be had from enclosure, forbidding the enclosure commissioners to buy land in the village until five years after their work.[37] Even for the few fields unenclosed by 1844 a commissioner in charge of commuting tithes held out to a Select Committee on Commons Inclosure the prospect of a rise in rents from their level of 15 or 16 shillings per acre to 30 shillings "by the mere simple re-distribution of land" that was "now incapable of cultivation according to improved rules of good husbandry."[38]

The best sources are account books of estates experiencing enclosure. The vigor with which estate studies have been pursued in England makes possible some general impressions. For an early instance,

[33] Thomas Davis, Sr., *Wiltshire* (1794), p. 83.

[34] John Wedge, *Warwickshire* (1794), pp. 20f.

[35] Michael E. Turner, "The Cost of Parliamentary Enclosure in Buckinghamshire," *Agricultural History Review* 21 (1973): 35–46, p. 36.

[36] J. R. Ellis, "Parliamentary Enclosure in Wiltshire," Ph.D. thesis, Bristol University, 1972, p. 93.

[37] 41 Geo. III, c. 109, para. II.

[38] *SP* 1844, vol. 5, question 257.

Table 1.2. *Rises in rents immediately after enclosure, 1765–1805, from* General Views *by the Board of Agriculture*

Village	County	Date of enclosure	Rise in rent	Source
Elford	Staffs.	1765	"Trebled"	W. Pitt, *Staffs.* (1796), p. 41
Lidlington	Beds.	1775	83% (12s. to 22s.)	T. Batchelor, *Beds.* (1808)
Coney Weston	Suffolk	1777	Doubled	A. Young, *Suffolk* (1794), p. 53
23 villages	Lincs.	Before 1799	92% (rise in rent from £15,504 to £29,760)	Young, *Lincs.*, pp. 77, 83
Risely	Beds.	1793	90%–157% (7–10s. to 18–19s.)	Batchelor, *Beds.* (1808)
Milton Bryant	Beds.	1793	88%	Ibid.
Queensborough	Leics.	1793	92%–130% (10–12s. to 23s. "now")	Pitt, *Leics.* (1809), pp. 70–76
Dunton	Beds.	1797	113% (8s. to 17s.)	Batchelor, *Beds.* (1808)
Enfield	Middx.	1803	33% (£18,000 to £24,000)[a]	J. Middleton, *Middx.* (1807), p. 142
Wendelbury	Oxon.	ca. 1805	140%–167% (9–10s. to 24s., latter free of tithes)	Young, *Oxon.* (1813), p. 37

[a]The second figure is for 1805. He laments that "many have unfortunately adopted [he means 'retained'] the old plan" of a two-field rotation.

John Broad used the Verney family papers to extract most of the relevant statistics on the enclosure by agreement of Middle Clayton, Buckinghamshire, in 1654–56. The rent rolls in 1646 imply rents of about 8 shillings an acre (depressed perhaps by the Civil War: A surveyor's evaluation in 1648 had put them at 11.6 shillings an acre). The actual rent paid in the three years after the enclosure was 17.8 shillings per acre, a rise of 53 percent on 11.6 shillings and 123 percent on 8 shillings.[39]

Sometimes, of course, enclosure was not such a good idea. Brenda Swann has given an eighteenth-century example.[40] A sixty-acre farm at

[39] John Broad, "Sir Ralph Verney and His Estates, 1630–1696," D.Phil. thesis, Oxford University, 1973.

[40] B. A. S. Swann, "A Study of Some London Estates in the Eighteenth Century," Ph.D. thesis, London University, 1964.

Tempsford, Bedfordshire, owned by Jesus College rented at £30 in 1747. It was enclosed in 1777 at a cost of about seven years of such rents. After enclosure the college was able to lease it for three years at £45, an advance of 50 percent on the earlier rent, but a modest 7 percent return on the costs. Furthermore, after this first lease expired the college had to settle for leases of £40 and then of £36. At the last the rise in rents was only about 20 percent and the 1.9 percent yield on the investment was a full percentage point below the yield on consols.

A bigger case is the Longleat estates in Wiltshire from 1773–1808, analyzed by J. R. Ellis.[41] Enclosure there produced *no* increase in rent. And at Warminster, for instance, rental surveys of 1781 and 1801, bracketing the enclosure of 1783, show a rise of 58 percent on land anciently enclosed, but a rise of only 28 percent on the newly enclosed lands.[42] Yet it must have been peculiar land to fall in price relative to the other lands after enclosure. Recall the remark by the reporter on Wiltshire that "the difference of rent and produce is not so great as in many counties." So it would seem. Ellis remarks that the earlier "rents" may have been mere notional figures, higher than equilibrium figures, with tenants being persuaded to accept holdings by the prospect of remissions and easy accumulation of arrears. We do not know.

A more typical figure was calculated from the Harcourt family papers by J. R. Walton, a rise in rents from £1,415 in 1773, a year before the enclosure of their lands, to £2,444 in 1777 – a 73 percent increase.[43] Swann's work provides other examples. Rents on a farm owned by Jesus College of about ninety acres in Great Wilbraham, Cambridgeshire, rose from 9 shillings an acre in 1796 to 30 shillings an acre in 1802, after enclosure, a rise of more than 200 percent. Holdings of St. Bartholomew's Hospital in Bottisham, Cambridgeshire, rented for £465 a year in 1794 and £1,100 in 1801, after enclosure, a rise of more than 130 percent; seven holdings in Northamptonshire "more than trebled" in rent after enclosure.[44]

The holdings from St. Bartholomew's of a Mr. Fiennes Trotman illustrate a number of points. Swann records that in 1753 he was granted a twenty-one-year lease on fifty-nine open-field acres at Heath,

[41] Ellis, "Enclosure in Wiltshire," pp. 119–25.
[42] Ibid., p. 135.
[43] J. R. Walton, "The Residential Mobility of Farmers and Its Relationship to the Parliamentary Enclosure Movement in Oxfordshire," in A. D. M. Phillips and B. J. Turton, eds., *Environment, Man and Economic Change* (London: Longman, 1975), p. 241.
[44] Swann, "London Estates," pp. 153f.; cf. pp. 167, 209.

Oxfordshire (with rights to graze a certain number of animals on a commons of eighty acres). Such long leases were usual, making rents a long moving average of the rack rent, though rack renting was not unheard of. The interpretation of the figures is not straightforward. The lease cost him a mere £4 per year on the holding in total but also a £160 fee in advance, an "entry fine." At 6 percent interest (for which there is evidence in the accounts) the entry fine amounted to an additional £13.6 a year, giving a total of 6 shillings per acre. The usual formulas for evaluating an annuity apply. The formula needs to allow for the possibility of Trotman dying. Under traditional rules for leases, the lease expired if Trotman died, and if he died the day after the lease was signed the entry fine would not be refundable. Allowing for such an eventuality would of course raise the pre-enclosure rent. In 1772 the village was enclosed, with forty-seven acres of closes allotted to Trotman in exchange for his fifty-nine acres of open field. (The other acreage probably went as compensation to the holders of agricultural tithes.) His new lease of 1774 extended for fourteen and a half years, at £14 total, the same price per acre (£17.6 × (47/59) = £14) as he paid before, "possibly [as] some compensation for the expenses he incurred in enclosing."[45] These expenses, as we have seen, were large relative to annual rents. When in 1789 the lease expired, the new rent finally acknowledged the underlying value of the now-enclosed land: It rented for 11.9 shillings an acre, double the preenclosure level.

A difficulty with the figures for the late eighteenth century is that the price of grain was rising, especially during the wars of 1793–1815. Leases were often for twenty-one years (though the authors for the Board of Agriculture complained that many counties had annual or short leases), and a long lease would be a bad bet if the acceleration of inflation had not been foreseen. Enclosure gave the landlords an opportunity to withdraw the bets. Inflation of 1 or 2 percent per year does not look large by recent standards, but it sufficed. Pitt's *Leicestershire* in 1809 noted that the Duke of Rutland's rent had increased from 6 shillings an acre before enclosure to 18 shillings after, "in part produced by the enclosure, but in part certainly by a change of times and circumstances."[46] Most of Leicestershire's and Rutland's enclosure took place before 1793, yet the 18-shilling figure was doubtless war-inflated.[47]

In the thirty years before the 1790s, also, the price of grain had been

---

[45] Ibid., p. 206.
[46] William Pitt, *Leicestershire* (1809), p. 15.
[47] Turner, *Parliamentary Enclosure*, p. 186, on enclosure in Leicestershire and Rutland.

19

rising somewhat relative to the price level. The chief landlord of Aspley Guise, Bedfordshire, enjoyed a rise in rents from £85 in 1759, on the eve of the enclosure, to £158 in 1781.[48] The rise looks less impressive when set beside the rise in the price of grain, from around 30 shillings per Winchester quarter to 45 shillings over the same span. The rent was the residual claimant, and would therefore rise more than the price of grain. The price of land, as Ricardo said, was high because the price of grain was high, not grain high because the price of land was high.

One possible way around the difficulty is to examine statistics on rents in open and enclosed villages, or on open and enclosed farms in different villages. Robert Allen has done so, using elegantly the data on a broad sample of large farms in the 1760s scattered through Arthur Young's tour books.[49] Some years ago I did a similar exercise with the mouthwatering statistics in Parkinson's *Rutland* (1808).[50] From the statistics on village differentials Allen and I both arrive at a low estimate of the rise in rent, much lower than the results from the time series. For instance, in my Rutland calculations the rent accruing to landlords in nine open villages was 14.9 shillings per acre as against 22.2 shillings in forty-four enclosed villages, a difference not far from the time series. As Allen and I have stressed, however, the "rent" relevant for productivity calculations must be the full economic rent, especially when comparing rents on farms in different villages, and must therefore include the poor rates and tithe. Including rates and tithes makes the figure for Rutland 21.9 shillings as against 26.0, a difference between open and enclosed villages of only 19 percent. (Attempts to control for land quality have little effect on the figures.)

The low differential is a puzzle. True, the "cross sections" have methodological difficulties of their own. The chief one is familiar from econometric studies of production functions, namely, that a "sample" of firms having to participate in the same market will be biased toward finding no differences of efficiency. The market pushes out the un-

---

[48] G. H. Fowler, "The Strip Map of Aspley Guise, c. 1745, with an Analysis of the Enclosure Award, 1761," *Quarto Memoirs of the Bedfordshire Historical Record Society* 2 (1928–36): 21–35.

[49] Robert C. Allen, "The Efficiency and Distributional Consequences of Eighteenth Century Enclosures," *Economic Journal* 92 (1982): 937–53, and "Enclosure, Capitalist Agriculture, and the Growth of Corn Yields in Early Modern England," University of British Columbia, Department of Economics, Discussion Paper 1986–39. Allen is writing a book on the subject.

[50] "Theses on Enclosure," *Agricultural History: Papers Presented to the Economic History Society Conference, Canterbury, April 1983* (Agricultural History Society), esp. pp. 69–71.

usually inefficient, with the result that the open fields that survived must have been especially suited to openness. To put it another way, the sample is self-selected: Places do not become enclosed by accident. It is suggestive, for instance, that all the nine open fields surviving in the tiny county of Rutland (eighteen miles across at its broadest) were in the southeastern part of the county, in Wrandyke hundred.

A better approximation to cross-sectional control is provided by rents on enclosed and open land *in the same village*. These tend to return to a figure of a doubling (or a little less: 50 to 100 percent would be a persuasive range). In Batchelor's *Bedfordshire* the open fields of Cranfield rented for 10 shillings an acre, the enclosures for 20; in Eversholt the figures were 12 and 23 shillings.[51] Pitt's *Worcestershire* (1813) reports "open field farms" at 20 shillings an acre (at the height of the wartime inflation), the same 20 for enclosed farms on inferior land, but 30 shillings, and a few 40 and 50, on better land.[52]

Of course such figures could be doubted, as irrelevant to open fields in their heyday. If the purpose is to explain the persistence of scattering through the centuries from the thirteenth to the eighteenth, a selection bias of another sort is introduced by focusing on the differential at the end. Since open fields in the end disappeared, one would expect if anything that late differentials would be greater than early differentials. Open fields in the fourteenth century would be more productive relative to enclosed farms than in the eighteenth century.

Gregory Clark has recently shed light on the problem, using probate records for the farms of manorial lords during the fourteenth century. In eleven cases (mainly in Wiltshire) the rents on acreage outside the open fields of a village were 128 percent on average above those inside.[53] The true figure is probably somewhat lower: Clark notes that open-field acreage carried with it a right to graze on the stubble after the harvest, apparently not valued in the probate records; and the enclosed acreage would probably have been better cared for. It is comforting, though, to see that the voluminous evidence in the twilight of the system is not contradicted by the scraps of evidence available at its noon.

The rise of rent on an enclosure, then, was 100 percent notionally, and probably a little lower in practice. Robert Allen, again, has argued

[51] Thomas Batchelor, *Bedfordshire* (1808), p. 34.
[52] William Pitt, *Worcestershire* (1813).
[53] From Gregory Clark, "The Cost of Capital and Medieval Agricultural Technique," Stanford University Department of Economics working paper, August 1986, Table 5, "Annual Value of Arable in Common and in Severalty," geometric average of ratios; the paper is forthcoming in *Explorations in Economic History*.

recently in a series of brilliant papers that contrary to the reasoning I introduced to the literature in 1972 the rise in rent does not measure a rise in productivity. As noted above, he reckons from a sample of 231 farms reported by Arthur Young in the 1760s (the selection bias that may afflict such samples has already been noted) that economic rent did *not* increase when a farm was enclosed. Why then did the rent paid increase? "Rents rose when villages were enclosed either because the efficiency of agriculture increased and hence the value of the land rose *or because open field rents were less than the value of the land and rents were raised at enclosure to eliminate the disequilibrium.*"[54] Allen is arguing that open fields rented below equilibrium.

It has long been recognized in the literature, as has been noted here, that parliamentary enclosure did truncate all leases in a village, and that in a period of accelerating inflation such as the late eighteenth century it is not strange to suppose that a parliament of landlords would enact a renegotiation of leases.[55] Yet Allen's argument and therefore his sample and method face the problem that the differential favoring enclosure seems to have been of long standing, not confined to the various French wars of the eighteenth century. However plausible would be a temporary disequilibrium in the 1760s, say, it would be odd for landlords to surrender land at rents below equilibrium for centuries. A landlord doing so would be spurning a doubling of his income. Such a man is not at any rate the grasping landlord of Ricardian theory or of Restoration comedy or of medieval poetry and preaching. The puzzle for future research will be to bring the Young sample into agreement with the other evidence, that landlords got higher rents from enclosures mainly on account of the higher productivity.

The physical rewards to enclosure, then, accrued to landlords. The change in rent divided by the value of total output will be the productivity change from enclosure. (Economists might worry that general equilibrium considerations would undermine the measure; but the statistics come out of a partial equilibrium experiment, the anticipated change in local rents from small changes in the nation's land.) Therefore, the productivity change in a village will be: the percentage change in rent (as estimated so far) multiplied by the share of the landlord's rent in total output (which remains to be estimated). The change in rent must be weighted by its importance.

---

[54] Allen, "Efficiency and Distributional Consequences," p. 939 (italics supplied).
[55] Compare McCloskey, "The Enclosure of Open Fields: Preface to a Study of Its Impact on the Efficiency of English Agriculture in the Eighteenth Century," *Journal of Economic History* 32 (March 1972): 15–35, p. 33.

Table 1.3. *Rent shares in total cost from circular letters of the Board of Agriculture, 1790–1813*

Date	Total cost (£)	Rent (£)	Share
1790	412	88	0.21
1803	548	121	0.22
1813	772	162	0.21

Source: Arthur Young's report of the results of the Board of Agriculture's circular letters, reported to the Committee on Petitions Relating to the Corn Laws (1814, "Evidence," p. 570).

The share of the landlord's rent (note that it is not the same as full economic rent including taxes) may be calculated in various ways. One way is to calculate it more or less indirectly from aggregate statistics. At the end of the eighteenth century the yield per acre of wheat was about 2.6 quarters (of 8 bushels each) per acre, barley about 4.2.[56] The price of wheat in the first decade of the nineteenth century was about 82 shillings per quarter, barley about 44 shillings per quarter. The rent of enclosed arable land was about 20 shillings, tithe-free (see Table 1.2 for some examples). Allowing for a fallow every third year gives:

$$\frac{20}{(0.33)(2.8)(82) + (0.33)(4.2)(44)} = 0.15$$

The other way to calculate the share of rents is more or less directly from farm accounts and contemporary testimony. Bowden's calculations in *The Agrarian History of England and Wales*, vol. 4, imply a share of rent of 0.14 during 1600–20, rising to double that in the 1640s.[57] Some such figure (that is, anything from 13 to 30 percent) seems to be typical. A dozen or so farm accounts 1790–1821 examined by Glenn Hueckel showed rents (apparently excluding taxes and tithes) of 23 percent of output.[58] In 1814 Arthur Young gave the estimates for a typical hundred-acre farm raising wheat shown in Table 1.3.

[56] Phyllis Deane and W. A. Cole, *British Economic Growth 1688–1959* (Cambridge: Cambridge University Press, 1964), p. 66, derived from the *General Views*; Allen's careful reestimation arrives at similar results ("Enclosure, Capitalist Agriculture," p. 47).

[57] Peter Bowden, "Agricultural Prices, Farm Profits, and Rents," in Joan Thirsk, ed., *The Agrarian History of England and Wales*, vol. 4, *1500–1640* (Cambridge: Cambridge University Press, 1967), pp. 653, 693.

[58] "War and the British Economy, 1793–1815: A General Equilibrium Analysis," *Explorations in Economic History* 10 (Summer 1973): 365–97, p. 385.

Table 1.4. *Rent shares for enclosed farms in Yorkshire, ca. 1823*

	Share of rent	Share of tithes and taxes	Rotation
Light soils	0.24	0.09	Turnips, barley, clover, wheat
Heavy soils	0.16	0.08	Wheat, clover, wheat, fallow

Source: J. S. Bayldon, *Art of Valuing* (1823), pp. 55, 68.

Bayldon's *Art of Valuing* gave the figures shown in Table 1.4 for hypothetical farms in 1823 – after enclosure, but after the French wars, too. The economic rent implied by these figures is 25 or 30 percent of the costs, but the rent to landlords – which is the relevant weighting on changes in rents to landlords – is lower. The correct figure is something between 13 and 30 percent, probably closer to the lower figure than the upper.

The consequences are as follows. Rents rose by 50 to 100 percent. Therefore efficiency rose by anything from 0.13 (50) = 6.5 percent to 0.30 (100) = 30 percent.

As usual in history (or in economics, if the truth be known), no heavy weight can be laid on the second or third digit in such estimates. Often enough the first is in doubt. The historical economist who lives by the second digit will die by the second digit. But what is clear is that the loss from open fields was not utterly trivial, 1 or 2 percent of output; nor was it immense, 50 percent. A defensible average for the eighteenth century would be, say, 13 percent, and something lower – perhaps 10 percent – for the centuries of prosperity in open fields. So be it.

This is no crushing burden of inefficiency. Little wonder. When inefficiencies become crushing the victims try to avoid them. One result of the light burden has long been known: The gains are so small that enclosure cannot be portrayed as the hero of the agricultural revolution.[59] If the gain from enclosure was 13 percent on villages still open in 1700, those were nonetheless only half of the villages. The gain to the efficiency of agriculture as a whole was therefore about 0.50 (0.13) = 6.5 percent. This is small relative to the evident gains in agricultural productivity during the eighteenth century (though not to be sneered at, either). Likewise it is small relative to the 73 percent

---

[59] See Allen, "Enclosure, Capitalist Agriculture," p. 45; McCloskey, "Enclosure of Open Fields," p. 35; and many earlier writers, such as Eric Kerridge, Chambers, and Mingay.

gain in overall British output per head from 1760 to 1830.[60] Around 1790 only 40 percent of income was earned from agriculture, and less from grain growing and cattle raising in open-field regions. This implies that enclosure raised national income less than $(0.40)(6.5) = 2.6$ percent. Three percent is not a contemptible return from the "mere simple re-distribution of the land," but neither by itself does it bulk large in the nature and causes of the wealth of nations.

Why scattering depends on missing markets

The national burden of inefficiency would have been more significant in the Middle Ages, though still not overwhelming. When perhaps four-fifths of income was earned in agriculture and when most of the agriculture took place in open-field villages a sacrifice of 10 or 15 percent from failing to enclose would translate into something under 10 percent of national income, but not far under.

Why would a starving peasantry throw away 10 percent of its output? This is the central puzzle.

The facts impose a discipline on the solutions. It is not enough to offer an explanation peculiar to England, since many agricultures have scattered their holdings. Nor again is it enough to offer an explanation merely for why scattering began. Scattering began in New England in the first generation of settlement, imported by habit from old England in the early seventeenth century, but it did not persist and was gone entirely by the third generation. The persistence of scattering, not its literal origin, is the puzzle. Peasants could have scattered land originally for reasons as trivial as their reasons for the local cure for warts. What is puzzling is that they stayed with so costly a custom for so many years. Nor, finally, is it enough to explain how the system persisted without telling how it came to an end. "Sheer custom" would have this difficulty: that it would go on working past its term. Farmers are bound by custom ever, as we all are.

The history is illuminated at once by the most abstract of economic theories. The abstract theory, proven with varying degrees of plausibility by Arrow and Debreu, Francis Y. Edgeworth, and Adam Smith, is that in a market with no transaction costs, and in which therefore everything is for sale, efficiency is achieved. Regardless of who owns them at the start, resources end up in the hands of the people who

---

[60] Charles H. Feinstein, "Capital Formation in Great Britain," in P. Mathias and M. M. Postan, eds., *The Cambridge Economic History of Europe*, vol. 7, *The Industrial Economies*, pt. 1 (Cambridge: Cambridge University Press, 1978), p. 84.

value them most. Income is maximized. Ronald Coase pointed out in 1959 to the astonishment of economists that the contrapositive of Smith's Theorem was therefore true: If inefficiency exists, then some market must be imperfectly realized, and it will matter who owns the resources at the start.

The historical point is this. Each explanation of scattering depends on a nonexistent or expensive market. If the market presumed to exist *does* exist, cheaply, then the explanation is wrong. The explanation cannot get to the conclusion, namely, an inefficient system of scattering. Take for example the oldest explanation of open fields, the alleged common plowing of the land. In 1883 Frederic Seebohm argued that the scattered strips were a consequence of the large number of oxen required to pull medieval plows. One contributor to the team, he said, would have the team for one day on his own land, another person the next day, and so on, distributing the penalty of inefficiently early or late plowing over the whole group.[61] The explanation has proven hardy, perhaps because it has an attractive air of technological determinism, and because the heavy clay lands of Northern Europe were in fact prime areas of open fields. The Orwins, Warren Ault, M. M. Postan, and Michael Mazur adopted it.[62]

It has difficulties, factual and logical. Joint plowing does not seem actually to have occurred, laming the theory at the starting gate. Ault, for instance, notes that cases before manorial courts make no mention of joint plowing, though they mentioned frequently other agreements among villagers (when the agreements were broken). Soon after Seebohm put forward the argument, Paul Vinogradoff noted that scattering occurred in regions with light soil, too, and on holdings large enough to support a full team.[63] Scattering long survived any documented need to share teams. Anyway, if plow teams came back to the village after a day's (really a morning's) plowing, as they often did, then there would be no advantage to laying out John's strips next to Richard's.

And, to get to the chief point, the coplowing explanation assumes

[61] *The English Village Community* (London: Longman, Green, 1883), pp. 113ff.
[62] C. S. Orwin and C. S. Orwin, *The Open Fields* (Oxford: Clarendon Press, 1938); Warren O. Ault, *Open-Field Farming in Medieval England* (London: Allen & Unwin, 1972), p. 20; M. M. Postan, *The Medieval Economy and Society* (Berkeley and Los Angeles: University of California Press, 1972), p. 49; and Michael P. Mazur, "The Dispersion of Holdings in the Open Fields: An Interpretation in Terms of Property Rights," *Journal of European Economic History* 6 (1977): 461–72.
[63] *Villainage in England* (Oxford: Oxford University Press, 1892), pp. 231ff.

that peasants could not rent oxen or plowing services from each other. This is false: They could and did. The missing market that supports inefficiency was not in fact missing.

Without pretending in this way to knock down serious scholarship in a few lines, the same point can be made of the other explanations, posing for them at least a problem to be researched. The explanations have proliferated, especially since economists have entered the field. An explanation with a flavor similar to Seebohm's, for example, has been put forward by Stefano Fenoaltea in papers critical of my work.[64] He has argued that the strips were scattered to spread not the oxen for plowing but the laborers for planting and harvesting. Fenoaltea cites with approval the argument of Charles Parain:

> At the outset [of the open field system], when each plot needed at least a day's work, the scattering was rather more advantageous than not. A single tenant's holding [consolidated] all on one kind of soil would often require to be worked quickly, when the soil was in the right condition, and harvested quickly. Plots with different soils are ready for working at different times.[65]

Again the argument has factual difficulties at the outset. Gregory Clark has recently calculated that the maximum cost saving from smoothing the peak was less than 1 percent of output, chiefly because only middling farmers would need *additional* labor for a consolidated holding: The small farmers needed no hired labor anyway, and the large farmers needed it regardless of the configuration of their holding.[66] But the main difficulty is that the argument supposes that hiring labor was especially costly. Fenoaltea agrees with other serious students of the matter that the myth of natural economy is false, and that the medieval West was saturated with markets in goods. But the same applies to labor. As was noted earlier, England had a large rural proletariat in the thirteenth and fourteenth centuries, people who lived by working on other people's land. There was nothing strange about hiring harvest labor. Fenoaltea's argument requires a bad market in labor, yet he offers scant evidence that the market in labor was anything but good.

---

[64] "Risk, Transaction Costs, and the Organization of Medieval Agriculture," *Explorations in Economic History* 13 (April 1976): 129–51, and recent unpublished work.

[65] Charles Parain, "The Evolution of Agricultural Technique," in M. M. Postan, ed., *The Cambridge Economic History of Europe*, vol. 1, 2d ed. (Cambridge: Cambridge University Press, 1966), p. 138 (Parain's text here is unmodified from the 1941 ed., p. 129).

[66] "Cost of Capital," pp. 39–43.

Carl Dahlman, in a tour de force of property-rights economics, has argued that common grazing was the key to scattering.[67] The common herd, he claims, was a source of economies of scale (this in contrast to most writers, who regard it as a source of economies of disease). To keep it together the strips were scattered, forcing a socialism of the herd on reluctant individualists. Gregory Clark has made a suggestion of a similar character, focusing on the economies of scale in fencing and on the individualized grazing that could go on within the fences.[68] Clark views the absence of fencing, not the presence of scattering, as the crucial feature of open fields. Both arguments, however, depend on a lack of market in grazing rights. Yet grazing rights were bought and sold with ease.

It is worth noting that any explanation that depends on the importance of animal products in medieval agriculture, as do Dahlman's and Clark's, is going to be in a certain amount of trouble from the start. English agriculture was a matter chiefly of grains, and to argue that advantages in the making of wool and meat and cheese led farmers to configure their grain fields in peculiar ways is probably a mistake. A serious estimate of the share of animal products in total product cannot be attempted here, but some back-of-the-envelope calculations illustrate the problem. Reckoning conservatively from the estimates of Gregory King in 1688 and the first crop returns in 1866, the close-packed population of England and Wales around 1300 worked on perhaps fifteen million acres of arable land, of which ten million were under crop.[69] Taking wheat and barley as the grain crops, and using yields and prices in southern England just after 1300, each acre would produce about 8.75 shillings' worth of grain.[70] The result is grain income of (8.75 shillings per acre) × (10 million acres) = 87.5 million shillings for England and Wales, without including the value of straw or fallow grazing. The animals yielded much less. Robert Trow-Smith,

---

[67] *The Open Field System and Beyond: A Property Rights Analysis of an Economic Institution* (Cambridge: Cambridge University Press, 1980).

[68] See Clark, "Cost of Capital." Compare McCloskey, "The Economics of Enclosure: A Market Analysis," in E. L. Jones and William Parker, eds., *European Peasants and Their Markets: Essays in Agrarian Economic History* (Princeton, N.J.: Princeton University Press, 1975), pp. 145n, 149.

[69] Lord Ernle (R. E. Prothero), *English Farming Past and Present*, 6th ed., ed. and introduced by G. E. Fussell and O. R. McGregor (Chicago: Quadrangle Books, 1961), pp. 503, 512.

[70] Yields from J. Z. Titow, *Winchester Yields: A Study in Medieval Agricultural Productivity* (Cambridge: Cambridge University Press, 1972), p. 149; prices from W. H. Beveridge, "The Yield and Price of Corn in the Middle Ages," *Economic History* 1 (May 1927): 155–67.

the leading historian of British livestock husbandry, noted that in the Middle Ages "the cow was primarily the source of the plow ox and only incidentally the source of what milk she had to spare for the cheese vat and the butter churn after she had fulfilled her most important function."[71] Cattle, in other words, were inputs into grain production, as was also the manure of sheep and cattle. Sheep were more important in their own right, but not enough to rise to much significance relative to grain. On the basis of export statistics of wool Trow-Smith put the national flock in 1310–11 excluding lambs at twelve million.[72] Wethers earned half a shilling a year in wool, ewes less in total (their milk was worth $3\frac{1}{2}$ pence).[73] The annual yield on sheep was therefore on a generous allowance some 6 million shillings. In other words, grain output was fourteen times more important.

A similar result can be achieved in another way. The average payer of tax in the thirteenth century would have been of above-average prosperity, yet had fewer than ten sheep, one or two oxen, two cows or calves, and a couple of pigs.[74] On his 19 acres (say), perhaps 60 percent of which was under crop in any year, he would produce (19 acres) × (0.60 crop land/acre of holding) × (8.75 shillings per acre of crop) = 100 shillings per year. But his sheep would yield him (10 sheep) × (0.5 shillings per sheep) = 5 shillings per year. That is, by this reckoning the grain output on the average prosperous peasant holding was twenty times more important than the most important animal product.

The result accords with what is known of medieval diets. A laborer was supplied with five pounds of bread daily. Consider that as a steady diet. Miller and Hatcher write:

> The average villager fed on large quantities of coarse dark bread, occasional dishes of pottage made primarily from oatmeal with a few vegetables or pieces of meat added to the pot when they were available, and copious draughts of weak ale made from the malt of wheat or more likely barley or oats. Families with a cow or ewes or goats would have a supply of milk, cheese and butter, and perhaps occasionally meat; but like the peasant's wheat crop, part of these animal products would have to be sold.[75]

The animal products were not sold for other consumption but for rent and taxes, half of agricultural income in the fourteenth century. All

[71] *A History of British Livestock Husbandry to 1700* (London: Routledge & Kegan Paul, 1957), p. 123.

[72] Ibid., p. 140.

[73] Ibid., p. 17.

[74] Edward Miller and John Hatcher, *Medieval England: Rural Society and Economic Change, 1086–1348* (London: Longman, 1978), p. 153.

[75] Ibid., p. 160 (5 lb); p. 159 (diet).

that could be reasonably asked was to get this day some daily bread, washed down with weak beer.

Though not a theory of scattering, one of the recent theories of the open fields depends heavily on a missing market (this time in land) and an exaggeration of the practical importance of animal products. It is the notion that open fields were cases of "overfishing." The argument rests in fact on a natural misunderstanding of the character of open fields, arising from their other name, "common fields." The terminology is confusing. The common fields were the open fields, plowed for crops, not the "commons," which were permanent grazing lands, frequently of an inferior and peripheral kind. To be sure, after the harvest was gathered the Lammas lands once under crop became common, in the sense that the common herd grazed on them. But otherwise they were as private as a suburban house lot.

Calling the open fields "common" makes them sound socialistic, or at least precapitalist. It makes them sound like a case of common property, to which the model of overfishing a lake applies. Garrett Hardin, a geographer, started this particular misapprehension in a classic paper in *Science* called "The Tragedy of the Commons," which drew on his notions of what things must have been like in England in olden times.[76] The model appeals in the abstract to both Marxist and procapitalist economists. B. D. Baack and R. P. Thomas (1974) have applied it from the capitalist side and J. S. Cohen and M. L. Weitzman (1975) from the Marxist side, reaching the same conclusion: What must have been wrong with medieval agriculture was that property was held in common (in those common fields); when in the sixteenth century, or perhaps in the eighteenth century, people started taking property seriously the inefficiency would of course disappear.[77]

The difficulties with the argument are numerous. The overgrazing would reduce the value of the animal crops, but these have been shown to be small. No one claims that the supposed overgrazing would affect the grain crops. Theoretically speaking, the overgrazing is said to have been a prisoner's dilemma, in which excessive numbers of cattle trampled the grass, killing it permanently, just as overhunting of whales brings the population below the level at which it can reproduce. Agronomically speaking, this is not quite right. The chief technical

---

[76] "The Tragedy of the Commons," *Science* 162 (December 1968): 1243–48.

[77] Baack and Thomas, "The Enclosure Movement and the Supply of Labor during the Industrial Revolution," *Journal of European Economic History* 3 (Fall 1974): 401–23; Cohen and Weitzman, "A Marxian Model of Enclosures," *Journal of Development Economics* 1 (February 1975): 287–336.

problem, however, is economic, namely, that the social milieu in which overgrazing is supposed to be taking place is unreasonable. The farmers of England are imagined to have tolerated big losses of grazing efficiency – a Cobb–Douglas specification implies a dissipation of two-thirds of the rent with as few as five graziers – yet not to have taken action. Theoretically the overgrazing model corresponds exactly to the Cournot model of oligopoly, term for term, and the criticism of the Cournot model therefore applies: No one would be so foolish as not to cooperate if cooperation were possible, which draws attention to the factual question of how easy cooperation was to achieve. Factually the Cournot/prisoner's dilemma model misdescribes villages in England: The farmers did in fact cooperate, because the existing institutions of the village or later of the king's court made cooperation easy. The common grazing land, whether the literal commons or the temporary common grazing on the open fields after the harvest, was "stinted," that is, limited in the number of animals allowed on it. The right to graze twenty sheep was attached to the Mill cottage and the right to graze three cows was attached to Tom's fifteen acres held of the lord in the open fields. The land was not overfished. A law of the sea was devised, village by village.

But the main problem with the overfishing argument is that it supposes that a market in land did not exist, that land in the Middle Ages was common property. It is difficult to convince educated people that this is not so. Somewhere early in their educations most people acquire a view of the Middle Ages prevalent in the nineteenth century, of the medieval economy as a "natural," nonmoney economy in which such a thing as owning land was foreign. Owning is supposed to have arrived with capitalism. Because of England's season of world eminence, English history provides the background for many other histories, and the freezing of attitudes toward medieval peasants in the configuration of around 1880 has therefore caused damage to people far removed from Oxfordshire and Kent.

Since the early years of this century medievalists have been fighting a losing battle against the popular notion that the Middle Ages was innocent of markets and that land was held communally. On sober consideration the subnotion that land was inalienable and common has never been very plausible: A society that marketed human beings and eternal salvation would be unlikely to have scruples about marketing land. But speculation is unnecessary, since the evidence of an active market in land among peasants is ample. Even serfs participated, though their lord taxed their gains and made certain that his ownership of their tenancies was not attenuated. M. M. Postan concluded that "the purpose of [the lord's] control was not to restrict, still less to

31

destroy, the village market... [but] to profit from his villein's transactions."[78] Rosamund Faith, summarizing work on the subject by herself and Postan among others, argues that in open-field villages of the late fourteenth century "land changed hands rapidly and on a large scale.... The chief function of the manorial court began to be that of land-registry for the virtually free market in peasant holdings that had come into being."[79] Even in the thirteenth century she believes "there is ample evidence of an active peasant land market," though she argues that before the coming of the plague in the mid-fourteenth century the exchanges were "predominantly small scale, involving odd acres and plots, a process which only marginally affected the ownership and structure of the basic family holdings."[80] The churning of the land was natural in view of the varying fortunes of individual families. The life cycle would alter the amount of land a family could profitably work; further, peasants were mobile in and out of the village and up and down the social scale.[81] In their survey Miller and Hatcher conclude that "the consequence was that the tenurial pattern of medieval villages, in the villeinage as well as in the free tenures, was in constant flux."[82]

Land was alienable, then, and it was private. More evidence comes from manorial court rolls, in which the peasants are reported quarreling endlessly about their *private* rights to land.[83] Did John make a way through Richard's field in the West Ing? Let him be bound to pay 3 pence. Did Thomas come into the field at night, for what cannot have been good reasons? Let him, too, be fined heavily, and made to offer a bond that he will pay it. The court rolls have the atmosphere of a police court, but a police court in a society that values everything in money. No one went to jail; he or she paid. That others had rights over John's land did not make the land common: Rights of passage or rights of early plowing were pieces of property, too, and alienable. Property rights were complicated in the open fields, but vividly present

---

[78] C. N. L. Brooke and M. M. Postan, eds., *Carte Nativorum*, Northamptonshire Record Society Publications 20 (1960), p. xlviii; compare D. Roden, "Field Systems in the Chiltern Hills and Their Environs," in Baker and Butlin, *Studies*, p. 356.

[79] "Peasant Families and Inheritance Customs in Medieval England," *Agricultural History Review* 14 (1966): 92.

[80] Ibid., p. 86.

[81] J. Ambrose Raftis, *Tenure and Mobility: Studies in the Social History of the Mediaeval English Village* (Toronto: Pontifical Institute of Mediaeval Studies, 1964).

[82] Miller and Hatcher, *Medieval England*, p. 142.

[83] See, for example, on quarreling about land rights, Warren O. Ault, "Open-Field Husbandry and the Village Community, a Study of Agrarian By-Laws in Medieval England," *Transactions of the American Philosophical Society* n.s. 55 (October 1965).

to the minds of the peasants as things to be bought and sold. The village land was no casually managed public park. A peasant owned unambiguously what he or she had planted – or rather what could be retained from the depredations of lord, church, and king. From the depredations of other peasants the owner had all the protection of the law. Haukyn the Active Man in *Piers Plowman* was no agrarian socialist:

> If I go to the plow I pinch so narrow
> That a foot of land or furrow fetch I would
> Of my next neighbor, take of his earth;
> And if I reap, overreach, or give him advice that reap
> To seize to me with their sickle what I never sowed.[84]

The private, alienable character of the land creates difficulties for other explanations of open fields, such as equality of inheritance or equality of the initial laying out of the fields.[85] F. W. Maitland asked in 1897, "Who laid out these fields?" and replied: "The obvious answer is that they were laid out by men who would sacrifice economy and efficiency at the shrine of equality."[86] Vinogradoff gave the usual formulation: "The only adequate explanation of the open-field intermixture . . . [is] the wish to equalize the holdings as to the quality and quantity of land assigned to [each peasant] in spite of all differences in the shape, the position, and the value of the soil."[87] Viewed merely as a theory of the origin rather than of the persistence of scattering, the egalitarian theory has difficulties well expressed in 1928 by George Fowler (who favored Seebohm's coaration theory): "I am not aware of any direct evidence in support [of the egalitarian theory]; and when one considers the handful of men who first settled in each township, and the abundance of land available, the theory seems to be unnecessary."[88] Nothing would be served, he was arguing, by distributing a free good equally. Furthermore, there is no evidence that medieval peasants were egalitarian as individuals or, as it is sometimes

---

[84] William Langland, *The Vision of Piers Ploughman*, the B text (ca. 1378), ed. A. V. C. Schmidt (London: Dent, 1978), passus xiii, 370–74 (p. 159) (modernized).

[85] Compare McCloskey, "Persistence of English Common Fields," in E. L. Jones and William Parker, eds., *European Peasants and Their Markets: Essays in Agrarian Economic History* (Princeton, N.J.: Princeton University Press, 1975), pp. 102–12.

[86] *Domesday Book and Beyond* (Cambridge: Cambridge University Press, 1897), p. 394.

[87] *Villainage*, p. 254; compare Vinogradoff, *The Growth of the Manor* (London: Allen & Unwin, 1911), pp. 175ff.

[88] G. H. Fowler, *Four Pre-Enclosure Village Maps*, Quarto Memoirs of the Bedford-shire Historical Record Society 2 (1928–36), pt. i, p. 4.

put to save the hypothesis, class by class. Holdings of village members varied radically from nothing at all to large holdings in several villages, serfs owning other serfs. It is hard to read Middle English literature and retain the view that the medieval peasantry was a band of brothers.

More important, viewed as a theory of the persistence of scattered strips, the egalitarian theory must deal somehow with the vigorous market in land. Scattering was an inefficient way of establishing equality. A community bent on equality might have chosen to simplify its task by distributing a bundle of strips drawn from all parts of the village land instead of adjusting the sizes of consolidated holdings to their quality. Inheritance by literal brothers often follows such a distribution to forestall backbiting. Yet after the original scattering had assured equality the peasants would benefit from trades to achieve consolidation – that is, they would benefit unless scattering had some advantage beyond equality. A peasant determined to acquire a consolidated holding could begin buying up contiguous strips, as occurred in the many cases of gradual enclosure by purchase. In other words, egalitarianism might have required scattering at the origin of the open fields, but it can hardly explain the scattering through eight or nine centuries of shifting ownership of land.

Open fields as behavior toward risk

A promising alternative is that strips were scattered to insure against disaster. The argument is that within a single English village there was enough variability to make it desirable to hold a diverse portfolio of strips.

The land and weather of England are notoriously variable, even over the two square miles or so of the typical village. A place with sandy soil on a rise would shed some year's excessive rain, yet one with clay soil in a valley would hold another's insufficient rain. An exposed place would have wheat likely to become tangled by rain and high winds at harvest but free of mold in a generally wet year. A sheltered place would be relatively immune from windy disasters but less dry and more moldy on that account. The average width of the English hailstorm is two hundred yards, one-sixth of the side of a typical field of three hundred acres; it cuts a swath of damaged grain through a consolidated holding three hundred yards on a side.[89] England has a

---

[89] F. R. A. Russell, *On Hail* (London: Stanford, 1893).

maritime climate and therefore feels sharp variations in temperature by altitude, and variations in the incidence of thaw and frost.[90] A place could be hit by birds, rust, moles, rabbits, thieves, flooding, insects, hunting parties, and wandering armies, to name a few more of the reasons an English peasant would value insurance, while another place close by would go free. A town dweller finds it hard to believe that crops could vary much over a small area; a country dweller does not.

When they have looked beyond peasant conservatism or peasant jealousy to explain why scattering persisted, a few historians and economists have come to risk aversion. The great French historian Marc Bloch was attached to an egalitarian theory but admitted, too, that "if the plots were dispersed . . . everyone had some hope of avoiding the full impact of natural or human disasters – hailstorms, plant diseases, devastation – which might descend on a place without destroying it completely."[91] Among the reasons Hungarian peasants rejected consolidation in the 1850s was their fear that natural disasters would destroy a family's whole crop.[92] Although regarded by its reporter as the prejudice of a benighted peasantry, the reason was given by a sample of villagers in modern Greece: "Why should the plots be all together? We are more secure this way: fire, bad weather, etc."[93] In 1970 John W. Thomas, an economist with the Development Advisory Service, was so bold as to *ask* peasants in what was then East Pakistan why they opposed consolidation, and found that their declared reason was protection against disaster, especially flooding that would leave untouched the higher plots (a mere six to ten feet above the rest).[94]

Anthropologists have been less liable than most historians or economists (or government planners) to dismiss scattering as irrational. The Hopi Indians of the American Southwest in the 1930s scattered their plots of maize: The Katcina clan in one village held six plots scattered over a six-by-six-mile area. C. Daryll Forde explained:

This dispersal is of very great practical importance since it reduces the risk of crop failure; where the crop on one group of fields may wither from drought or

[90] Gordon Manley, *Climate and the British Scene* (Glasgow: Collins, 1952).
[91] *French Rural History*, trans. J. Sondheimer (Berkeley and Los Angeles: University of California Press, 1966; first published in French, 1931), p. 255. Compare p. 233.
[92] E. Molnar, ed., *Magyarorszag Története*, 3d ed., vol. 2 (Budapest: Gondolat, 1971), p. 37.
[93] Thompson, *Farm Fragmentation in Greece*, pp. 8, 170–73; cf. Papageorgiou, "Greece," p. 546; J. Roche for France, also in Parsons et al., eds., *Land Tenure*, p. 536; Hyodo for Japan, p. 559.
[94] Personal communication.

be washed away by floods there remains the chance that the others will be spared. In particular, disastrous floods rarely occur in all the flats in the same season. The lands close in to the mesa and those out in the middle are still more definitely reciprocal. In an abnormally wet year, when many of the latter are liable to be destroyed by the high floods, the scarp plots are well watered, while, on the other hand, in [a?] dry season when they in their turn are likely to be parched out, enough water is usually brought down by the streams to afford a harvest for the mid-valley fields.[95]

Another anthropologist, Alan Hoben, argues that the scattering of plots by the Amhara farmer of Ethiopia "is highly desirable . . . for by providing him with fields of different qualities it enables him to diversify his crops and to reduce the risk of total crop failure." Repeated attempts to impose land reform on the Amhara, in 1967–68, for example, were bloody failures. As Hoben remarks, "If a program of land reform is to be effective it must be based on a model . . . illuminating the rational process through which people make decisions about land instead of simply attributing these decisions to the dead hand of tradition."[96] Anthropologists elsewhere have noted that risk aversion explains scattering, in Tanzania, for example, and southwestern Switzerland and Brazil.[97] So have poets and prophets. The Merchant of Venice did not "think upon his merchandise," because

> My ventures are not in one bottom trusted,
> Nor to one place; nor is my whole estate
> Upon the fortune of this present year:
> Therefore my merchandise makes me not sad.

"Give a portion to seven, and also to eight," said Jesus, son of Sirach, "for thou knowest not what evil shall be upon the earth."

The question is whether giving a portion to six effective strips in one of three open fields made the peasant not sad by avoiding the evils of this earth.[98] The answer is that it did. A consolidated holding would

---

[95] *Habitat, Economy and Society* (London: Methuen, 1934), p. 234.

[96] "Social Anthropology and Development Planning: A Case Study in Ethiopian Land Reform Policy," M.S. thesis, Boston University, n.d. [ca. 1972], pp. 2, 11–12, 34.

[97] Beidelman, *Karugu*, p. 16; R. M. Netting, "Of Men and Meadows: Strategies of Alpine Land Use," *Anthropological Quarterly* 45 (1972): 132–44, p. 134; A. W. Johnson, *Sharecroppers of the Sertao* (Stanford, Calif.: Stanford University Press, 1971), pp. 69–72; and other evidence on Tanzania in articles by Hawkins and by Heijnen and Kates in Gilbert F. White, ed., *Natural Hazards: Local, National, Global* (London: Oxford University Press, 1974).

[98] What follows is a radical condensation of pp. 131–61 in McCloskey, "English Open Fields as Behavior Towards Risk," *Research in Economic History* 1 (Fall 1976): 124–70.

Table 1.5. *The average and standard deviation of medieval grain income on consolidated and on scattered holdings*

	When disaster is 50			
	Average income	Standard deviation	Distance from disaster	Frequency of disaster
Consolidated	110	48.4	1.24σ	Every 9.3 years
Scattered	100	34.7	1.44σ	Every 13.4 years

Source: Detailed calculations in McCloskey, "Risk," pp. 132–51.

have a higher average income but also a higher variance; the less productive but safer option was to scatter. If the scattering was very expensive and its reduction of risk small, then the deal would be a bad one. But for the conditions facing medieval peasants it was good in that it reduced the probability of falling below a disastrous level of income. The results are given in Table 1.5.

Some of the entries in the table are relatively straightforward. The 10 percent increase in productivity that might be expected from consolidation has been discussed at length above. The standard deviation on the index of 100 as the average yield is based on the ample evidence of medieval yields, especially Titow's magnificent compilation of yields 1209–1349 from the Bishop of Winchester's forty-odd manors in southwestern England.[99] That the level of disaster was about 50 percent of average output can be established in various ways.[100] The simplest and surest derives from the widespread agreement among English medievalists that the subsistence holding for a family was about ten acres.[101] If the average holding was nineteen acres, then subsistence income was about half of the average.

The exercise hinges, however, on the difference between the standard deviation of 34.7 observed on the typical scattered holding and the 48.4 claimed to hold on a consolidated holding. The variability on a holding depends on the correlation among strips. If the yields on strips move in lockstep from year to year, then scattering is useless.

[99] See ibid., pp. 132–36.
[100] Ibid., pp. 141–45.
[101] Miller and Hatcher, *Medieval England* (pp. 147f.), mention Bennett, Kosminsky, Hilton, and Titow as authorities for such a figure, to whom may be added M. M. Postan.

Donald N. McCloskey

The lower the average correlation of yields the lower is the variance on the portfolio of strips.

Call the variance of the entire bundle S^2, the variance of the ith strip s_i^2, and covariance between the ith and the jth strip s_{ij}. If the average output of each strip is defined to be 1.0, then s_i will be the coefficient of variation of the ith strip and S will be the coefficient of variation of total grain output. Supposing that each strip makes an equal contribution to output, the weight of each strip's output in the total will be $1/N$. Since the definition of the correlation coefficient, R_{ij}, is $s_{ij}/s_i s_j$, one can make the substitution $s_{ij} = s_i s_j R_{ij}$. With these bits of notation, it follows from the algebra of variances that:

$$S^2 = (1/N)^2 \left[\sum_{i=1}^{N} s_i^2 + \sum_{\substack{i=1, j=1 \\ i \neq j}}^{N} \sum s_i s_j R_{ij} \right]$$

The equation looks less enlightening than it is. The typical term of the first sum inside the brackets will be simply s^2, the average variance (that is, s^2, without a subscript, is the average of all the s_i^2). Further, because $s_i s_j$ will typically be close to s^2, the average variance, the typical term of the second, double, sum will be $s^2 R$, the average variance multiplied by the average correlation coefficient. There are $N(N-1)$ of these in the double sum (not N^2 because terms with $i = j$ are excluded). The double sum can therefore be approximated by $N(N-1)s^2 R$. The upshot is:

$$S^2 = (1/N)^2 [Ns^2 + N(N-1)s^2 R] = s^2[1 + (N-1)R]/N$$

Or, taking square roots,

$$S = s \{[1 + (N-1)R]/N\}^{\frac{1}{2}}.$$

This relation between the coefficient of variation of single strips (s) and of a bundle of strips (S) is approximate, but the inaccuracy can be shown to be trivial.

Observe that if $R = 1$ or $N = 1$, then $S = s$. That is, the coefficient of variation is not reduced if the yields of the various strips move in lockstep or if, equivalently, only one strip is held. When $R = 0$ the equation is simply $S = s/N^2$, the usual equation for the sample standard deviation. The risk falls steadily, though at slower and slower rates, as the number of strips rise. As N gets large then S approaches $sR^{\frac{1}{2}}$, this being the maximum effect of diversification in lowering the variability of income. When two types ($N = 2$) move exactly inversely ($R = -1$) then the variance is zero: By holding two such perfectly inversely correlated assets all of the variability of income is eliminated.

38

Most items in the equation are easily calculated from the Winchester yields and similar medieval sources. What is difficult is R. One sort of evidence is agronomical. R. A. Fisher's pioneering work *The Design of Experiments* was in large part devoted to a similar problem. One hears echoes of a cautious medieval peasant laying out long strips in a part of Fisher's advice for handling the problem: "Each [experimental] plot must . . . sample fairly the whole area of the block in which it is placed. It is often desirable, therefore, . . . to let the plots lie side by side as narrow strips running the whole length of its block."[102] He remarks that an area as small as an acre has "considerably greater soil heterogeneity" than a quarter-acre.[103] His elaborate care to minimize the uncertainty due to such variation was justified by earlier spoiled experiments. In reporting the experiments in rotation on a field at Woburn beginning in 1881, for example, J. A. Voelcker complained repeatedly that despite its apparent uniformity "the soil of Lansome Field . . . has been found to be not really uniform enough and the land not level enough to make a really satisfactory experimental field."[104] Plots 1 and 4 were quarter-acres a little over a hundred yards apart, treated to precisely the same unfertilized rotation. Yet the average yield from the four crops of barley taken from 1885 to 1897 was 13 percent higher on plot 4 than on plot 1 (perhaps plot 4 was enclosed and plot 1 open). The correlation of yields on plots 1 and 4 was only .78, despite the care taken to cultivate the plots in the same thorough and expensive way. Even the more successful experiments in the continuous growth of barley in the Stackyard field at Woburn could produce a correlation coefficient of only .84 from 1877 to 1884 between the two unfertilized plots, 1 and 7, a hundred yards apart.[105] The correlation drops sharply for plots treated with different fertilizers but cultivated otherwise in an identical careful fashion. For example, the correlation at Rothamsted between yields of wheat grown continuously without fallow on plot 3 (unfertilized) and plot 2 (fertilized with dung) from 1844 to 1883 was only .55.[106] Plot 2 could stand for the fertilized

---

[102] (New York: Hafner, 1947; first published 1935), p. 65.

[103] Ibid., p. 104.

[104] "The Woburn Experimental Farm," *Journal of the Royal Agricultural Society of England* 58 (1897): 258–93; 59 (1898): 622–55 and 678–726, p. 640, and "Report," *Journal of the Royal Agricultural Society of England* 45 (1884): 337–60, p. 360.

[105] Voelcker, "Woburn," pp. 722, 690–97.

[106] J. B. Lawes and J. H. Gilbert, "Report of Experiments on the Growth of Wheat for 20 Years in Succession on the Same Land," *Journal of the Royal Agricultural Society of England* 25 (1864): 93–185, and "On the Continuous Growth of Wheat on the Experimental Plots at Rothamsted during the 20 years, 1864 to 1883, Inclusive," *Journal of the Royal Agricultural Society of England* 45 (1884): 391–481.

infield and plot 3 for the unfertilized outfield in the runrig arrangement of upland Britain.

The experimental evidence, though, has the defects of its virtues. Cultivation was carefully controlled over a small area, but with the result that the effects of variations among plots, such as local attacks of mold and local peculiarities of drainage, were intentionally minimized. If the experimental evidence is relevant at all, it is to give upper bounds on the correlations to be expected in an agriculture lacking the knowledge or resources to achieve laboratory standards. The experiments suggest an upper bound on R of .70 or .80.

The best evidence on R is from open-field agriculture itself, scarce and ambiguous though the evidence is. Practically never do the records for a crop of wheat, say, specify yields in different parts of a village, yet this is what is wanted. Even so methodical a record keeper as Robert Loder, farming in Harwell, Berkshire, in the early seventeenth century, kept records on separate portions of his many different crops only for hay. On three crops of hay not more than a mile or so from each other the mutual correlations 1611–20 were .90, .66, and .37, giving an average of .64.[107] Loder interpreted a reduction in the crop from the Padocke in 1612 as "the loving and fatherly chastisements of the Lord my God,"[108] but the Lord did not lay on the lash everywhere: The yield in the Town Meade rose by over 50 percent in the same year.

In the absence of more evidence of this sort – which in any case could be expected to exist only in an age of literate and reflective farmers, and which therefore would be to some extent anachronistic – one must turn again to the medieval records of the manorial farms, the farms of the lord of the manor from which our evidence on yields always comes. Many manorial farms with records were close to others with records. This makes it possible to infer from the correlations between villages what the correlation might have been within them.

The procedure has difficulties, to be sure. The neighboring villages must be quite close, no more than three miles or so apart, to be relevant to the inside of anything but a long, thin village. Since few are less than two miles apart (measuring distances from church to church on the modern Ordnance Survey maps) and since, as will be shown in a moment, the correlation falls with distance, the calculated correlations may be too low to represent the correlation facing a peasant in

---

[107] G. E. Fussell, ed., *Robert Loder's Farm Accounts 1610–1620*, Camden Society Publications, 3d ser., 53 (1936), *passim*, e.g. pp. 5–6, 184.
[108] Ibid., p. 36.

one open field in a village. On the other hand, since the manorial farm usually took the best land (bottomland in a valley, for example), the correlations may be too high, because the bottomland in one village may be more similar to the bottomland in another than to the land on the village hill. Although Twyford and Stoke are the most distant pair of the Bishop of Winchester's neighboring manorial farms considered below (3.3 miles church to church), the correlation of their wheat crops is the second highest observed, .84. If the manorial farms were consolidated and near the center of each village, then the observed high correlation would be misleading, for the centers of both are on the same bank of the River Itchen with the same (southeasterly) exposure relative to nearby hills.

The evidence, nonetheless, is suggestive. The first insight that can be wrung from it is that the correlation of yield of a crop between two villages, R, does fall as the distance between the two increases. Were this not the case it might be possible to achieve insurance without scattering, for if R were, say, .60 both at a distance of two hundred yards and two thousand yards a peasant could hold a sufficient diversity of land within a small area. One presumes that R would indeed fall with distance, and it is pleasing to have the presumption confirmed for the villages on the Winchester estates 1335–49. Choosing the dozen under 3.3 miles apart and setting aside the two pairs (East Meon–East Meon Church and Twyford–Stoke) that fall far off the fitted line for the good reason that they were in different parts of Hampshire from the others, the regression of R for wheat on miles of distance is:

$$R = .95 - .14 \text{ (distance)} \quad r^2 = .66$$
$$n = 10$$
$$SEE = .07$$

For each mile of distance of one crop of wheat from another, therefore, the R fell 14 points. Errors in variables cannot be ignored, in particular the error in measuring crop distances with church-to-church distances. Reversing the regression to allow for the bias due to error leads to a coefficient of .22 rather than .14, a more powerful effect of distance on correlation.

The correlations would not, of course, go on falling indefinitely as distance rose. The correlations in six randomly selected pairs of villages (from ten to forty-five miles apart), compared in Table 1.6 with the correlations in close villages, imply a lower limit on R in Hampshire for the three major crops taken together of about .40. The last line in the table gives the probability of observing such differences by the chances of the sample if the correlations between pairs of the distant and near villages were in truth the same. That the distant

41

Table 1.6. *Comparisons of correlations between yields in close and far villages, Winchester manorial farms, 1335–49*

	Wheat	Barley	Oats	Average equally weighted
Distant villages (N = 6)				
Average R	.55	.15	.38	.38
(Standard dev.)	(.18)	(.23)	(.90)	(.09)
Near villages (N = 9)				
Average R	.68	.57	.66	.64
(Standard dev.)	(.15)	(.15)	(.22)	(.09)
Level of significance of difference	.074	.001	.01	.0001

villages have lower R's is additional testimony to the inverse relationship between R and distance. By this test there is more room for skepticism about the testimony on wheat than on the other crops, although by the regression test less room. Regressions of R against distance work poorly for barley and oats, possibly because spring crops depend more than does wheat on variations of soil and the like within distances smaller than the mile-or-more minimum distance church to church in the Winchester estates.

This last possibility finds some confirmation in still another test of the inverse relationship between R and distance, relying on correlations between different crops. If correlations fall with distance one would expect correlations between crops of, say, wheat and barley to be lower between two close villages than within each village. For instance, one would expect the correlation of the wheat crop in Alresford with the barley crop in Sutton (these two crops being about one and a half miles apart) to be lower than the correlation of the wheat crop in Alresford with the barley crop in Alresford itself (these crops being closer: a mile or less apart). Remarkably (to someone with mature experience in such matters) the expectation is fulfilled (see Table 1.7). The differences between the within- and between-village correlations for oats–barley fall with greater distance (the correlations involving the winter crop, wheat, display no uniform pattern). Regressing the excess of the within-village correlations of oats and barley over the between-village correlation on the church-to-church distance in miles (d) for the seven pairs gives:

$$R_{\text{within}} - R_{\text{between}} = -.16 + .12 \text{ (distance)} \quad r^2 = .61$$
$$SEE = .07$$

Table 1.7. *Correlations between crops within and between seven pairs of close villages, Winchester manorial farms, 1335–49*

	Average correlations between			
	Wheat & barley	Wheat & oats	Oats & barley	Average of these
Within the villages	.39	.26	.43	.36
Between the villages	.35	.21	.32	.29

For each mile of distance, in other words, the oats–barley correlation falls twelve points further below the same correlation within a village. Notice how similar the coefficient is to the comparable coefficient in the wheat regression given above. That the difference would be negative (rather than what it should be, zero) when the distance is zero comes from extrapolating a straight line beyond the data (compare Gregory Clark's strictures, which make much of the point). A linear specification could easily be wrong for small distances, flattening out at distances below the observed minimum of the sample (1.5 miles, alas). The R^2 of $R_w - R_b = .008d^{2.72}$ is in fact a little higher, .65. In any event, the correlations do fall with distance.

The other insight that can be wrung from the experience of neighboring manorial farms is that the correlation for a single crop over the distances relevant to scattering in open fields is indeed about .60. Since the experimental correlations over small distances are not much above this level, the assertion is not surprising. On the neighboring Winchester estates, to be sure, the average (given in Table 1.7) is a little higher, about .64, implying a still higher figure at lower distances. Yet these manorial farms, as was noted earlier, were located on chalk soils, inherently less variable and hazardous in their response to the weather than the clay soils further north (on which open fields persisted longest). On the four Woodstock manors at about the same time located on the edge of the clay soils of the Midland plain, the average R was well below .60, as Table 1.8 shows. The average over the three crops for the six pairs (from 1.25 to 3.6 miles apart) ranges from 0 (for Combe–Wooton) to .52 (for Bladon–Wooton), the average over the six pairs for the three crops, from .10 (for oats) to .48 (for wheat). The overall average correlation is .24. The evidence justifies a choice of R as low as .60.

The rest of the argument requires mere manipulation of these findings. The coefficient of variation on manorial farms is observed to be about .46, and was of course the result of holding many diverse

Table 1.8. Correlations between yields of neighboring manorial farms of the Woodstock manors, 1243–49

	Combe			Handborough			Wooton		
	Wheat	Barley	Oats	Wheat	Barley	Oats	Wheat	Barley	Oats
Bladon wheat	.12								
barley		.60							
oats			−.29						
Combe wheat				.76					
barley					−.51				
oats						.046			
Handborough wheat							.50		
barley								.48	
oats									.37

Source: A. Ballard, "Woodstock Manors in the Thirteenth Century," *Vierteljahrschrift für Sozial- und Wirtschaftsgeschichte* 6 (1908): 424–59, as compiled in B. H. Slicher van Bath, *Yield Ratios, 810–1820,* Afdeling Agrarische Geschiedenis Bijdragen 10 (1963).

types of land. The manorial farms were themselves often scattered, and in any case were much larger than a peasant farm with a mere half-dozen plots in each field. Suppose the manorial farm contained fifteen types of land (it would make little difference if it contained ten or twenty), each having the correlation of .60 with the others on average. With such figures the expression derived above for the coefficient of variation of a portfolio,

$$S = s\{[1 + (N - 1)R]/N\}^{\frac{1}{2}},$$

translates into

$$.46 = c\{[1 + (15 - 1)(.60)]/15\}^{\frac{1}{2}}.$$

We have gotten down to the coefficient of variation on one type of land, c. It can be solved for in the equation, and here it is $c = .58$.

Now build back up to a peasant holding of nineteen acres. If a peasant had a crop on one type of land, the coefficient of variation, as just shown, would be .58. If he had only one crop that would be that. But peasants had two or three crops, wheat for the rent, barley for beer and black bread, and oats for porridge. On consolidated holdings the average correlation, R, of yields among crops was .36 (see Table 1.7, the end of the "Within the villages" row). So according to the formula just used, the coefficient of variation on the consolidated holding would be

$$S = .58\{[1 + 2 (.36)]/3\}^{\frac{1}{2}} = .58 (.76) = .44.$$

Applied to an average yield of 110 (relative to 100 on the scattered holding), the .44 implies a standard deviation of .44 (110) = 48.4, as given in the master Table 1.5. That is the consolidated row.

The scattered row uses the formula still again. If a scattered peasant holding had five types under one crop (it makes little difference if it has four or six: Five seems reasonable for the six effective plots per field) his coefficient of variation for that crop would be $.58\{[1 + 4(.60)]/5\}^{\frac{1}{2}}$ – notice how the correlation of yields, R, fits in. The result is .48. But again there are three crops. So reapply the formula for the last time:

$$.48\{[1 + 2(.29)]/3\}^{\frac{1}{2}} = .48 (.73) = .347,$$

as again in the master table.

So: The table was correct. So: Scattering made sense. But after such measures a sensitivity analysis is surely in order. In forty-eight permutations of the variables R (from .43 to .73), disaster (from .41 to .60 of the average), the additional income with consolidation (from 7 to 13

45

percent), and so forth, only three yield a probability of disaster higher on scattered than on consolidated holdings.[109] Furthermore, when the model is supplemented by specifying the way productivity varies with the number of plots, the predicted number of plots can be derived. It is 6.2 plots per field, with variations from 5.3 to 11 for reasonable variations in the critical parameters.[110]

Risk aversion, in short, explains the open fields. A peasant who scattered his land was not behaving irrationally. He was buying insurance, and paying a reasonable premium. The open field was not egalitarianism or work spreading or a communalism of the herd or plow. It was behavior toward risk.

The costliness of alternative insurance: the storage of grain

The explanation in terms of risk aversion is not immune to the criticism leveled at the other explanations: Was the market missing? The market in question is insurance. Was there no insurance that could have saved peasants the bother of the expensive self-insurance of scattering their plots?

The operative words in the last sentence are "could have" and "expensive." Anything could have been. In some world the crops of medieval peasants could have been insured by State Farm Insurance Company or the United States Department of Agriculture. It misunderstands the scholarly task to merely imagine possibilities without testing them. There are dozens of possibilities, some more plausible than State Farm. Most social institutions have elements of insurance in them, for we live otherwise in a wildly uncertain world. The institution of the family, the greatest of insurors, *could* have helped a peasant in need; the Church could have, and was supposed to. The lord of the manor could have remitted rents in bad years, and he sometimes did. The whole village could have joined forces in a socialist commonwealth, achieving of course the variance of the village's output as a whole. It is easy to imagine why this could not have worked, for the reasons the numerous utopian communities in the American Midwest dissolved in the second or third generation – but that is more "could have," misunderstanding the role of economic theorizing.

The question is how expensive the self-insurance of scattering was compared to some alternative. If God is good, any alternative in use will do, because at the margin all must cost the same.

---

[109] Compare McCloskey, "Risk," pp. 152–53.
[110] Ibid., pp. 154, 158–59.

The one sort of alternative insurance we can know about is storage of grain. A man with seven years' worth of grain in his barn need not fear. Grain must be stored anyway until the next harvest. The issue is the carryover into the next harvest year, and it has been asserted that the carryover was large and cheap enough to obviate the need for scattering.[111]

This proves to be incorrect. But bear in mind that if it were correct, not all self-insurance would therefore be foolish. One does not smoke in bed because one's house and life insurance are paid up.

The way to show that storage of grain was in fact quite expensive, more expensive than scattering plots, is to exploit the price statistics of Europe. Historians have been transfixed by the long-term averages, which tell little more than the value of money. They have overlooked the use of the price movements within a harvest year.[112]

If a manorial lord keeps his grain in store from December to January he will have to earn what it costs to store the grain for that month. If he does not expect to earn so much he will sell the grain early. Everyone similarly placed will do so, driving down the price in December and correspondingly raising it in January, until the equilibrium of entry and exit is reestablished. Imposing rational expectations (and recalling that it was this context, agricultural markets, in which John Muth first spoke out loud and clear), the observed prices should reflect on average the cost of storage per month. In the spring they will become unreliable as people get some information about what the next harvest will be like. But before the spring the price should march up at the cost of storage.

It does. In the thirteenth and the early fourteenth centuries we have from the pioneer in price statistics, J. E. Thorold Rogers, some twenty-seven thousand quotations of grain prices, two thousand of which are more or less precisely dated within the year.[113] One can find numerous pairs of wheat prices at two dates within the same harvest year and in the same village. At Elham, Kent, in 1331, for example, the price of wheat rose from 6s. 8d. per quarter (eight bushels) in May to 6s. 10d. in July. There are 1,075 such wheat pairs in the Rogers data. They rise at 2.37 percent per month, irregularly (the standard deviation is 1.87 percentage points).

[111] Fenoaltea, "Risk, Transaction Costs."

[112] Another précis follows, here of D. N. McCloskey and John Nash, "Corn at Interest: The Cost and Extent of Grain Storage in Medieval England," *American Economic Review* 74 (March 1984): 174–87.

[113] *The History of Agriculture and Prices in England*, vol. 1 (Oxford: Clarendon Press, 1866).

Something going up at 2.37 percent per month will rise at 32 percent per year. This is a high cost of storing grain – a third of the harvest, as against the 10 percent or so sacrificed by scattering in the open fields. Barley goes up at a higher rate in the data, too high to be quite believable; rye goes up at 4.17 percent per month, and similarly with minor grain – the grains the peasants ate seem to go up at about 4 percent per month, some 60 percent a year.

It can be shown that the cost of storage fell dramatically in more modern times. The same calculations can be performed on the prices from the Oxford town market 1618–44, yielding only 11.3 percent per year. For Namur, Belgium, we have data over most of the seventeenth century, 1614–92, and the August-to-June rise is 14 percent a year. In Diest in Belgium 1718–36 the rates of annual rise are 10.9 percent for wheat, 14.8 percent for barley, 14.5 percent for rye, 15.4 percent for oats, and 18.1 percent for buckwheat. In the nineteenth century the gradients are shallower still. Storage was not a cheap way to protect oneself from disaster in the Middle Ages but became so in modern times.

The fall in storage costs, incidentally, seems to be the result of an unheralded but large and important drop in interest rates from the fourteenth to the sixteenth century. Most of the cost of storage was the interest rate: that is to say, the opportunity cost of tying up 6 shillings in a quarter of wheat for a month. The high interest rates were of course pervasive, finding their way also into the prices and profitability of animals and land.[114] Scattering was the cheapest way to insure because the interest rate in the Middle Ages was high.

The story of open fields

The fall of interest rates is one among many reasons that the diversification from scattering became less valuable in early modern times. The fall of interest itself bespeaks an improved capital market (for which there is direct evidence), and a good capital market is another substitute for self-insurance.[115] One need not fear a bad harvest if the friendly local moneylender stands ready to repair the shortfall with a loan at moderate rates.

---

[114] For animals, see McCloskey and Nash, "Corn," pp. 183–85; for land, see Clark, "Cost of Capital."

[115] B. A. Holderness, "Credit in a Rural Community, 1660–1800," *Midland History* 3 (1975): 94–115; Elaine Clark, "Debt Litigation in a Late Medieval Village," in J. A. Raftis, ed., *Pathways to Medieval Peasants*, Papers in Mediaeval Studies 2 (Toronto: Pontifical Institute of Mediaeval Studies, 1981), pp. 247–82.

There were also direct reductions of risk in early modern times. The riskiness of plant disease and weather, for example, was being reduced by the introduction of new varieties of grain from the sixteenth century on.[116] A red-stalked wheat was developed in the south Midlands in the early seventeenth century that was resistant to smut, a fungus that destroyed whole stands.[117] Early-ripening barley was another among many other innovations in the seventeenth century that reduced risk, the risk – cricketers would say the certainty – of wet, cold springs in England.[118]

The advances in the control of water reaching the crop, beginning with floating (that is, repeatedly flooded) meadows in the seventeenth century and ending with clay-pipe underdrainage in the nineteenth century, reduced the risk of unseasonable rain. Drainage is especially difficult in clay soils. It is significant therefore that from 1650 to 1850 grain production moved off the clay lands, a move made possible in turn by new and cheap animal fodder, and its resulting manure, from turnips and swedes and clover.

Most powerfully, the new affluence of farmers that came in the seventeenth and eighteenth centuries, and the new opportunities for employment outside agriculture, reduced the value of insurance from scattering. For all the decline in real wages during the sixteenth century, the last medieval famine occurred in England in the 1590s (in Scotland the relief came a century later, in France a century and a half later). Gregory King believed that the farmers and lesser freeholders in 1688 earned about £50 a year.[119] Yet eleven farmers of mid-Essex 1666–1743 held at their deaths movable wealth not including land and standing crops of twice this figure.[120] With such a store of wealth a harvest failure was less dangerous. Such men were comfortably well off, and it must be noted that most people did not share so largely in the increasing yields of grain. The thirty-acre farmers, however, were the men deciding whether or not an enclosure should go forward. Two or three centuries earlier they would have resisted enclosure; now they approved.

The enclosures did not take place immediately, of course.[121] The

---

[116] Eric Kerridge, *The Agricultural Revolution* (New York: Kelley, 1968).
[117] Joan Thirsk, "Farming Techniques," in Joan Thirsk, ed., *The Agrarian History of England and Wales*, vol. 4, p. 168.
[118] Ibid., p. 170.
[119] Thirsk and Cooper, eds., *Seventeenth Century Economic Documents*, p. 780.
[120] From F. W. Steer, *Farm and Cottage Inventories of Mid-Essex 1635–1749*, 2d ed. (London: Phillimore, 1969), p. 52.
[121] For an elaboration and qualification of what follows, see McCloskey, "Economics of Enclosure."

land law was tangled, until, as Maitland put it in another connection, "the transcendent power of Parliament was called in to cut the Gordian knot." The knot was that owners and even tenants in a village could veto an enclosure under the common law. The common law quite reasonably required that a man be consulted before his property was meddled with. The intermixture of property in the open fields, however, made the reasonable rule an incentive to unreason. Enclosure was everybody's business and therefore, as the saying goes, nobody's business. A single holdout could block an enclosure, and could therefore demand all the gains. Anyone could, and all did.

Parliamentary procedures in the middle of the eighteenth century sharply reduced the height of this obstacle. They made enclosure dependent on merely a majority, not a unanimity. Enclosure was a landlord's enthusiasm. The hurt to laborers was small, and probably on balance a gain (the old notion that people were driven off the land and into factories by enclosure has long since been cast aside by the evidence, though like the notion of medieval communalism it survives). The hurt to small landlords may have been large, though the matter depends critically on when smallholders could sell out. If they could sell out at the right time they could profit from the doubling of the price of land that came with the doubled rent. But the gain to the rich from hurting the laborers or the small owners had nothing to do with the timing of enclosure. Large increases in rent, and quarrels with the holders of the tithe, not scraps of land purchased at bargain prices from widows or common lands stolen from the goose, motivated the owners to arrange at considerable expense for the redistribution and enclosure of the land. The poor were too poor to influence the juggernaut.

"Juggernaut" is too strong. After all, the decline of open fields was a long process, from the fifteenth to the eighteenth century, a land reform in slow motion. The reform was the other side of the system's long duration. To explain open fields satisfactorily one must give an account of why they declined, and to explain the decline one must give an account of why they flourished.

The explanation is a story of reasonable people – one hesitates to write "rational" because the word is so charged with political and methodological emotion; "reasonable" will do. It was reasonable for a medieval peasant to scatter his plots, because he lived dangerously and it was hard to arrange for a better way to be safe. Presently it became easier, and open fields lost their charm. By that time, however, they were expensive to eradicate. Much of the new husbandry could be adopted on them anyway. At last the state – or, to be exact, an executive committee of the landed class – intervened, though even then with proper British regard for law and muddle.

The new story of open fields and enclosure does not have a novel moral. By now the moral that medieval people were canny and calculating has lost its novelty. Students of the matter have been saying it for eighty years. In 1971 David Herlihy spoke for many medievalists in declaring that "research has all but wiped from the ledgers the supposed gulf once considered fundamental, between a medieval manorial economy and the capitalism of the modern period."[122] Where was Jack's brother peasant when Jack had to borrow at 20 to 50 percent per year? Where was the ancient Germanic community when he had to scatter his land for safety? Where was the tradition-bound unreasonableness of medieval men when their behavior danced to an R^2? "You know, Ernest, the poor in medieval times were different from you and me." "Yes, Scotty, they had less money."

---

[122] "The Economy of Traditional Europe," *Journal of Economic History* 31 (March 1971): 153–64, pp. 154–55.

2

Labor market behavior in colonial America: servitude, slavery, and free labor

David W. Galenson

At the very outset of English settlement in North America, employers were introduced to the colonial labor problem. English planters accustomed to an economy that enjoyed abundant labor had to learn to cope in a New World in which labor would be scarce. The key to economic success in colonial America, for individual planters as well as entire colonies, was to obtain an adequate supply of agricultural labor to grow crops that would satisfy the demands of the large European market. Stark contrasts appeared among the solutions to this problem that were developed in colonial America; these solutions were far-reaching in their implications for virtually all facets of life in the colonies, as well as in their consequences for the later history of the United States. Considerable attention has recently been devoted to two of the major solutions, white servitude and black slavery, while the third, free labor, remains relatively neglected. This essay will draw on the available information about each of these labor systems in an attempt to improve our understanding of how labor markets functioned in colonial America.

The Jamestown experiment and the colonial labor problem

In the years following its establishment of a settlement at Jamestown in 1607, the Virginia Company set out to build an agricultural colony that would earn profits for investors. To this end, the company drew up a

I am grateful to Lois Carr, Stanley Engerman, Robert Fogel, Walter Galenson, Robert Gallman, Farley Grubb, Daniel Levy, Peter Lindert, Robert McColley, Russell Menard, Larry Neal, Theodore Schultz, Daniel Scott Smith, Daniel Vickers, and Lorena Walsh for discussions of the issues treated in this essay and comments on an earlier draft. Joseph Ferrie provided capable research assistance. Financial support for the research was provided by an Alfred P. Sloan Research Fellowship. Earlier versions of the essay were presented at seminars at the University of Chicago, the University of Illinois, the University of North Carolina, Northwestern University, and the University of Texas.

detailed plan for the colony's operation.[1] All land was to be owned by the company and farmed collectively. The workers, all men, were to be treated as bound servants of the company for lengthy terms. They were to be housed in barracks and provided with strict rations. For building fortifications and growing crops they were to be divided into work gangs, in military fashion, each of which was to be supervised by an overseer. The company would govern the colony under martial law, and punishments for misdeeds would be harsh and summary.

Within little more than a decade after first settlement, however, sweeping changes – recently described as no less than a social revolution – had transformed the economic and social organization of Virginia.[2] By 1620 the company had freed the earlier settlers from their contracts and given them their own land and houses. The company had also brought women to Virginia to become the colonists' wives. Martial law had been abolished, and a General Assembly, which included representatives from each of Virginia's ten settlements, had been convened.[3]

The reason for these changes was clear: The company had recognized that greater inducements were necessary to permit the recruitment and motivation of a labor force sufficient to reverse the economic decline that had begun during the company's earlier regimen.[4] The company had begun with the intention of paying workers little more than the low prevailing English wage rates and transporting them to America, where abundant land would greatly increase the value of their labor. The substantial difference between the workers' high productivity in Virginia and their low English wages would reimburse the company for the cost of transportation and leave a handsome surplus that would accrue to the company as profits. Although the company's scheme provided the workers with relatively little incentive to work hard in the hope of future gain, the company believed the workers would have no choice but to cooperate because of their total reliance on the company in the hostile American wilderness. What the company had failed to anticipate, however, was that the workers would rebel against their treatment in Virginia by finding alternative employments, whether by running away to live with the Indians or simply

[1] Edmund S. Morgan, *American Slavery, American Freedom: The Ordeal of Colonial Virginia* (New York: Norton, 1975), pp. 79–81.

[2] Sigmund Diamond, "Values as an Obstacle to Economic Growth: The American Colonies," *Journal of Economic History* 27, no. 4 (December 1967): 565.

[3] Morgan, *American Slavery, American Freedom*, pp. 93–97.

[4] Lyon Gardiner Tyler, ed., *Narratives of Early Virginia, 1606–1625* (New York: Scribner, 1907), pp. 432–35.

starting their own small settlements. Faced with this effective competition for the workers' labor, the company had to recognize that it did not enjoy the monopsony position it had hoped for in the region's labor market, and was forced to respond by offering workers higher wages and better living and working conditions.[5]

The Virginia Company was only the first of many employers to encounter the colonial labor problem. But out of its subsequent efforts to reduce labor costs came indentured servitude, an institution that became the first significant solution to the labor problem.

Indentured servitude

Indentured servitude was a credit system under which labor was leased. Servants signed contracts, called indentures, promising to work for a recruiting agent or his assigns in a particular colony for a specified period under stated conditions. The servant was then transported to the agreed destination, where his contract was sold to a colonial planter, who provided the servant with food, lodging, and clothing during the time the servant worked for him. Recent research has revealed how the design and practice of indentured servitude successfully overcame major obstacles, in the form of capital market imperfections and principal–agent problems, to make indentured servants a key element in the early economic growth of colonial America. A consideration of its development and functioning can indicate what problems the system solved and how the efficiency of the system was achieved.

Ten years after the initial settlement at Jamestown, Virginia's plan-

---

[5] An observer described the brutality of the punishments handed out by the governor of Virginia in 1612 to a group of settlers who had run away to live with the Indians and been recaptured, and then explained that the cruelty of the tortures was intended "to terrify the reste for Attempting the Lyke" (Morgan, *American Slavery, American Freedom*, p. 74). The crime was alarming to the Virginia Company in part because it directly threatened its position as monopsonist in the colony's labor market.

The Virginia Company did not prosper by using a scheme in which profits would derive directly from the fees paid by immigrants who rented land or became tenants, and the same was true later of many large investors in the colonies. Over time, however, some wealthy investors recognized that large profits could better be made from land sales after a new settlement had successfully been established. This led to more successful schemes in which initially land would be sold at very low prices – or even given away to early settlers in a locality – and later the proprietor would sell land at much higher prices, after the first settlers had created such public goods as roads and schools and established key enterprises like sawmills. For discussion of some examples, see Bernard Bailyn, *The Peopling of British North America: An Introduction* (New York: Knopf, 1986), pp. 65–85.

ters began to export tobacco to England. The introduction of the crop produced an economic boom in the colony, and the value of labor rose sharply. In September 1619 the secretary of the colony wrote of its new prosperity that "all our riches for the present doe consiste in Tobacco," but then corrected himself, noting that "our principall wealth (I should have said) consisteth in servants."[6]

To meet the lively demand for labor, in November 1619 the Virginia Company sent one hundred new workers to the colony, each bound to the company for a term of years. In order both quickly to disperse the workers after their arrival, so as to reduce the danger from contagious disease, and to provide food and lodging for them in the Virginia winter, the company decided to rent the majority out to private planters for a year at a fixed rate.[7] This arrangement had a severe defect, for it created a new principal–agent relationship, between the company and the private planters, that could prove costly to the company. That rentals of this kind were not subsequently repeated was apparently a result of the company's recognition that the planters lacked sufficient incentives to protect the company's substantial investment in the labor of their hired workers, both in providing adequate maintenance and provision for health care in the colony's unhealthy disease environment and in preventing runaways.[8] In the summer of the following year, the Virginia Company announced that it would send to the colony "one hundred servants to be disposed amongst the old *Planters*."[9] This was the earliest example on a significant scale of the characteristic form of the indenture system, as colonists paid a lump sum to the importer and in return received title to the services of an immigrant for a fixed term of years.[10] This transaction solved the agency problem the Virginia Company had encountered earlier, for in making the servant's immediate supervisor the owner of the labor

---

[6] Susan Myra Kingsbury, ed., *The Records of the Virginia Company of London*, vol. 3 (Washington: U.S. Government Printing Office, 1933), p. 221.

[7] Ibid., pp. 226–27, 245–46, 257–58.

[8] On the unhealthiness of the early Chesapeake, see Morgan, *American Slavery, American Freedom*, ch. 8; Carville V. Earle, "Environment, Disease, and Mortality in Early Virginia," in Thad W. Tate and David L. Ammerman, eds., *The Chesapeake in the Seventeenth Century: Essays on Anglo-American Society* (Chapel Hill: University of North Carolina Press, 1979), pp. 96–125. For evidence of the Virginia Company's awareness of the problems of the illness of servants and of runaways, see Kingsbury, ed., *Records of the Virginia Company*, vol. 3, pp. 167, 226–27.

[9] Ibid., p. 313.

[10] Abbot Emerson Smith, *Colonists in Bondage: White Servitude and Convict Labor in America, 1607–1776* (Chapel Hill: University of North Carolina Press, 1947), p. 13.

contract, it gave him a direct incentive to prevent the servant from running away.

The form of this transaction was an important early solution to the labor problem of colonial America, for it provided a means by which English labor supply could be connected to colonial demand. Recent estimates have indicated that a majority of all hired labor in preindustrial England was performed by "servants in husbandry" – youths of both sexes, normally in the teen years and early twenties, who lived and worked in the households of their masters on annual contracts.[11] Passage fares to Virginia in the early seventeenth century were high relative to the earnings of these servants in husbandry, and few prospective migrants were able to pay the cost of their voyage out of their accumulated savings.[12] The Virginia Company's solution was to use its own funds to advance the cost of passage to prospective settlers in the form of a loan to the migrants, who contracted to repay this debt out of their earnings in America.

The large size of the debt for passage meant that repayment would take substantially longer than the single year that characterized the employment of farm servants in England, and this raised new problems of work incentives. The migrant faced a term of four or more years as a bound laborer after he had received the major benefit from the bargain, passage to America. One historian has recently argued that under the circumstances, with the servant lacking the motivation of either future wages or the desire to be rehired, masters had to resort to the use of physical violence to extract work from indentured servants.[13]

Available evidence does not provide a firm basis for comparison, but corporal punishment of servants may have been more common in the colonies than in England; although colonial laws protected servants from excessive punishment, masters were permitted considerable latitude in beating their servants. Yet it would be surprising if such

---

[11] Ann Kussmaul, *Servants in Husbandry in Early Modern England* (Cambridge: Cambridge University Press, 1981).

[12] The passage fare typically quoted through the mid-seventeenth century was £6; e.g., see John Smith, *The Generall Historie of Virginia, New-England, and the Summer Isles* (London, 1624), p. 162. Daily wages for unskilled laborers in southern England in 1620 ranged from 8d. to 12d. (British Library of Political and Economic Science, London: Records of International Scientific Committee on Price History [Beveridge Price Commission]). Implied annual wages for full-time adult laborers would be approximately £10–15. The wages of unskilled servants in husbandry in the teen years would generally have been lower; see Kussmaul, *Servants in Husbandry*, pp. 36–39.

[13] Morgan, *American Slavery, American Freedom*, p. 126.

physical abuse had been common, for harming their servants would obviously have reduced the profits masters could derive from their work. There is furthermore considerable evidence that significant positive work incentives for servants were created within the operation of the indenture system. Masters typically appear to have exceeded the legally required minimum levels of food and clothing they provided to their servants, and the freedom dues given to favored servants could also be raised above the legally specified levels.[14] Wages were sometimes paid to servants during their terms, and masters sometimes made bargains with their workers under which the servants could be released early from their terms of servitude.[15] The frequency with which these and other positive incentives were used cannot be determined, but the opportunities they afforded clearly contributed to the flexibility of the indenture system in practice.

Although the Virginia Company first developed the method by which the indenture system operated, once the practice of outright sale of the contracts had been established a large company no longer had any significant advantage in servant transportation, and the indenture transaction was quickly borrowed by private merchants and planters. The capital requirements for European merchants who made the advances to finance immigrant transportation were reduced from the long periods of years for which the servants were bound to the relatively short period between the signing of the contracts in England and their sale in the colonies – principally the two or three months during which the servant was on the ship. The trade in servants was a natural one for European merchants who imported sugar, tobacco, or rice from the colonies, for servants could be exchanged directly for colonial produce. The servant trade was apparently a lucrative return-haul operation for merchants engaged in the colonial trade, and merchants competed for recruits. There were no legal barriers to entry into the trade, and economic barriers to entry were small for merchants or captains already involved in transatlantic shipping. In consequence, throughout the colonial period in the principal European ports there were normal-

---

[14] Gloria Main, *Tobacco Colony: Life in Early Maryland, 1650–1720* (Princeton, N.J.: Princeton University Press, 1982), p. 113. The payment of freedom dues, which was virtually universal in colonial servitude, obviously served to discourage servants from running away.

[15] David W. Galenson, *White Servitude in Colonial America: An Economic Analysis* (Cambridge: Cambridge University Press, 1981), pp. 207–209; Russell R. Menard, "From Servant to Freeholder: Status Mobility and Property Accumulation in Seventeenth-Century Maryland," *William and Mary Quarterly* 3d ser., 30, no. 1 (January 1973): 50.

ly large numbers of recruiters involved in the servant trade.[16] The result was that servant recruitment and transportation were typically carried on in highly competitive markets.

Contemporary fare quotations indicate that the charges for passage from England to America were uniform for all servants at a given time; they did not vary either with individual characteristics or across colonial destinations.[17] As a result, all servants who migrated to America incurred debts of similar value. With recruitment under competitive conditions, the present discounted value of every servant's contract should have been approximately the same at the time the contracts were negotiated. Since individual productivity varied across servants, the conditions of their indentures had to vary: The higher the servant's expected marginal value product in the colonies, the faster he could repay the loan made to him, and the shorter the contract he should have received.[18]

Evidence on the functioning of the market for servants can be drawn directly from the bargains made between recruiting agents and servants. Two large surviving collections of contracts preserved among English legal records, one from Middlesex County in 1683–84, the other from London during 1718–59, provide detailed evidence about the characteristics of several thousand servants and the conditions on which they agreed to migrate to America.

Multiple regression analysis of the length of the servants' contracts confirms the prediction of an inverse relationship between the term of servitude and individual productivity.[19] In both samples, the length of

---

[16] David Souden, "English Indentured Servants and the Transatlantic Colonial Economy," in Shula Marks and Peter Richardson, eds., *International Labour Migration: Historical Perspectives* (London: Institute for Commonwealth Studies, 1984), p. 29; Galenson, *White Servitude in Colonial America*, p. 97. For evidence on competition in the eighteenth-century trade in German indentured servants, see Farley Grubb, "The Market Structure of Shipping German Immigrants to Colonial America," *Pennsylvania Magazine of History and Biography* 111, no. 1 (January 1987): 27–48.

[17] Galenson, *White Servitude in Colonial America*, pp. 251–52.

[18] For more detailed treatments of both the theoretical analysis of the indenture bargain and the empirical results reported concerning the length of indenture, see Galenson, *White Servitude in Colonial America*, pp. 97–102, and "The Market Evaluation of Human Capital: The Case of Indentured Servitude," *Journal of Political Economy* 89, no. 3 (June 1981): 446–67.

[19] This statement and the following results apply to the minors in these samples of contracts, who accounted for 22 percent of the 785 servants with known ages in the earlier sample and 67 percent of the 3,040 in the later sample. Inspection of the contracts indicates that for minors the greatest variation in the conditions occurred in the duration of term, whereas for adults this was not the case, as four years was the

indenture was negatively related to both age and skill: Ceteris paribus, older servants, those who recorded skilled trades, and those able to sign their contracts received shorter terms. Detailed analysis of the relationship between age and skill in the later sample furthermore shows that, whereas servants with skilled trades received shorter terms at all ages, the length of indenture fell more rapidly with age for the skilled than for the unskilled. This result, which implies that the age–earnings profile of skilled servants was steeper than that of the unskilled, is consistent with a result typically found in studies of modern labor markets, of a positive relationship between training and the steepness of age–earnings profiles.[20]

In both samples, holding individual characteristics constant, servants bound for the West Indies received considerably shorter terms than those bound for the colonies of the North American mainland. This reduction in term was clearly a compensating wage differential paid to the servants who traveled to a less desirable destination. Whereas both working conditions for servants and economic opportunities for freedmen were known to be poor in the Caribbean islands after the introduction of large-scale sugar cultivation in the mid-seventeenth century – with the attendant slave gangs and consolidation of small farms into large plantations – the mainland long continued to be considered a land of opportunity for poor immigrants, where freed servants could hope to own land and become prosperous members of society. The higher mortality rates of the West Indian colonies made servants even more reluctant to go there. Although the high mortality also lowered the servants' expected productivity in the islands, sugar planting was the most profitable activity in colonial America, and the planters' demand for labor was great.[21]

The length of indenture furthermore responded to changes over time

normal term assigned. For adults, cash payments were apparently substituted for further reductions in the term of servitude; for a combination of legal and clerical reasons, however, these do not always appear to have been recorded in the contracts. For discussion of the format of the data, and for analysis of wage payments that were specified in the two samples that reinforces the results discussed in the text, see Galenson, *White Servitude in Colonial America*, pp. 200–203, 207–209.

[20] E.g., see Gary S. Becker, *Human Capital: A Theoretical and Empirical Analysis, with Special Reference to Education*, 2d ed. (New York: Columbia University Press, 1975), pp. 221–22.

[21] It might be noted that the substantial differences in the length of indenture accounted for by destinations run counter to the view often expressed by historians that servants had little say in determining their destinations. For example, a recent study concluded that "the servant's individual desires played little part in determining where he

David W. Galenson

in the colonial demand for labor. The terms of servants bound for the West Indies in the eighteenth century varied inversely with the price of sugar. With the region's virtual monoculture in sugar, high prices for the staple generally signaled periods of prosperity in the islands, and the high demand for labor during these periods improved the conditions on which servants could travel to the region.[22] Additional evidence that the market for servants operated efficiently comes from recently analyzed evidence on short-run fluctuations in the volume of the servant trade over time. Specifically, the number of servants arriving annually in the Chesapeake Bay colonies of Virginia and Maryland during the seventeenth century was found to have varied positively with tobacco prices. As for sugar in the West Indies, the dominant position of tobacco in the early Chesapeake made tobacco prices good indicators of the state of the region's economy. That high prices resulted in high levels of immigration again testifies to the efficiency with which the transatlantic market for servants transmitted information about the state of colonial labor demand to Europe.[23]

eventually ended up. Instead, it was the trading community that was responsible for directing and regulating emigration in response to the needs of the colonies" (James Horn, "Servant Emigration to the Chesapeake in the Seventeenth Century," in Tate and Ammerman, eds., *The Chesapeake in the Seventeenth Century*, p. 92). Another historian recently concluded that "servants invariably went where the dealers in human cargoes knew there was a ready market. . . . [The servants] were not making the choices, for power in the commercial transaction that brought labor across the Atlantic resided in the hands of the supplier and the buyer" (Gary B. Nash, *The Urban Crucible: Social Change, Political Consciousness, and the Origin of the American Revolution* [Cambridge: Harvard University Press, 1979], p. 111). Yet the shorter terms of servants bound for the West Indies indicate that higher implicit wages were paid to servants there than in the mainland colonies. If servants had had no preferences as to destination, or no influence on their destinations, wages would not have varied across colonies, and no differences would have existed in contract lengths by destination; that significant differences did appear contradicts the statements of Horn and Nash.

[22] The empirical success of the economic analysis of the indenture bargain summarized here again contradicts views expressed by historians concerning the operation of this market. One recent example is a historian's statement that "the length of indenture seems generally to have been socially rather than economically determined, reflecting prevailing ideas of when young people could be expected to come of age" (David Souden, "'Rogues, Whores, and Vagabonds'? Indentured Servant Emigrants to North America and the Case of Mid-Seventeenth-Century Bristol," *Social History* 3, no. 1 [January 1978]: 26).

[23] Russell R. Menard, "British Migration to the Chesapeake Colonies in the Seventeenth Century" (unpublished paper, University of Minnesota, 1984). Menard also reported in this study that the number of migrants brought annually to the Chesapeake varied inversely with English real wages.

Although the directions of the adjustments of the length of servants' contracts discussed above are consistent with the operation of an efficient market in servant transportation, information on the prices for which the contracts were sold in the colonies is necessary to determine whether the magnitudes of the adjustments were appropriate. Several questions can be asked in this regard. One is whether the market was sufficiently competitive to reduce the lengths of contracts to the point at which servants were sold in America for no more than the real cost of their transportation. The available evidence suggests that it was. The prices for which servants were sold upon arrival in the colonies appear to have been only slightly higher than the fares charged free passengers; the difference could have been a premium received by merchants for bearing the risk of servant mortality on the ocean voyage.[24] A related question concerns the quality of the forecasts made by recruiting agents in Europe: Was their knowledge of colonial labor market conditions adequate to allow them to adjust the contract lengths so as to equalize the expected colonial sale prices of all contracts at the time of binding the servants? Limited evidence on the English servant trade in the seventeenth century shows that the typical sale prices of servants in the colonies did not vary with either the sex of the individuals or their colonial destinations, suggesting that recruiters did make appropriate adjustments of contract lengths.[25] More abundant evidence on the trade in English and Irish indentured servants to Philadelphia in the eighteenth century points to the same conclusion. A series of variables that represented information known by recruiting agents at the time the servants' bargains were made in Europe – characteristics both of the individual servants and of the contracts they

[24] Galenson, *White Servitude in Colonial America*, p. 100; Farley Grubb, "Redemptioner Immigration to Pennsylvania: Evidence on Contract Choice and Profitability," *Journal of Economic History* 46, no. 2 (June 1986): 411–17. It might be noted that the empirical evidence considered in the studies cited here supports the theoretical prediction that in this competitive setting servants would be sold in the colonies for the full cost of their passage, i.e., their fare plus a normal profit and the risk premium discussed in the text. This evidence contradicts Abbot Emerson Smith's view that servants were "grievously exploited" by being sold for sums far above the cost of passage (*Colonists in Bondage*, p. 39). Some recent historians persist in describing the indenture system as exploitive of the servants, though it is often impossible to test these assertions because of their failure to define the nature of the alleged exploitation; e.g. James A. Henretta, W. Elliot Brownlee, David Brody, and Susan Ware, *America's History* (Chicago: Dorsey, 1987), p. 47.

[25] Galenson, *White Servitude in Colonial America*, pp. 99–100.

signed – were found to have a jointly insignificant effect on the sale prices of the servants' contracts in America.[26]

An important question in the study of any migration concerns how the migrants fared at their destination. This clearly also bears on the efficiency of the market that permits their migration, for it can serve to indicate how well information is transmitted to the migrants at their places of origin. The question of the indentured servants' achievements is particularly interesting in view of the substantial sacrifices they were willing to make, for the servants surrendered their freedom to choose where to live and work for periods of four years and more in order to migrate to America.

The best systematic evidence on this question comes from several studies that have traced the careers of sizable groups of indentured servants who migrated to Maryland during the seventeenth century.[27] These studies found that servants who arrived in the colony early in the century and who escaped the substantial risk of premature death in the early Chesapeake generally prospered: 90 percent of those who arrived in Maryland by 1642 and who remained in the colony for at least ten years after completing their terms of servitude became land-owners, typically on a scale that afforded them at least a comfortable living. Some gained considerable wealth, and a few eventually accumu-lated estates that placed them among the wealthiest men in the colony. Nearly all the group who remained in Maryland at least ten years after gaining their freedom also held political office or sat on a jury – not major accomplishments in most cases, but nonetheless substan-tially above what these men could have expected had they remained in England. Some of these early servants actually gained entrance

[26] Farley Grubb, "The Market for Indentured Immigrants: Evidence on the Efficiency of Forward-Labor Contracting in Philadelphia, 1745–1773," *Journal of Economic History* 45, no. 4 (December 1985): 855–68. It might be noted that a number of the variables included in this analysis were found to have had a substantial impact on the lengths of the servants' contracts in the same samples; see Grubb, "Colonial Labor Markets and the Length of Indenture: Further Evidence," *Explorations in Economic History* 24, no. 1 (January 1987): 101–106.

[27] The following evidence on the opportunities for freedmen in seventeenth-century Maryland is drawn from Menard, "From Servant to Freeholder"; Lois Green Carr and Russell R. Menard, "Immigration and Opportunity: The Freedman in Early Colonial Maryland," in Tate and Ammerman, eds., *The Chesapeake in the Seven-teenth Century*, pp. 206–42; Lorena S. Walsh, "Servitude and Opportunity in Charles County, Maryland, 1658–1705," in Aubrey C. Land, Lois Green Carr, and Edward C. Papenfuse, eds., *Law, Society, and Politics in Early Maryland* (Baltimore: Johns Hopkins University Press, 1977), pp. 111–33, and "Staying Put or Getting Out: Findings for Charles County, Maryland, 1650–1720," *William and Mary Quarterly* 3d scr., 44, no. 1 (January 1987): 89–103.

into the group that ruled early Maryland, even joining the colony's Council.

Opportunities for immigrants to Maryland deteriorated over time, however. Parallel analysis of the careers of a group of servants who arrived in the colony during the 1660s shows less impressive accomplishments, as more than half of those who remained in Maryland for at least ten years as freedmen failed to become landowners. None of these former servants acquired great wealth. A smaller proportion than of the earlier group participated in government, and none rose above minor public office. The opportunity for former servants to become prosperous independent farmers in Maryland was much less late in the seventeenth century than it had been earlier, and freedmen increasingly faced a choice between remaining in the colony as hired workers or moving elsewhere, most often to the Middle Colonies, in search of their own land.

Several important general conclusions might be drawn from these studies of the success of migrants. One is the simple recognition that the time and place chosen by an immigrant were important determinants of his experience. This point, which emerges strongly from the history of Maryland over six decades, becomes even more obvious when differences among colonial regions are considered: Whereas the availability of good farmland caused Pennsylvania to become known to eighteenth-century Europeans as the "best poor man's country," the high cost of land and undesirable conditions for hired workers caused servants very early to avoid traveling to the West Indies. A second point is that although the degree of opportunity available to immigrants declined over time in the Chesapeake, the authors of these studies emphasize that even in the last two decades of the seventeenth century there was no shortage of employment opportunities. Although the rapid expansion of the tobacco economy that earlier had made the sparsely settled Chesapeake a good place for poor settlers had given way to slower growth in a more heavily settled region where the choicest land had become occupied, freedmen could still find work at good wages. This point again seems subject to wider generalization, for although there were differences over time and across space in the extent of opportunity for immigrants, colonial English America appears throughout its history to have remained a genuine land of opportunity where European migrants might considerably improve their condition if they were willing to run the risk of premature death in the transatlantic passage and the often dangerous disease environment of the New World. That the colonies continued to attract skilled Europeans in considerable numbers throughout the seventeenth and eighteenth centuries thus appears to have been another consequence of the efficient transatlantic market for migration, as migrants made choices that appear in general to have been well considered and well informed.

That these transatlantic markets in indentured labor operated efficiently should perhaps come as no surprise, for the value of indentured servitude as an early solution to the colonial labor problem led to its widespread adoption and use throughout English America in the seventeenth and eighteenth centuries. Although the total numbers of servants are not known precisely, an indication of their quantitative significance is given by one historian's estimate that between one-half and two-thirds of all white immigrants to the American colonies between the 1630s and the Revolution came under indenture; this would imply that a total of between three and four hundred thousand Europeans migrated to English America as servants during the colonial period.[28] Their importance at times in particular regions was even greater, as is suggested by other recent estimates that three-quarters or more of European immigrants to the Chesapeake Bay region during the seventeenth century were servants.[29] Whereas initially all the servants came from England, in the course of the colonial period migrants from other countries joined the flow of servants to English America, and especially in the eighteenth century substantial numbers of Scottish, Irish, and German immigrants arrived in the colonies under indenture.

In the course of the seventeenth century an addition to the indenture system had arisen, under which felons were sent to the colonies as servants.[30] English courts would grant pardons to those convicted of capital crimes on condition that the convicts remain in the colonies for substantial terms, normally seven years, as bound laborers. The actual transportation of the convicts was arranged by private merchants, who made profits from the trade by selling the convicts as indentured servants in the colonies. During the seventeenth century the number of convicts involved in this trade was small – perhaps no more than a total of five thousand – in part because of the reluctance of many colonies to accept shipments of criminals. In the early eighteenth century, how-

---

[28] Smith, *Colonists in Bondage*, p. 336; Galenson, *White Servitude in Colonial America*, p. 17.

[29] Wesley Frank Craven, *White, Red, and Black: The Seventeenth-Century Virginian* (Charlottesville: University Press of Virginia, 1971), p. 5; Russell R. Menard, "Economy and Society in Early Colonial Maryland" (Ph.D. thesis, University of Iowa, 1975), p. 162.

[30] For more detail on the system described in this paragraph, see Smith, *Colonists in Bondage*, chs. 5–6; also A. Roger Ekirch, *Bound for America: The Transportation of British Convicts to the Colonies, 1718–1775* (Oxford: Clarendon Press, 1987).

ever, to make convict labor more attractive to the colonies parliament passed a law increasing the number of crimes punishable by transportation, lengthening the term many convicts would serve as bound laborers to fourteen years, and granting a subsidy to merchants for shipping convicts to the colonies. A regular trade now sprang up in convict labor, and it has been estimated that fifty thousand felons were sent to America during the eighteenth century. The saving to England's penal system was substantial, as 70 percent of those convicted at the Old Bailey in the mid-eighteenth century were transported. The major destinations for the convicts were Maryland and Virginia, where they provided an inexpensive source of indentured labor for many small planters who lacked the capital to purchase slaves. The convict trade was interrupted in 1775, but interestingly after the end of the Revolution the English planned to resume the shipment of convicts to America. The former colonists indignantly rejected this proposal, and, seeking another outlet for its criminal population, England soon established penal colonies in Australia.[31]

Although indentured servitude was an important initial solution to the problem of colonial American labor supply, it was not a definitive solution. In precisely those regions that had initially depended most heavily on white servants for their labor needs, planters eventually turned to black slaves as their principal source of bound labor. As will be discussed in the next section of this essay, these substitutions of slaves for servants occurred at different times and at different speeds, but in each case the functions of indentured servants evolved in similar ways over time.[32]

Indentured servants were quantitatively most important in the early development of those regions that produced staple crops for export. The major demand was for workers to grow the staple, and initially planters relied on indentured labor. As time went on there was also a growing demand for skilled workers – carpenters, coopers, blacksmiths, potters, sawyers, masons, weavers, tanners, and practitioners of a multitude of other crafts – to do the work of building plantations, processing, refining and shipping products to market, and caring for the needs of the inhabitants.

A second stage in the evolution of the function of indentured servi-

---

[31] A. G. L. Shaw, *Convicts and the Colonies: A Study of Penal Transportation from Great Britain and Ireland to Australia and Other Parts of the British Empire* (London: Faber & Faber, 1966), chs. 2–3.

[32] The following discussion of the evolution of the role of indentured servitude in the colonial labor market is based on Galenson, *White Servitude in Colonial America*, chs. 8–9.

tude occurred in the West Indies after the introduction of sugar, in the Chesapeake after the 1680s, and in South Carolina and Georgia in the eighteenth century, after planters had replaced their European field workers with Africans. In each case this substitution caused the majority of the bound labor force to change from white to black, but this initial transition from servants to slaves was not a complete one, for the newly arrived Africans lacked many of the skills required by planters. Colonial planters typically did not train adult African slaves to perform skilled jobs, preferring instead to wait and train either those imported as young children or American-born slaves. In an intermediate period in the growth of staple-exporting colonies, a racial division of labor by skill therefore existed, as unskilled labor forces were made up increasingly of black slaves while white servants continued to perform skilled crafts and often acted as plantation managers and supervisors of the slaves.

But this was not the final phase of development. As output continued to increase, the demand for both skilled and unskilled labor grew further. The eventual outcome in the plantation economies was widespread investment in the training of slaves to take over the skilled work. Although there were differences in the timing of this evolution across regions, by the time of the Revolution the substitution of slaves for servants had been largely completed in all the staple-producing colonies of English America. In the West Indies and the southern mainland colonies there were many large plantations based almost exclusively on black labor, with considerable numbers of skilled slaves as well as unskilled slave field hands. The adoption and growth of slavery in those regions of English America that were characterized by plantation agriculture did not bring a complete end to the immigration of white servants, but it did produce systematic shifts over time in their composition by skill, and eventually in their principal regions of destination. By the end of the colonial period, the West Indies had ceased to import white servants on a significant scale, and among the plantation economies only the Chesapeake Bay colonies continued to receive sizable flows of indentured labor. Among the economies not characterized by staple production for export, only Pennsylvania received large numbers of servants for an extended period, beginning in the late seventeenth century and continuing through the end of the colonial period.[33]

[33] For quantitative indications of changes in the servants' destinations over time, see Smith, *Colonists in Bondage*, pp. 307–37; Galenson, *White Servitude in Colonial America*, ch. 6; Bernard Bailyn, *Voyagers to the West: A Passage in the Peopling of America on the Eve of the Revolution* (New York: Knopf, 1986), ch. 6; and Farley

Indentured servitude dwindled to quantitative insignificance in the late eighteenth and early nineteenth centuries, and despite several attempts later in the nineteenth century it was not subsequently revived for use in the United States.[34] Both the decline of the use of servitude and the failure of later attempts to revive it appear explicable on economic grounds. As discussed earlier, indentured servitude arose to allow the long-distance migration of people who could not pay the costs of migration out of their own wealth and were unable to borrow the necessary funds from other individuals or financial institutions. In these circumstances, the use of indentures provided a source of capital to finance migration, as the intermediation of merchants effectively allowed migrants to borrow the cost of their passage from those who demanded their services in their region of destination, in the form of advances against their future labor. Yet entering an indenture entailed substantial sacrifices of personal freedom during the term of servitude; servants in colonial America generally had no say in determining their masters or the work they would do and were forbidden to marry without their masters' permission.[35] In light of these disadvantages of indentures, the disappearance of servitude from the nineteenth-century United States appears to have been an understandable result of the rising wealth of Europeans and the falling cost of transatlantic migra-

---

Grubb, "The Incidence of Servitude in Trans-Atlantic Migration, 1771–1801," *Explorations in Economic History* 22, no. 3 (July 1985): 332–37. It has recently been argued that a similar evolution in the occupational employment of indentured servants also occurred in Pennsylvania, where the use of slaves was much less than in the regions discussed in the text; Farley Grubb, "Immigrant Servant Labor: Their Occupational and Geographic Distribution in the Late Eighteenth-Century Mid-Atlantic Economy," *Social Science History* 9, no. 3 (Summer 1985): 245–75.

[34] Charlotte Erickson, "Why Did Contract Labour Not Work in the Nineteenth-Century United States?" in Marks and Richardson, eds., *International Labour Migration*, pp. 34–56. For discussion of an exception in which an effective extralegal indenture system was used, see Patricia Cloud and David W. Galenson, "Chinese Immigration and Contract Labor in the Late Nineteenth Century," *Explorations in Economic History* 24, no. 1 (January 1987): 22–42.

[35] For detailed discussions of the restrictions on servants, see Smith, *Colonists in Bondage*, chs. 11–12, and Richard B. Morris, *Government and Labor in Early America* (New York: Columbia University Press, 1946), chs. 7–9. Because these restrictions constituted disadvantages of servitude relative to other forms of migration, it might be expected that at times when servitude was an option, the probability that a migrant would travel under indenture would vary inversely with the migrant's wealth. Farley Grubb has argued that this was the case among Germans migrating to Pennsylvania in the late eighteenth century ("The Incidence of Servitude in Trans-Atlantic Migration," pp. 319–26).

tion.[36] Whereas many Europeans had found it necessary to indenture themselves in order to migrate to America in the seventeenth and eighteenth centuries, this was no longer the case in the nineteenth century, and the great migration of that century from Europe to the United States consisted almost exclusively of free workers and their families.

Slavery

The transatlantic slave trade began long before the English colonization of America. Portuguese merchants had begun to trade for slaves on the coast of West Africa as early as the middle of the fifteenth century, and a transatlantic trade in slaves in sizable numbers arose in the course of the sixteenth century, with Portuguese ships carrying African workers to Spanish America and Brazil. By the end of the sixteenth century the Portuguese had been joined in the trade by Spanish merchants, and soon thereafter by Dutch traders. It has recently been estimated that more than a hundred thousand African slaves had been brought to the Americas by the end of the sixteenth century and another half-million by the middle of the seventeenth, still before significant English involvement in the trade had begun.[37]

When the English entered the transatlantic slave trade in the second half of the seventeenth century, they therefore found a highly competitive international business in the process of rapid expansion. The spread of sugar cultivation from Brazil to the West Indies after 1640 produced a booming demand for labor, and more African slaves were sold to Europeans in the five decades following 1650 than in the preceding two hundred years combined.[38] The desire of English merchants to capture a share of the lucrative trade in slaves, added to an existing interest of the English royal family in the African trade,

---

[36] For evidence and further discussion, see David W. Galenson, "The Rise and Fall of Indentured Servitude in the Americas: An Economic Analysis," *Journal of Economic History* 44, no. 1 (March 1984): 13–24.

[37] Philip D. Curtin, *The Atlantic Slave Trade: A Census* (Madison: University of Wisconsin Press, 1969), p. 116; Paul E. Lovejoy, *Transformations in Slavery: A History of Slavery in Africa* (Cambridge: Cambridge University Press, 1983), p. 47; James A. Rawley, *The Transatlantic Slave Trade: A History* (New York: Norton, 1981), chs. 2–4.

[38] Lovejoy, *Transformations in Slavery*, p. 46. The large numbers of slaves exported from Africa on a continuing basis make it clear that slave catching within Africa was a business, and recent scholarship has come to just this conclusion. Lovejoy stresses the importance of the political fragmentation of Africa as a background for this industry, for in many cases enslavement was a result of hostilities between warring states. He

eventually led to the grant in 1663 by Charles II of a charter to the Company of Royal Adventurers Trading into Africa, for the purpose of trading in slaves.[39] This company was badly organized, however, and its operations were interrupted by the outbreak of war between the English and Dutch in 1664. When peace was restored in 1667 the company was beyond saving, and its liquidation began in 1670.

The Company of Royal Adventurers was succeeded by the Royal African Company, which received a charter from Charles II in 1672. The new company was granted a legal monopoly of the slave trade to English America in return for agreeing to establish and maintain fortified settlements on the West African coast. The forts, where company factors would purchase and hold slaves prior to shipment, were desired by the government to maintain an English presence in West Africa and to prevent the military domination of the region, and possible exclusion of the English, by France or another European power.[40]

In the event, the expected monopoly of the slave trade to the English colonies failed to materialize. From the beginning of its career the Royal African Company suffered a stream of damaging infringements of its monopoly in the form of illegal deliveries of slave cargoes by smaller traders, referred to by the company as "interlopers." Surrounded by wealthy planters who favored an open trade in slaves, the company's resident agents in the West Indies fought a losing battle to stop these illegal shipments; they could rarely persuade colonial governors to apprehend the interlopers, and when they did colonial juries made up of planters rarely gave judgments against the smaller traders.

---

furthermore points to regional differences in the process of enslavement. In some places, wars or organized slaving raids were carried out by governments against neighboring states; these might result in depopulation and exhaustion of the slave supply, but in some instances the balance between warring states might remain even enough to avoid this, and instead produce a continuing supply of slaves to both states. In other cases, slaves were supplied from within societies, as enslavement became a punishment for convicted criminals. Detailed evidence on the process of enslavement within Africa has been scarce; it is obviously critical for understanding this major source of American labor supply, and this will undoubtedly remain an active area of investigation. For a summary of recent research and references, see ibid., ch. 4; for an interesting case study of the economics of slave supply within Africa, see Philip D. Curtin, "The Abolition of the Slave Trade from Senegambia," in David Eltis and James Walvin, eds., *The Abolition of the Atlantic Slave Trade: Origins and Effects in Europe, Africa, and the Americas* (Madison: University of Wisconsin Press, 1981), pp. 83–97.

[39] George Frederick Zook, *The Company of Royal Adventurers Trading into Africa* (Lancaster, Pa.: New Era, 1919), pp. 8–13.

[40] K. G. Davies, *The Royal African Company* (London: Longman, 1957), chs. 3, 6.

As a result, at most times the Royal African Company does not appear even to have carried a majority of the estimated totals of slaves delivered to the English sugar islands.[41] Having failed to produce adequate profits for its shareholders, and suffering from outstanding debts from West Indian planters that grew steadily over time, the Royal African Company saw its role in the transatlantic slave trade dwindle after the 1680s, it became altogether inactive in that trade after 1730, and it was finally wound up in 1752.

The economic history of the Royal African Company's legal monopoly has long been misunderstood. A notable early misinterpretation was offered by Adam Smith in *The Wealth of Nations*. Part of Smith's famous attack on mercantilism was devoted to an exposition of the unfortunate economic consequences that ensued when legal monopolies were granted to groups of merchants to set up joint-stock companies to carry on England's foreign trade. In summarizing the Royal African Company's career, Smith stated that it had enjoyed a monopoly of the slave trade until 1688, when the flight of James II nullified royal monopolies. Exposed to competition, the company was unable to survive, even in spite of a parliamentary act of 1698 granting the company the proceeds of a tax levied on its English competitors in the slave trade. In Smith's view the reason for the company's economic failure upon being exposed to competition was not hard to find; he believed the company to have been twice cursed by inefficiency, with the "negligence and profusion" of both a joint-stock company and a legally protected monopoly.[42]

Smith's analysis of the Royal African Company's history appears incorrect; its failure was not caused by inefficiency spawned by a sheltered monopoly position, but on the contrary by the very competitiveness of the transatlantic slave trade. The company's African forts proved an expensive liability that raised the company's expenses relative to those of its smaller competitors, while the compensating benefits the royal charter was supposed to confer on the company were never realized, as neither Charles II nor his successor, James II, proved willing to override the strenuous lobbying of colonial planters and effectively enforce the company's exclusive right to deliver slaves to the English colonies. In consequence, company employees convincingly reported to African House in London that interlopers were able

---

[41] David W. Galenson, *Traders, Planters, and Slaves: Market Behavior in Early English America* (Cambridge: Cambridge University Press, 1986), ch. 1.

[42] Adam Smith, *An Inquiry into the Nature and Causes of the Wealth of Nations* (New York: Modern Library, 1937), pp. 700–701, 712–13.

both to outbid the company for slaves in Africa and to undersell it in the West Indies.[43]

A long-standing belief that the Royal African Company held an effective economic monopoly of the slave trade to English America has often served to obscure the fact that the transatlantic slave trade to the colonies was a highly competitive industry, and has consequently resulted in significant misunderstandings of one of colonial America's major sources of labor supply.[44] Recent investigations have produced evidence of the conduct of the trade that contrasts with many earlier views, by pointing to a number of outcomes that suggest careful and efficient approaches to the business of slave trading. Much of this evidence for the early colonial period comes from the records of the Royal African Company, which have been preserved in the English Public Record Office. These include not only records of each of more than sixteen thousand individual transactions in which the company sold seventy-five thousand slaves in English America between 1673 and 1725, but also dozens of volumes of minutes of company committee meetings and correspondence with company employees in West Africa and the West Indies that together offer a remarkably detailed portrayal of the workings of one of the largest joint-stock companies of the preindustrial world.

The mortality of slaves on the transatlantic crossing has long been one of the most intensively studied aspects of the slave trade. The debate over mortality dates back to the British parliamentary hearings on the abolition of the slave trade that began in the late eighteenth century. The slaves' passage mortality rates appear to have been high

[43] Davies, *Royal African Company*, p. 114.
[44] A common treatment in the historical literature not only joins Adam Smith in the incorrect assumption that the Royal African Company's legal privilege gave it an effective economic monopoly of the slave trade to the English colonies, but unlike Smith fails to recognize that the legal privilege lost its force after the Revolution of 1688. (For the company's reaction to the Revolution, see ibid., p. 123.) These errors together have often led to the belief that the company held an effective economic monopoly until this was terminated by the act of parliament of 1698 that opened the English slave trade to all. Many statements of this view could be cited; for examples, see Wesley Frank Craven, *The Colonies in Transition, 1660–1713* (New York: Harper & Row, 1968), p. 290; T. H. Breen, *Puritans and Adventurers: Change and Persistence in Early America* (New York: Oxford University Press, 1980), p. 145; Bailyn, *The Peopling of British North America*, pp. 101–102. The error of this interpretation is ironic, for far from being a blow to the Royal African Company's position, the act of 1698 resulted from prolonged lobbying in parliament by the company and was intended to restore some degree of privilege to it; the act placed a duty on all independent traders, and the proceeds were to accrue to the Royal African Company for the maintenance of its African forts.

compared to the mortality suffered by other travelers crossing the Atlantic: Although the Royal African Company's records show a decline in average slave mortality per voyage from 24 percent during the 1680s to 13 percent in the 1720s, the latter figure remained far above the 4 percent suffered by a group of German migrants traveling to Pennsylvania in the eighteenth century.[45] The earliest explanation for these high mortality rates, first offered by the abolitionists, attributed them to "tight-packing," or overcrowding, of the slaves. Yet recent quantitative investigations of the activities of the Royal African Company and other traders have failed to reveal any systematic relationship between the rate of slave mortality on a voyage and the ratio of the number of slaves carried to the ship's size or capacity.[46] Another traditional explanation for the slaves' high mortality rates concerned the poor provisioning of the slaving ships, suggesting that the depletion of inadequate supplies of food and water would have produced extremely high losses on unusually long voyages. Yet again quantitative analysis has not found evidence of an increase in the mortality rate in the latter stages of long voyages.[47]

The absence of an impact of either overcrowding or inadequate provisioning on slave mortality does not appear surprising in view of the attention paid by slave traders to these aspects of their business. The Royal African Company's records clearly demonstrate the com-

---

[45] Galenson, *Traders, Planters, and Slaves*, pp. 38–39; Farley Grubb, "Morbidity and Mortality on the North Atlantic Passage: Eighteenth-Century German Immigration to Pennsylvania," *Journal of Interdisciplinary History* 17, no. 3 (Winter 1987): 565–85. Another recent study found a passage mortality rate of 2.5 percent among English convicts sent to Maryland during the late eighteenth century (Kenneth Morgan, "The Organization of the Convict Trade to Maryland: Stevenson, Randolph & Cheston, 1768–1775," *William and Mary Quarterly* 3d ser., 42, no. 2 [April 1985]: 213). The figures given in the text in comparing the mortality of slaves and white migrants may exaggerate the difference somewhat, because the passage mortality rates for both groups may have declined during the eighteenth century; e.g., see Raymond L. Cohn, "Deaths of Slaves in the Middle Passage," *Journal of Economic History* 45, no. 3 (September 1985): 685–92; Herbert S. Klein, *African Slavery in Latin America and the Caribbean* (New York: Oxford University Press, 1986), pp. 141–42; Ekirch, *Bound for America*, pp. 104–8.

[46] Galenson, *Traders, Planters, and Slaves*, p. 42; Herbert S. Klein and Stanley L. Engerman, "A Note on Mortality in the French Slave Trade in the Eighteenth Century," in Henry A. Gemery and Jan S. Hogendorn, *The Uncommon Market: Essays in the Economic History of the Atlantic Slave Trade* (New York: Academic Press, 1979), pp. 264–67; Johannes Postma, "Mortality in the Dutch Slave Trade, 1675–1795," in ibid., pp. 249–50.

[47] Royal African Company records show a positive relationship between the length of a voyage and the percentage of its slave cargo that died in passage, but no evidence of an association between voyage length and the average mortality rate per day of the voyage (Galenson, *Traders, Planters, and Slaves*, pp. 40–42).

pany's awareness of the potential dangers of loading too many slaves aboard its ships, and instructions to its factors in West Africa often specified the maximum number of slaves particular ships would be allowed to carry.[48] Similarly, the company expressed considerable interest in the kinds and amounts of provisions that would be provided for slaves.[49] In general, the company paid close attention to all aspects of its slaving voyages that might have an influence on the passage mortality of their human cargoes. In correspondence with its agents, the company was always concerned with finding out how well its captains and other employees conducted their voyages, for as it commented, "Wee find that those Masters that looke well after the Negroes bring them in Good Condition . . . whereas others that are not Carefull do loose the greatest part of the Negroes."[50]

The seasonality of the slave trade further appears to have reflected the interest of the Royal African Company in limiting slave mortality. Although slaving voyages occurred throughout the year, a relatively large number of shipments arrived in the West Indies in late winter, spring, and early summer, whereas relatively few cargoes reached there from August through early winter. This meant that shipments from West Africa were low during the region's rainy season, when higher disease levels among the African population would have tended to raise passage mortality among slaves sent to America. The lower levels of activity during these months might have been a sign of greater care in selecting slaves for shipment, and the company's ships do appear to have avoided a seasonal increase in passage mortality.[51]

Recent years have witnessed a great increase in the use of quantitative evidence to test both old and new hypotheses about the causes of slave mortality on the infamous Middle Passage, and this remains an active area of research. What the results obtained up to this point appear to suggest is that slave traders were not negligent or careless in the ways often charged in the past, as evidence of the conduct of the Royal African Company and others reveals reasoned and systematic actions designed to minimize the costs of some of the risks and difficulties characteristic of their industry.[52]

---

[48] E.g., see ibid., pp. 42–43.

[49] E.g., see Colin Palmer, *Human Cargoes: The British Slave Trade to Spanish America, 1700–1739* (Urbana: University of Illinois Press, 1981), p. 50.

[50] Quoted in Galenson, *Traders, Planters, and Slaves*, p. 50.

[51] Ibid., pp. 33–35, 45–47; Palmer, *Human Cargoes*, p. 45.

[52] Recent hypotheses concerning the high passage mortality rates of slaves have tended to focus on the deadly results of the fact that the trade brought together people from different disease environments; e.g., see Philip D. Curtin, "Epidemiology and the Slave Trade," *Political Science Quarterly* 83, no. 2 (June 1968): 190–216. Apparent

David W. Galenson

Similar evidence of intelligent economic behavior appears in other aspects of the conduct of the early slave trade. An example concerns the selection of the slaves purchased in Africa for transportation to America. In the case of the Royal African Company, this selection was done either by factors resident on the West African coast or by ships' captains. African traders would bring groups of slaves to the coast, and the company employees would buy some and refuse others. In deciding which slaves to purchase, the factors and captains had to keep in mind that slaves could profitably be shipped to America only if their West Indian prices exceeded their African prices by at least the cost of transporting them. In order to ensure the proper selection of slaves, the factors would therefore have to be kept informed of the current levels of slave prices in the West Indies.

We cannot directly examine how well the selection was done because of a lack of evidence on African slave prices. With evidence on West Indian slave prices, transportation costs, and the age composition of slave cargoes, however, we can test for the existence of one relationship that would have resulted from the proper selection of slave cargoes. A necessary condition for the profitability of transporting a slave was that the slave's American price be greater than the cost of passage. Transportation costs across the Atlantic were sufficiently high relative to West Indian slave prices so that throughout the period of the Royal African Company's activity there were always minimum and maximum ages that defined the pool of African slaves eligible on economic grounds to be transported to America: Younger and older slaves' American prices were below transportation costs, and these slaves should not have been selected for shipment in Africa. An increase in West Indian slave prices would widen the range of ages at which slaves could profitably be shipped by adding both some young and some old slaves to the eligible pool. Because there were many more children than adults in the African population, however, this increased the share of children within the pool of all slaves eligible for transportation. If the selection of slaves was done properly, therefore, an increase in the level of slave prices in America should have resulted

support for epidemiological explanations was afforded by the finding that crew members on slave ships suffered higher passage mortality rates than the slaves in the French and Dutch slave trades of the American colonial period (Curtin, *The Atlantic Slave Trade*, pp. 282–83; Klein and Engerman, "A Note on Mortality in the French Slave Trade in the Eighteenth Century," pp. 266–67; Postma, "Mortality in the Dutch Slave Trade, 1675–1795," pp. 259–60). Evidence from Royal African Company records has furthermore shown that captains of company ships suffered a mortality rate of 10.5 percent on the Middle Passage during 1720–25, not far below the slaves' rate of 13 percent (Galenson, *Traders, Planters, and Slaves*, p. 116).

in an increase in the share of children among the slaves carried to America.

Combining evidence on the age composition of Royal African Company slave cargoes with a time series of West Indian slave prices estimated from the company's records of slave sales reveals that there was a strong positive effect of changes in American slave prices on the share of children in the slave trade.[53] Inspection of the Royal African Company's correspondence again suggests that this result should not be surprising, for the company was well aware of the economics underlying the hypothesis described here: The company's central office in London repeatedly stressed the need for its agents in the West Indies to keep factors on the West African coast informed about the status of slave markets in their colonies, and insisted that the factors use this information in selecting the slaves they purchased and loaded on the company's ships. Departures from this behavior, as for example when factors purchased slaves too young or too old to yield a profit in the West Indies, elicited sharp rebukes from London for the company's overseas employees.[54]

The format of slave sales in the West Indies further illustrates the pragmatic response to the Royal African Company to practical problems. The company requested its agents in the West Indies to sell the slaves delivered to them individually, in ascending-bid auctions, in order to maximize the revenue they received from the sales. The company quickly recognized the impracticality of using this system, however, for a chronic shortage of currency in the colonies meant that the requirement of immediate payment excluded many potential purchasers and lowered the prices paid for slaves. The normal format of the company's slave sales came to be one in which the agents negotiated credit transactions individually with planters. An interesting pattern invariably appeared in these sales, each of which consisted of the sale of the slaves from a single ship over one to two weeks' time, as the prices of the slaves sold declined over the course of the sales. The reason for this was that the best slaves were selected first for purchase by the wealthiest planters. The wealthiest planters placed the highest value on their time and demanded first service from the agents; that these planters selected the best slaves appears consistent with com-

---

[53] This evidence and further discussion of the analysis of the demographic composition of the slave trade is presented in Galenson, *Traders, Planters, and Slaves*, ch. 5. It might be noted that the analysis described here furthermore implies that a decline in transportation costs should have had an effect similar to rising American slave prices, namely, increasing the share of children among slave cargoes; this prediction is also confirmed by the empirical evidence.

[54] For example, see ibid., pp. 110–14.

plementarity of the quality of inputs in sugar production, for these planters generally also owned the best land. The company's agents also had an interest in selling the most expensive slaves to the wealthiest planters, for the agents' incomes were determined as a percentage of the funds they remitted to London from the sales; because the wealthier planters were generally better credit risks, the observed pattern contributed to the maximization of the agents' expected incomes.[55]

Although some slaves were present in nearly all the colonies of English America from very early in their settlement, there came to be pronounced differences in the quantitative importance of slavery among the major regions. Large-scale slavery appeared earliest and most prominently in the West Indies. All the English colonies there had black majorities in their total populations by the end of the seventeenth century, and all reached black shares of over 80 percent in total population during the eighteenth century. On the North American mainland only South Carolina attained a black majority in its population during the colonial period, although slaves also came to make up substantial shares of more than one-third of total population in Maryland, Virginia, North Carolina, and Georgia. The Middle Colonies – Pennsylvania, Delaware, New York, and New Jersey – had much lower black shares in total population, generally between 5 and 10 percent; New England never had more than 3 percent of its population made up of blacks.

The growth of slavery in the West Indies and the southern mainland colonies had implications as far-reaching for those societies as any other event of the colonial period, and in consequence the causes of that growth have been the subject of many historical investigations. Some cases appear relatively straightforward. In the West Indies, the growth of slavery was one consequence of the sugar revolution that began in Barbados in the 1640s and spread to the other islands. The introduction of sugar produced an enormous increase in the demand for labor, but it also required heavy work, most efficiently done in gangs, and white workers soon learned to avoid the rigors of sugar cultivation in the tropics. Another effect of the sugar revolution on white labor supply to the islands was more indirect. The technology of sugar cultivation, with high fixed capital requirements for sugar mills, boiling and curing houses, and distilleries, resulted in considerable economies of scale; as a result, the sugar islands ceased to be places of real economic opportunity for former servants, for small farms could not compete with the great plantations that swallowed up the islands' land. Finally, Englishmen were reluctant to risk premature death in

[55] For further discussion and evidence on the slave sales, see ibid., ch. 4.

the harsh demographic regime of the West Indies. With a rising demand for labor and a declining supply of those laborers who could choose their destinations, West Indian planters readily turned to the use of laborers who did not have this ability, and slavery quickly came to dominate the labor forces of the sugar islands.[56]

Although less detailed information is available on the growth of slavery in South Carolina, the causes there may have been similar to those of the West Indies. As in the islands, the increase in the black share of the labor force coincided with the rise of a single crop – rice – to dominance of the colony's economy. As in the West Indies, the nature of the work involved in production of the staple crop might have been a key element in the transition from servants to slaves in South Carolina, for the hard work of growing rice in labor gangs in the heat of the colony's summers appears to have deterred English servants from migrating to the colony after rice became its main product. And like the West Indies, South Carolina quickly gained a reputation for unhealthiness that further reduced white labor supply. In sum, South Carolina appears to have been another case in which a staple crop both increased the demand for labor and reduced the supply of indentured servants, thus pushing planters toward the large-scale purchase of slaves.[57]

Yet although the rise of staple crops might have been responsible for the growth of slavery in the West Indies and South Carolina, the same was not true of the Chesapeake Bay colonies. Tobacco was introduced into Virginia by 1620 and soon became the basis of the Chesapeake region's economy, but it was cultivated primarily by white farmers and their indentured servants for at least the first five decades. Tobacco

---

[56] For evidence on the growth of slavery in the seventeenth-century West Indies, see Richard S. Dunn, *Sugar and Slaves: The Rise of the Planter Class in the English West Indies, 1624–1713* (Chapel Hill: University of North Carolina Press, 1972); Richard B. Sheridan, *Sugar and Slavery: An Economic History of the British West Indies, 1623–1775* (Bridgetown, Barbados: Caribbean Universities Press, 1974); Carl and Roberta Bridenbaugh, *No Peace Beyond the Line: The English in the Caribbean, 1624–1690* (New York: Oxford University Press, 1972).

[57] On the growth of slavery in South Carolina, see Peter H. Wood, *Black Majority: Negroes in Colonial South Carolina from 1670 through the Stono Rebellion* (New York: Norton, 1974); a considerable amount of additional evidence on the transition from servants to slaves is provided by Russell R. Menard, "The Rise of Plantation Society in the Carolina Lowcountry" (unpublished paper, University of Minnesota, 1986). Even less information is available on the growth of slavery in Georgia, but circumstances similar to those in South Carolina – the cultivation of rice on large plantations under conditions unattractive to white servants – might have had similar effects there. For some evidence, see Betty Wood, *Slavery in Colonial Georgia, 1730–1775* (Athens: University of Georgia Press, 1984).

David W. Galenson

was a more delicate plant than sugar or rice and was not well suited to the routinized labor of work gangs. Tobacco production furthermore required much less fixed capital than did sugar, and as a result apparently offered no significant economies of scale; throughout the colonial period, tobacco was grown profitably on small farms as well as on large plantations.[58]

Because of the slower emergence of a labor force based significantly on slavery in the Chesapeake, as well as the fact that the Chesapeake was the first region to adopt slavery in what would later become the United States, the issue of labor choice there has received considerable attention from historians. Recent analysis of the composition of the estates of decedents in the region during the late seventeenth century from the evidence of probate records has shown that the most rapid period of transition was concentrated in the 1680s, as planters' holdings of bound labor shifted from a ratio of 3.9 servants to each slave in the late 1670s to a ratio nearly the reverse, of 3.6 slaves for each servant in the early 1690s. Changes in the conditions of supply of both servants and slaves appear to have caused this dramatic change. The supply of servants to the region appears to have fallen as a result of both improving labor market conditions in England and deteriorating prospects for migrants to the Chesapeake late in the seventeenth century; while the former reduced the total numbers of migrants leaving England, the latter was harming the Chesapeake in competing for migrants relative to more recently settled Pennsylvania, which offered the inexpensive land that Virginia and Maryland no longer did. The result of this shift in servant supply was a sharp increase in servant prices together with falling numbers of new arrivals.[59] At the same

[58] The absence of economies of scale in tobacco production is further indicated by the fact that even the Chesapeake's large plantations were typically broken up into smaller units called quarters. Each quarter was effectively operated as a small farm, with an overseer and perhaps twenty to thirty slaves; gang labor was not used. On the organization of tobacco plantations, see Gerald W. Mullin, *Flight and Rebellion: Slave Resistance in Eighteenth-Century Virginia* (London: Oxford University Press, 1972), pp. 47–50; Allan Kulikoff, *Tobacco and Slaves: The Development of Southern Cultures in the Chesapeake 1680–1800* (Chapel Hill: University of North Carolina Press, 1986), pp. 330–40, 386–87.

[59] On dating the Chesapeake's transition and for an explanation that stresses the falling supply of servants, see Russell R. Menard, "From Servants to Slaves: The Transformation of the Chesapeake Labor System," *Southern Studies* 16, no. 4 (Winter 1977): 355–90. For estimates that point to a decline in total immigration to the colonies in the final decades of the seventeenth century, and to the falling share of those migrants bound for the Chesapeake, see Galenson, *White Servitude in Colonial America*, pp. 216–18; Henry A. Gemery, "Emigration from the British Isles to the New World, 1630–1700: Inferences from Colonial Populations," *Research in Economic History* 5 (1980): 215–16.

78

time the supply price of slaves to Chesapeake planters appears to have fallen. The 1680s marked the lowest point of a secular decline in West Indian slave prices, apparently due to falling sugar prices in European markets, and slave traders dissatisfied with the prices they were receiving for their cargoes in the West Indies appear to have begun to bring the tobacco planters a steady supply of Africans at low prices.[60] The Chesapeake's rapid transition in the 1680s from primary reliance on white servants to the large-scale use of black slaves was therefore fueled by a substantial decline in their price relative to that of servants.[61]

Evidence from the probate inventories of four counties on Maryland's lower western shore in the late seventeenth century adds some interesting detail on the growth of slavery in the region.[62] Table 2.1 shows that the rising prices of servants caused planters at all levels of wealth to reduce their holdings between the 1660s and the 1680s, but that the impact was greatest at lower wealth levels, as the proportional decline in the probability of owning servants varied inversely with wealth. The probability that a planter would own slaves also rose quite steadily at all but the lowest wealth levels, but the proportion of slave owners remained low in all but the highest wealth categories; around 1700 only one-third even of decedents with wealth in the range of £100–150 owned slaves. Table 2.2 furthermore shows that the number of slaves held by planters below the highest wealth level also remained low. Among decedents around 1700 worth £100–150, the mean num-

[60] Galenson, *Traders, Planters, and Slaves*, ch. 3.
[61] Historians have sometimes argued that dissatisfaction with indentured labor led Chesapeake planters to substitute slaves for servants. In one variant of this argument, fear of the politically revolutionary potential of a growing class of discontented former servants led planters to reduce their demand for new indentured servants; e.g., see Breen, *Puritans and Adventurers*, p. 150; Joseph Douglas Deal, "Race and Class in Colonial Virginia: Indians, Englishmen, and Africans on the Eastern Shore during the Seventeenth Century" (Ph.D. thesis, University of Rochester, 1981), pp. 105–106. At a theoretical level, the logic of this argument might be questioned, because of the presence of a free-rider problem: Since the threat posed by the former servants was a collective one, no planter would perceive his own labor choice as having a significant impact on the extent of the danger, and individual planters would be unlikely to be influenced by this factor in their labor choices. Empirically, the argument appears weak because of the substantial increase in servant prices that occurred during the principal period of transition; see Menard, "From Servants to Slaves," p. 372. Although it is of course theoretically possible for a price increase to occur in spite of declining demand, the increase of 50 percent in servant prices between 1675 and 1690 indicates that any hypothetical decline in demand was overwhelmed by a decline in the supply of servants.
[62] I am grateful to Russell Menard for providing me with abstracts of the probate inventories from which Tables 2.1 and 2.2 were calculated. The original records are held at the Maryland Hall of Records, Annapolis.

David W. Galenson

Table 2.1. *Percentages of householders who owned servants and slaves by total estate value, 1658–1705*

Total estate value (£)	1658–59	1660–69	1670–79	1680–89	1690–99	1700–1705
0–19.9						
Servants	0	0	0	2	2	0
Slaves	0	0	0	0	1	2
No. householders	4	21	82	94	127	63
20–39.9						
Servants	0	17	28	9	9	9
Slaves	0	2	1	0	0	0
No. householders	1	46	79	75	107	58
40–59.9						
Servants	0	61	40	36	8	27
Slaves	0	4	0	2	5	2
No. householders	1	23	63	50	78	45
60–99.9						
Servants	0	74	47	49	30	50
Slaves	0	5	7	11	9	14
No. householders	0	19	55	71	46	36
100–149.9						
Servants	100	88	89	66	69	76
Slaves	0	6	11	9	31	33
No. householders	1	17	28	35	32	33
150+						
Servants	100	100	84	88	65	85
Slaves	0	37	38	54	70	72
No. householders	1	27	91	68	96	78

Source: Probate inventories from Calvert, Charles, St. Mary's, and Prince George's counties, Maryland.

ber of slaves held by those who owned any was not substantially greater than the mean number of servants held by servant owners.

What these data demonstrate clearly is that it was the wealthy planters who brought large-scale slavery to the Chesapeake. Planters at all wealth levels remained interested in holding servants throughout the late seventeenth century, but the wealthiest were able in addition to begin buying slaves. By the 1680s, a majority of decedents with total wealth of more than £150 held slaves, and from the 1690s the proportion of this group with slaves is similar to the proportion with servants. The typical number of slaves held by slave owners in this group came to exceed the mean number of servants held by wealthy servant owners during the 1680s, and by the turn of the century the mean slaveholding was more than twice the mean holding of servants.

80

Table 2.2. *Mean numbers of servants and slaves owned by house-holders who owned any of the respective type of labor, by total estate value, 1658–1705*

Total estate value (£)	1658–59	1660–69	1670–79	1680–89	1690–99	1700–1705
0–19.9						
Servants				1	1.5	—
Slaves				—	1	1
20–39.9						
Servants		1	2	1.1	1.1	1.2
Slaves		1	1	—	—	—
40–59.9						
Servants		1.5	1.2	1.2	1.3	1.3
Slaves		1	—	1	1.3	1
60–99.9						
Servants		1.9	2	1.5	1.4	3.2
Slaves		1	1.5	2.4	1.5	1.9
100–149.9						
Servants	2	2.9	2.5	1.8	1.8	2.1
Slaves	—	1	1.7	1.8	2.3	2.6
150+						
Servants	2	4.6	3.6	4.6	2.7	3.7
Slaves	—	4.3	3.5	5.7	5.9	8.2

Source: Probate inventories from Calvert, Charles, St. Mary's, and Prince George's counties, Maryland.

Information drawn from the probate inventories of the members of colonial Maryland's legislature, shown in Table 2.3, tells a similar story of the importance of the wealthy in bringing slavery to the Chesapeake. Few legislators with total wealth at death of less than £150 owned slaves in the seventeenth century, whereas in contrast half the decedents worth more than £150 owned slaves as early as the 1650s. Many wealthy legislators held both servants and slaves in the late seventeenth century, but the proportion with slaves became consistently greater than the proportion with servants after 1700. These data also clearly show both the dwindling ownership of servants and the nearly universal ownership of slaves by the wealthy as the eighteenth century went on.[63]

[63] I am grateful to Daniel Levy for providing me with the data on which Table 2.3 is based.

For additional evidence on the Chesapeake's transition to slavery, and for discussion of regional variation within Maryland and Virginia, see Menard, "From Servants to Slaves," pp. 385–87, and Main, *Tobacco Colony*, pp. 102–106.

David W. Galenson

Table 2.3. *Percentages of Maryland legislators who owned servants and slaves, by total estate value, 1630–1779*

| Decade beginning | Total estate value (£) | | | | | |
| | 0–149.9 | | | 150+ | | |
	Servants	Slaves	N	Servants	Slaves	N
1630	—	—	0	0	0	1
1640	0	0	2	—	—	0
1650	0	0	4	25	50	4
1660	20	0	5	50	50	8
1670	11	0	9	89	67	18
1680	17	17	6	63	63	8
1690	20	20	5	67	67	15
1700	25	0	4	40	52	25
1710	14	29	7	26	77	35
1720	17	67	6	52	83	23
1730	27	36	11	21	66	29
1740	0	33	6	23	87	31
1750	17	57	7	19	59	32
1760	0	0	4	28	90	39
1770	17	17	6	13	81	31

Source: Edward C. Papenfuse, Alan F. Day, David W. Jordan, and Gregory A. Stiverson, *A Biographical Dictionary of the Maryland Legislature, 1635–1789*, vols. 1–2 (Baltimore: Johns Hopkins University Press, 1979–85).

There are a number of possible explanations for the failure of poorer planters to substitute slaves for servants as early and as thoroughly as their wealthier contemporaries. One follows from possible differences in the interest rates faced by planters of differing wealth.[64] The higher the interest rate a planter faced, the lower the present value of a slave relative to that of a servant. If poorer planters had faced higher credit costs as a result of their generally higher default risks, the present value of slaves relative to servants would have been lower for them than for wealthier planters who could borrow at lower interest rates. At given market prices of servants and slaves, some poorer planters might therefore have found servants a more profitable investment at the same time wealthier planters found the purchase of slaves more advantageous. Another possible element involves the riskiness of own-

[64] Some early records of trade in the Chesapeake show that slaves might be sold either for bills of exchange or on credit (Jacob M. Price, "Sheffeild v. Starke: Institutional Experimentation in the London–Maryland Trade c. 1696–1705," *Business History* 28, no. 3 [July 1986]: 19–39). The terms of the credit transactions remain to be determined.

ing slaves in the high-mortality environment of the late-seventeenth-century Chesapeake.[65] Smaller planters might have chosen to forgo a higher return to slave ownership in order to avoid the concentration of a large share of their wealth in one or two slaves, preferring instead to own the less expensive servants. A third factor that could have contributed to the earlier adoption of slavery by larger planters concerns differences in information. The early growth of slavery on the mainland may have been slowed by many planters' doubts about the productivity of African slaves. If this was an important obstacle, it might have been overcome earlier by wealthier planters, who would have had access to more information about the successful experiences of West Indian planters with slaves. Indeed, some wealthy planters who were among the early large slaveholders in the Chesapeake had immigrated there directly from the West Indies. Two notable examples, Thomas Notely and Jesse Wharton, arrived in Maryland from Barbados well after the large-scale adoption of slavery there. Both were wealthy men, and both owned substantial numbers of slaves in Maryland during the 1670s. Their example may have been particularly influential, for both were prominent members of Maryland's political elite; both held a number of important positions, including the colony's deputy governorship.[66] A fourth possible reason for the earlier adoption of slavery by the wealthy involves living and working conditions in the early Chesapeake. Smaller planters housed their bound laborers in their own dwellings and supervised their work themselves. In contrast, wealthier planters often had separate living quarters for their laborers and hired overseers to direct their work. Because of their greater physical separation from their workers, the wealthy may have been less reluctant to purchase Africans, who were culturally more alien to them than their own countrymen, just as they might have been less concerned with the problems of overcoming language barriers and teaching the Africans farming methods that many English servants already knew.[67] These hypotheses are obviously not mutually exclu-

---

[65] On the continuing high mortality rates in the colonial Chesapeake in the late seventeenth and eighteenth centuries, see Daniel S. Levy, "The Life Expectancies of Colonial Maryland Legislators," *Historical Methods* 20, no. 1 (Winter 1987): 17–27.

[66] See the entries for Notely and Wharton in Edward C. Papenfuse, Alan F. Day, David W. Jordan, and Gregory A. Stiverson, *A Biographical Dictionary of the Maryland Legislature, 1635–1789*, vol. 2 (Baltimore: Johns Hopkins University Press, 1985), pp. 616, 880–81. Notely, who had served as personal attorney to Charles Calvert, 3d Lord Baltimore, held twenty-nine slaves at the time of his death in 1679. (I am grateful to Russell Menard for these references.)

[67] On the relevant living and working conditions, see, e.g., Carr and Menard, "Immigration and Opportunity," p. 228; Main, *Tobacco Colony*, pp. 112, 131–32, 160–

sive. It is to be hoped that additional evidence will be collected to determine whether they are relevant to understanding this important instance of a systematic difference by wealth in the demand for types of labor.[68]

The transatlantic trade that supplied the American colonies with African laborers was one of the preindustrial world's major international industries. Between first settlement and the American Revolution, an estimated total of one and a half million slaves were brought to English America.[69] The consequences for the different regions of the colonies contrasted sharply: In 1770, blacks made up less than 5 percent of the total population of New England and the Middle Colonies, compared with more than 40 percent of the population of the southern mainland colonies and more than 90 percent of the population of the West Indies.[70] The economic commitment of the West Indies and the southern mainland colonies to slavery was thorough: At the time of the Revolution, slaves made up fully one-third of total physical wealth in the southern colonies, and a larger share in the West Indies.[71] The operation of the colonial labor market had therefore clearly created one economic basis for the differing cultures of north and south, and had laid down the geographic lines along which later rhetorical and military battles would be waged over the abolition of slavery.

Free labor

The least-studied sector of the colonial workforce has been free labor. This appears to have been the result of both a lesser degree of interest – free labor has often appeared a less dramatic subject than servitude

62; Lorena Seebach Walsh, "Charles County, Maryland, 1658–1705: A Study of Chesapeake Social and Political Structure" (Ph.D. thesis, Michigan State University, 1977), pp. 176–78.

[68] For additional discussion, see David W. Galenson, "Economic Aspects of the Growth of Slavery in the Seventeenth-Century Chesapeake" (unpublished paper, University of Chicago, 1987).

[69] Curtin, *The Atlantic Slave Trade*, pp. 119, 216.

[70] For population estimates by race for the mainland, see U.S. Bureau of the Census, *Historical Statistics of the United States: Colonial Times to 1970* (Washington, D.C.: U.S. Government Printing Office, 1975), pt. 2, p. 1168; for the West Indies, John James McCusker, Jr., "The Rum Trade and the Balance of Payments of the Thirteen Continental Colonies, 1650–1775" (Ph.D. thesis, University of Pittsburgh, 1970), pp. 692–99.

[71] Alice Hanson Jones, *Wealth of a Nation To Be: The American Colonies on the Eve of the Revolution* (New York: Columbia University Press, 1980), pp. 97, 114–15; Sheridan, *Sugar and Slavery*, p. 231.

or slavery – and a more limited supply of evidence – the smaller amounts of money involved in hiring labor for short periods generally attracted less interest from the government and the courts than the larger amounts involved in the long-term leasing or purchasing of human capital, and records of transactions in free labor are consequently scarcer than those in indentured and slave labor. The discussion of this section will therefore necessarily be based on less detailed evidence than the discussions above, but it appears useful nonetheless to raise some questions about the operation of free-labor markets in the colonies in light of the evidence that is available.

Free labor was present in all the colonies, but its importance varied considerably across regions. This discussion will be restricted to the one region of colonial America where free labor can be studied almost in isolation from other labor types. Among the colonial regions, New England not only imported the least bound labor but received the fewest immigrants of any kind. Although New England's total population was only about 10 percent below that of the Chesapeake colonies at the close of the colonial period, and was nearly 50 percent larger than that of the West Indies, the region had lower levels of net immigration than these other regions in every decade of the colonial period after the initial Puritan migration of the 1630s.[72] Unlike the southern regions, which increased their populations in spite of high mortality rates, largely through persistently high rates of immigration, New England enjoyed low mortality rates throughout the colonial period, and grew as a result of high rates of natural increase.[73] As a consequence, New England was distinctive among the colonial regions in the eighteenth century in having nearly all its work performed by native-born whites.[74] A recent study of probate inventories from the mainland colonies in 1774 found that only 20 (or 5.2 percent) of 381 New England decedents sampled had owned slaves and that none had owned servants; the latter finding is hardly surprising, for of 3,709 indentured servants enumerated by English customs officers as they departed for America during 1773–75, none had the destination listed

---

[72] Gemery, "Emigration from the British Isles to the New World, 1630–1700," p. 215; Galenson, *White Servitude in Colonial America*, pp. 216–18.

[73] Daniel Scott Smith, "The Demographic History of Colonial New England," *Journal of Economic History* 32 (March 1972): 165–83; Maris A. Vinovskis, *Fertility in Massachusetts from the Revolution to the Civil War* (New York: Academic Press, 1981), ch. 2.

[74] Richard S. Dunn, "Servants and Slaves: The Recruitment and Employment of Labor," in Jack P. Greene and J. R. Pole, eds., *Colonial British America: Essays in the New History of the Early Modern Era* (Baltimore: Johns Hopkins University Press, 1984), p. 183.

as New England.[75] The absence of servants was clear to contemporaries; one visitor to the colonies as early as 1660 remarked that although "Virginia thrives by keeping many Servants . . . New England conceit they and their children can doe enough, and soe have rarely above one Servant."[76]

An interesting preliminary question to raise about New England's labor market in fact concerns why the region had so few bound laborers. The detailed evidence necessary for a complete explanation has not been collected, but hypotheses can be suggested to explain the scarcity of both slaves and servants. The overwhelming majority of slaves imported to the Americas in the colonial period were brought to sugar-producing regions. Although there appear to have been considerable fluctuations over time in labor productivity in sugar cultivation, it appears that this always remained sufficiently high relative to productivity in New England's diversified agricultural economy to ensure that it simply was not profitable for most of the region's farmers to buy slaves. The exceptions appear to have occurred in those areas of New England where proximity to a large port resulted in unusually large-scale agricultural production for urban consumption or export to other colonies, thus raising labor productivity considerably. A notable example of this was the Narragansett country in Rhode Island, where the largest concentration of slaves in colonial New England worked on large plantations, producing dairy products and raising livestock for export to the West Indies and a number of mainland colonies.[77] The

---

[75] Jones, *Wealth of a Nation To Be*, pp. xxiv, 113–14; Galenson, *White Servitude in Colonial America*, pp. 220–27. New England received very few free immigrants in the same period, as fewer than a hundred of nearly five thousand unindentured British migrants to the colonies included on these lists had the region recorded as their destination (Bailyn, *Voyagers to the West*, pp. 212–13).

[76] "Certaine Notes and Informations concerning New England," ca. 1660–64, British Museum, Egerton Mss. 2395, fol. 415v.

[77] Lorenzo Johnston Greene, *The Negro in Colonial New England* (New York: Columbia University Press, 1942), pp. 81–82, 88, 104–108; Percy Wells Bidwell and John I. Falconer, *History of Agriculture in the Northern United States, 1620–1860* (New York: Peter Smith, 1941), pp. 109, 116; Edward Channing, *The Narragansett Planters: A Study of Causes*, John Hopkins University Studies in Historical and Political Science, 4th ser., vol. 3 (Baltimore: Johns Hopkins Press, 1886); Rhett S. Jones, "Plantation Society in the Narragansett Country of Rhode Island, 1690–1790: A Preliminary Study," *Plantation Society in the Americas* 2, no. 2 (December 1986), 157–70.

 This generalization about New England can in large part be extended to the incidence of slaveholding in the middle colonies. Blacks generally made up somewhat higher shares of the middle colonies' population than was the case in New England – in 1720, for example, blacks were 2.4 percent of the population of Massachusetts, compared with 6.5 percent of Pennsylvania's, 8.0 percent of New Jersey's, and 15.5

great majority of all indentured servants who came to colonial America were bound for the Chesapeake Bay colonies, and increasingly in the eighteenth century Pennsylvania. As discussed earlier in this essay, unlike slaves, servants did not simply flow to the areas of highest labor productivity, but rather chose destinations also on the basis of the opportunities they offered for economic and social mobility after servitude. New England's failure to bid servants away from the mainland regions to the south might have resulted from a combination of low wages in most parts of the region and a reputation for being hostile to newcomers who did not share the Puritan beliefs of the region's original settlers.[78]

Because of the absence of bound labor on a significant scale, an interesting point of comparison for New England's labor market is that of England. Preindustrial England had two distinct types of hired labor. One, service in husbandry, was made up of unmarried youths in the late teen years and early twenties who lived and worked in the households of their employers, typically on annual contracts. The second was made up of adults, principally men, who worked for hire by the week, or more commonly by the day. Both these types of labor were used in New England, but their relative neglect by historians makes it difficult to judge their importance. We might ask, however, how underlying economic differences between Old and New England might have been expected to affect their importance in America.

Although English historians' views of service in husbandry have varied, a straightforward interpretation appears to be that it was a relatively efficient method of labor allocation, for it allowed workers to move among farms at minimal cost in order to increase their productivity. Children could move from the smaller farms of their parents to the larger farms of neighbors or nearby villages. The direct costs of migra-

percent of New York's – but they never rose to levels comparable to those of the colonies from the Chesapeake to the south. (For estimates of the racial composition of the mainland colonies' populations over time, see U.S. Bureau of the Census, *Historical Statistics of the United States: Colonial Times to 1970*, p. 1168.) As in New England, in the middle colonies slaves appear to have been present in the largest numbers in urban areas and those areas nearby that produced for the cities. A recent study furthermore argued that New York relied on slave labor to a greater extent than did Philadelphia because of a relative shortage of white immigrants to New York and attributed this to a relative shortage of land in New York on which new immigrants could establish their own small farms (Jean R. Soderlund, *Quakers and Slavery: A Divided Spirit* [Princeton, N.J.: Princeton University Press, 1985], pp. 75–78). This serves as a reminder of the importance of the labor supply of white immigrants in determining the extent of slavery in a region or colony; for a general analysis, see Galenson, *White Servitude in Colonial America*, pp. 141–49.

[78] Smith, *Colonists in Bondage*, pp. 28–29.

tion were lower for these individuals than for whole families, for there were no tied movers, and the residence of the individual with the employer eliminated time lost in walking from home to work. Annual contracts allowed farmers to assure themselves of a supply of labor for the growing and harvest seasons without interfering with their ability to change the scale of their operations from year to year.[79]

A common belief has been that labor was scarcer throughout the American colonies than in England. The evidence of Table 2.4 provides some support for this assertion. Wages generally appear to have been considerably higher relative to land prices in New England than in England in the late seventeenth and early eighteenth centuries. This may have had significant implications for the incidence of service in husbandry in New England. It has been found that in preindustrial England wealthier farmers were less likely than poorer laborers to send their children into service.[80] In part, this could have been the result of greater wealth allowing parents to retain their children at home in spite of a sacrifice in wages forgone from more productive employment elsewhere. More likely, however, is that the larger farms of the wealthier parents meant that they could use their children's labor more productively, thereby not sacrificing income by retaining their children at home. The considerably higher value of labor relative

[79] More sinister views of service in husbandry have been offered by some historians. For example, Peter Laslett has argued that "the practice of the poorer families offering up their children to the richer families at the very time when those children were at the height of their productive powers must certainly be called exploitation of one set of persons by another set" (*Family Life and Illicit Love in Earlier Generations: Essays in Historical Sociology* [Cambridge: Cambridge University Press, 1977], p. 45). Though the ambiguity of Laslett's use of "exploitation" here precludes a test of his argument, it might be noted that the movement of children from poorer families – that owned little or no land – to richer families – that owned larger farms – is consistent with the efficient allocation of labor. Observing this same phenomenon, Alan Macfarlane commented that "the institution of servanthood might, therefore, be regarded as a disguised means whereby wealth and labour flowed from the poorer to the richer: husbandmen and their families were left precariously devoid of any adult support [by the departure of their children], while the households of the wealthier villages were stabilized against the effects of illness and death by the presence of young men and women whom they had not raised, and who replaced their absent children" (*The Family Life of Ralph Josselin. A Seventeenth-Century Clergyman: An Essay in Historical Anthropology* [New York: Norton, 1977], pp. 209–10). Macfarlane's contention that service in husbandry transferred wealth to richer families appears to neglect the ability of the servants to capture their marginal product in what were clearly competitive labor markets; he similarly appears to ignore the fact that the total income of the members of the poorer families would have been increased if the children moved to larger farms where their productivity was greater than at home.

[80] Kussmaul, *Servants in Husbandry in Early Modern England*, pp. 75–78.

Table 2.4. *Price of land relative to laborers' wages, rural areas of England and New England, 1650–1715*

Date	Price of land per acre (£)	Laborers' wages per day (d.)	Ratio of land price to laborers' wages
England			
(1) 1650–59	4.16–4.53	8–14	71–136
(2) 1651–67	2.79–8.64	10–14	48–207
(3) 1677	2.87–8.88	12–14	49–178
(4) 1690–91	5.27	12–14	90–105
(5) 1695–96	4.75–5.86	12–14	81–117
(6) 1705	5.25	8–15	84–158
(7) 1706	3.26–10.08	8–15	52–302
(8) 1714	4.42	14–15	71–76
New England			
(1a) 1651–59	1.33	16–35	9–20
(1b) 1651–59	1.87	16–35	13–28
(2a) 1660–69	2.75	12–30	22–55
(2b) 1660–69	4.72	12–30	38–94
(3a) 1670–75	2.85	12–36	19–57
(3b) 1670–75	6.63	12–36	44–133
(4) 1685	1–3	18–30	8–40
(5) 1700–1709	1.59	18–30	11–18

Notes

1. England land prices were obtained by multiplying annual rental charges by the "number of years' purchase," i.e., the ratio of the price to the annual rental. The estimates of the number of years' purchase were taken from Christopher Clay, "The Price of Freehold Land in the Later Seventeenth and Eighteenth Centuries," *Economic History Review* 2d ser., 37, no. 2 (1974): 174. Following Clay, the number of years' purchase was taken to be 18 for 1650–59 and 1651–67, 18.5 for 1677, 19 for 1690–91 and 1695–96, and 21 for 1705, 1706, and 1714.

2. The land prices used in rows 1a, 2a, and 3a were calculated by William Davisson as the mean price per acre of all land listed in Essex County probate records in the appropriate years; as he noted, this included pasture, meadow, orchards, and cultivated land. The lower population density in New England than in England might be expected to result in a higher proportion of such land not having been improved, however, and this would impart bias to the comparison discussed in the text, owing to the lower average quality of the New England land. As a result, the probate inventories used by Davisson were searched for itemized quotations of the price of "planting land." The means of all such prices by decade are presented in rows 1b, 2b, and 3b. Because all this land was cultivated, use of these prices in calculating the ratios discussed in the text should yield results biased against the finding of higher wages in New England relative to land prices. Interestingly, the ratios shown in rows 1b and 2b are still generally far below those of England; only in row 3b is this not the case. The latter may have been a consequence of the growth of Salem as a seaport and the resulting increase in land values there.

David W. Galenson

Notes to Table 2.4 (*cont.*)

Sources:

England: English land prices were derived from rental rates; see n. 1 above for procedure.

(1) Land rent: Eric Kerridge, "The Movement of Rent, 1540–1640," in E. M. Carus-Wilson, ed., *Essays in Economic History*, vol. 2 (New York: St. Martin's, 1962), pp. 216–17.

Wage: Henry Phelps Brown and Sheila V. Hopkins, *A Perspective of Wages and Prices* (London: Methuen, 1981), p. 11; British Library of Political and Economic Science, London: Records of International Scientific Committee on Price History (Beveridge Price Commission).

(2) Land rent: J. E. Thorold Rogers, *A History of Agriculture and Prices in England*, vol. 6, *1583–1702* (Oxford: Clarendon Press, 1877), p. 716.

Wage: Same as (1).

(3) Land rent: Same as (2).

Wage: Same as (1).

(4) Land rent: Peter H. Lindert, "Some Economic Consequences of English Population Growth, 1541–1913" (unpublished paper, University of California, Davis, 1983), p. 33.

Wage: Same as (1).

(5) Land rent: Joan Thirsk and J. P. Cooper, eds., *Seventeenth-Century Economic Documents* (Oxford: Clarendon Press, 1972), p. 765.

Wage: Same as (1).

(6) Land rent: Arthur G. Ruston and Denis Witney, *Hooton Pagnell: The Agricultural Evolution of a Yorkshire Village* (New York: Longmans, Green, 1934), p. 193.

Wage: Same as (1); also Elizabeth W. Gilboy, *Wages in Eighteenth Century England* (Cambridge: Harvard University Press, 1934), pp. 277, 280.

(7) Land rent: Same as (2).

Wage: Same as (6).

(8) Land rent: Lindert, "Some Economic Consequences of English Population Growth," p. 34.

Wage: Same as (1).

New England:

(1a) Land price: Calculated as decadal mean of annual land prices given by William I. Davisson, "Essex County Price Trends: Money and Markets in 17th Century Massachusetts," *Essex Institute Historical Collections* 103, no. 2 (April 1967): 165.

Wage: Mean of quotations of wages of unskilled labor for appropriate years from Essex Institute Historical Collections, *Record of the Quarterly Court of Essex County, Massachusetts*, 8 vols. (Salem, Mass.: Essex Institute, 1918).

(1b) Land price: Mean price of "planting land" from probate records for appropriate years, as recorded in Essex Institute Historical Collections, *Probate Records of Essex County, Massachusetts*, 3 vols. (Salem, Mass.: Essex Institute, 1916–21). See n. 2 above for discussion.

Wage: Same as (1a).

(2a) and (3a): Same as (1a).

(2b) and (3b): Same as (1b).

(4) Land price: Stephen Innes, *Labor in a New Land: Economy and Society in*

90

Notes to Table 2.4 (*cont.*)

Seventeenth-Century Springfield (Princeton, N.J.: Princeton University Press, 1983), pp. 46–47.
Wage: Ibid., pp. 307–35.

(5) Land price: Terry L. Anderson, "Economic Growth in Colonial New England: 'Statistical Renaissance,'" *Journal of Economic History* 39, no. 1 (March 1979): 257.
Wage: Same as (4).

to land in New England might have meant that rather than sending their children to larger farms, more colonial parents could behave like wealthy families in England and expand their landholdings to take advantage of the labor of their children. This logic suggests that service in husbandry would have been less common in New England than in England.[81]

The evidence is much too slight to draw any firm conclusions, but the available data do appear consistent with the prediction. For England, a total of ten population enumerations of rural parishes are

---

[81] It should be observed that the prediction made here could be negated by wealth differences between England and New England. In addition to its indirect influence through the size of the family's landholding, wealth may also have had a direct effect on the decision to retain or send out the child. At given levels of wealth, English families would have been more likely than colonial families to send their children into service because of their smaller landholdings. Per capita wealth levels were greater in England than in the colonies, however, so in some places higher English wealth levels might have offset the higher relative cost of land in England, thus negating the prediction stated here.

An extension of the argument made in the text would further predict that the time typically spent in service by those who did enter the status was less in New than in Old England. A principal determinant of the age of exit from service in England was the ability of the individual to establish an independent household (ibid., pp. 78–85). The higher ratio of wages to land prices in New England implies that the time needed to accumulate savings sufficient to buy a farm should generally have been shorter in America than in England.

Purchasing land was of course not the only way of expanding the scale of a family's farming. Several recent studies have emphasized the importance of leasing and land tenancy in colonial New England. These were in part ways of overcoming capital constraints, but they are of course consistent with the argument made here, because the relative abundance of land in the colonies should have improved the terms on which land could be rented.

Another extension of the argument in the text provides a prediction concerning differences in the incidence of service in husbandry within New England. To the extent that the value of labor relative to that of land varied inversely with population density, it might be predicted that at any time the importance of service in husbandry would have declined with increasing distance from the older, coastal settlements of New England toward the frontier. Closer to the frontier more farms would have been expected to operate exclusively with family labor than with any kind of hired or bound labor.

known for the late seventeenth and early eighteenth centuries. In these enumerations, servants in husbandry made up an average of 10 percent of these parishes' total population.[82] For New England, even less evidence is available. One recent study of Essex County, Massachusetts, estimated that less than 5 percent of that county's population in the seventeenth century was made up of male servants in husbandry.[83] Another study, of Dedham, Massachusetts, reported that servants in husbandry, captive Indians, and black slaves together made up less than 5 percent of the town's population.[84] A third study, based on an analysis of a listing of the population of Bristol, Rhode Island, in 1689, found that servants accounted for 13 percent of the town's residents.[85] Of these estimates for New England, Bristol's status as a seaport may make it least comparable to the rural English parishes, for towns like Bristol were precisely the parts of New England where labor productivity was greatest; later in the colonial period Bristol became a major New England center of slaveholding.[86] But additional estimates of the importance of service in husbandry will clearly be needed to allow a genuine test of the prediction made here.

Evidence on colonial New England's market for hired day laborers is no more abundant than that on servants in husbandry. New England does appear to have had active markets for hired labor from a very early date, and these operated with little effective government intervention. As early as 1641 John Winthrop noted the inability of the Massachusetts General Court to legislate against "the excessive rates of laborers' and workmen's wages," commenting (in terms that indicate that the colonial labor problem was not unique to Virginia) that "being restrained, they would either remove to other places where they might have more, or else being able to live by planting and other

---

[82] Ibid., pp. 12–13. In all, servants made up 9 percent of the total population of the parishes taken together. In only one parish did they make up less than 5 percent; in five they made up more than 10 percent.

[83] Daniel Vickers, "Working the Fields in a Developing Economy: Essex County, Massachusetts, 1630–1675" (unpublished paper, Memorial University, St John's, Newfoundland, 1986), p. 8. Vickers also comments that children in Essex County departed from home at older ages than they might have in England (p. 15).

[84] Kenneth A. Lockridge, *A New England Town: The First Hundred Years* (New York: Norton, 1970), p. 72.

[85] John Demos, "Families in Colonial Bristol, Rhode Island: An Exercise in Historical Demography," *William and Mary Quarterly* 3d ser., 25, no. 1 (January 1968): 43–44.

[86] In 1774, slaves made up more than 9 percent of the town's population (ibid., pp. 50–51).

employments of their own, they would not be hired at all."[87] It appears to have been common for farmers to hire out for wages for short periods. A recent study concluded that almost every man in seventeenth-century Essex County performed hired labor at some time in his career; this most often involved younger farmers doing occasional work for their older and wealthier neighbors.[88]

Yet although markets for hired labor appear to have been an important feature of New England's economy throughout the colonial period, the high level of wages relative to the price of land would also be expected to have had significant implications for these markets. Specifically, the greater ease of purchasing farms in New England should have meant that fewer adults worked as hired laborers there than in England. Although few studies of the occupational distributions of adult males have been done either for the colonies or for England, it might again be noted that what evidence is available does appear consistent with this prediction. In 1688 Gregory King estimated that 27 percent of all heads of English families were "labouring people and out servants" and another 30 percent were "cottagers and paupers," yielding a total of 57 percent of adult males who would have had to rely substantially on wage labor for their livelihood.[89] A recent revision of King's estimates has suggested that the share of these groups was somewhat lower, and reduces it to 43 percent of adult

---

[87] James Kendall Hosmer, ed., *Winthrop's Journal, 1630–1649*, vol. 2 (New York: Scribner, 1908), p. 24. Also see J. R. T. Hughes, *Social Control in the Colonial Economy* (Charlottesville: University Press of Virginia, 1976), pp. 98–99. One historian of the economy of early New England concluded: "All the colonists wasted much governmental strength in fruitless efforts to regulate prices, and especially the prices of wages" (William B. Weeden, *Economic and Social History of New England, 1620–1789*, vol. 1 [Boston: Houghton Mifflin, 1890], p. 115).

[88] Vickers, "Working the Fields in a Developing Economy," pp. 10–12; Stephen Innes, *Labor in a New Land: Economy and Society in Seventeenth-Century Springfield* (Princeton, N.J.: Princeton University Press, 1983), ch. 4.

Some knowledge of the extent of women's labor-force participation, including evidence on its variation over time and space, is also critical to a better understanding of free-labor markets in the colonies. It might be predicted that high labor productivity in agriculture in many of the colonies raised the value of field work relative to that in the home, and resulted in higher rates of participation for women in agricultural labor in America than in England. Although evidence on women's work in the colonies is scarce, Lois Green Carr and Lorena S. Walsh have suggested that women in the early Chesapeake were more likely than their counterparts in England to do field work ("The Planter's Wife: The Experience of White Women in Seventeenth-Century Maryland," *William and Mary Quarterly* 3d ser., 34, no. 4 [October 1977]: 542–71).

[89] Peter Laslett, *The World We Have Lost*, 2d ed. (London: Methuen, 1971), pp. 36–37.

David W. Galenson

males.[90] In contrast, however, a recent study concluded that at most one-third of free adult men in colonial Connecticut would have had to perform hired labor regularly in order to support their families.[91] Although more evidence should be examined before firm conclusions are drawn, the substantial difference between these estimates for England and the colonies does suggest that a significant difference might be confirmed when studies are done with the explicit intention of developing standardized occupational distributions that can be used in such comparisons. A great many primary data are available from surviving sources, and such studies would be of considerable interest. It should also be considered, however, that in many colonial areas increasing population densities over time may have produced increasing shares of laborers in the adult male population. Some evidence suggestive of this appears in a recent study of rural Pennsylvania, where nonhouseholders – most of whom would have worked as hired laborers – rose from one-tenth of the adult male population during 1715–30 to one-third in 1774, a period in which the county's population grew rapidly.[92]

Considerable work remains to be done in tracing the development of New England's free-labor market and measuring the importance of both service in husbandry and hired day labor in colonial New England – and indeed elsewhere in the colonies. Little information on colonial wages and employment has been collected, but a great deal is available in legal records and account books.[93] Although the lack of quantitative evidence makes firm conclusions inappropriate, several recent studies

[90] Peter H. Lindert and Jeffrey G. Williamson, "Revising England's Social Tables, 1688–1812," *Explorations in Economic History* 19, no. 4 (October 1982): 388–89; also see Lindert, "English Occupations, 1670–1811," *Journal of Economic History* 40, no. 4 (December 1980): 685–712.

[91] Jackson Turner Main, *Society and Economy in Colonial Connecticut* (Princeton, N.J.: Princeton University Press, 1985), p. 175. Studies of smaller areas have produced similar estimates. Charles S. Grant found that hired laborers accounted for 25–33 percent of adult males in Kent, Connecticut, at a number of dates during 1740–77; interestingly, he also found that the majority of these men were typically only temporarily in the status of hired laborer (*Democracy in the Connecticut Frontier Town of Kent* [New York: Norton, 1972], pp. 96–97). Vickers points out that in seventeenth-century Essex County the employment of hired labor was so irregular that the identifying designation "laborer" almost disappeared from county records ("Working the Fields in a Developing Economy," p. 11).

[92] Lucy Simler, "Tenancy in Colonial Pennsylvania: The Case of Chester County," *William and Mary Quarterly* 3d ser., 43, no. 4 (October 1986): 546–49.

[93] The most abundant evidence on wages in preindustrial England has been drawn from the account books of great institutions that hired workers for construction and agricultural production over long periods. Thus, for example, when the Beveridge Price Commission set out to examine long-run trends in English wages, its principal

94

of localities point toward the intriguing possibility that free-labor markets played a major role in colonial New England, and that the availability of free labor for hire contributed substantially to the prosperity and flexibility of the region's economy.

Conclusion

The economic history of colonial English America is a success story. Although our view of the aggregate economy remains clouded, cautious estimates have suggested that the second half of the colonial period was characterized by annual rates of growth of per capita net national product of 0.3–0.5 percent. Although modest by the standards of the modern economic growth that came later, these rates were impressive by the standards of Europe in the centuries preceding the colonization of the New World. The achievement of this intensive growth is even more impressive in view of colonial rates of population growth that averaged more than 3 percent per year, so that in sum net national product increased between seventy-five-fold and a hundred-fold from 1710 to 1840.[94] One consequence of this was the achievement of a level of per capita income in the United States in 1840 significantly greater than that of France, and perhaps little below that of Great Britain.[95] Yet these economic accomplishments have received little attention from students of economic growth. It is of some interest to ask why colonial economic history is so often either ignored or dismissed summarily as a stagnant and uninteresting prelude to the nineteenth-century onset of modern economic growth.

Until quite recently, much of the research on the history of colonial America was done by intellectual and theological historians. Although they might discuss the colonial economy, few directed much energy to the subject, and fewer still brought with them the expertise in economic research that would have enabled them to perceive that economy's achievements. This situation is now changing. During the past two

sources were the accounts of the expenditures made by major city governments, colleges, and hospitals. Such records of accounts may exist for institutions in colonial America, but they do not yet appear to have been used for the study of wages and prices.

94 Robert E. Gallman, "The Pace and Pattern of American Economic Growth," in Lance E. Davis, Richard A. Easterlin, William N. Parker et al., *American Economic Growth: An Economist's History of the United States* (New York: Harper & Row, 1972), p. 22.

95 Robert E. Gallman, "Gross National Product in the United States, 1834–1909," in Peter Temin, ed., *The New Economic History* (Harmondsworth: Penguin Books, 1973), pp. 20–23.

decades more historians trained in demography and economics have turned their attention to the colonial period, and many striking findings have emerged. The nature of the surviving data has dictated that much of this research be carried out at a micro level, and the results have consequently often given us close-up views of individual markets and local economies. The accumulation of these has now begun to make it possible to make some wider generalizations and to offer some hypotheses for future study.[96]

The labor markets that have been the subject of this essay have been perhaps the most intensively studied part of the colonial economy. The existence of large and efficient markets in bound labor – both indentured and slave – has now been documented. Some signs of efficient local markets in free labor have also been uncovered. Contrary to many traditional interpretations that have stressed departures from efficiency and the dominance of noncompetitive structures, it now appears that colonial America benefited from highly competitive transatlantic markets for both European and African labor that helped colonial farmers and planters minimize the labor costs that posed the major constraint on their economic opportunities. The precise extent of the penetration of labor markets into the colonial economy remains to be determined, but a guess might now be hazarded that before long evidence will be forthcoming to contradict a recent assertion that colonial farmers who hired or bought labor in order to make profits were an exception.[97]

Some work has been done on the behavior of colonial product markets and other factor markets, but much remains to be done. As for labor markets, some recent examples of this work have increasingly challenged older views that stress the inefficiencies of the colonial economy.[98] Although much research and many debates undoubtedly lie ahead, the economic success of the colonial period may come to be more fully appreciated, and the existence of markets that produced efficient allocations of resources may be recognized as a central ingredient of this success.

---

[96] For a recent comprehensive literature survey, see John J. McCusker and Russell R. Menard, *The Economy of British America, 1607–1789* (Chapel Hill: University of North Carolina Press, 1985).

[97] James A. Henretta, "Families and Farms: Mentalité in Pre-Industrial America," *William and Mary Quarterly* 3d ser., 35, no. 1 (January 1978): 18.

[98] On capital markets, for example, see Jacob M. Price, *Capital and Credit in British Overseas Trade: The View from the Chesapeake, 1700–1776* (Cambridge: Harvard University Press, 1980); on product markets, see Winifred B. Rothenberg, "The Market and Massachusetts Farmers, 1750–1855," *Journal of Economic History* 41, no. 2 (June 1981): 283–314.

3

Productivity in American whaling: the New Bedford fleet in the nineteenth century

Lance E. Davis, Robert E. Gallman, and
Teresa D. Hutchins

In economics, productivity change is often associated with technical change. Looking at the matter from the level of the firm, where, after all, the principal relevant decisions are made, it is customary to focus on the choice of an appropriate technology, with attention devoted to the role of factor prices in determining the combination of factors employed.[1]

Life in the firm, however, is likely to be more complex than this model suggests. Frequently there are many productive operations, and each could be affected by a variety of alternative techniques. Each technique, in turn, may employ a range of types of labor and forms of capital. Over time, techniques, factor prices, and output prices all can change. New opportunities crop up and new problems appear. The

Davis and Gallman are Research Associates of the National Bureau of Economic Research. Most of the research on which this paper is based was funded by the National Science Foundation and the NBER project Productivity and Industrial Change in the World Economy. Grants to Gallman from the Kenan Foundation helped finance the construction of the capital-stock estimates. The Division of Humanities and Social Sciences at the California Institute of Technology provided funds for the collection of the labor data. The Carolina Population Center helped plan and carry out the computer operations. We thank in particular Judith Kovenock, Karin Gleiter, Kathleen Gallagher, and Billie Norwood. Paul Cyr, of the New Beford Public Library, was a kind and helpful guide through the whaling data. Evidence from the Joseph Dias manuscript is published with the permission of the Baker Library of the Graduate School of Business, Harvard University. We thank Michael Butler, Emil Friberg, and Eugene Dyar for research assistance.

The paper was presented to the Triangle Workshop in Economic History, the Washington Area Seminar in Economic History, the Conference on the Evolution of Firms and Industries (NBER), and seminars at Brown University, the University of Chicago, the University of Illinois, the University of Michigan, the University of Rochester, and Yale University. We thank the participants in these seminars for their comments and suggestions.

[1] For a criticism of this approach, see Edward Ames and Nathan Rosenberg, "The Enfield Arsenal in Theory and History," *Economic Journal* 78, no. 312 (December 1968): 827–42.

defensive actions of the firm faced by a new problem may be as important (by preventing the deterioration of productivity) as the firm's decision to exploit a new opportunity. Finally, the level of productivity may be importantly influenced by decisions that are only peripherally (if at all) related to matters of production technique in the usual sense of the phrase. Decisions to open a new source of a raw material or to exploit a new market are two obvious examples.

This essay examines productivity in the context of the complete web of entrepreneurial decisions influencing production. We are interested in the reactions of entrepreneurs to shifting opportunities and problems, the ways in which decisions about technique are related to other business decisions, and the relative weights of the factors influencing productivity.

Whaling was competitive – the industry was made up of many relatively small firms. Major decisions were in the hands of the whaling agent who hired the crew, rigged and provisioned the vessel, laid plans for the voyage, and provided the captain with access to overseas credit and with information and guidance before and during the voyage.[2] We are interested in the choices the agent made, the influence of exogenous developments on these choices, and the impact of the agent's decisions on the productivity of the venture. The unit of analysis is the individual whaling voyage, for the voyage was the focus of all of these decisions.

The first section provides a brief historical and economic background. The second describes the data set, and the third, the system for measuring productivity. The fourth section lays out the opportunities and problems facing agents and the choices they were obliged to make. It also develops the variables that figure in the empirical analysis. The fifth section contains the empirical analysis, and the last is a summary of conclusions.

Historical and economic background

In July of 1842 seaman Herman Melville deserted the whaler *Acushnet* in the Marquesas, where he spent a month with the natives of the Taipi Valley. He subsequently treated this experience in his novel *Typee*. Before he finally reached home he had material for three more books, *Omoo, Mardi*, and *Moby-Dick*. The first two were based on visits to Tahiti and Eimo, occasioned by a second desertion (this time from an

---

[2] See, for example, the papers of Matthew Howland, held by Baker Library, Graduate School of Business, Harvard University. Howland was an agent who kept a particularly firm grip on the activities of his captains.

Australian whaler); the last, on Melville's life aboard the *Acushnet* and later the Nantucket whaler *Charles and Henry*, on which he served as boatsteerer. The dates of Melville's sailing from Fairhaven aboard the *Acushnet*, January 1841, and of his publication of *Moby-Dick*, October 1851 (in London, under the title *The Whale*), nicely delineate the apogee of American whaling.

Although the peak of American whaling occurred in 1841–51, the history of the industry spanned centuries. It began with the first colonial settlements along the East Coast of North America and persisted, albeit weakly, until 1974, when whaling was finally outlawed.[3] Long before whaling became illegal, the mode of whaling celebrated by Melville had disappeared and had been replaced by modern methods pioneered by the Norwegians. The Americans never adopted the new techniques on a large scale and were effectively out of whaling by the beginning of World War I. The industry has changed in other ways as well. Modern whalers seek whale meat and cooking oils rather than the illuminants, lubricants, and structural materials brought back by Melville's whalemen. Modern whaling is therefore an entirely new industry, prosecuted by new techniques in pursuit of new ends.

By the outbreak of the Revolution, the American whaling industry had evolved from a land-based operation into a deep-sea industry. In its earliest stages whalemen stuck close to shore. Whales were sighted from the beach and hunted down from small boats. The process of rendering the blubber into oil took place on land. Gradually, however, whalemen left the shore, and instead of waiting for whales to swim close to land, went looking for the whales. Technological change and geographical expansion occurred rapidly. By the 1770s the process of rendering blubber had been moved aboard the vessel, and Yankee whalemen were routinely cruising the Atlantic from Newfoundland to the Falkland Islands.[4]

Favorable market conditions helped to foster these developments. Blessed with a growing export market in Great Britain, the colonial whale fishery expanded until 1774, when, in the words of Alexander Starbuck, the Revolutionary War caught the industry in its "full tide of success."[5] For the next forty years it suffered a series of major econo-

[3] Robert Owen Decker, *Whaling Industry of New London* (York, Pa.: Liberty Cap Books, 1973), 119.

[4] Ibid., p. 19.

[5] Alexander Starbuck, *History of the American Whale Fishery* (Waltham, Mass.: The Author, 1878), p. 57. Starbuck's *History* was first published in part IV of the *Report of the U.S. Commission on Fish and Fisheries* (Washington, D.C., 1878).

Lance E. Davis, Robert E. Gallman, & Teresa D. Hutchins

Table 3.1. *Annual average vessel tonnage: USA and New Bedford whaling fleets, 1816–1905*

| Years | Tonnage | | Percentage New Bedford of USA |
	USA	New Bedford	
1816–25	27,775	9,906	35.7
1826–35	70,352	35,272	50.1
1836–45	159,788	64,796	40.6
1846–55	202,143	94,382	46.7
1856–65	156,129	93,770	60.1
1866–75	67,602	53,074	78.5
1876–85	42,967	33,934	79.0
1886–95	28,380	7,838	27.6
1896–1905	14,311	3,143	22.0
1816–45	85,971	36,665	42.6
1846–75	144,719	80,408	55.6
1876–1905	27,968	14,972	53.5
1816–1905	86,694	44,046	50.8

Sources: USA: Walter S. Tower, *A History of the American Whale Fishery* (Philadelphia: University of Pennsylvania Press, 1907). New Bedford: Davis, Gallman, and Hutchins tape (see note 15).

mic reversals, and at no time were conditions stable long enough to allow it to experience any period of sustained growth.[6]

Although our subject is the American whaling industry, most of the material used in this paper refers to vessels that sailed from New Bedford, Massachusetts. Nantucket had been the principal American whaling port at the beginning of the nineteenth century, and San Francisco assumed that position at the end. In the years between 1825 and 1890, however, New Bedford dominated the industry. Subject to some year-to-year variation, over those sixty-five years the port's vessels, on average, represented more than 50 percent of the nation's whaling tonnage (see Table 3.1). Moreover, whereas vessels from other ports tended to specialize in certain whaling grounds and in either sperm or baleen whales, the New Bedford whalers ranged over all the world's hunting grounds and sought both species of whales. Thus the New Bedford whalers not only constitute a representative sample of the American industry, but they also present a microcosmic

[6] Walter S. Tower, *A History of the American Whale Fishery* (Philadelphia: University of Pennsylvania Press, 1907), Table I, p. 129. For the first year for which he has tonnage statistics, Tower lists the tonnage of the U.S. fleet at 4,129. At the end of the war it was 1,168. The maximum value reached during this period was 12,339 (1804).

100

picture of the behavior of the firms that made up the industry.

Our study encompasses more than half of the American industry; the Americans, in turn, operated about eight-tenths of the world's whaling fleet over the last eight decades of the nineteenth century. There had been some British competition before the 1840s; the Australians hunted whales throughout the period; and after the mid-1890s the Norwegians dominated the industry; but between 1820 and 1890 the industry was virtually an American monopoly.

Marine biologists inform us that there are two types of proper whales: the baleen (suborder Mysticeti) and the catchelot (suborder Odonoceti). In the nineteenth century the Americans hunted one variety of catchelot (the sperm whale) and four varieties of baleen (the right, the gray, the bowhead, and the humpback).

The five varieties do not all inhabit the same parts of the ocean. Sperm whales are found in the tropical and subtropical regions of the Atlantic, Pacific, and Indian oceans. The rights prefer cooler waters. They travel in the North Atlantic from Bermuda to Greenland, in the North Pacific from Japan to the Pacific Northwest and as far north as the Arctic Circle, and in the South Atlantic from Brazil and in the South Pacific from Chile to the Antarctic Ocean. The whalers looked for bowheads in the Arctic Ocean, the Okhotsk Sea, the Bering Strait, and the North Pacific above the fifty-fourth parallel; however, since those animals had discovered the Northwest Passage centuries before Martin Frobisher began his fruitless search, they also appeared in Hudson's Bay and in Davis Strait. Like the sperms and rights, the humpbacks and grays inhabit the more temperate climes.

During the first few decades of the nineteenth century, sperm oil and spermaceti were used primarily as illuminants. Spermaceti, a solid, made the highest-quality candles; sperm oil was burned in lighthouses and public buildings where high-intensity illumination was required. In the second and particularly in the third quarter of the century, sperm oil came to be used increasingly as a lubricant to ease the movements of light, rapidly moving machines (the spindles of cotton and woolen mills, for example). In fact, the expansion of sperm-oil production after 1830 matches very closely the rise of the cotton textile industry.

Whale oil, obtained from the blubber of baleen whales, was the illuminant chosen by the average consumer. Although it was technically inferior to sperm oil both as an illuminant and as a lubricant, its relatively low price made it one of the most popular lamp fuels in the 1820s, 1830s, and early 1840s.[7] By the last of these decades whale oil

[7] Edgar Winfield Martin, *The Standard of Living in 1860* (Chicago: University of Chicago Press, 1942), p. 95.

101

Table 3.2. *New Bedford whaling fleet average annual catch, 1816–1905*

Years	Sperm oil (1,000 gal.)	Whale oil (1,000 gal.)	Whalebone (1,000 lb.)	Real value ($1,000)[a]
1816–25	352	466	11	360
1826–35	1,209	1,200	80	1,340
1836–45	1,867	2,087	299	2,591
1846–55	1,404	3,322	1,377	4,256
1856–65	1,421	2,483	828	4,159
1866–75	968	1,320	440	2,236
1876–85	844	773	233	1,797
1886–95	344	87	78	632
1896–1905	224	11	10	195
1816–45	1,143	1,251	130	1,430
1846–75	1,264	2,375	882	3,550
1876–1905	471	290	107	875
1816–1905	959	1,305	373	1,952

[a] Real value expressed in 1880 dollars.
Source: Davis, Gallman, and Hutchins tape.

began to face ever stiffening competition from new illuminants (coal oil, coal gas, and, in the 1850s, kerosene), but total sales held up fairly well as manufacturers began to use it to lubricate their heavy machinery.[8]

Whalebone, or baleen, is not really bone but the bonelike screen that the whale uses as a filter to separate its food (krill) from sea water. In the nineteenth century, whalebone was used in the manufacture of stays, corsets, hoops, whips, umbrellas, carriage shades, and almost any other product that required a strong, flexible material – needs now met by plastics and specialty steels.

The quantity of sperm oil that the fleet brought home increased rapidly from 1820 until the late 1830s. Then growth ceased, although output remained fairly constant until the middle of the next decade. By the late 1840s, however, the catch had begun to decline. The fall continued, although with some significant pauses, until the end of the century (see Table 3.2).[9] The real price of sperm oil doubled between 1820 and 1850 but then began to fall; by the end of the century the price was no higher than it had been in 1820.

The quantity of whale oil that the captains brought back to New

[8] Louis S. Russell, *A Heritage of Light* (Toronto: University of Toronto Press, 1968), p. 58.
[9] Tower, *Whale Fishery*, p. 126, Table III.

Bedford increased until the early 1850s, stabilized until the Civil War, and then began an almost continuous decline. In no postbellum year did output come close to matching its prewar peak. Over the nine decades the real price of whale oil displayed a profile that was similar to that of sperm oil except that the decline in the second half of the century was more gentle. Over most of the period the ratio of the price of sperm oil to the price of whale oil averaged about 2:1; by 1900, however, the ratio had fallen to 3:2.

At the beginning of the nineteenth century whalebone was in such small demand that captains often refused to surrender the valuable storage space needed to bring it back. Gradually, as demand increased, returning cargoes contained more and more of the strong, flexible material. By the Civil War, high prices – prices inflated by the fashions of the day – made whalebone a very desirable addition to a whaler's catch. Indeed, the case can be made that it was the growing demand for whalebone that kept the fishery profitable and encouraged the pursuit of the Arctic bowhead. Like that of whale oil, the quantity of whalebone brought back increased yearly until the mid-1850s, peaked at that time, and then began to decline. Output recovered some ground in the 1880s, but even at that time it did not reach the levels attained before the war. Because of the rapid rise in price, however, the value of the bone brought back continued to rise.[10] The real price, in fact, rose from ten cents a pound in 1820 to more than five dollars a pound in 1905. Exports of baleen (primarily to England, France, and Germany) commanded a significant proportion of total output over the entire nineteenth century.[11]

Given the similarity in the production paths of all three of the industry's major products, it should not come as a surprise that the fortunes of the industry improved steadily from the end of the War of 1812 until sometime in the mid-1850s and then gradually declined. The industry had, in fact, all but disappeared by the time of the archduke's assassination in the streets of Sarajevo. The real value of the industry's total output was about $1.2 million in 1820; it had reached $12 million by mid-century, but it had fallen to less than $1.2 million fifty years later.

The geographic dispersion of the stock of whales meant that New Bedford whalers could be found all over the world. The chronicler of the port's fleet lists no fewer than fifty-one whaling grounds, but for our analysis the fifty-one have been grouped into four: (1) the Atlantic

---

[10] Ibid., p. 127, Table IV. Until 1862 Tower's whale-oil statistics include data on "other fish oil."

[11] Ibid., pp. 126, 127, Tables III and IV.

Table 3.3. *Vessel tonnage returning by ground (3,369 New Bedford voyages)*

Years	Percentage of returning tonnage			
	Atlantic	Indian	Pacific	Arctic
1816–25	55.5	0.3	43.2	0.0
1826–35	51.7	2.4	46.0	0.0
1836–45	22.7	20.9	56.0	0.2
1846–55	3.6	21.6	65.0	9.7
1856–65	10.8	13.1	58.2	18.0
1866–75	25.3	10.0	37.7	15.9
1876–85	41.3	6.6	36.5	15.7
1886–95	45.5	6.3	48.3	0.0
1896–1905	100.0	0.0	0.0	0.0
1816–45	43.6	7.9	48.4	0.1
1846–75	13.9	14.9	53.6	14.5
1876–1905	62.2	4.3	28.3	5.2
1816–1905	24.2	14.3	52.0	9.4

Source: L. E. Davis, R. E. Gallman, and T. D. Hutchins, "The Structure of the Capital Stock in Economic Growth and Decline," in Peter Kilby, ed., *Quantity and Quiddity* (Middletown, Conn.: Wesleyan University Press, 1987), p. 364.

Ocean, Hudson's Bay, and Davis Strait, (2) the Indian Ocean, (3) the Pacific Ocean, and (4) the western Arctic.

If interest centers on relative contribution to New Bedford's prosperity over the entire ninety-year period, the list, in order of importance, would read the Pacific, the Atlantic, the Indian, and finally the Arctic; however, within those nine decades the contribution of individual grounds ebbed and flowed (see Table 3.3). There were, for example, no voyages to any of the western grounds in the last decade of the period. The Indian Ocean drew a significant fraction of the city's fleet only in the middle decades, a period that saw almost no vessels hunting in the Atlantic. Finally, although the Arctic drew whaling captains from New Bedford in only four of the nine decades, during those four decades it was by far the most profitable.

It is a long way from New Bedford to the Arctic Ocean. The vessels employed in the trade depended on the wind for power, and once on station it was still necessary to find the whales. As a result, voyages were long, averaging almost three years (see Table 3.4). Over time, the length of a typical voyage increased. Although the increase was due in part to the opening of grounds further and further removed from the New England coast, it was also due to a nontrivial increase in

Table 3.4. *Average voyage length in months by ground (New Bedford ships and barks)*

Years	Atlantic	Indian	Pacific	Arctic
Ships				
1816–25	12.2	—	24.2	—
1826–35	12.2	14.8	33.3	—
1836–45	20.7	24.9	36.3	21.0
1846–55	26.9	33.7	37.5	34.8
1856–65	20.5	41.0	43.6	41.3
1866–75	22.0	42.0	47.2	46.9
1876–85	36.3	40.5	37.6	8.8
1886–95	37.6	—	33.6	—
1896–1905	—	—	—	—
1816–1905	17.0	32.1	37.6	38.9
Barks				
1816–25	12.3	—	32.0	—
1826–35	12.6	23.0	30.3	—
1836–45	18.7	22.4	35.5	21.0
1846–55	24.0	34.0	37.6	38.1
1856–65	23.7	40.3	44.4	42.4
1866–75	27.6	41.4	45.2	52.1
1876–85	32.9	38.8	33.4	16.2
1886–95	32.6	35.7	34.7	—
1896–1905	28.3	—	—	—
1816–1905	26.4	36.1	39.8	36.2

Source: L. E. Davis, R. E. Gallman, and T. D. Hutchins, "The Structure of the Capital Stock in Economic Growth and Decline," in Peter Kilby, ed., *Quantity and Quiddity* (Middletown, Conn: Wesleyan University Press, 1987), p. 375.

the length of stay in each ground. A trip to the Atlantic averaged less than two years, whereas a typical voyage to the Arctic or Pacific, which might have taken only two years when the ground first opened, took almost four in the 1870s.

As the whaling fleets of New England began to hunt more extensively in the Pacific, captains found it efficient to restock and refit during a voyage. In response to these needs the ports of Honolulu and Lahaina emerged as rendezvous points. There whalers could pick up fresh provisions, recruit new seamen, and repair their vessels. Beginning about 1840 the Hawaiian ports and Panama also became important centers for transshipments of oil and bone.[12] Captains wishing to

[12] Ralph S. Kuykendall, *The Hawaiian Kingdom*, vol. 1, *1778–1854: Foundation and Transformation* (Honolulu: University of Hawaii Press, 1968), p. 309.

continue whaling were able to ship their catch on whalers or merchant ships returning to New England.

Despite the widespread innovation of iron ships and steam power in the passenger and carrying trades, the New Bedford whalers that undertook those three- and four-year voyages were virtually all sailing vessels. Ships, barks, brigs, sloops, and schooners all found employment in whaling, but most of the fleet was made up of ships and barks. Taken together, the brigs, sloops, and schooners made up less than 5 percent of the number of vessels in the New Bedford total, and they represented only 2 percent of the city's total whaling tonnage.

Ships accounted for 56 percent of the number of vessels that sailed from New Bedford. They were relatively large vessels, averaging about 350 tons, but they were set apart from the barks, brigs, sloops, and schooners not so much by their relatively greater size as by their rigging. They had three square-rigged masts (that is, sails were set on yardarms attached at the center to the masts). The barks that made up 39 percent of the vessels operating out of New Bedford were on average, at 285 tons, smaller than the ships. More important, they were square-rigged on the fore- and mainmasts and fore-and-aft-rigged on the mizzen (that is, on the rear mast sails were set vertically and were attached directly to the mast and to the stern of the vessel). The average size of both classes of vessel rose over the first four decades. For ships the increase was about 20 percent; for barks, about twice that. Thus by the 1860s, when a typical ship had attained a size of about 380 tons, an average bark was 320.

Ships were the rigging of choice when the industry emerged from the wartime doldrums, and they retained that position through most of the period of expansion (see Table 3.5). Gradually, however, the number of barks increased in absolute and, even more impressively as the fleet began to contract, in relative terms. In 1845 there had been 1 bark for every 5.3 ships; by 1875 the ratio had been reversed, and there was 1 bark for every 0.53 ship.

The postbellum increase in the proportion of barks underscores two characteristics of the whaling fleet. First, the capital stock was very malleable. Even as vessels shifted from whaling to the merchant marine and the whaling fleet contracted, new barks were constructed and ships were rerigged as barks. Second, as the demand for whalebone rose, the bowheads of the Arctic became an ever more favored target; the rise in the importance of that northern ground, with its icebergs and icepack, put an increased premium on maneuverability – an important feature of the bark-rigged vessel.

Although barks were better able to escape the winter freeze, losses at sea of all types of vessels were very high. Of the approximately

106

Table 3.5. *Vessel rigging types: annual averages of percentage distribution (New Bedford fleet)*

Years	Percentage of total tonnage		
	Ships	Barks	Other
1816–25	87.0	5.2	7.8
1826–35	87.5	9.8	2.8
1836–45	83.4	15.0	1.6
1846–55	75.2	23.9	0.1
1856–65	56.5	42.8	0.6
1866–75	34.3	64.0	1.8
1876–85	25.6	67.6	6.8
1886–95	23.1	65.0	11.9
1896–1905	0.0	73.3	26.6
1816–45	85.1	12.4	2.5
1846–75	59.0	40.1	0.9
1876–1905	23.4	67.5	9.1
1816–1905	62.2	35.5	2.4

Source: Davis, Gallman, and Hutchins tape.

seven hundred and fifty vessels that sailed at least once from New Bedford in search of whales, no fewer than two hundred and thirty-one were lost. The crude loss rate per voyage averaged almost 9 percent; the loss rate per year at sea was 3.2 percent (2.6 for ships, 3.5 for barks, and an astounding 8.6 percent for the brigs, schooners, and sloops that made up the remainder of the fleet – see Table 3.6).

No summary of the industry could be complete without some mention of the men who manned the whalers. On average, twenty-seven men (including three or four officers) were needed to sail and hunt a ship. Because a bark was, on average, smaller, it required only about twenty-three (see Table 3.7). However, although the bark used a smaller crew, it actually represented a more labor-intensive technology; the trade-off faced by the agent who planned the voyage was between greater maneuverability and higher labor costs. Over time, average crew size increased for both classes of vessel. In the case of ships, for example, the figure rose from twenty-one to thirty-three. Although average vessel size was increasing, the size of the crew was rising even more rapidly; between 1820 and 1905 the labor–capital ratio rose by about 15 percent.

Whaling was a risky enterprise. A sailor risked life and limb. The owner risked the loss of his vessel, and, depending upon the luck of the hunt, he also faced financial feast or famine. In an attempt to

Lance E. Davis, Robert E. Gallman, & Teresa D. Hutchins

Table 3.6. *Annual loss rate (New Bedford fleet)*

Years	Ships	Barks	Other
1816–25	3.0	0.0	3.1
1826–35	1.5	2.7	17.4
1836–45	1.7	0.8	11.2
1846–55	3.0	3.8	7.9
1856–65	2.7	3.7	27.3
1866–75	3.5	5.4	8.0
1876–85	3.8	2.6	10.4
1886–95	0.0	0.5	1.8
1896–1905	—	3.1	4.7
Average[a]	2.6	3.5	8.7
Average[b]	2.4	2.8	10.2

Note: The annual loss rate is the number of vessels lost per vessel year of voyaging × 100.
[a] Vessel weights.
[b] Decade weights.
Source: L. E. Davis, R. E. Gallman, and T. D. Hutchins, "The Structure of the Capital Stock in Economic Growth and Decline," in Peter Kilby, ed., *Quantity and Quiddity* (Middletown, Conn.: Wesleyan University Press, 1987), p. 382.

Table 3.7. *Average crew size (New Bedford fleet)*

Years	Average crew size		
	Ships	Barks	Other
1816–25	20.9	14.3	14.0
1826–35	23.4	19.8	14.8
1836–45	26.3	22.7	16.8
1846–55	29.1	25.8	18.3
1856–65	30.0	27.1	20.1
1866–75	30.9	27.4	17.7
1876–85	31.1	27.8	18.3
1886–95	33.0	28.4	16.5
1896–1905	—	26.4	17.0
1816–1905	27.5	26.5	17.1

Source: L. E. Davis, R. E. Gallman, and T. D. Hutchins, "The Structure of the Capital Stock in Economic Growth and Decline," in Peter Kilby, ed., *Quantity and Quiddity* (Middletown, Conn.: Wesleyan University Press, 1987), p. 361.

spread the risk, the owners and seamen adopted a system of labor payments that made remuneration depend on the success of the voyage.

Every member of the crew was entitled to a fraction (a lay) of the net receipts of the voyage. On average, the total labor share amounted to slightly more than one-third of the receipts from the sale of the catch. Although there are examples of total lays as low as 26 percent and as high as 37 percent, the average was about 34. Individual crewmen were compensated on the basis of the position held and their level of skill and experience. Thus a captain's share was typically about one-sixteenth, but there were voyages where the captain received as much as one-eighth and others where his pay fell as low as one-twentieth. Progressively smaller shares were allocated to the other officers, the cooper, the boatsteerers, seamen, other artisans (blacksmiths, carpenters, sailmakers, and so on), ordinary seamen, green hands, and boys. The last named, the youngest and least-skilled crewmen, typically received a share of about one two-hundred-and-fiftieth.

The industry expanded and then contracted, and that pattern is reflected in the catch and profit figures. In the case of sperm oil, there is evidence of some decrease in the catch as new vessels entered, but as exit reduced competition it appears to have rebounded strongly (see Table 3.8). For whale oil, however, the pattern is one of fairly continuous decline. Finally, the pattern for whalebone is somewhat mixed; it appears that the "catch" increased to about 1850, remained at those levels until the mid-1880s, and then fell as the New Bedford fleet, faced with competition from vessels based on the West Coast, began to withdraw from the Arctic grounds.

The trends in catch correlate closely with the movements in profits (see Table 3.9). Profits appear to have declined through the mid-1850s – a decline most likely associated with increased competition – and then, as competition lessened, increased once again. The postbellum increase was sufficient to return industry profits to the levels that had prevailed in the earlier years.

Of perhaps even greater interest, however, is the average level of the industry's profits. Although subject to a great deal of year-to-year (and voyage-to-voyage) variation, the average appears to have been about 45 percent per year (with allowance for vessels lost at sea). That figure is consistent with contemporary observations; it provides some insight into the level of "normal" profits in a risky, but competitive, industry. Certainly it does suggest the motivation that induced shipowners to continue to send their vessels out in search of whales even when there was one chance in ten that the vessel would not return. As late as 1900, although ships appear to have proved no longer profit-

109

Table 3.8. *Average catch per ton year of hunting: physical quantities (New Bedford fleet)*

Years	Sperm oil (bbl.)			Whale oil (bbl.)			Bone (lb.)		
	Ships	Barks	Other	Ships	Barks	Other	Ships	Barks	Other
1816–25	1.2	2.1	1.7	4.3	0.1	3.2	3.0	0.5	0.0
1826–35	1.4	1.8	2.2	3.2	1.8	0.4	6.3	10.3	0.9
1836–45	1.1	1.1	1.7	1.8	1.7	0.3	7.0	6.4	0.9
1846–55	0.6	0.8	0.5	1.7	1.0	0.2	17.0	9.8	0.0
1856–65	0.5	0.8	1.3	1.1	0.7	0.7	11.3	7.8	8.0
1866–75	0.7	0.9	1.3	1.1	0.7	0.7	11.8	5.8	2.6
1876–85	0.9	1.0	1.6	1.0	1.5	0.4	9.1	13.4	3.2
1886–95	1.0	1.4	2.9	0.3	0.4	0.2	2.8	2.4	0.6
1896–1905	—	3.6	3.5	—	0.1	0.1	—	0.6	3.9
1816–45	1.2	1.7	1.9	3.1	1.2	1.3	5.4	5.7	0.6
1846–75	0.6	0.8	1.0	1.3	0.8	0.5	13.4	7.8	3.5
1876–1905	1.0	2.0	2.7	0.7	0.7	0.2	6.0	5.5	2.6
1816–1905	0.9	1.0	2.0	1.9	1.0	0.5	10.6	8.2	2.1

Source: L. E. Davis, R. E. Gallman, and T. D Hutchins, "The Structure of the Capital Stock in Economic Growth and Decline," in Peter Kilby, ed., *Quantity and Quiddity* (Middletown, Conn.: Wesleyan University Press, 1987), p. 390.

Table 3.9. *Average profit rates (percentages; New Bedford fleet)*

Years	Ships	Barks	Other
1816–25	40.5	22.6	30.5
1826–35	54.8	54.1	28.9
1836–45	39.7	34.5	21.1
1846–55	38.3	32.1	LOSS
1856–65	45.4	46.8	68.7
1866–75	51.9	42.2	44.7
1876–85	70.2	92.5	50.2
1886–95	33.5	38.3	57.5
1896–1905	—	70.9	69.2
1816–1905	43.7	48.7	39.6

Source: L. E. Davis, R. E. Gallman, and T. D. Hutchins, "The Structure of the Capital Stock in Economic Growth and Decline," in Peter Kilby, ed., *Quantity and Quiddity* (Middletown, Conn.: Wesleyan University Press, 1987), data underlying Table 10.22.

able, the owners of the fifteen or so barks, brigs, sloops, and schooners that remained in the fleet were earning nearly 70 percent per year on their investment.

Sources of data

At the heart of the analysis presented in this paper is a set of measurements of productivity computed at the level of the individual voyage. Most, but not all, of the whaling voyages that ended at New Bedford in the years 1820–1906 are represented in the data set. The productivity estimates enter as dependent variables in a regression analysis designed to explain the variations of productivity across voyages.

The principal source of data is a Baker Library manuscript produced by Joseph Dias, probably a whaling captain himself, and certainly the son and grandson of whaling captains.[13] Dias apparently took his data from ships' logs, newspapers, and port records, as did those better-known students of whaling Alexander Starbuck and Reginald B. Hegarty.[14] The Dias manuscript covers a longer period of time than do the works of Starbuck or Hegarty, and it is organized by vessel. Both the Starbuck and Hegarty volumes are organized by voyage, a much less convenient system. The Starbuck and Hegarty volumes, together with *Whaling Masters*, were used to check Dias and to fill out his record, but Dias is the primary source of the analyses in this essay.[15]

---

[13] Joseph Dias, "Mss.: The New Bedford Whaling Fleet, 1790–1906," on deposit at Baker Library, Graduate School of Business, Harvard University. See "The New Bedford Whaling Fleet, 1790–1906," *Bulletin of the Business History Society* 6 (December 1932): 9–14, for a discussion of the manuscript. A. B. C. Whipple (*Tall Ships and Great Captains* [New York: Harper Bros., 1951], pp. 179–85) says that Joseph Diaz [*sic*], Jr. (then only twenty-eight years old) was captain of the *Pocahontas* in 1850 when that vessel was rammed and nearly sunk by a large whale in the South Atlantic.

[14] Starbuck, *Whale Fishery*; Hegarty, *Returns of Whaling Vessels Sailing from American Ports* (New Bedford, Old Dartmouth Historical Society, 1959).

[15] Federal Writers' Project, Works Progress Administration of Massachusetts, *Whaling Masters* (New Bedford: Old Dartmouth Historical Society, 1938). Where Dias disagrees with Starbuck or Hegarty or *Whaling Masters*, we accepted Dias unless there was very good reason to prefer the other. Hegarty's records for the late nineteenth century and early twentieth century are more complete than Dias's; we therefore filled out our data set with Hegarty's data. The Dias records for the period before 1876 are also probably incomplete (perhaps 10 to 15 percent), but less seriously so, and we made no effort to complete them. It should be said that matters of completeness are not easily settled. The ports of Dartmouth, Fairhaven, Mattapoisett, and New Bedford were within a few miles of each other, and whether a vessel belonged to one or the other of these ports on any given voyage was not always easily settled. For example, Dias lists some voyages as beginning from New Bedford that *Whaling*

Lance E. Davis, Robert E. Gallman, & Teresa D. Hutchins

Dias recorded the following information for each New Bedford whaling vessel:

1. the dates of each voyage (sailing and return)
2. the names of the captain and agent at each voyage
3. the vessel type (ship, bark, brig, sloop, schooner)
4. the date and place of construction (usually)
5. incidents of rerigging (ships were sometimes rerigged as barks)
6. the mode of exit from the fleet (condemnation, transfer to another port, loss by sinking, running aground, fire, and so on)
7. the product of each voyage, in physical units (sperm oil, whale oil, whalebone, occasionally other products)
8. hunting grounds visited (Dias identified fifty-one, which we combined into four: (a) the Atlantic Ocean, Hudson's Bay, and Davis Strait; (b) the Indian Ocean; (c) the Pacific Ocean; (d) the Arctic Ocean north of the Pacific, Bering Strait, and the Okhotsk Sea)
9. the tonnage of the vessel (a measure of capacity)[16]
10. quite rich notes on events of the voyage, particularly touching the loss of men to disease, accidents aboard, desertion, and the attacks of whales, mutineers, and islanders of the northern and southern seas

The mode of entry into the fleet – construction or transfer in from another port or the merchant marine – can be inferred from the construction and voyage data.

The Dias data set contains a good deal of information on capital, output, and firm organization, as well as various vessel traits and

Masters attributes to Fairhaven, across the Acushnet River from New Bedford, and vice versa. This type of disagreement appears to be of a random nature and should have absolutely no importance to the statistical estimates described in this paper. Henceforth the data set analyzed in this essay will be cited as: Davis, Gallman, Hutchins tape.

[16] The official procedure for measuring vessels changed in 1865. In most cases Dias recorded the tonnage of the vessel when it entered the fleet; since most entered before 1865, the tonnages of most of the vessels in our data set are "old" tonnages. In virtually every one of those few cases where Dias chose to report "new" tonnage, we were able to adjust to the old standard by consulting Starbuck. A few cases remain, however, of vessels that were built or transferred from the merchant marine into the whaling fleet after 1865. The old tonnages of these vessels are unknown, and although we have developed formulas for translating new into old tonnages that work quite well for many purposes (L. E. Davis, R. E. Gallman, and T. D. Hutchins, "The Structure of the Capital Stock in Economic Growth and Decline," in Peter Kilby, ed., *Quantity and Quiddity* [Middletown, Conn.: Wesleyan University Press, 1987], p. 349 n. 10), we decided that they are not sufficiently exact for the purposes of this paper. We therefore left the capacities of these few vessels expressed in new tons and recognized the problem in the regression analysis by entering a dummy variable.

activities that might have affected productivity, but it does not report output prices, factor shares in income, or labor and land (that is, the stock of whales) inputs – information necessary to estimate productivity and interpret the estimates. Price data are readily available, notably in Starbuck and Tower. Officers and crewmen were paid subsistence and a share of the product. We assumed a total lay of 34 percent for all voyages. Subsistence has been estimated to have been about $35–60 per man per year, in prices of 1844.[17] As between these two values the choice does not appear important. The productivity results obtained are virtually identical regardless of which is used.

There are three important sources of labor data; none is perfect; the two that appear most comprehensive were used.[18] Two caveats: first, although the labor data cover all of the years under consideration, they are more nearly complete for the periods 1820–34 and 1840–80. Second, the data refer chiefly to crewmen recruited before vessels left New Bedford. Extra crewmen were sometimes added in the Canaries or Hawaii; more often, crewmen who died or deserted were replaced at a port of call. The data provide, therefore, no more than a rough index of the average number of men aboard during a voyage, but there is no reason to believe that errors in the labor data bias our results.

Productivity indexes

The measure of productivity chosen is a translog multilateral productivity index, a so-called superlative index.[19] The index has characteristics that are very well suited to the industry and the problems under analysis. It is designed to handle multiproduct firms and industries of the type represented by nineteenth-century American whaling. The

---

[17] Rough estimates derived from Elmo Paul Hohman, *The American Whalemen* (New York: Longman Group, 1928), pp. 315, 325, assuming that the provisioning described on p. 325 for sperm whalers was to cover twenty-nine months, and for right whalers, twenty-three months (see p. 327 [1843]). The estimates were carried to other years than 1844 on the basis of the Warren and Pearson food-price index (*Historical Statistics of the United States, 1789–1945*).

[18] We took our data from port records, held by the National Archives, and from the New Bedford Public Library's collection "Whalemen's Shipping Papers." The two sources overlap. Where they gave contradictory accounts, we used the larger of the two values. We did not make use of the records of the New Bedford Port Society, since they appear to be less comprehensive than the records of the other two sources.

[19] Douglas W. Caves, Laurits R. Christensen, and W. Erwin Diewert, "Multilateral Comparisons of Output, Input, and Productivity Using Superlative Index Numbers," *Economic Journal* 92 (March 1982): 73–86.

We thank Douglas W. Caves, V. Kerry Smith, Richard Hydell, and David Guilkey, all of whom discussed productivity indexes with us.

underlying model assumes optimizing behavior and is, therefore, clearly suited to competitive activities of the likes of American whaling. The measure was developed to permit multilateral comparisons and as a result it is not subject to base-reversal problems, a very important characteristic because the voyage productivity estimates were to be used in a regression analysis. Moreover, it is readily computed and economical of data, requiring no more evidence than is available.

There are, however, few examples of absolute perfection, and the index, although superlative, is not one of them. It poses one minor and readily handled computational problem. Two other difficulties arise out of the application of the index to whaling and to individual whaling voyages.

As to the computational problem, whalers typically returned with whale oil, sperm oil, and whalebone, but not infrequently they returned with only two, say, whale oil and bone, or one, say, sperm oil. Occasionally they even came back "clean," that is, with no marketable catch. Since the superlative index cannot handle zeroes, these cases posed problems. The first two might have been solved by distinguishing three separate whaling industries, one specializing in baleen whales and one in sperm whales, and the third a generalist baleen-sperm industry.[20] Such an approach, however, would distort the reality of nineteenth-century New Bedford whaling. Whalers did not regularly specialize to the exclusion of one type of whale. It is true that a vessel setting out for the Arctic was after bowheads (baleens), but between New Bedford and the Arctic it passed through waters inhabited by sperm whales and was prepared to take them as opportunity afforded. Once the western Arctic was opened, a common pattern was to hunt bowheads and then, in the off season, move to California to take gray whales, or to the coasts of New Zealand and Australia for humpbacks and sperm whales. Moreover, as prices and opportunities shifted, vessels emphasized one type of activity over another. Thus it appears that New Bedford whaling should be regarded as one industry, not three.

A better solution to the computational problem is to substitute small positive values for the zeros. If values much less than e (the base of natural logs) are selected, large negative weights are assigned to the shares accorded the missing products, and the results that emerge are counterintuitive. For example, with a value of 0.001, a relatively un-

---

[20] The possibilities for specialization were greater than this statement suggests. Among baleens, bowheads were taken in the Arctic; grays and humpbacks, in temperate and tropical waters. Bowheads produced large amounts of high-quality baleen (whalebone); grays and humpbacks, much less per whale, and of lower quality.

successful voyage that resulted, nonetheless, in three types of output might register a higher level of productivity than a successful voyage with only two. These anomalies disappear with values in excess of e. The values 3 and 10, both very small when compared with typical whaling output levels, were tried. The results of the two sets of calculations were similar, suggesting that the index is not very sensitive to the specific value selected as long as it is small but greater than e.[21]

A second and more serious problem emerges because there is no obvious way to introduce land – that is, the stocks of whales – directly into the productivity calculations. Thus, the indexes do not measure total factor productivity but only the productivity of labor and capital. In an attempt to work around this problem, whale stocks were introduced on the right-hand side of the regression as independent variables helping to explain the level of productivity of labor and capital.

Finally, and most serious, the calculations do not include the effects of truly disastrous voyages – voyages from which vessels failed to return. The indexes refer only to vessels that came back to New Bedford. The omission is unlikely to have affected the long-term drift of our productivity measurement for the industry as a whole, since, over time, loss rates do not seem to have changed dramatically, on average (see Table 3.6). Of course, the level and the year-to-year variations are affected, but the former is unimportant and the latter are not the chief concern of this essay.

Of more importance, however, is the effect of the exclusion of disastrous voyages from the regressions. Whaling was a risky business in which luck and the skill of the agent and captain – neither figuring directly in our regression analysis – played important roles. One therefore has to expect a substantial amount of unexplained variance. If the disastrous voyages were introduced into the analysis, the unexplained variance would, no doubt, increase. Moreover, since older vessels had higher loss rates than younger ones, and since loss rates varied among hunting grounds, the age and hunting-ground variables would also be affected but, happily, in predictable ways.[22]

The form of the productivity index is as follows:

$$\ln \eta_{kn} = \tfrac{1}{2}\Sigma_i (R_i^k + \bar{R}_i)\,(\ln Y_i^k - \overline{\ln Y_i})$$
$$- \tfrac{1}{2}\Sigma n\,(W_n^k + \bar{W}_n)\,(\ln X_n^k - \overline{\ln X_n}),$$

where the R's are the shares of total revenue produced by the three individual outputs; the Y's are quantities of individual outputs; the W's

---

[21] Nonetheless, the possible significance of output mix – degrees of specialization – is explored in the regression analysis described below.

[22] Davis, Gallman, and Hutchins, "Structure."

115

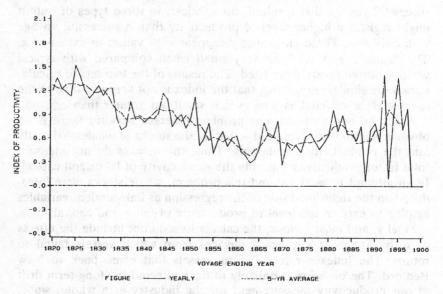

Fig. 3.1. Index of total factor productivity: New Bedford whaling voyages ending 1818–98.

are factor shares of income; the X's are quantities of factor inputs; the $\bar{R}$'s, $\bar{Y}$'s, $\bar{W}$'s, and $\bar{X}$'s are average values across all observations. Three outputs – sperm oil, whale oil, and baleen – and two inputs – labor and capital (man months and ton months) – are distinguished.[23]

The sources of the evidence and our estimating decisions were discussed above.

Influences on productivity

The productivity index for the whole New Bedford industry declines from 1820, when the industry was still very small, to the mid-1830s, when the industry was quite large. During the period of its maturity (1835 onward), New Bedford whaling exhibited less pronounced changes in productivity. Plotted, the productivity index describes a profile like that of a dinner plate: It declines, gradually flattens out, and finally rises again (see Fig. 3.1). Although a trend line fitted to the index in the years of maturity exhibits little movement, the industry was by no means quiescent in the period. It changed dramatically in size, in the composition of its capital stock, in the structure of its

---

[23] Whale oil includes oil taken from blackfish and walruses.

116

output, in the relative importance of the hunting grounds it visited, in the sources of its labor supply, in the ways in which production was organized, in its techniques of production, and no doubt in other ways as well. The changes reflected responses to shifts in the environment in which the New Bedford whalers operated, and represented the efforts of whaling men to cope with new problems and to exploit new opportunities. The central concern of this essay is with the estimation of the direction in which, and the strength with which, each of these influences pressed productivity. We want to understand the forces affecting the industry and the ways in which its entrepreneurs and managers responded to them. The following subsections consider the factors that influenced productivity and attempt to capture them in a series of variables that can be used in the regression analysis.

Whale stocks

The drift of the industry productivity index across time, the persistent search for new hunting grounds, contemporary complaints, and even the structure of output, all suggest that as the industry expanded there were pressures on the stock of whales. The evidence on stocks before large-scale hunting began, on the procreative capacities of the whales, and on the amount of hunting conducted in the nineteenth century suggests that there was no global problem, no general ecological disaster resulting from American whaling in the nineteenth century.[24] Depletion of some hunting grounds and possibly some species of whales, however, might have required whalers to seek out new grounds, the search raising costs and reducing the productivity of capital and labor.

To test this proposition we developed annual indexes of hunting pressures on the whale populations of the four hunting grounds. Pressure index numbers reflecting hunting dates and destinations were attached to each voyage. Thus a vessel that hunted in the Pacific had assigned to it sperm and baleen pressure index numbers relevant to the Pacific and to the dates of the voyage. If excessive hunting was reducing the productivity of whaling capital and labor, the regression coefficients of these indexes should have negative signs. (Details are in Appendix 1.)

Vessel competition

There is a second possible effect of hunting on measured productivity. Even if whale stocks were not being depleted, increased hunting

---

[24] L. E. Davis, R. E. Gallman, and T. D. Hutchins, "The Decline of U.S. Whaling: Was the Stock of Whales Running Out?" *Business History Review*, Winter 1988/89.

might lead to lower productivity simply because of greater competition among vessels. One vessel coming upon a pod of sperm whales might be able to take all the largest whales by itself; however, if it approached the pod in company with other vessels, it would be less likely to come away with as many barrels of oil. The one case slides over into the other, of course. One vessel alone would be unable completely to destroy a pod, but three or four vessels might do so. Still, it appears useful to distinguish analytically between the two cases. To that end a second index reflecting whaling competition in each year and in each hunting ground was constructed. The index number for any given ground and year is a ratio: The numerator is the number of vessel tons leaving for the hunting ground two years previously, divided by 300 (to convert the tons to "standardized vessels"). The denominator is the number of whales (all species combined) in the ground before intensive hunting began, per one hundred square miles in the hunting ground. Thus the index can be interpreted as the number of standard-sized vessels per whale per hundred square miles per hunting ground. Since the index is designed to measure competition in the ground, it could be expected to carry a negative coefficient in the regression if competition affected productivity unfavorably. (Appendix 1 provides more details of the construction of the index.)

Specialization

The degree to which whalers specialized in a particular type of whale varied from vessel to vessel and voyage to voyage. In an effort to see how far specialization mattered we included dummy variables indicative of the degree and type of specialization. Specifically, we divided voyages into three groups (of roughly equal size): those in which sperm oil contributed at least 90 percent of the value of output, those in which whale oil and baleen contributed at least 90 percent of the value of output, and all others. This device also helps to deal with a technical problem. All productivity indexes have trouble dealing effectively with output mixes far removed from the mean mix, and the superlative index is no exception. The specialization dummies segregate voyages in which the degree of specialization was pronounced and permit the regression to standardize for them. (The issue is discussed further below.)

Hunting grounds

The search for whales carried New Bedford whalers from the Atlantic to the Indian and Pacific oceans, and finally to that bonanza ground, the western Arctic. One would expect to find productivity varying initially from ground to ground, the differences disappearing as the fleet adjusted its hunting activities. In the case of the Arctic, however, equilibrium was probably not achieved before the New Bedford whalers began abandoning their home port for the West Coast port of San Francisco. Furthermore, the Arctic was by far the most dangerous ground, exhibiting much higher rates of vessel loss than the other grounds. Thus, even if whalemen, owners, and agents were risk-neutral, it should have taken higher rates of gain, gross, to attract whalers to the Arctic. Therefore, since the analysis excludes vessels that were lost while whaling, one would expect that vessels hunting in the Arctic would appear to be more productive than vessels that avoided that ground. Among other grounds, differences might be slight, with the new grounds of the Indian and Pacific oceans perhaps displaying modestly higher average productivities than the Atlantic.

One word of warning: Although acknowledged mixed voyages (that is, voyages reported to have been to the Pacific and Arctic, for example) are excluded from the regression data set, to some extent all voyages to any ground but the Atlantic were mixed. That is, even if the vessel was sent to hunt in the Arctic, Indian, or Pacific ocean, it was forced to pass through other grounds, and captains seldom passed up a chance to catch a whale. Moreover, if weather or catch proved discouraging captains frequently steered to adjacent grounds for short periods of time. Thus the assignment of ground should not be thought to have precluded the possibility that the vessel hunted at least a little in other grounds.

Rig types

As time passed, hunting grounds shifted, and so did the way vessels were rigged. There had never been more than one or two of the smaller vessels – brigs, sloops, and schooners – in the Pacific and Indian oceans, and there were none at all in the western Arctic, but by the middle of the period they had all but disappeared from the Atlantic as well. Over the first half of the period barks gradually eroded the dominant position previously held by ships in all grounds, but they really came into their own in the western Arctic, where the relative ease of handling and of launching the two stern boats were matters of great importance.

In the regression, barks, brigs, sloops, and schooners are grouped together. It should be kept in mind however that the three smaller classes represented only a tiny fraction of the total. Thus the comparison is really between ships and barks (excluding all but barks does not affect any result).

The performance of this somewhat heterogeneous group was compared with the performance of ships. The expectation as to sign is somewhat ambiguous. Ships dominated in the Atlantic, Indian, and Pacific grounds in most years, but barks were more important in the Arctic and ultimately pushed their competitors from the other grounds as well. On net for all grounds and all years the coefficient on the ship dummy was thought likely to be positive.

Vessel size

The shift toward ships and toward more distant grounds was associated with an increase in the size of whalers, but vessel size also rose independently of these developments. That is, standardizing for rig and hunting ground, vessel size increased. The shift seems not to have been a pure scale phenomenon.[25] Tonnage was entered (squared, since tonnage also appears in the formula used to estimate productivity) as an independent variable. Given the shift toward larger vessels, we expected a positive sign on the coefficient of this variable.

Mode of entry into the fleet

Some vessels were built for whaling, others transferred into the fleet from the merchant marine, and still others, vessels that had originally entered by one of these two routes, were rerigged (ships were often rerigged as barks, particularly to hunt the Arctic). Ceteris paribus, one would expect vessels built for the fleet to be most productive. Whether one should expect this result to emerge from the statistical analysis, however, is not so clear. In the flush times of New Bedford whaling, particularly when the Arctic was opened, many vessels were quickly transferred into the whaling fleet and many ships were rerigged as barks to fit them for Arctic hunting. It took longer to design and build vessels to exploit this rich ground, and by the time these entrants were in service some of the first-arrival gains had almost certainly evapo-

---

[25] See L. E. Davis, R. E. Gallman, and T. D. Hutchins, "Technology, Productivity, and Profit: British–American Whaling Competition in the North Atlantic, 1819–1848," *Oxford Economic Papers* 39 (December 1987): 149. Since the productivity formula assumes no scale economics, this point is an important one. It should be said that, although the size of whalers increased, the range through which the increase occurred was quite limited. The typical ship, for example, ran between 300 and 350 tons, although some were as much as 500 tons.

rated. Transferred and rerigged vessels may, then, exhibit unusually high productivity levels, for market as opposed to technical reasons.

Age of vessel

The age of the vessel (entered as age and age squared) also captures the effects of more than a single set of forces. Elements of wear and tear that influenced productivity, a technical characteristic that one might hope to capture in the age variable, are confounded with the consequences of qualitative differences among vessels. Effective vessels were presumably survivors; ineffective vessels were transferred by their owners to other activities, were condemned at an early age, or were destroyed in service. The regression should pick up this influence as well as capital consumption. Thus one could expect to find a positive sign on the coefficient for age, as poor vessels were screened out with advancing age, and a negative sign on the coefficient for age squared, as wear and tear reduced even an efficient vessel's effectiveness.

As a second device for uncovering the influence of the deterioration of a vessel's productive capacity, the last voyage of each vessel was identified. If poor productivity performances eventually led to condemnation or to transfer to other activities, the variable should have a negative sign.

Innovations

Although they were not equally important, three types of technical innovations were widely adopted in the whaling fleet between the 1820s and the 1880s. The first reflected improvements in maritime technology in general; the other two were associated with improvements in whaling narrowly defined. Although the years between 1820 and 1845 have been viewed by some specialists as technologically unprogressive, the period was, in fact, marked by substantial technical progress. There were a series of advances that were first tested in the merchant fleet and then borrowed by the builders of whaling vessels. These advances included, in addition to the substantial gains realized by improvements in the techniques of ship construction, "patented rigging, deck machinery, and fittings. Such things as geared capstans and windlasses, iron strapped blocks, geared steering, . . . geared winches, new mast and spar ironwork . . . rod rigging and turnbuckles, screw- or lever-operated, were [also] introduced."[26] In addition, the

---

[26] Howard I. Chapelle, *The Search for Speed under Sail: 1700–1850* (New York: Norton, 1967), p. 279.

number of sails was increased (the topsail, for example, was divided into an upper and a lower half) for ease in handling.[27]

The second set of innovations was in vessel design: Barks were specifically designed for whaling. These new vessels were first built in the vicinity of New Bedford in the mid-1850s. They were constructed with raking stems and with sharper lines than the usual whalers. "The hull design of these vessels had much in common with that of the clippers. Their sailing qualities were disguised by the heavy appearance of the hull, above water, which was emphasized by the deck houses and the whale boats carried on strong davits [another innovation] or on skids above the deck. These American whalers were built of wood, copper sheathed below the waterline."[28] They were, in fact, medium clippers, "sharp floored and easy bilged to make them roll down when 'cutting out' a whale."[29]

The third group of innovations was in "whalecraft," the implements employed to capture and kill the whale – harpoons, lances, whale guns of various types.[30] According to Scammon (see Appendix 2), in a period of twenty years these innovations had as revolutionary an impact on whaling as had all the changes in vessel design that took place between the seventeenth and the late nineteenth century. The successful inventions were made in the relatively short period 1848–65 and were widely diffused by the mid-1870s. The most significant of the group, the darting gun, was invented last (1865) and did not begin to diffuse rapidly until the early 1870s. (See Appendix 2.)

Unfortunately, the Dias data do not indicate the equipment carried on the various whaling voyages. The period during which the innovations diffused is clear, however, as well as the fact that they diffused very widely. In the regression, therefore, a dummy was entered to distinguish voyages sailing before January 1, 1870, by which date the chief design and whalecraft innovations had been made and most had been widely diffused. If these new techniques had affected productivity favorably, the coefficient on the variable would be positive.

---

[27] Gordon Grant, *Ships under Sail: An Outline of the Development of the Sailing Vessel* (New York: Garden City Publishing, 1930), p. 24.

[28] B. W. Bath, "The Clipper's Day," in Joseph Jobe, ed., *The Great Age of Sail* (London: Patrick Stephens, 1967), pp. 205–206.

[29] Howard I. Chapelle, *The History of American Sailing Ships* (New York: Norton, 1935).

[30] Thomas G. Lytle, *Harpoons and Other Whalecraft* (New Bedford: Old Dartmouth Historical Society, 1984).

Competition for labor

A frequently told story attributes the collapse of the American whaling fleet to the qualitative deterioration of the vessel crews as the best labor was bid away by improving onshore opportunities. Real wage rates ashore certainly were rising through a substantial part of this period, and our preliminary analysis of whaling lays suggests that the return to whalemen may not have been keeping pace. The pool of seamen available to man the whalers may very well have deteriorated, with unfavorable consequences for whaling productivity. With measures of labor quality, we could test this proposition directly, and we hope to be able to do so in future. At present, however, we must settle for an indirect test, employing wage-rate data alone. We first entered wage indexes of common and skilled labor on shore as independent variables.[31] Since the two proved to be collinear, we reran the regression, using only one wage series at a time. The choice between the two mattered little: The results are virtually identical, whether the common or the skilled index is employed. The coefficient should be negative if the New Bedford whaling industry really did have a labor problem.

Time at sea

As the fleet moved into more distant waters, the organization of hunting was revised to cope with the problems raised by the greater distances. Resupply and transshipment points were developed; by using these bases, a vessel could hunt for longer periods and catch more than it could bring home itself. Organized resupply and transshipment were important institutional innovations. To capture their influence on productivity, the interval at sea (actually, the square of the interval) was entered as an independent variable in the regression equation. Unfortunately, the variable also picks up other influences, including, for example, the bad luck (or poor performance) that kept a vessel long at sea before an adequate cargo was obtained. If the first in-

---

[31] The wage-rate indexes entered the regression with a lag. That is, a voyage beginning in year n was associated with wage-rate index numbers for year $n - 1$. The common wage-rate series was computed from Paul A. David and Peter Solar, "A Bicentenary Contribution to the History of the Cost of Living in America," *Research Economic History* 2 (1977), data on p. 59 divided by data on p. 16. The skilled-wage-rate index was derived by multiplying the series on p. 59 of David and Solar by the skill ratios on p. 307 of Jeffrey G. Williamson and Peter H. Lindert, *American Inequality* (New York: Academic Press, 1980) and then dividing by the price index on p. 16 of David and Solar.

fluence – the innovation of the transshipment point – predominated, the coefficient on this variable should have a positive sign; otherwise, it should have a negative sign.

Measurement errors

The "tonnage" for most vessels in the data set refers to old admeasurement tonnage; in a few cases, however, it refers to new admeasurement tonnage (see note 16). A dummy was introduced to deal with the problem. The coefficient of this dummy should have a negative sign.

Time

Finally, time was entered as an independent variable. As will be evident, the technology variable – which is a time dummy – leaves something to be desired and might pick up any of a variety of time-dependent processes other than technical change. Although the comprehensiveness of the model both theoretically and empirically reduces the chances of such an eventuality, we decided to reduce them further by entering time as a device for detrending (the issue is taken up further below). The analysis is limited to voyages leaving New Bedford in 1820 or later. The time variable is, therefore, the year the vessel sailed from New Bedford minus 1820.

Statistical results

General considerations

The general New Bedford data set contains evidence on over 4,100 whaling voyages in the period 1790–1906, but this essay is concerned with only some of them. First, since the industry was unduly affected by political and military events during the early period, the years before 1820 have been excluded (reducing the universe to fewer than 3,900 voyages). Second, a number of incomplete observations were dropped. As a result, the regression analysis is based on fewer than 2,400 observations confined to the period 1820–96. The sample is a very large one, but is it representative? If it is representative, of what is it representative? Of New Bedford voyages? Of East Coast voyages? Unlike many other northeastern ports, New Bedford engaged in diversified whaling. It sent vessels to every hunting ground, and the port was regarded as representative of the East Coast ports taken together. The sample, however, was certainly not randomly drawn from all of

124

the East Coast voyages. Indeed, it was not even randomly drawn from the list of New Bedford voyages.

To test the extent to which the sample resembles the universe of New Bedford voyages 1820–96, we compared average sample and universe values for each of the outputs, the data on crew numbers, vessel tonnage, and average voyage time, by hunting ground. On the whole, we found that the sample overrepresents successful voyages.

To test whether this feature of the sample made the regression results unrepresentative of the behavior of the entire New Bedford fleet, we reran the regression analysis on the relatively unsuccessful voyages alone; that is, on the thousand voyages with the lowest levels of productivity. In all but five cases (intercepts and independent variables), the coefficient signs were the same for the full sample and for the sample of unsuccessful voyages. In three of the remaining five cases, the interpretation of the variable was left essentially unchanged, despite the sign change (for example, low significance levels; very small coefficients). We concluded, therefore, that although some features of the full sample may make it imperfectly representative for some purposes, nonetheless the regression results do adequately describe New Bedford whaling. Although we cannot demonstrate the matter rigorously, we also believe that the regressions capture the nature of East Coast whaling as a whole.

The model

The results of the first regression (no. 1) appear in Table 3.10. The equation explains almost half of the productivity variance, a level of explanatory power that is excellent for a pooled cross-section–time-series data set, particularly given the nature of this industry. It is well known that the variation between the performances of one vessel and another could be extremely wide and that whalemen attributed such variations in some considerable measure to luck. The Dias data also show that certain vessels – and probably certain agents and captains – typically performed above standard, and others typically below. Even in these cases, however, performance varied from one voyage to the next. No attempt has yet been made to sort these matters out and to see how far the quality of the vessels, agents, and captains differed one from the other (these are feasible projects). The regression equation leaves luck out of account and deals only indirectly with the quality of captain and crew. Not all of the variables conform precisely to the theoretical requirements. With these matters in mind the degree of

Table 3.10. *Productivity in New Bedford whaling, 1820–96 (regression no. 1)*

$F = 103.1$; adj. $R^2 = .478$; dependent mean = 0.733; observations = 2,343

Productivity depends on: Variable	Parameter estimate	Significance level
Intercept	+2.2091	***
Vessel type: ships compared with all other vessels	+0.1055	***
Hunting ground (compared with Pacific)		
Atlantic	−0.1544	***
Indian	−0.0638	***
Western Arctic	+0.1704	***
Time	−0.00039	
Mode of entry into the fleet		
Built for fleet	−0.0298	
Rerigged (compared with vessels transferred into the fleet)	+0.0942	***
Hunting pressures		
On baleens	+0.1070	***
On sperms	+0.0539	
Competition among whalers	−0.0037	
Technological dummy	+0.3103	***
Vessel size (tons squared)	+0.0000015	***
Voyage length (months squared)	−0.00029	***
Vessel age	+0.00421	***
Vessel age squared	−0.000089	***
Last voyage	−0.0762	***
Real common wage rate ashore	−0.0060	***
Ratio, skilled wage to real common wage	−0.5732	***
Specialization		
In baleens	−0.0948	***
In sperms	−0.7005	***
Measurement dummy	−0.0314	

*** Significantly different from zero at the 1 percent level.
Durbin–Watson D 1.823
1st order autocorrelation   0.086

Notes: (a) The t statistics were adjusted to allow for the large size of the sample:

Adjusted t = coefficient/adjusted standard error

$$\text{Adjusted } s.e. = s.e. \times \sqrt{\frac{\text{Population} - \text{sample size}}{\text{Population} - 1}}$$

(b) The equation was also run in natural logs. The fit was poorer, and the results did not change substantially.

(c) A priori there is no strong reason to expect heteroskedasticity or, if it exists, to expect serious problems with it, in view of the enormous size of the sample compared with the universe. Nonetheless, since the data are panel data we tested for heteroskedasticity by regressing the variances of the error terms against the continuous explanatory variables, and the test turned up evidence of heteroskedasticity. We made corrections by dividing the dependent and independent variables by the standard errors

126

Notes to Table 3.10 (*cont.*)

of the residuals and ran the regression again. The significance levels did not deteriorate.
Source: See text.

explanatory success attained by the equation seems very high.[32]

Average productivity dropped sharply from the 1820s to the 1860s and then rose to the 1890s (see Fig. 3.1). A second way to judge the power of the regression model is to test to see how far the equation explains this pattern of falling and then rising productivity. We devised a test of the following form. First, we estimated a regression with productivity as the dependent variable and dummies standing for the decades of the 1820s (the comparison base), 1830s, 1840s, etc. as the independent variables.[33] We then re-estimated the equation, including the decadal dummies and all of the independent variables of the equation in Table 3.10 (except time, whose place is taken by the decade dummies). The changes in the coefficients of the dummies between the first and the second runs measure the extent to which the comprehensive equation explains the pattern of productivity change across time. The results we obtained are as follows:

| Decade | Coefficients | | % explained by complex equation |
	Simple equation	Complex equation	
1830s	−.302	−.205	32
1840s	−.289	−.207	28
1850s	−.629	−.384	39
1860s	−.649	−.285	56
1870s	−.596	−.306	49
1880s	−.460	−.279	39
1890s	−.484	+.113	100

The comprehensive equation explains between 28 percent and 100 percent of the deviations in productivity among decades, not a bad performance. In fact, however, the performance is better than these figures suggest. Only about a third of the drop between the 1820s and 1830s is explained, but notice that the productivity curve described in the second column of figures is much flatter between the 1830s and 1880s than is the curve described by the first column. This characteristic of the second column of figures can be exhibited most clearly if one

---

[32] The superlative index is said to represent outliers badly, which could distort our results. To test to see how large were the effects of outliers, we dropped the 240 voyages (about 10 percent of all voyages) with the highest productivities and the 240 voyages with the lowest productivities and ran the regression on this restricted data set. The results were not markedly different.

[33] The test was suggested to us by Robert Evenson of Yale University.

Lance E. Davis, Robert E. Gallman, & Teresa D. Hutchins

looks at the decrements (or increments) in the coefficients between the 1830s and each of the subsequent decades:

Decade	Changes in coefficients from 1830s		% explained by complex equation
	Simple equation	Complex equation	
1840s	+.013	−.002	100
1850s	−.327	−.179	45
1860s	−.347	−.080	77
1870s	−.294	−.101	66
1880s	−.158	−.074	53
1890s	−.182	+.318	100

It appears, then, that the equation in Table 3.10 explains about one-third of the drop in productivity between the 1820s and 1830s, but that it is much more successful in accounting for the subsequent movements in productivity. Indeed, the degree of success attained is so high that the equation seems clearly worthy of considerable confidence.

Strong priors. We had strong expectations as to the signs on the coefficients of six of the variables in the equation. Specifically, we expected positive signs on the vessel-size variable, on the Arctic dummy, and on the technological-date dummy, and we expected negative signs on the wage series and on the tonnage measurement and last-voyage dummies. In every case the signs are as expected, the coefficients are large, and, in all cases but one, they are significantly different from zero at the 1 percent level.[34]

Weak priors. We had expected productivity in the Indian and Pacific oceans to exceed productivity in the Atlantic, and the regression confirms our expectations. The Pacific, the ocean to which most voyages were made, proves to have been, on average, a more productive hunting ground than the Indian Ocean, but not by a wide margin. Satisfying our expectations, ships were more productive, on average, than other vessels.

Tests of hypotheses in the literature. Contemporary comment and the subsequent literature on whaling suggest that productivity may have been adversely affected by overhunting on the one hand and heavy competition among whalers on the other. Our study of data on whale

---

[34] As to size, compare the coefficients with the dependent mean. Bear in mind that the vessel-size variable is the square of vessel tonnage and the coefficient of the common-wage-rate variable refers to each point of the index number. The concluding section of the essay treats these issues in more detail.

stocks, the procreative capacities of whales, and the level of hunting in the nineteenth century led us to doubt that overhunting was a major problem;[35] the possibility that competition may have reduced productivity seemed more likely to us, a priori.

In the cases of the hunting-pressure indexes, our guesses are shown to have been correct. Both indexes carry small coefficients of the wrong sign, not significantly different from zero at conventional levels of significance. The coefficient of the competition variable has the sign that a reading of the literature would lead one to expect, but it is very small, as is the *t* value associated with it.[36]

Complex variables. Three sets of variables capture the effects of more than one influence, which made the signs and values of the coefficients of the variables difficult to predict. The favorable influence of the transshipment innovation was apparently overborne by the unfavorable influence of long, unsuccessful hunts (the coefficient on voyage length is negative). The large catches associated with the opening of the Arctic appear to have formed the measured effect of mode of entry on productivity. The regression shows no significant productivity difference between transfers and vessels built for the fleet. Rerigged vessels, however, exhibit a modest but significant advantage, an advantage that presumably reflects as much the date of their entry to the fleet as any underlying technical superiority.

Finally, the age variables no doubt reflect the experience of successful survivors, but it is clear that the unfavorable effects of aging also figure in the results. The measured level of productivity turns down at about the age of fifty, if the coefficients on age and age squared are to be believed. That figure would probably not have surprised whaling men of the nineteenth century, who were accustomed to vessels that lasted much longer than this in the whaling trade.[37] It may be that, properly refitted, an old vessel was, indeed, only very modestly inferior to what it had been when new. Certainly there is some suggestion of this idea in the literature, and these results appear to add additional support.

[35] Davis, Gallman, and Hutchins, "Decline of U.S. Whaling."

[36] The possibility that the variable voyage length was capturing over hunting and competition led us to drop the variable in one run, to see if the signs, coefficients, and significance levels of the pressure and competition indexes changed dramatically. They did not

[37] For example, the *Charles Morgan* served eighty years as a whaler; the *Rousseau*, eighty-seven; the *Maria*, ninety. The *Canton* was lost in its seventy-sixth year (Albert Cook Church, *Whale Ships and Whaling* [New York: Norton, 1938; reissued 1960), pp. 19, 20.

No priors. Time was entered as a detrending variable, and the specialization indexes were incorporated in our effort to cope with an undesirable feature of the productivity index. The coefficient on time is very small – even allowing for the number of years covered by the equation – and is not significantly different from zero (the *t* value is very small). There is the suggestion here that the equation is comprehensive, leaving no role for time; but we return to this point below.

Both of the specialization dummies carry negative coefficients, the one for sperm whalers a very large one. Since there is no good reason to believe that sperm whalers were, indeed, at so dramatic a disadvantage, the strong suggestion is that the productivity index, even with missing values supplied (see above), understates the productivity of specialist vessels. The specialist variables correct for this feature of the index, however, so that the regression results should not be unduly influenced by the problem.

Interaction terms

In two respects it appeared before the fact that the model could be improved by introducing interaction terms. Specifically, the advantages of the bark were said to be pronounced only in the Arctic, whereas ships were believed to have important advantages in the Indian and Pacific oceans. The matter could be explored by interacting the vessel-type and hunting-ground dummy variables. Furthermore, the institutional advantage of the refitting and transshipment port was exploited only by vessels sailing to the Indian, Pacific, and Arctic oceans. Interacting voyage length and hunting ground might, then, reveal the favorable consequences of this institutional innovation, consequences that are not exhibited in the coefficient of the voyage-duration variable of the first equation.

In fact, these procedures throw no new light on the problem of whaling productivity. The signs on the voyage-duration–hunting-ground interactions are all negative. We are unable to separate out the favorable effects of the institutional innovations. The vessel-type–hunting-ground interactions have the correct signs, but the differences among them are not large. Little additional is learned from them.

Technical changes and labor quality: some further thoughts

The regression analysis unfolds reasonably and seems to reveal important aspects of forces at work on U.S. whaling productivity, but some of the variables are less than perfect and pose interpretive problems.

Two sets of these variables – measuring technical changes and labor quality – deserve further attention.

New technology did diffuse very rapidly, so that the use of a time dummy to proxy technical changes is certainly reasonable (see Appendix 2). The fact remains, however, that the dummy is only an indirect indicator of technical change and could be picking up the effects of some other time-dependent process. It would be helpful to have direct evidence of the tools and methods employed by the whalers in our sample.

Most whalers had an outfitting book that listed the gear aboard the vessel at the beginning of each voyage. One part of the book was devoted to whalecraft, the implements used to capture the whale. As we have indicated, among the three sets of technical changes those that appear to have had the greatest impact on productivity were innovations in whalecraft. Whales were frequently lost because a harpoon failed to hold or because the whale smashed the attacking boat before the boatheader was able to dispatch it. Innovations were devised to make the harpoon more secure and the lance more deadly. The two-flued harpoon was partly replaced by the more secure one-flued harpoon, and that device was, in turn, replaced by the toggle iron. Boatheaders shifted from common lances to steel lances to bomb lances shot from guns to the deadly darting gun. (See Appendix 2.)

Some outfitting lists have survived, and we have managed to assemble seventy-five that can be used to establish the gear that was actually aboard the vessels in the sample. Unfortunately, however, the range of experience depicted in these lists is very narrow: There is, for example, little usable evidence on the darting gun. Thus the comparisons that can be drawn depend on very little hard evidence:

	N	Average productivity index
Vessels with toggle irons	69	.655
Vessels w/o toggle irons	6	.481
Vessels with bomb lances	68	.649
Vessels w/o bomb lances	7	.567

The mean productivity of the voyages using advanced gear was greater than the mean productivity of the rest, but the sample sizes are small and the differences between the sample means are not significant (Student's *t*). We also ran various regressions in which the technological-date dummy was replaced by dummies relating to the use of toggle irons and whale guns. Not surprisingly, none was very illuminating. The regression in Table 3.11 is characteristic.

131

Table 3.11. *Productivity in New Bedford whaling, 1820–96 (regression no. 2)*

$F = 3.115$; adj. $R^2 = .3519$; dependent mean $= 0.641431$; observations $= 75$

Productivity depends on: Variable	Parameter estimate	Significance level
Intercept	+1.704420	
Vessel type: ships compared with all other vessels	+0.198935	
Hunting ground (compared with Pacific)		
Atlantic	−0.741689	**
Indian	+0.241176	
Western Arctic	+0.120425	
Time	+0.042115	
Mode of entry into the fleet		
Built for fleet	−0.275912	***
Rerigged (compared with vessels transferred into the fleet)	+0.228511	
Hunting pressures		
On baleens	+0.464618	**
On sperms	−0.209942	
Competition among whalers	+0.003333	
Whaling-guns dummy	−0.141948	
Toggle-irons dummy	+0.032362	
Vessel size (tons squared)	+0.00000145	
Voyage length (months squared)	−0.0005028	***
Vessel age	−0.016567	
Vessel age squared	+0.000425	
Last voyage	−0.154950	
Real common wage ashore	−0.027653	**
Measurement dummy	+0.467091	

*** Significant at the 1 percent level.
** Significant at the 5 percent level.
Source: See text.

It will be observed that only one of the technological variables has the right sign and that neither carries a coefficient significantly different from zero at a conventionally acceptable level. In view of the very limited number of vessels outfitted with the earlier technology, and in the absence of evidence on the darting gun, the regression results cannot be taken to be a very serious challenge to the view that improved whalecraft technology did indeed raise whaling productivity. Settling the matter definitively will require the acquisition of more outfitting books; but if, as we believe, the new technology did diffuse very rapidly, even more outfitting evidence may not make it possible to distinguish the effects of technical change from other time-dependent processes.[38]

The wage variables were introduced into the regressions to test a hypothesis drawn from the whaling literature: As wage rates ashore went up, the best men were bid out of whaling, the quality of crews deteriorated, and productivity fell. Our modeling of this hypothesis seems straightforward enough, linking, as it does, the underlying cause (higher wage rates ashore) with the ultimate consequence (lower productivity). We also believe, as we indicated above, that wage rates ashore rose relative to the earnings of whalemen. The middle step in the argument, however, is bypassed: the deterioration of the quality of crews. Did crews really decline in quality? We are now exploring this question by collecting signatures and marks as well as stations from the crew lists. The data assembled so far strongly suggest that both literacy and the skill level among crewmen fell markedly in the 1840s and 1850s. If the analysis confirms these conjectures, we should be able to conclude that the testimony of the whaling literature and of the coefficients on the wage variables in the regressions is correct: The quality of whaling crews did decline as time passed.

The wage series poses a second problem. We know that the productivity index for the fleet as a whole declined from 1820 to the 1860s while the wage rate ashore was rising. The strong negative association between the wage series and the vessel-productivity series may, therefore, describe only the numerical relations between two trends that, in fact, have no true theoretical connection. The latter proposition could be tested by differencing or detrending the data. Such a procedure is not appropriate in the present case, however. The hypothesis in the literature is, in fact, a hypothesis relating to trends. That is, the argument is not that a rise in wages ashore in year 1 reduced the quality of whaling seamen in year 1 and that a decline in wages ashore in year 2 raised the quality of seamen in that year. The argument is that a persistent strong increase in the wage rate ashore led to the deterioration of whaling crews.

Nonetheless, we did attempt a species of detrending, above and beyond that attempted in equation no. 1. First, we restricted the regression to voyages departing after 1833 – a period that saw productivity first fall and then rise, finally reachieving in the 1890s the levels attained sixty years before. Second, in order to allow for the remaining

---

[38] Unfortunately, there may be little more evidence to exploit. We have collected data from virtually all the outfitting books at the New Bedford Public Library, the New Bedford Whaling Museum, and the G. W. Blunt White Library at Mystic. There may be more evidence in vessel logs and agents' papers.

long-term variations in productivity, we entered time and time-squared variables. The regression appears in Table 3.12.

It will be observed that the common-wage coefficient retains a large negative value and is significantly different from zero at better than the 1 percent level. The correlations between the coefficients of the two time variables and the common-wage coefficient are also very small (−.082 and −.035). The wage series appears to be capturing something other than time. The suggestion that the quality of whalemen deteriorated as opportunities ashore improved, and that the decline in the quality of crews tended to lower productivity, ceteris paribus, is strengthened.[39]

Two other features of the regression are worthy of notice. First, the signs, coefficient values, and significance levels of most of the variables are very similar to those in Table 3.10, which is reassuring, since it suggests that we have identified stable relationships. The significance levels are also very high across the board.

Second, one might have supposed, before the fact, that the introduction of time squared might displace the technological dummy − a dummy that divides the observations at January 1, 1870. The reason for this expectation is that productivity turned up late in the period (see Fig. 3.1), so that one could expect time squared to carry a positive coefficient, which it does. Notice, however, that the technological dummy retains a large coefficient, significantly different from zero at the 1 percent level. The correlation matrix also shows clearly that the technological dummy is not simply a version of time squared. The correlation between the coefficients on the technological dummy and time squared is only 0.0144.

Conclusions

After 1820 a series of changes in the economic environment pressured whaling agents to change their ways. The rapid growth of the demand for lubricants and illuminants led agents to send their captains farther and farther from home in search of whale and sperm oil. The whalemen opened rich grounds in the South Atlantic, the Indian Ocean, and the Pacific. The subsequent change in the structure of demand for whaling products − a change that favored whalebone over sperm oil

---

[39] The *t* value on the ratio of the skilled- to common-wage indexes drops to a low value, however, and the correlations between this coefficient and the time coefficients become large. These are quite unimportant matters, however, compared with the results with respect to the common-wage series.

Table 3.12. *Productivity in New Bedford whaling, 1833–96*
(regression no. 3)

$F = 85.6$; adj. $R^2 = .465$; dependent mean $= 0.686$; observations $= 2,144$

Productivity depends on:

Variable	Parameter estimate	Significance level
Intercept	+1.7694	***
Vessel type: ships compared with all other vessels	+0.1021	***
Hunting ground (compared with Pacific)		
Atlantic	−0.1968	***
Indian	−0.0276	
Western Arctic	+0.1069	***
Time	−0.00821	***
Time squared	+0.000259	***
Mode of entry into the fleet		
Built for fleet	−0.02708	
Rerigged (compared with vessels transferred into the fleet)	+0.0999	***
Hunting pressures		
On baleens	+0.1915	***
On sperms	+0.1555	*
Competition among whalers	+0.00112	
Technological dummy	+0.1485	***
Vessel size (tons squared)	+0.00000153	***
Voyage length (months squared)	−0.000278	***
Vessel age	+0.00628	***
Vessel age squared	−0.000120	***
Last voyage	−0.0981	***
Real common wage ashore	−0.0058	***
Ratio, real skilled wage ashore to real common wage ashore	−0.2111	
Specialization		
In baleens	−0.0805	***
In sperms	−0.7044	***
Measurement dummy	−0.0338	

*** Significantly different from zero at 1 percent level.
* Significantly different from zero at 10 percent level.
Durbin–Watson D 1.862
1st order autocorrelation   0.067

Note: See Table 3.10, note (a).
Source: See text.

and whale oil – sent captains to the North Pacific in search of right whales. One of them was venturesome enough to push through the Bering Strait into the Bering Sea, where he found a profusion of the greatest of the bone whales, the bowhead. He was quickly followed by many other captains.

These shifts in demand and in hunting grounds, coupled with emerging labor problems, led the agents to reorganize the industry. In place of the fourteen-month voyage to Davis Strait and the Atlantic typical of the early nineteenth century, voyages of two, three, and even four or more years to the Indian Ocean, the Pacific, and the western Arctic had become common by mid-century. Different vessel types (ships in the Pacific; barks in the Arctic) and new designs of each type (clipper style, with heavy use of power winches) were adopted. The new designs came in part from unspecialized builders for the merchant marine, and in part from ship architects specializing in whalers. Longer voyages meant the adoption of larger vessels of each type and the development of resupply and transshipment points in Hawaii and Panama. In the whaleboats, the whaling gun replaced the hand-held lance, and toward the end, the darting gun, the most effective American whalecraft innovation, was widely adopted. The agents responded to the economic and technical stimuli. They reacted quickly and effectively. For example, when the writing was on the wall – when the Arctic had become the most profitable hunting ground, when steamers proved the most effective whalers, and when the transcontinental rail lines were in place – they abandoned New Bedford and reberthed their vessels in San Francisco.

These changes in environment and the reactions to them by the agents affected productivity in ways nicely captured in the regression appearing in Table 3.10. The clearest and most powerful environmental change was the deterioration in the quality of labor occasioned by competition ashore. According to the coefficient on the common-wage variable, productivity fell 0.006 points for every point the real wage ashore went up. Since the real common wage ashore rose by 52 points between 1820 and 1860 and another 34 points between 1860 and 1895, the effect was a strong one. Thus, if we press these results as far as we can – perhaps harder than they should be – the common-wage variable "accounts for" a decline of 0.504 in the productivity index across the full period. Given a dependent mean of 0.733, this is a very powerful effect indeed.

The changing quality of labor may also be hidden in a second variable, the one concerned with voyage length. This essay had been completed to this point in its present form when we encountered

Charles Nordhoff's little book *Whaling and Fishing*.[40] Nordhoff's account strongly suggests that the quality of crews deteriorated as voyage length went up. Except when whales were actually under attack, whaling was immensely boring, particularly for seamen accustomed to the constant activity of a merchantman or a naval vessel or even a fishing smack. As voyages increased in length, the boredom became unbearable and the rate of desertion increased dramatically, a point made by many students of the industry. Nordhoff claims that the problem became so serious that recruiters began to bypass seamen and recruit the greenest of green hands. These hands, since they had not had the experience of merchant service, might be less likely to be unfavorably affected by the tedium of the voyage, and also their prospects on desertion were dim. A seaman could desert and easily pick up another vessel. Not so a green hand who had nothing but his brief whaling experience.

Whether or not Nordhoff is right as to the recruitment practices of agents, the variable "voyage length" may pick up the unfavorable consequence of the rising desertion rate, in addition to the factors previously discussed. Indeed, it may well be that this factor is the most important one influencing the coefficient on the variable "voyage length."

The reactions of agents to these – and other – environmental changes are also captured nicely in the regression. There are, first, the shifts in hunting ground, the movement first into the Pacific, with its vast supplies of sperm whales, and then into the western Arctic in pursuit of the bowhead. These changes can be thought of as the results of a persistent search for better hunting grounds, the agents adjusting activities in ways that raised productivity. There is also, however, another aspect of them: They reflect the changing structure of demand. The drive into the Pacific in the 1820s, 1830s, and 1840s was motivated by the high price of sperm oil; the drive into the western Arctic after 1848, by the market for baleen.

All of the preceding discussion of the regression, although it is concerned with productivity change, leaves technical considerations aside. This point is an important one. The principal environmental influences on productivity and some of the chief actions taken by agents to raise productivity had nothing to do with technology. That point is worth stressing. Nonetheless, agents also manipulated tech-

---

[40] (New York, 1895). See also Elmo Hohman, *The American Whaleman: A Study of Life and Labor in the Whaling Industry* (New York: Longman Group, 1968), p. 239.

nological variables, and the results they obtained show up in the coefficients of the regression in Table 3.10.

Thus the adoption of ships, as opposed to other rig types, increased productivity (ceteris paribus) by a substantial amount (coefficient of +0.11, as compared with a dependent mean of +0.733), presumably reflecting the advantage of ships in the Indian and Pacific ocean hunting grounds, the grounds that were most important throughout the full period. The choice to rerig to bark specification with the opening of the Arctic also is shown to have been an important factor promoting higher productivity (coefficient of +0.09), and the adoption of improved vessel design and, perhaps more important, better whalecraft, had an enormous effect, according to the regression (+0.310). The change in vessel size was also favorable, although of a smaller order of importance. For example, the rise in average ship size between 1821–35 and 1871–75 improved productivity only +0.006, according to the regression coefficient.

The regression, then, effectively describes the chief influences bearing on whaling productivity, including the activities of agents. A substantial part – a little over half – of the variance is left unexplained, however. The place to seek for further enlightenment is surely among the human actors in this drama. How far did the identity of the agent matter? Presumably there were good agents and bad ones. How far did the quality of the agent determine the result of the voyage? The same question may be asked with respect to the captain. Did crews regularly break up after each voyage, or were some crews kept together to sail a second and a third time? If so, were such crews more effective? All of these queries can be treated with the data set detailed in this paper, and all will be the subject of our attention in the months ahead.

Appendix 1

Whale-stock pressure indexes

General procedures

We began by assembling Frost's data on the initial stock of mature female sperm whales for each of the oceans in which sperm whales are found: the Atlantic (Frost's divisions 1 and 2), Indian (divisions 3–5), and Pacific (divisions 6–9).[1] We then used the parameters from Frost's sperm-whale model (pp. 254–56 and especially 257–60) to estimate the maximum sustainable yield in each ocean. Next we distributed the U.S. catch of sperm oil among the three oceans on the basis of the New Bedford catch, which we derived from the

---

[1] Sir Sydney Frost, *The Whaling Question* (San Francisco: Friends of the Earth, 1979), pp. 266–67. For a discussion of these estimates, see Davis, Gallman, and Hutchins, "Decline of U.S. Whaling."

Dias–Hegarty data set described in the text. We converted the catch into numbers of whales killed, following Starbuck's procedure, and computed four-year moving averages.[2] These averages, dated to the year following (for example 1816–19 equals 1820), were expressed as ratios of the maximum sustainable yield relevant to the particular hunting ground. The ratios, which reflect relative pressures on whale stocks (differing by year and by ground), were then associated with the voyage data. Thus, a vessel leaving New Bedford in 1820 to hunt in the Pacific would have an associated "pressure index" of 1820 (reflecting average hunting 1816–19) for the Pacific Ocean. We used four-year averages so that the indexes would reflect the hunting pressures over an extended period, but there is nothing sacrosanct about the number four. It could easily have been a larger or a smaller number.

There are many things wrong with the sperm-hunting "pressure index," but it is clearly the best option open to us, and we think that it is a satisfactory proxy for the relative degree of sperm population depletion by hunting ground and by year.[3] Similar procedures were followed in the case of baleens.

Maximum sustainable yield

In order to produce indexes of the pressure placed on whale stocks by U.S. hunting in the nineteenth century, we were obliged to estimate the maximum sustainable yields of the sperm-whale populations inhabiting the Atlantic, Pacific, and Indian oceans (a separate estimate for each population) and the

[2] Starbuck, *Whale Fishery*, p. 661. The procedure leads to overestimates of the number of whales killed. See Davis, Gallman, and Hutchins, "Decline of U.S. Whaling."

[3] The shortcomings of the index:

(1) A more subtle index would allow the whale stock of each ground to decline with hunting, and the fertility rate gradually to rise. But to carry through with such a model would require judgments as to the identity of the whales (by age and sex) captured each year. We opted for a simpler, more straightforward calculation, which calls for fewer judgments about the nature of whale hunting.

(2) The procedure implicitly assumes that each ocean contains a single population group, whereas each contains more than one. But our hunting-ground data do not permit us to draw distinctions so narrow.

(3) The division of the U.S. catch among hunting grounds on the basis of the New Bedford catch involves the assumption that New Bedford was typical of U.S. sperm whaling. It probably was, but we are unable to demonstrate that. If we had the data to do so, we would be able to work out a better method of division. Our procedure here is less than perfect, but it is the best we could produce.

(4) The use of an average annual catch in the index is readily defended, but there is no good defense for the selection of four years as against other possibilities, a point already made in the text.

(5) Vessels sailing, for example, to the Pacific might kill whales in the Atlantic and the Indian ocean, on the way to and from the Pacific. Thus New Bedford "Pacific" catches probably include whales from other oceans.

(6) Only U.S. hunting is accounted for. Whereas the United States was far and away the leading hunter, other nations also participated in the hunt and accounted for between 20 and 25 percent of the total catch.

baleen-whale populations inhabiting the Bering Strait and Okhotsk Sea (taken together) and the Atlantic, Pacific, and Indian oceans (taken together). The absolute levels of these estimates matter not at all; all that matter are the relative levels among hunting grounds and years for each of the two broad whale types. (Even relative levels *between* the two broad whale types do not matter.) Since the initial population numbers establish these relative differences, we could have adopted procedures producing only rough estimates of the true maximum sustainable yields. Our actual methods, while entirely adequate, were probably too elaborate for the purpose.

According to Frost, the natural rate of mortality of sperm whales is about 0.133 for the first two years of life and 0.05 thereafter (p. 257 – but see, also, Allen, pp. 9, 10).[4] We assumed a static population with an unchanging number of births each year. Given Frost's death-rate data and the assumption of numerical equality between the sexes at each age, we were able to estimate the age–sex structure of the population. Frost says that the sperm-whale population models assume females reach the age of sexual maturity at between 8.5 and 10 years (p. 257). We chose 10 years, which implies an average pregnancy rate of 0.22 in the stationary population (a figure 0.03 higher than the one used by Frost). Since the maximum pregnancy rate is 0.25, according to Frost, the implied ratio of net increase to the sexually mature female population is 0.03 (assuming that the structures of the stationary and maximum-yield populations are the same).

The maximum sustainable yield is achieved at various female population levels, depending upon the form in which the yield is to be obtained (that is, in females alone, or in males alone, or in females and males combined, or in weight) (Frost, p. 260). We assumed that the yield was to be taken in females alone, and therefore computed the yield against a mature female population 60 percent of the original level (Frost, p. 260).

Without any doubt, our sperm MSY estimates are too low. One could make a good case that the Frost "net pregnancy rate" of 0.06 should have been used in place of our derived 0.03, and that we should have computed the yield on the assumption that it was to be taken disproportionately in the form of males. Moving to these assumptions would have produced much larger MSY estimates and much lower indexes of hunting pressure on the sperm-whale stocks. But it would not have altered the relative levels of the indexes from year to year or from hunting ground to hunting ground.

The regression requires that there be a pressure index for each hunting ground for each type of whale. Since there are virtually no sperm whales in the Arctic, we were obliged to produce a synthetic value for this type of whale for this ocean. We used the average value of the indexes for all other oceans. The coefficient on this index for the Arctic has no substantive meaning.

We used the same mortality rates and population structure in the estimating procedures for baleens. We assumed a maximum pregnancy rate of 0.50 (e.g., Burton, p. 86) and an age of sexual maturity of 10.5. Both these estimates may

[4] K. Radway Allen, *Conservation and Management of Whales* (Seattle: Washington Sea Grant Publication, 1980).

be too high (for example, see Matthews, p. 84), but the errors tend to offset and, in the event, they seem to have offset very well.[5] At least it is true that the crude birth rate implied by our simple model is almost identical with the crude birth rate observed by D. W. Rice and A. A. Wolman among the California gray whales during the recovery of this group from overhunting.[6] The implied crude death rate, however, although at the level of the average for sperm whales (Allen, p. 10), is about two percentage points below the death rate found by Rice and Wolman among the grays. The difference may reflect the fact that smaller whales, such as the grays, have higher mortality rates than larger ones (Allen, p. 9), presumably in part because they suffer the depredations of the killer whales, whereas the larger types do not. It is also possible that our mortality estimate is too low and that, as a result, our estimated MSY level is too high. Once again it is worth remarking that for our purposes such an error matters not at all, as long as the relative levels of the hunting-pressure index numbers among years and hunting grounds are correct. Whether they are depends not on the MSY estimates but on the estimates of the initial population levels.

Estimates of whales killed

The estimates of the numbers of whales killed were based on the quantity of sperm and baleen oil brought back by hunters, following procedures established by Alexander Starbuck. That technique works well for sperm whales, and for baleen whales through the 1870s. After 1880 the ratio of oil to baleen brought back drops sharply. Whalers were probably abandoning blubber, a rational response to the dramatically changing relative prices of baleen and oil. For the years after 1878, therefore, the estimate of the number of whales killed was based on the amount of baleen brought back. To produce the estimate it was necessary to infer from the baleen returned the amount of oil that could have been obtained from the whales that produced the baleen. This estimate (3.49 gallons per pound of bone) was derived from the returns of U.S. hunting in the period immediately preceding the 1880s.

Competition index

The number of exploitable sperm whales in each hunting ground (Atlantic, Pacific, and Indian) was taken from Frost. We defined the Atlantic as Frost's divisions 1 and 2; the Indian, 3, 4, and 5; and the Pacific, 6, 7, 8, and 9. We then converted exploitable whale stocks to total whale stocks, following James Scharff.[7] Gray whales were allocated to the Pacific and bowheads to the

[5] Robert Burton, *The Life and Death of Whales*, 2d ed. (New York: Universe Books, 1980); and L. Harrison Matthews, *The Natural History of the Whale* (New York: Columbia University Press, 1978).

[6] *Life History and Ecology of the Gray Whale*, American Society of Mammalogists, Special Publication 3, 1977.

[7] James E. Scharff, "The International Management of Whales, Dolphins, and Porpoises: An Interdisciplinary Assessment," pt. 1, *Ecology Law Quarterly* 6 (1977):

western Arctic and to the North Atlantic, following Frost (pp. 266–67). We accepted Allen's estimates (p. 19) of the number of humpbacks and rights in the North Pacific, and the latter were allocated to the Arctic.[8] Frost's estimates of the number of humpbacks and rights in the Southern Hemisphere (converted from exploitable to total numbers, following Scharff) were divided among the Atlantic, Pacific, and Indian oceans in proportion to the number of sperm whales in these oceans.

Whales are not of equal size or equal value, but we made no attempt to adjust for these matters. On the whole, baleens were bigger but yielded less valuable output, ton for ton, than sperm whales. Summing up without weighting is a reasonable enough procedure.

Hunting voyages differed in duration, from time to time, hunting ground to hunting ground, and voyage to voyage. Again, we made no effort to introduce these subtleties into our index numbers. We assumed that a vessel arriving in New Bedford from the Pacific, in, say, 1830 was affected during its whaling voyage by the amount of competition from vessels leaving for the Pacific in 1828. Thus if the vessel had hunted in the Pacific and had returned to New Bedford in 1830, it was assigned the "competition index number" for 1828. We were unable to allow for competition offered by vessels other than those sailing from New Bedford.

We assumed that the western Arctic encompassed about 2.17 million square miles (one-ninth of the Arctic Ocean – representing the Chukchi Sea – the Bering Sea, the Sea of Okhotsk, and the Bering Strait); the Atlantic, about 10 million square miles (roughly one-third of the area of the Atlantic); the Pacific, about 22 million square miles (roughly one-third of the area of the Pacific); the Indian, about 7 million square miles (roughly one-quarter of the area of the Indian Ocean). These estimates rest on data from the *Columbia Gazeteer of the World* (New York, 1962) and maps showing whale migration routes in *The Times Atlas of the World*, comprehensive ed. (New York, 1980).

Appendix 2

The diffusion of whalecraft innovations

"There has been as great a revolution in the mode of killing whales during the past twenty years, as there has been in the art of naval warfare; were it not for this, but few whalers would now be afloat."[1]

323. Scharff asserts that the ratio of the total population to the exploitable population was 2 to 1 in the case of sperm whales, and 1.5 to 1 in the case of baleens. Scharff uses these ratios to convert both current (i.e., disequilibrium) and initial (i.e., equilibrium) figures. One would expect that ratios to vary from the first to the second case, but for present purposes the coefficients are adequate.

[8] The geographic definition of the Arctic used here – including all of the Bering Sea as well as the Bering Strait – is probably somewhat too broad. To compensate, we included in the region the North Pacific right whales, whose migration route takes them through the Bering Sea.

[1] Charles M. Scammon, *The Marine Mammals of the North-Western Coast of America*, (San Francisco: Carmany, 1874), p. 216.

Scammon refers to whalecraft innovations, which he believes produced effects in twenty years roughly equivalent to the changes in vessel design and other aspects of outfitting that took place in the period between the seventeenth and the late nineteenth century. This appendix describes the principal innovations and investigates the speed of their adoption.[2]

The American style of whaling involved (1) a sailing vessel (later in the period some had auxiliary steam power) and (2) several small (28 to 30 feet by 6 feet), light whaling boats, from which the attack on the whale was made. The equipment in the boat and the attack on the whale depended somewhat on the type of whale involved and the place of the attack. Gray whales and humpbacks were typically taken in bays in shallow water, which required certain types of equipment (for example, humpbacks sank when killed, so that boats had to carry gear to mark them and hold their bodies in place until, eventually, they rose again; bay hunting called for the use of anchors, useless in the open sea, where most hunting went on) and permitted the use of other gear that was not very effective in the rougher waters outside the bays (the Greener swivel harpoon gun, for example). Sperm whales were regarded as much more ferocious than rights, requiring special caution in the attack. Bowheads posed peculiar problems, since they could – and did – seek escape from the hunters under the Arctic ice.

Despite these variations, the fundamental character of the American system is clear. It can be described best if we consider the case of, say, a large bark hunting the Pacific. Slung from davits above the decks of the bark are four whaling boats; two or three spares are stored elsewhere. Men are in the crosstrees on watch for whales. When whales are sighted, the boats are lowered to give chase. Each boat carries six men, five oarsmen (three starboard and two port) and a steersman, called a boatheader. The boatheader of each boat is normally a mate. With all four boats on the sea, there are typically five or six men left to sail the vessel, keep lookout, and signal the movements of the whales to the boats.

Whaleboats were sailed and sometimes rowed. If there was danger that the sound of the oars would frighten the whale, they were paddled. The boat crew attempted to approach the whale closely; if possible, they would run the boat onto the whale's back, when the forward starboard oarsman – known as the boatsteerer or harpooner – would rise and thrust two harpoons into the whale. Boatsteerer and boatheader would then change places in the boat and, in the early days of whaling, the latter would slash at the whale with a sharp implement called a spade, in an effort to sever the tendons in the whale's flukes (tail) and cripple it. This dangerous practice was later generally abandoned.

The purpose of the harpoon was to hook the whale and attach it by a line to the whaleboat. The weight of the line and the whaleboat was intended to tire the whale and permit it to be approached once again. The dispatching of the

---

[2] Much of the information on the innovations comes from Thomas G. Lytle, *Harpoons and Other Whalecraft* (New Bedford: Old Dartmouth Historical Society, 1984).

whale was then left to the boatheader, who killed it with a tool called a lance, originally a long, hand-held stabbing implement.

Whereas the technique remained essentially unchanged, the implements were improved in important respects. The principal innovations were introduced between the late 1840s and the mid-1860s, and they diffused during the period of decline of the American fleet.

The most important innovations in harpoons (called "irons" by whalemen) centered on the mode by which the implement was conveyed from the boat to the whale, and on the features of the head of the harpoon that affected its ability to hook the whale.

Most American harpoons were thrust or thrown – darted, the whalers said – by hand. The harpoon was attached to a cut sapling, with bark left on to improve the grip. The harpooner then thrust or threw the pole. If he was successful, the harpoon hooked the whale and the pole was detached and floated away.

Harpoon poles could not be thrown very far; thus attempts were made to shoot the harpoon from swivel guns and from rocket launchers that closely resembled the World War II bazooka. The swivel gun was invented at a very early date and figured importantly in the Scotch and English fisheries, but it never established itself in the American fisheries except in the hunt for gray whales in the California bays. Success with the swivel depended upon calm seas (otherwise aim was thrown off) and sturdy boats, neither common in the American fisheries.[3]

The rocket launcher seems to have been a more promising line. It was light and it did not have the kick of a swivel gun, an important matter for American whalemen in view of the small, light boats in which they hunted. According to Lytle, notable whalemen from Scoresby to Rotch to Roys reported great success with various rocket launchers. Yet there appears to have been no rush among American whalemen to adopt this innovation, and its general impact seems to have been negligible.

Innovations respecting the head of the harpoon were numerous, and some were widely and rather quickly diffused. Although the variations on each style were great, there appear to have been only three basic styles of harpoon head: the two-flued, the one-flued, and the toggle. The terms are descriptive. The head of a two-flued harpoon was shaped like an arrowhead, with sharp leading edges and dull following edges, the latter intended to lodge in the flesh of the whale. Sometimes, however, the two-flued harpoon pulled out. The one-flued harpoon – with only one following edge – was designed to minimize the chances that that would happen, and it was widely regarded as superior to its predecessor. The toggle iron had a head that turned on a pivot. When the harpoon was being thrown, the head was held in a fixed position – sharp edges forward – by a small, light piece of wood. When the head entered the whale, the wood broke, the head turned, and the whale was securely hooked.

---

[3] Ibid., chs. 4, 6. The *Florida* was outfitted with a Greener swivel gun and twenty irons in 1858, and Mrs. Williams describes the first mate shooting the gun from time to time, chiefly at fin whales and always from the deck of the *Florida*. She does not report that

The crucial innovation – dated to 1848 – appears to have been the toggle iron.[4] James Durfee, a leading New Bedford manufacturer of whalecraft, produced 22,133 harpoons between May 15, 1830, and October 29, 1844, all two-flued. Between October 29, 1844, and May 9, 1850, only two years after the invention of the toggle, he produced 7,526 two-flued harpoons and 265 toggle irons; between May 9, 1850, and October 27, 1862, the numbers were almost equal: 20,462 two-flued versus 20,191 toggle. The outfitting books of the bark *Ospray* list 190 "common" irons and 50 toggle in 1854; 40 two-flued, 10 one-flued, and 60 toggle in 1866; and 10 two-flued, 11 one-flued, and 90 toggle in 1880.[5] The bark *Louisa* carried all common irons in 1850; 130 common and 50 toggle in 1853; 42 each of the one- and two-flued and 100 of the toggle in 1856; 36 two-flued, 20 one-flued, and 100 toggle in 1865; and 10 two-flued, 3 one-flued, and 120 toggle in 1874.[6] The bark *Globe* listed 36 toggle in 1869.[7] Scammon says that a first-class whale ship on a Cape Horn voyage in the early 1870s should carry 15 two-flued and 150 toggle harpoons.[8]

The examples could readily be multiplied. The lessons seem clear. According to these records, the two-flued and toggle irons were the important designs, the one-flued having limited transitional significance. A clearer and firmer finding is that the toggle iron was adopted quickly and achieved equal importance with the two-flued iron in the 1850s, but did not clearly dominate the other forms until the 1870s, a quarter of a century after its innovation. Even then, outfit books typically called for a few common irons in addition to the toggles.

Harpoons were made of iron, the shank being of soft iron to allow it to bend under pressure and thus to reduce the likelihood that the head would pull out of the whale. Hand lances, however, were to serve not as hooks, but as stabbing devices, being easily thrust into the whale and easily withdrawn, so that subsequent thrusts could be made. The lance was typically made of tough wrought iron and mounted on a pole, but the head was frequently of steel. Lytle says steel was preferred – for obvious reasons – and that it completely displaced wrought iron, "once steel was produced in quantity in this country," a development presumably associated with a decline in the price of steel relative to iron.[9] In fact, the timing is almost right. Relative steel prices fell particularly sharply after 1867. If the ratio of steel to wrought-iron prices in

he hit anything with it (Harold Williams, ed., *One Whaling Family* [Boston: Houghton Mifflin, 1964]). The book consists chiefly of the diary of Mrs. Williams, who went whaling with her husband and raised a family at sea.
[4] Lytle, *Harpoons*, p. 33.
[5] New Bedford Whaling Museum, James Durfee Mss. 56, box 22, ser. D, subser. 13; Swift and Allen Mss. 5, box 37, vol. 85. Lytle (*Harpoons*, p. 11) calls Durfee a typical New Bedford whalecraft maker.
[6] Lytle, *Harpoons*, p. 16.
[7] G. W. Blunt White Library, Mystic Seaport, Inc., Outfit Book of bark *Globe*, 3d voyage, 1869, New Bedford, VFM 425.
[8] *Marine Mammals*, p. 316.
[9] *Harpoons*, p. 133.

145

1867 is taken as the base of an index number series (100), the index fell to 71 in 1870 and to 59 in 1875.[10] Outfitting lists immediately reflected the change: The lists for the *Emily Morgan*, 1842–45, and the ships *Julius Caesar*, 1837, *Magnolia*, 1842, and *Frances Henrietta*, 1843, mention no steel-headed lances, and those for the barks *Globe*, 1869, and *Mary Frazier*, 1876, mention no iron-headed hand lances.[11] Scammon's list for the early 1870s also contains no hand lances with iron heads.[12] The *Ospray* carried half common and half steel-headed lances in 1854, but its outfit had changed to all steel-headed lances by 1868.

There were other proposals to make the lance deadlier: Heat it, electrify it, poison it. None of these plans came to much, for fairly obvious reasons: For example, crewmen reasoned (correctly) that if the poison killed the whale, it might kill them, too, when they handled their victim. The proposal to make the lance explosive, however, did come to something. Explosive devices were commonly innovated with new modes of delivering the lance to the whale: guns of various kinds.

The first set of guns consisted of shoulder guns, similar to shotguns, and they were intended to be managed by the boatheader. Unfortunately they produced a substantial kick that frequently threw the boatheader to the bottom of the boat, sometimes broke his collarbone, and occasionally capsized the boat. Much inventive effort was directed toward dealing with these problems, and eventually the Allen gun – usually called the Brand gun because C. C. Brand developed and promoted it – achieved a wide acceptance. The progress of the shoulder gun is exhibited nicely in the outfitting lists of the bark *Ospray*: The lists for 1851 and 1854 show no whale guns; those for 1866 and 1868 refer to three (fewer than one per boat), presumably all shoulder guns. The number rises to six at the end of the 1860s and the beginning of the 1870s, and remains at six in 1880, one per boat plus two spares. The bark *Globe* carried four in 1869, Scammon (early 1870s) calls for four on his Cape Horn whaler, and John Williams, around 1880, allowed one gun per boat. The *Lottie Beard*, a resupply vessel, carried eight boxes of guns and lances in 1886. The order books of Frank E. Brown, a New Bedford seller of whaling implements, show the sale of 1,906 feathered lances – lances for shoulder guns – and only 921 long lances and unspecified lances – presumably hand lances – in 1877 and 1878. By the fall of 1899 and the spring of 1900, Brown listed only feathered lances and lances for darting guns (discussed below).[13]

[10] James M. Swank, *History of the Manufacture of Iron in All Ages* (Philadelphia: American Iron & Steel Association, 1892), p. 514.
[11] G. W. Blunt White Library, Charles W. Morgan Papers, 1798–1861, Account Book, 1842–48, coll. 27, vol. 35, *Emily Morgan*; vol. 24, ship *Magnolia*, December 1842, ship *Frances Henrietta*, November 1843; *Mary Frazier* (bark), Memorandum of Whaler's Outfits, 1876, VFM 1461; *Julius Caesar* (ship) Papers, New London, coll. 167, box 1/8.
[12] *Marine Mammals*, p. 316.
[13] Swift and Allen, op. cit.; Outfit Book of bark *Globe*; Scammon, *Marine Mammals*, p. 316; G. W. Blunt White Library, John L. Williams, List ca. 1882, "Provisions

The final whalecraft innovation of note combined in one instrument most of the important characteristics of harpoon and whaling gun. It consisted of a gun – called a darting gun, or a Pierce gun, for its inventor – mounted on the staff of a harpoon. When the harpoon was darted into the whale, a lever was depressed. The gun was fired and an explosive lance was driven deep into the whale. The Pierce gun could deliver an explosive lance more accurately than a shoulder gun. The location of the gun – close to the whale when it went off – meant that the lance was delivered with great power, without conveying a kick to harpooner or boat. Finally, the apparatus usually stopped the whale, preventing the long struggles common when a standard harpoon was placed. In the Arctic, where there was always danger that a harpooned whale would dive under the ice, this feature was particularly important.

The darting gun was probably the most effective piece of whalecraft introduced in the American fishery in the nineteenth century. It developed late, however. It was invented in 1865 and its diffusion did not begin on a large scale until the 1870s. The outfitting books of the bark *Ospray* in the late 1860s and early 1870s make no mention of darting guns, but two of them plus fifteen lances appear in 1880. None are on John Williams's list for around 1882, despite the fact that Williams had in mind an Arctic voyage, but Scammon (early 1870s) called for four – one per boat – and fifty darting-gun bomb lances. Clearly Scammon saw important uses for the darting gun but did not conceive of its replacing all its predecessors: His list includes 35 steel-headed hand lances, 4 whaling guns other than the darting guns, and 150 shoulder-gun bomb lances. The Frank E. Brown order books show a steady increase in the relative importance of the darting gun: The fraction of the total lances supplied by Brown that fit the darting gun rose from 7 percent in 1877 to 9 percent in 1878 to 14 percent in 1879 to 41 percent in the fall of 1899 and the spring of 1900. A clearer indication of the change under way is that Brown sold only eight Brand shoulder guns in the period 1877 through 1879 while disposing of eighty-one Pierce darting guns.[14]

In summary, the important whalecraft innovations were made in the period between 1848 and 1865, and they diffused in the 1850s through at least the 1880s. The order of adoption ran about as follows: toggle iron (1848–70), steel-head lance (1845?–70), shoulder gun (1855?–80), darting gun (1865?–85?). From the time when the diffusion of the toggle iron was clearly well under way to the time when the darting gun had made a substantial impact is an interval of about thirty years. The process began at about mid-century and was over in the early 1880s.

Needed to Outfit a Whaling/Sealing Vessel for Sea," vfm 1430; Harvard University, Graduate School of Business Administration, George F. Baker Foundation, 1878–86, schooner *Lottie Beard*, New Bedford, Mss. 252, and Order Book, Frank E. Brown, New Bedford Whaling Implements, 1877–1922, Mss. 252, vol. 1.

[14] Swift and Allen, op. cit.; John L. Williams, op. cit.; Scammon, *Marine Mammals*, pp. 228, 316; Frank E. Brown, op. cit.

4

Households on the American frontier: the distribution of income and wealth in Utah, 1850–1900

Clayne L. Pope

The settlement of Utah, from the start of the Mormon migration in 1847 until the turn of the century when virtually all the current communities had been formed, provides economists and economic historians with an unusual experiment worthy of close study. Utah was isolated from most U.S. markets for two decades after settlement before integration with the rest of the U.S. economy by way of the transcontinental railroad. It was largely settled by migrants who chose to move to Utah out of religious conviction. These migrants were drawn from virtually all parts of the United States and much of Europe. In part because of the hasty exit from Illinois and the high cost of migration from the Midwest, most families arrived in Utah with little or no wealth, so that Utah was an egalitarian, though poor, economy in 1850. Real property averaged $189 in Utah in 1850 in contrast to $832 in the old Northwest, $352 in a frontier Iowa county, and $626 in Wisconsin.[1] The Gini coefficient of .69 for property wealth

Most of the research reported in this essay was conducted jointly with J. R. Kearl. Larry Wimmer and Dwight Israelsen helped us to create the Utah data set. Larry Wimmer also was involved in much of the early research in the project. Research grants from the College of Family, Home and Social Sciences, Brigham Young University, and the National Science Foundation (SES8218799) supported much of the work on the Utah Income and Wealth Project. Many research assistants have worked on this project over the years – most recently James Liu and Kathy Moon. David Galenson, Stanley Engerman, and Larry Wimmer provided useful comments on drafts of this essay, as did seminar participants at the University of Illinois and Indiana University and members of the economic history workshop at the University of Chicago. Errors are my responsibility.

[1] See Lee Soltow, *Men and Wealth in the United States, 1850–1870* (New Haven, Conn.: Yale University Press, 1975), p. 81; J. R. Kearl, Clayne L. Pope, and Larry T. Wimmer, "Household Wealth in a Settlement Economy," *Journal of Economic History* 40 (September 1980): 484; David W. Galenson and Clayne Pope, "Economic and Geographic Mobility on the Nineteenth Century Farming Frontier: Evidence from Appanoose County, Iowa, 1850–1870," working paper, 1987; Lee Soltow, *Patterns of Wealthholding in Wisconsin since 1850* (Madison: University of Wisconsin Press, 1971),

was 80 percent of the U.S. average of .86. Moreover, 70 percent of the Utah households held real estate compared with 41 percent for the United States.[2] The wealthy's share of aggregate wealth was much lower in Utah than in the United States.[3] Given the low levels of initial wealth and relative equality, the effects of settlement and establishment of a viable economy on economic inequality can be observed in Utah in a very pure form.

The institutional peculiarities of Utah add interesting variance to nineteenth-century U.S. experience.[4] The practice of polygyny by a significant share of the population allows the observation of unusual marriage markets as well as insights into the influence of large multi-marriage families on economic achievement and intergenerational linkages.[5] The Mormon theology of the nineteenth century carried strong impulses toward economic equality that powerful church leaders tried sporadically to put into practice.[6] (The terms "Mormon" and "LDS", or Latter-day Saints, are used interchangeably in this paper to refer to the Church of Jesus Christ of Latter-day Saints – the dominant religion of Utah.) Church leaders also attempted to coordinate settle-

---

p. 77. The figures for the USA are for free males aged twenty or over. The figures for Appanoose County and Utah are for household heads.

[2] Soltow, *Men and Wealth*, ch. 4; Kearl et al., "Household Wealth in a Settlement Economy," p. 484.

[3] The original allocation of land was fairly independent of the wealth a household brought to Utah. Land was originally allocated by the leaders of the Latter-day Saints church. They typically divided the land into quite small parcels of perhaps forty or eighty acres for farmers and smaller parcels for craftsmen and artisans. Allocation was done by random drawings. Access to water was critical to the value of land. Water rights were allocated in a similar way. Federal laws governing property rights were not in force in Utah until 1869. See Leonard J. Arrington, *Great Basin Kingdom: An Economic History of the Latter-day Saints, 1830–1900* (Lincoln: University of Nebraska Press, 1968), pp. 45–48, 50–53, 90–95.

[4] Arrington, *Great Basin Kingdom*, is a fine history of the Utah economy and the impact of the institutional peculiarities on the economy during this period.

[5] Gary S. Becker, *A Treatise on the Family* (Cambridge: Harvard University Press, 1981), ch. 3; James E. Smith and Phillip R. Kunz, "Polygyny and Fertility in Nineteenth-Century America," *Population Studies* 30 (1976): 465–80. A group of scholars at the University of Utah have studied the demography of Utah extensively. For examples of their work, see Lee Bean, Geraldine P. Mineau, Douglas L. Anderton, and Yung-Chang Hsueh, "The Fertility Effects of Marriage Patterns in a Frontier American Population," *Historical Methods* 20 (Fall 1987): 161–71, and Geraldine P. Mineau, Lee Bean, and Mark Skolnick, "Mormon Demographic History II: The Family Life Cycle and Natural Fertility," *Population Studies* 33 (November 1979): 429–66.

[6] See Leonard Arrington, Feramorz Y. Fox, and Dean L. May, *Building the City of God: Community and Cooperation among the Mormons* (Salt Lake City: Deseret, 1976).

ment and promote economic development through cooperative activities of church members. Certainly, the power of Brigham Young, the leader of the LDS church, and of the church hierarchy was used to promote development of an otherwise economically unattractive region. With annual rainfall of less than fifteen inches in the valleys where farming was feasible, definition of property rights for water in streams fed by deep mountain snow was crucial to land values and economic success. A system of publicly constructed ditches and canals was combined with the appointment of watermasters who oversaw the allocations of water associated with each plot of land.[7] Property rights for grazing land for cattle and sheep also had to be defined.[8]

These unusual institutional and demographic features of Utah are combined with statistical records that are extraordinary for the nineteenth – or any other – century. The mid-nineteenth-century census manuscripts of 1850, 1860, and 1870, which fortuitously include families' own estimate of their wealth, provide a very useful point of departure, since the settlement of Utah begins in earnest in 1847. These censuses also provide a basis for comparison with the rest of the United States. To these censuses are added good tax-assessment records for the rest of the century giving some observation of wealth over the whole period. Estimates of household income are extremely rare before the twentieth century. In Utah, however, LDS church records yield reasonable estimates of income for as much as 90 percent of the state's population in the early years and perhaps 75 percent of population at the turn of the century.[9] Finally, LDS genealogical records make the necessary intergenerational connections so that the economic relationships of fathers, sons, brothers, in-laws, and so on can be studied in rich detail.

Given some of the unusual characteristics of Utah, it may be tempting to assume that the Utah experience is irrelevant to the larger American experience. This assumption would be in error, however, for Utah appears to have gone through essentially the same settlement process as other states or regions – a process vital to American de-

---

[7] Arrington, *Great Basin Kingdom*, pp. 52–53.

[8] Ibid., pp. 91–92.

[9] It is difficult to know the exact percentage of the Utah population that was LDS. Nels Anderson in *Deseret Saints: The Mormon Frontier in Utah* (Chicago: University of Chicago Press, 1968) inferred that Mormons were 94 percent of the population in 1870 by comparing the vote of a political party that was Mormon to one that was "gentile" (the Mormon term for non-Mormons). Gustive O. Larson in *The Americanization of Utah for Statehood* (San Marino, Calif.: Huntington Library, 1971), p. 100, put Mormons at 85 to 90 percent depending on whether or not one includes apostates. Not all LDS contributed funds to the church.

velopment before the twentieth century. The American economy, like the economies of Canada, Australia, and much of Latin America, has a history embedded in a process of continuous settlement of vacant or sparsely settled lands. Most frontier settlements coped with similar problems of developing transportation systems, adjusting to a new health environment, defining property rights and land policies, coping with scarce labor, and integration of the frontier economy into the larger market economy. The settlers of Utah faced these same problems. The church's influence on household decisions can be easily overstated. Much of the church's effort was directed at resistance to the inevitable market forces that moved the Utah economy after its economic integration with the rest of the United States. Certainly Utah's unusual religion created some very large households, selected out immigrants through conversion, and inculcated cooperative values. Nonetheless, the process of settlement seems in other ways to be quite typical of economic development on the frontier.

The importance of this settlement process in the American experience has not been overlooked. The existence of a frontier, the shift of the frontier westward by settlement, and the development of frontier or settlement institutions are important themes in American history. Turner's frontier thesis, however specified, has employed a significant portion of several generations of historians.[10] Economic historians have certainly placed transportation, labor institutions, migration, and property-right definition near the top of their research agenda. Scholars have examined the influence of the frontier or the settlement process on fertility, migration, technological change, and wages.[11] The purpose here is not to examine all of the effects of settlement, but rather to examine in detail the distributions of income and wealth for an economy going through the settlement process. The focus is upon

[10] Merle Curti, *The Making of an American Community* (Stanford, Calif.: Stanford University Press, 1959); Allan G. Bogue, *From Prairie to Corn Belt* (Chicago: University of Chicago Press, 1963); Margaret Walsh, *The American Frontier Revisited* (London: Macmillan, 1981); Ray A. Billington, *The Genesis of the Frontier Thesis* (San Marino, Calif.: Huntington Library, 1971), and *America's Frontier Heritage* (New York: Holt, Rinehart & Winston, 1966).

[11] Richard A. Easterlin, "Population Change and Farm Settlement in the Northern United States," *Journal of Economic History* 36 (March 1976): 45–75; David W. Galenson, *White Servitude in Colonial America* (Cambridge: Cambridge University Press, 1981); Gary Libecap, "Property Rights in Economic History: Implications for Research," *Explorations in Economic History* 23 (1986): 227–52; Bogue, *From Prairie to Corn Belt*; Richard Steckel, "The Economic Foundations of East–West Migration during the 19th Century," *Explorations in Economic History* 20 (1983): 14–36; H. J. Habakkuk, *American and British Technology in the Nineteenth Century* (Cambridge: Cambridge University Press, 1967).

the income and wealth of individual households rather than upon the overall development of the Utah economy. What were the trends in inequality? What factors were most important in generating the observed inequality? Were the economic positions of households fixed or did they fluctuate widely? Did Utah achieve the equality expected on the frontier?

The language of analysis

"I've been rich and I've been poor and believe me, rich is better." This phrase must describe most individuals' attitude toward wealth and income. The assumption that households prefer more to less seems to be one of the more innocent assumptions economists use to spin theory. Yet even if everyone makes choices consistent with the desire to be rich, everyone does not end up with anything like the same wealth or income. Inequality, often extreme inequality, of wealth, income, and consumption is the common characteristic of market economies. Indeed, reducing inequality is usually the first target of social reformers.

Undoubtedly, a significant part of the inequality can be accounted for by difficulties in measuring income, wealth, and consumption in a context of nonpecuniary income differentials, labor–leisure choices, costs of education, and so forth. Even poor observation of income, wealth, and consumption is rare and often difficult. Household wealth has been observed historically in probate records, tax rolls, and census manuscripts,[12] but the omission of human capital has made the relationship of wealth to income tenuous. Income was rarely recorded until the imposition of income taxes, and consumption, the most relevant measure of well-being, is most often not observed at all. Still, much inequality would remain even if every measurement were made perfectly. The presence of so much inequality in market economies is somewhat puzzling, for there are some forces within a market economy that narrow or level the distributions of income and wealth.

Since a market economy is one with minimal barriers to choices and actions, one would expect households operating in a pure market economy to observe market returns to various characteristics and make choices or take actions that would increase their lifetime consumption and, therefore, their income and wealth in most instances.[13] Choices

---

[12] Alice Hanson Jones, *Wealth of a Nation To Be* (New York: Columbia University Press, 1980); Edward Pessen, *Riches, Class and Power before the Civil War* (Lexington, Mass.: Heath, 1973); Soltow, *Men and Wealth*.

[13] A consideration of lifetime consumption would also need to include intergenerational transfers through bequests and gifts. The importance of these transfers remains in

152

about occupation, investment in human capital, residence, and so forth are surely made with an eye to their effect on income, wealth, and ultimately consumption. In general, if any characteristic would increase income or wealth, households would be expected to acquire that characteristic unless the cost of acquisition is greater than the gross return, causing a decline in consumption rather than an increase. This simple idea leads to the supposition that markets that give information as to which attributes are valuable are a force for equality in the distributions of income and wealth. Indeed, should not markets and individual choice produce near-equality if income, consumption, and wealth are properly measured? The answer is, unfortunately, no. Maximization of lifetime consumption (properly measured) is maximization under a multitude of constraints. These constraints, which include sex, race, age, cohort, some basic capacity for learning or intelligence, and birthplace, vary widely across individuals and households, producing much of the inequality observed in market economies.

One common approach to the constraints listed above is to view them as fixed characteristics that earn a rent. If characteristics are given and unacquirable from the point of view of the individual or particular assets are fixed in supply and unproduceable, inequality in the ownership of these fixed characteristics and assets (which might be thought of as Ricardian characteristics or assets) will be a major source of inequality in income and wealth. Ricardo, the master of this type of analysis, focused on land as a fixed asset and developed a model that related land rents to population.[14] In principle, rents to fixities in the economy could either rise or fall as the supply of other factors and technology changed in the economy. From the individual's point of view, these fixed characteristics would include birthplace, race, sex, IQ, cohort, and aging.

A team headed by Christopher Jencks, using contemporary data, conducted a study that provides a good illustration of the measurement of rents. Most of the results can be interpreted as measurement of rents or, more precisely, the percentage of variance in income or earnings accounted for by several of the most common Ricardian characteristics – family background, race, and IQ.[15] They found that

dispute (Laurence J. Kotlikoff and Lawrence H. Summers, "The Role of Intergenerational Transfers in Aggregate Capital Accumulation," *Journal of Political Economy* 89 [August 1981]: 706–32; Andrew Abel, "Precautionary Saving and Accidental Bequests," *American Economic Review* 75 [September 1985]: 777–91; B. Douglas Bernheim, Andrei Shleifer, and Lawrence H. Summers, "The Strategic Bequest Motive," *Journal of Labor Economics* 4 [July 1986]: S151–S182).

[14] David Ricardo, *On the Principles of Political Economy and Taxation* (London, 1817).

[15] Christopher Jencks, Susan Bartlett, and Mary Corcoran, *Who Gets Ahead?* (New York: Basic, 1979).

family background accounted for 15 to 35 percent of the variance in earnings.[16] In other words, a significant rent is earned by the individual who has the good fortune to have been born of superior parents. They also found that a fifteen-point difference on a normalized IQ test was associated with a 30 percent difference in earnings.[17] They also found a substantial rent for whites relative to blacks.[18]

Treating the effect of these fixed characteristics on distributions of economic rewards in terms of the distribution of such characteristics and the importance of their rents is, in one sense, too mechanistic, for it misses the behavior of households in response to these constraints. Households undoubtedly realize that certain traits are liabilities and take reasonable steps to mitigate their effect. Similarly, other fixed characteristics of the household may be advantageous. Households then try to maximize the advantage of fortuitous characteristics. In other words, there are strong interactive effects between the fixed characteristics of an individual and the choices that are made.

Consider birthplace as an illustration. Birthplace is a fixed characteristic that, for certain broad categories such as country or region of birth, has a noticeable effect on income and wealth. How do households ameliorate the effect of a bad birthplace? They migrate. One of the great attractions of an unsettled area or of the frontier was its ability to mitigate the disadvantage of a poor birthplace and, perhaps, a poor family background. Were there no migration, birthplace would be a powerful determinant of wealth, income, and consumption. With migration, birthplace has a minor, though statistically significant, effect on economic fortunes. Similar responses can be found for the other constraints. The economist's usual device of analyzing behavior in response to a set of constraints is as useful for the examination of the distributions of income and wealth as it is for the more common applications such as explanations of expenditures on various consumer goods or the combinations of factors of production.

Markets should have systematic effects on distributions of income and wealth. Choices households make in response to constraints seem to level the distributions of economic rewards. Market forces increase

---

[16] Ibid., p. 217.

[17] Ibid., p. 220.

[18] The problems of measuring discrimination are well known. For example, see Ronald L. Oaxaca, "Theory and Measurement in the Economics of Discrimination," in Leonard J. Hausman, ed., *Equal Rights and Industrial Relations* (Madison, Wis.: Industrial Relations Research Association, 1977), pp. 1–30; James J. Heckman and Richard Butler, "The Government's Impact on the Labor Market Status of Black Americans: A Critical Review," ibid., pp. 235–81.

or decrease rents to the Ricardian elements or the constraints and widen or narrow the dispersion of income or wealth.

The efforts to secure income, wealth, and consumption take place in a most uncertain world where luck plays a powerful role. Luck will increase inequality, especially in the cross-sectional, but even in the long-term, distributions of income and wealth. In fact, luck is a dominant factor in any statistical examination of the factors influencing the distributions of income, earnings, or wealth. The scholar using all the statistical tricks of the trade will, in the end, attribute much if not most of the variance in wealth or income to luck.[19]

Each of these three categories of influence on the distribution of economic rewards – luck, choice, and fixed characteristics – is approached differently in this essay. Luck, or the stochastic element, is treated as a residual where the ideal is to remove variance due to any variable, observed or unobserved, with systematic influence in order to reduce the unexplained variance to that which is truly stochastic. In practice, this ideal is rarely approached. The level and time trend of rents and the factors influencing those rents are important to the analysis of the role of the constraints on the distributions and will occupy a major portion of the essay. Choices are viewed as responses to the constraints facing households. It will be shown that households make reasonable choices in order to mitigate the influence of the constraints, thereby leveling the distributions of income and wealth.

The data set

Four primary sources were combined to create the data set used in the analysis reported here.

(1) The manuscript censuses of 1850, 1860, and 1870 have been collected for all household heads in Utah. These censuses report wealth, occupation, birthplace, age, and household size. County and town of residence are acquired at the point of collection. Then households that appeared in more than one census were linked together to form the basis of a longitudinal panel. The censuses of 1880 and 1900

---

[19] For examples, see Arleen Leibowitz, "Family Background and Economic Success: A Review of the Evidence," in Paul Taubman, ed., *Kinometrics: Determinants of Socioeconomic Success within and between Families* (Amsterdam: North Holland, 1977), pp. 9–34; Jencks et al., *Who Gets Ahead?* p. 54; Jere R. Behrman, Z. Hrubec, Paul Taubman, and T. J. Wales, *Socioeconomic Success* (Amsterdam: North Holland, 1980). There are always unobserved or unmeasured variables so that the error term may include systematic effects of such things as values, ambition, and so forth. With panel data, some of these effects may be removed.

have been used to fill in the occupational history for this and other subsets of the population that could be followed in the data sources for extended periods of time. However, these later censuses of 1880 and 1900 do not contain estimates of wealth. (The census manuscripts of 1890 were burned.)

(2) Tax-assessment records have been used for an estimate of wealth for 1870, 1880, 1890, and 1900 for the households that we have been able to trace through time. The mean of tax-assessment wealth is 40 percent lower than the mean of census wealth for 1870. However, the correlation between the two sources is very high.[20] Census manuscripts and tax assessments are the basic sources for the wealth estimates in the data set.

(3) Financial records of the LDS church give the amount contributed to the church by each individual in each year. Access to these data was obtained for twelve years – 1855, 1857, 1859, 1861, 1866, 1870, 1875, 1880, 1885, 1890, 1895, and 1900. Members of the church were to contribute a tithe, or one-tenth of their income, to the church. Income estimates may be derived by assuming all paid a full tithe. Assuming contributions are a full tithe (income calculated as ten times contribution) when a partial tithe was actually paid (income more than ten times contribution) will produce biased measures of incomes, with a lower mean than that of actual incomes. Inequality measures will also be biased, but the direction of the bias will depend on the relationship of tithe paying to income. Fortunately, in eight of the twelve years, the tithing owed or the percentage of a full tithe paid was also recorded, giving better estimates of income.[21] Algorithms have been used to impute the percentage paid when it is not given by using the information for other years for that individual. Regression results reported here are not particularly sensitive to alternative procedures for estimating income.

It is important to note that tithe paying was done at the local level and was monitored by the "bishop" or local lay leader of the church.

---

[20] The correlation coefficient between census wealth and tax-assessment wealth of households for which we have both observations in 1870 is .664. The simple regression between the two is ln (census wealth) = 1.767 + .787ln (tax-assessment wealth) with an R^2 of .44.

[21] Even though the Utah data are remarkable for the nineteenth century, they present many difficulties. One of the foremost is that the tithing records from which income is measured can only be a partial coverage of Utah households. In any given year, not all Mormon households paid tithing or were listed in the records. The specification of a full tithe or the percentage of a full tithe was not always given even in the years when it was generally recorded. Consequently, coverage was partial even though the records covered the majority of Utah households in any year.

The individual making the contribution was questioned by the bishop as to the degree to which his or her contribution was a full tithe. All data on income are derived from these church records. Consequently, no empirical work on income or its distribution can be done for the non-Mormons in Utah or on Mormons who did not make contributions to the church. Since Mormons were such a dominant group in the state in the nineteenth century, it is unlikely that conclusions could be turned by differences in the behavior or outcomes for non-Mormons compared with Mormons even though the records of the church do not include as many as half of the households by the end of the century.

(4) The final source of data is the large collection of "family group sheets" found in the Genealogical Library of the LDS church. These demographic records give vital dates on three generations and allow linkages of kin. In the research reported here, the genealogical records have been used to create samples of brothers and of father–son combinations in the data set. These samples are the basis for the measurement of the effect of the family on the distributions of income and wealth.

To summarize, the data set contains the population of Utah for the censuses of 1850, 1860, and 1870. It also contains the LDS population of Utah that contributed to the church in the twelve years listed above. From these population sources, a linked sample has been created that forms a longitudinal sample of about 17,000 households.[22] The primary observations are:

1. Gross household wealth, drawn from census manuscripts and tax-assessment records.
2. Income, based on tithing paid to the LDS church. Contributions as a percentage of a full tithe were also recorded for selected years.
3. Occupation, drawn from the census and classified into a standard three-digit code, which has been further aggregated for analysis.
4. Birthplace, found on the family group sheets and in the census.
5. Vital dates of birth, marriage, and death, drawn from the family-group records.

---

[22] In general, the sample size in any two years (for example, 1875 and 1880) of the longitudinal sample cannot be used to calculate persistence rates, because we have looked for households that persisted in the various data sets for a number of years rather than finding everyone who happened to be in any two years. The persistence rates for the census files can be calculated. They are 34 percent for 1850–60 and 38 percent for 1860–70. We know that a significant percentage of individuals were missed by the census, because they were found in other records and reappeared in a later census in the same location. We are examining the extent of this problem.

157

6. Residential histories, based on observations of county and town of residence in the censuses and the church records.
7. Kinships, drawn from the family-group sheets establishing brother and father–son combinations in the longitudinal sample.

A panel of the kind described here has obvious selection biases. Households enter and leave the sample in what is likely to be a nonrandom fashion, for persisters are economically different from those who exit the economy. The most serious weaknesses of the data set include lack of income observations for non-Mormons and lack of data on educational attainment. Nevertheless, this panel is a very rich data set that can address a number of important distributional issues.

The economic structure of early Utah

Table 4.1 summarizes the economic structure of Utah households for the first two decades after settlement. Population grew rapidly, with population in 1870 nearly eight times that of 1850. Such population growth was not unusual, states as diverse as Alabama, Colorado, Iowa, and Washington having grown much faster than Utah during the initial periods of settlement. In Utah, an increasing number of households were headed by females as the population aged slightly and polygyny became more widespread.[23] Many converts to the LDS faith from Great Britain, Germany, and Scandinavia made the difficult trek to Utah in the 1850s and 1860s, increasing the households headed by the foreign-born from 27 percent in 1850 to 65 percent in 1870. Settlement in Utah began in Salt Lake, which quickly became something of a city, with a population of 12,900 by 1870 and 20,800 by 1880.[24] As land was occupied around Salt Lake City, settlements were begun in outlying regions that had some access to water. By 1870 Salt Lake County was home to only 23 percent of the households.

The occupational structure of early Utah changed in an odd way. There were proportionally more craftsmen in the primitive Utah economy of 1850 than in 1870, when exchange had become more extensive. Many of these craftsmen actually turned to farming for a living. By 1860 the percentage of male household heads who listed themselves

---

[23] Polygyny increased through time, and a polygynous wife was often listed as the head of the house with an occupation of "keeping house." Of course some of the heads of households so listed were widows. In the longitudinal sample, we have combined polygynous wives into a single household but retained a record of the multiple dwellings.

[24] Thomas G. Alexander and James B. Allen, *Mormons and Gentiles: A History of Salt Lake City* (Boulder, Colo.: Pruett, 1984), p. 87.

158

Table 4.1. *Characteristics of early Utah households*

Year	1850	1860	1870
Population[a]	11,247	39,321	85,288
Households[a]	2,713	7,750	19,137
Mean household size	4.1	5.1	4.5
Household heads			
Male	91%	90%	84%
Foreign-born	27%	56%	65%
Farmers	41.8%	48.3%	36.2%
White-collar	4.5%	4.5%	5.5%
Craftsmen	25.9%	18.2%	20.9%
Laborers	22.1%	23.5%	24.5%
Not in labor force	5.6%	5.6%	13.0%
Urban[b]	52%	29%	23%
Mean real wealth	$189	$476	$563
Mean personal wealth	NA	$439	$338
Mean total wealth	NA	$915	$901
Gini coefficients			
Real wealth	.71	.69	.77
Personal wealth	NA	.62	.75
Total wealth	NA	.62	.73

[a] Based on the census manuscripts of the current boundaries of Utah. In the nineteenth century Utah included some territory that is now in other states.
[b] Salt Lake County.
Source: Census manuscripts of Utah for 1850, 1860, 1870.

as craftsmen had fallen from 28 percent to 18 percent, though by 1870 it had risen to 25 percent. The religious motivation for much of the Utah migration may be the source of this odd pattern of occupational change. Many of the converts to the LDS religion were European craftsmen who changed to farming as they entered the less specialized Utah economy of the early years. As the economy developed and Salt Lake City grew, the demand for skilled labor grew, allowing more of the craftsmen to remain in their occupations. The white-collar segment of the population slowly increased, as did the percentage of household heads not in the labor force. Farming was always the dominant occupation in nineteenth-century Utah.

Mean nominal household wealth as reported in the census manuscripts grew quite rapidly between 1850 and 1860 but stagnated between 1860 and 1870.[25] The stagnation was caused by a decline in

---

[25] Moving from nominal values to real values is not easy for Utah because the state was not integrated economically with the rest of the nation until after the full economic

mean personal wealth in both Salt Lake County and the outlying region, accompanied by an offsetting rise in real-estate wealth in Salt Lake with no change in mean real-estate wealth outside of Salt Lake County. However, those who had arrived in 1850 or 1860 enjoyed good growth in the value of the real estate and modest gains in the value of other wealth. Consequently, it is the low wealth of migrants in each decade that gives a growing economy the appearance of low rates of wealth accumulation. Wealth-to-income ratios were low initially but rose quite rapidly.

Trends in inequality

If conditions for a natural egalitarian society ever exist, they should have existed in Utah in the nineteenth century. The migration to Utah was unusually costly because of the overland distances for travel and shipping. In a sense, Utah was beyond the normal frontier in its first two decades of settlement. It had a population of nearly 87,000 in 1870 at a time when surrounding territories were populated by a few ranchers, miners, Native Americans, and a few outlying Mormon settlements. Because of these high costs of migration and settlement, Utah started as a fairly egalitarian society, as reflected in the data of 1850. Land ownership was high, with 70 percent of household heads holding real estate compared with 18 percent in the West and 41 percent for the nation as a whole. The distribution of real wealth was relatively equal, with a relatively low Gini coefficient and with the richest 1 percent of households owning only 14 percent of the wealth in Utah but 30 percent in the United States as a whole.[26] Occupation made little difference: The wealth of white-collar households was less than twice the mean.

Moreover, Utah was a frontier society with free land and expansive economic opportunity. Turner's vision of frontier economic equality should clearly have been fulfilled in Utah. Mining, an avenue to large fortunes and immediate inequality, played a small role in Utah compared with most far-western states. Furthermore, the pervasive LDS

impact of the transcontinental railroad was achieved in the 1870s. Some work has been done on a price index for Utah before 1870 by L. Dwight Israelsen ("Economic Stabilization in a Theocracy: The Great Basin, 1847–1900," Utah State University Department of Economics Working Paper, 1981). In this essay, we have tried to avoid the price-deflator problem by using year dummies in longitudinal regressions or relying on cross-sectional regressions where appropriate. More work is planned on the real rate of growth in the Utah economy, where the first order of research is the price-index problem.

[26] Soltow, *Men and Wealth*, p. 41; Kearl et al., "Household Wealth," p. 484.

culture believed in economic equality and took some steps to promote more equality, in terms of both opportunity and results. In the early decades, the church "called" prosperous and established individuals with some entrepreneurial ability to open new areas for settlement, easing the way for new migrants by providing new land and reducing the concentration in the settled areas.[27] The church established a revolving fund to assist immigrants with their resettlement costs. In the 1870s and 1880s the church experimented with cooperatives and a few communal settlements.[28] Throughout the period, the rich and the fortunate were expected to affirm the unity of the church by helping the poor and less fortunate. Thus, conditions were ripe for perpetuation of an egalitarian society.

In spite of these forces that should have led to relative equality in Utah, there was a clear trend toward more inequality during the first two decades of settlement, as seen in Table 4.2. Most of the inequality came from enrichment of the upper tail of the distribution, where the richest 1 percent of the households doubles its share of real wealth. The Gini coefficient for real wealth rises by 12 percent, from .69 in 1860 to .77 in 1870, and by 18 percent for total wealth, from .62 to .73. This rise in wealth inequality was partially generated by an influx of poor migrants, often foreign-born, an increase in female-headed households, the settlement outside of Salt Lake County, and the re-establishment of the normal age–wealth profile.

There also appears to have been an increase in income inequality over time, though measurement problems make this result more tenuous. Measurement of income and hence income inequality raises three difficult problems. First, the church financial records do not distinguish between household heads and other contributors. Through time more young children and teenagers contributed small sums to the church. If the incomes of such children are included in the population for the calculation of income inequality, they add spurious inequality and will affect the trend, because the practice of contributions by children increased with time. A crude, and as yet the only, approach to this problem is to eliminate all annual contributions below some value such as $5 or $10.

Second, the relationship of tithing paid to a full tithe was recorded sporadically in some years and not at all in others. Consequently, one cannot develop a reliable series for all years that moves solidly from

[27] Arrington, *Great Basin Kingdom*, p. 89.
[28] See Arrington, Fox, and May, *Building the City of God*; L. Dwight Israelsen, "An Economic Analysis of the United Order," *Brigham Young University Studies* 18 (Summer 1978): 536–62.

Table 4.2. *Trends in inequality: income and wealth*

Year	Income			Real estate wealth			Total wealth		
	G	Top 5%	Top 1%	G	Top 5%	Top 1%	G	Top 5%	Top 1%
1850	—	—	—	.69	37	14	—	—	—
1855	.32	16	5	—	—	—	—	—	—
1860	.375	17	6	.69	43	22	.62	37	20
1870	—	—	—	.77	50	24	.73	46	22
1880	.44	24	8	—	—	—	—	—	—
1890	.45	23	7	—	—	—	—	—	—
1900	.50	27	8	—	—	—	—	—	—

Notes: "G" is the Gini coefficient. "Top 5%" is the percentage of total or real wealth held by the richest 5% of the households.
Source: Utah Income and Wealth Project.

contributions to income. However, one can use the relationship of tithing paid to a full tithe to gauge the error one makes in the distribution by assuming that everyone pays a full tithe. For the years where the percentage of a full tithe paid was recorded, comparisons of the distributions of tithing paid and income are possible. The relationship of these two distributions will depend on the relationship of contributions to income.[29] Tithing paid was always more unequally distributed than income in nineteenth-century Utah because there was no strong relationship between income level and the percentage of income contributed to the church.

Finally, the church records did not cover the whole population. If the non-tithe-paying population was changing in terms of its position in the income distribution, a trend in income distribution for tithe payers would be misleading. Tithe payers are a declining share of the total population as more non-Mormons and less-committed Mormons increase proportionately in the population. However, there is no evidence to indicate that the relationship of the income distribution of tithe payers to the income distribution of the population was changing over time.

All the measures point to an increase in inequality from 1850 to 1870, but the timing of the inequality increase is different for income and wealth. The Gini coefficient for the income distribution shows a marked increase in the 1850s. Tithe paying cannot be directly adjusted for income in the 1860s, but the Gini coefficient and other inequality measures for tithe paying rise modestly from 1850 to 1870. Measures of wealth inequality rise little during the 1850s but increase substantially from 1860 to 1870.

After 1870, there was little increase in the inequality of tithes paid, but there was an increase in the inequality of income (where it is possible to move from tithes paid to income). When the income Ginis of the early period (1855–61) are compared with those of the later period (1880–1900), one is left with a clear conclusion that inequality increased as settlement continued. Although the measures of economic inequality in Utah for this period have problems, together they give a fairly robust conclusion of increasing dispersion of income and wealth. Thus, in spite of the opening of a frontier and the pressure of the

---

[29] It is likely, but not certain, that the distribution of income will be more equal than the distribution of contributions. If there were no correlation between contributions as a percentage of a full tithe and income, contributions would be distributed more unequally than income because income is incorrectly measured by tithing paid. If there were a strong negative correlation between contributions as a percentage of a full tithe and the level of income, it is possible tithing paid would be distributed more equally than income.

religion for more equality, inequality grew with settlement. This trend away from the egalitarian beginning leads to consideration of the forces that promoted this increase in inequality of income and wealth.

Ricardian forces

The search for explanations of inequality begins with a search for fixities or constraints within economic life over which the individual had little or no control. Here, the constraints of age, nativity, duration in Utah, and common family background are considered. Clearly, the division of characteristics between those that are acquired by choice and those that are fixed or not amenable to choice is to some extent arbitrary. Duration in Utah could easily be considered to be a choice variable where individuals chose their entry into the Utah economy through migration. In this analysis, duration is considered to be a nonchoice variable on the premise that most early migrants to Utah jointly chose migration and conversion to the Mormon faith. It is possible that some individuals may have changed religions to pursue economic opportunities. If so, they were probably misinformed, for the economic opportunities within Utah were at best meager compared with those in other parts of the United States.

Each of these fixed characteristics can influence both the level and trend of inequality in the economy. If the distribution of a fixed attribute becomes more dispersed or the rents to the attribute increase or both, the distribution of income or wealth will become more unequal. If, on the other hand, households pursue strategies that limit the handicap of a negative attribute, the distributions of economic rewards should narrow. In short, there are two questions of interest that will be pursued here. What factors are important in determining the level or degree of inequality in an economy? Since inequality rose in Utah, what factors are important in explaining this rise in inequality? The first question is easier to answer than the second.

The constraint of age

The biological process of aging represents a fundamental constraint on households in their efforts to improve their income and wealth position. Indeed, much of the decision making of the household is a struggle to ward off the inevitable but postponable effects of aging per se. The evidence from mortality and morbidity rates as well as physical measures suggests that individuals reach their biological peak very early in life – perhaps in their twenties.[30] With life expectation at age twenty of another fifty years or more for many populations, most of one's productive life is spent slowly deteriorating biologically. It is important, from the point of view of the household, that productivity not closely follow biological capacity, for once an individual reaches a physical peak, aging has an increasingly negative effect on labor productivity, holding all other factors constant. Consequently, the typical household takes a series of measures to offset the effects of aging. Experience or learning by doing will by itself offset the aging process for a time. There are few tasks at which experience does not increase productivity. The gain in productivity from experience will more than offset the decline in physical capacity in early years, so that productivity rises. One would, however, expect diminishing marginal productivity from years of experience. Eventually, the gains from experience are not sufficient to overcome the negative effects of aging, so that earnings peak and then fall.[31] Without other actions to offset aging, such as conscious investment in human capital, the peak in earnings will come rather early.

Robert Fogel and Stanley Engerman found a peak in productivity for their cross-sectional sample of the U.S. slave population at about thirty-five years of age.[32] In our Utah sample, the male age–earnings peak, computed by controlling income for occupation, residence, nativity, duration in Utah, and wealth, was between thirty-six and forty-three years of age depending on the cross section or the specification of a longitudinal sample, the most common peak being at about forty years of age.[33] (Table 4.5, built from regressions like those

---

[30] The biological peak is probably difficult, if not impossible, to measure. Human physical performance peaks at different ages for different feats. Sprinters in track events seem to peak quite early. Marathon runners, on the other hand, are able to maintain their ability at later ages. Peaking has strong mental and psychological components. Most model life tables have the lowest mortality between ages ten and fourteen, well before physical maturity.

[31] There is a large age-profile literature in economics. For examples, see Giora Hanoch and Marjorie Honig, "'True' Age Profiles of Earnings: Adjusting for Censoring and for Period and Cohort Effects," *Review of Economics and Statistics* 67 (August 1985): 383–94; Yoram Weiss and Lee A. Lillard, "Experience, Vintage and Time Effects in the Growth of Earnings: American Scientists, 1960–1970," *Journal of Political Economy* 86 (1978): 427–43; A. F. Shorrocks, "The Age–Wealth Relationship: A Cross-Section and Cohort Analysis," *Review of Economics and Statistics* 57 (1975): 155–63.

[32] Robert W. Fogel and Stanley L. Engerman, *Time on the Cross* (Boston: Little, Brown, 1974), p. 74.

[33] Neither the cross-sectional nor the longitudinal profile of age and earnings or other economic measures is suitable for most interesting questions. The longitudinal profile

165

reported in Tables 4.3 and 4.4, summarizes the peaks in the various age profiles.) This slightly later peak, compared with that for a slave population, is to be expected, for the age–earnings and age–income profiles of the Utah sample are mixed, with more investment in human capital through more education and probably more on-the-job training than would be the case for a slave sample.

Investment in human capital through formal schooling and on-the-job training undoubtedly postpones the peak in productivity as individuals move to occupations where physical strength and hence age are less important than knowledge and experience. In Utah, the peak in earnings was one to three years later when one does not control for occupation and other choice variables. This change in the peak substantially underestimates the total effect of investment in human capital on the peaking of the age–earnings profile because of the investment in human capital that occurred prior to entry into the labor force or investment in human capital not reflected in occupational class. To sum up, heads of households in Utah were able to shift the peak in earnings or labor productivity from the age of physical maturity to about forty-two years of age through experience, more conscious investment in human capital through education and on-the-job training, and occupational change.[34]

Another factor, independent of household behavior, shifts the peak of an individual's productivity to a later age. Economic growth post-

confounds age and growth effects. The effect of age on income and earnings profiles must be disentangled from two other possible effects that are associated with time and therefore age. In any cross section of data, the effect of age will be confounded with a cohort or vintage effect. Individuals aged fifty entered the economy at a particular time with a particular vintage of education or skills, making such individuals differ from the twenty-five-year-olds of the cross section not only in age but also in vintage or cohort. Fortunately, this problem is minimized in the early Utah data because the effects of vintage and cohort are largely eliminated by the arduous and expensive migration to Utah. Since formal investment in human capital was negligible and the primitive nature of the early economy made some skills acquired through apprenticeship or on-the-job training economically irrelevant, duration in Utah is a good measure of the vintage or cohort effect. Thus, the effect of age can be measured quite well in the Utah economy. For a discussion of the vintage and growth issues, see Hanoch and Honig, "'True' Age Profiles of Earnings" and Weiss and Lillard, "Experience, Vintage and Time Effects in the Growth of Earnings." We have controlled for wealth by directly entering wealth into the income regression or, alternatively, by subtracting a return on wealth from income to estimate earnings directly. The peaks in the age profiles do not vary significantly across techniques.

[34] Modern issues of discrimination, job segmentation, and implicit contracts that could obviously affect the age profiles of earnings, income, and wealth do not arise in the Utah data. Since most of the Utah households were self-employed, the profiles should be quite accurate. Labor–leisure choices are still a part of the observed profiles.

Table 4.3. *Cross-sectional regressions on income*

Variable	1855	1861	1866	1870	1875	1880	1885	1890	1895	1900
Age	.047	.058	.078	.070	.052	.063	.049	.047	.044	.030
Age^2	−.00053	−.00067	−.00086	−.00076	−.0006	−.00070	−.00055	−.00054	−.00046	−.00033
Foreign birth	.084	−.027*	−.0071*	−.085	.065	.047	.055	.032*	.086	−.012*
Time in Utah	.024	.034	.018	.026	.030	.016	.013	.012	.0065	.00083*
White-collar	.032*	.064*	.236	.238	.319	.378	.29	.593	.56	.600
Craftsmen	.05*	−.121	.070*	−.037*	.023*	.005*	−.07*	.017*	−.086*	−.026*
Service	−.159*	−.136*	.103*	−.046*	−.012*	−.131*	−.14	.107*	.111*	−.238
Laborers	−.144	−.222	−.212	−.173	−.255	−.274	−.300	.209	−.147	−.294
Rural county	−.032*	−.057*	−.236	−.150	−.189	−.336	−.354	−.52	−.369	−.400
Constant	5.27	4.94	4.708	4.30	4.72	4.68	5.14	5.20	4.83	5.61
R^2	.05	.08	.06	.07	.10	.11	.10	.14	.09	.13
N	1,448	3,160	2,891	2,854	2,959	4,004	3,325	2,826	2,327	2,382

*Not significant at the .05 level.
Note: The control group is U.S.-born/farmers residing in Salt Lake County.
Source: Utah Income and Wealth Project.

Table 4.4. *Cross-sectional regressions for total wealth*

Variable	1860	1870	1880	1890	1900
Age	.022	.026	.050	.064	.078
Age^2	−.0002	−.0002	−.0005	−.0006	−.0007
White-collar	.617	.563	.305	.292	.076*
Craftsmen	−.326	−.160	−.228	−.126	−.430
Service	−.209	−.097*	−.069*	.020*	−.260
Laborers	−.734	−.591	−.515	−.325	−.455
Foreign birth	−.284	−.192	−.052*	.002*	−.010*
Time in Utah	.067	.033	.031	.016	.008
Rural county	−.083	−.526	−.557	−.599	−.126*
Constant	6.04	6.48	5.425	5.87	4.77
R^2	.28	.21	.25	.14	.06
N	4,005	4,014	2,609	2,609	2,209

*Not significant at the .05 level.
Notes: All regressions are OLS with ln of total wealth as the dependent variable. All counties are considered rural except Salt Lake County. The control group is native farmers residing in Salt Lake County.
Source: J. R. Kearl and C. L. Pope, "Choices, Rents and Luck: Economic Mobility of Utah Households," in Stanley Engerman and Robert Gallman, eds., *Long Term Factors in American Economic Growth* (Chicago: University of Chicago Press, 1986), p. 227.

Table 4.5. *Summary of life-cycle patterns*

	1860	1870	1880	1890	1900	Mean
1. Age peak of earnings	38	43	36	41	43	40.2
2. Age peak of earnings with occupational and residential change	39	45	39	44	44	42.2
3. Age peak in income	42	49	46	49	49	47.0
4. Age peak in wealth	53	60	56	56	60	57.0

Notes: 1. Age peak of earnings controls for all characteristics including wealth.

ln income = f(age, age squared, time in Utah, dummies for foreign birth, white-collar, craftsmen, service workers, unskilled laborers, and residence in a rural county)

2. Age peak of earnings with occupational and residential change does not control for any variables except age and wealth.

ln Y = f(age, age squared, ln wealth)

3. Age peak of income does not control for wealth.

ln Y = f(age, age squared)

4. Age peak of wealth is simply the age profile of wealth.

ln TW = f(age, age squared)

pones the peak in earnings if the increase in productivity from the growth process is greater than the decline in productivity due to aging.[35] Nevertheless, biology eventually wins in spite of the positive effects on productivity of economic growth, investment in human capital, and experience. Households anticipate the decline in productivity by accumulating wealth to generate income from sources independent of labor and therefore not subject to the age constraint. Consequently, income may well continue to rise after earnings have peaked because the decline in labor income is more than offset by the rise in income from nonhuman wealth. Eventually, there will be sufficient decline in earnings to cause total income to peak. For Utah, the peak in income came about seven years after the peak in earnings. Wealth will, of course, continue to rise until the household consumption pattern causes dissaving and a decline in wealth. Wealth for Utah households peaked about ten years after income and seventeen years after earnings. This is the common life-cycle story in economics, and it played out well in the Utah economy.[36]

To summarize, earnings, given occupational and locational decisions as well as birthplace and duration in the economy, peaked at about age forty in the cross sections. Earnings peaked about two or three years later if the control factors listed above are relaxed. Income peaked about seven years later than earnings, at about age forty-seven, reflecting the effect of wealth accumulation on income. Wealth peaks about ten years after income, suggesting that consumption was below income, allowing positive savings and wealth accumulation to continue well after the peak in income.

Clearly, the constraint of age adds to inequality in any distribution of income or wealth.[37] Does a change in the "rents" to certain ages

[35] Growth and the effect of technology on age profiles are such that many modern profiles do not have peaks before retirement, though obviously they do sometime before death (Nancy D. Ruggles and Richard Ruggles, "The Anatomy of Earnings Behavior," in Thomas Juster, ed., *The Distribution of Economic Well Being*, Studies in Income and Wealth, vol. 41 [Cambridge, Mass.: NBER, 1977], pp. 115–57).

[36] The life-cycle literature is large. For a sample including a better summary of our data, see J. R. Kearl and Clayne L. Pope, "Life Cycles in Income and Wealth," working paper, 1987; Shorrocks, "The Age–Wealth Relationship"; Thad W. Mirer, "The Wealth–Age Relationship among the Aged," *American Economic Review* 69 (1979): 435–43; James J. Heckman, "A Life Cycle Model of Earnings, Learning and Consumption," *Journal of Political Economy* 84 (1976): S14–S44; Mervyn A. King and L. D. Dicks-Mireaux, "Asset Holdings and the Life-Cycle," *Economic Journal* 92 (June 1982): 247–67.

[37] There is a series of articles in the *American Economic Review* on correcting for the effect of age on inequality, with Morton Paglin, "The Measurement and Trend of Inequality: A Basic Revision," *American Economic Review* 65 (1975): 598–609, the

change through time, thereby explaining part of the rise in inequality? After 1870, there is no clear time trend in the age profiles. However, the profile for 1860, especially the wealth profile, peaked earlier in every specification. One would expect a more mature or developed economy to afford individuals more opportunity to shift the peak in earnings, income, and wealth to later ages because of the decline in physical strength as a determinant of productivity. Such appears to have been the case in the Utah economy. Of more importance for Utah households, the migration west had distorted the wealth-accumulation profile so that older households were not able to shift their peak in income very far from the peak in earnings. Consequently, dissaving occurred earlier in age, and wealth began to decline three to seven years earlier in 1860 than it did in later profiles. The change in the age pattern and the change in the rents to various ages probably contributed slightly to the rise in inequality over time.

The constraint of nativity

The foreign-born paid higher costs to migrate and tended to migrate to Utah later than natives. At first glance, the foreign-born appear to have been quite disadvantaged economically. In 1850 their wealth in real estate was only 77 percent of that of natives. In 1860 their mean total wealth was only 75 percent of that of natives, and it had fallen to 70 percent of native wealth in 1870. These cursory statistics suggest strong disadvantages for the foreign-born. In fact, the Utah panel provides a striking picture of the success of the foreign-born over time within the Utah economy. Part of the disadvantage of the foreign-born is explained by their shorter duration in the economy. For example, as shown in Table 4.4, the foreign-born wealth deficit in 1870 of 30 percent falls to 19 percent when one controls for duration in Utah. Presumably, much of the rest of the wealth deficit of the foreign-born was accounted for by the heavy costs of migration relative to their wealth prior to migration.

Once the foreign-born were in Utah, they displayed some striking differences from natives. They tended to live in clusters within the community. They also showed a marked tendency to reside at their original point of settlement and were less likely than natives to change county of residence, controlling for wealth, age, occupation, urban or

seminal article. The issue of correcting measures of inequality for age-related inequality is normative. Age inequality could be viewed as benign or serious depending on one's value judgments.

rural residence, and duration in Utah. Since the foreign-born tended to live in enclaves sharing the same nationality, there were fewer opportunities to move and still retain the benefits of living near individuals with a similar culture. However, the foreign-born were just as likely to change occupation as natives, given age, residence, and initial occupation.

One might expect the disadvantages of lower wealth and a lower propensity to change county of residence to be translated into lower incomes for the foreign-born. Such was not the case. As shown in Table 4.3, the foreign-born had higher incomes than natives from 1870 onward when the effects of occupation, duration, residence, and age are held constant. When the dependent variable is earnings rather than income, the foreign-born had an advantage after 1860. Either the foreign-born chose to substitute work for leisure because of their wealth disadvantage or the process of conversion to the LDS church and subsequent migration selected out more able individuals from European populations than it did from the native-born. After 1880, wealth differences between the foreign-born and natives had largely disappeared, as is seen in Table 4.4. The rates of wealth accumulation for the foreign-born were substantially above those of natives (on the order of 18–20 percent in 1860–70). The foreign-born probably worked harder, and, in any case, they had higher incomes and saved more. Thus, the period from 1860 to 1900 is striking in that the foreign-born, initially disadvantaged economically, moved quite quickly to mitigate and overcome any disadvantage.[38]

The influx of the foreign-born into the Utah economy from 1850 to 1870 increased the overall level of inequality of wealth and, to a lesser extent, income. But the effects were quite quickly diluted by the ability of the foreign-born to earn high incomes and accumulate wealth more quickly than natives. Nevertheless, a significant part of the rise in inequality between 1850 and 1870 can be attributed to the dramatic change in the percentage of the population that was foreign-born.

---

[38] Our results are consistent with Barry R. Chiswick, "The Effect of Americanization on the Earnings of Foreign–Born Men," *Journal of Political Economy* 86 (October 1987): 897–921. George J. Borjas in "Assimilation Changes in Cohort Quality and the Earnings of Immigrants," *Journal of Labor Economics* 3 (October 1985): 463–89, has an alternative hypothesis resting on a secular decline in the quality of migrants. Utah migrants are selected out largely through religious affiliation throughout the nineteenth century. This religious factor may have affected the quality of migrants but is unlikely to have affected the trend in that quality except through different conversion rates in different countries or regions at different points in time.

Clayne L. Pope

The effect of duration in the Utah economy

Getting to Utah early mattered and mattered a lot. As shown in Table 4.4, each year of duration in Utah added over 3 percent to the household's wealth in 1870. This effect declined through time but was still significant in 1900. Table 4.3 suggests that the effect of duration was not limited to capital gains on wealth, for income was also positively affected by duration. If one controls for wealth in income regressions (not shown in Table 4.3), duration still adds to the income of the household. About half of the effect of duration on income is accounted for by wealth, leaving a sizable effect of duration on the earnings of Utah households.

This effect of duration on income and wealth could have worked through a variety of channels. Obviously, early arrivers had better chances of making capital gains by owning real estate that was of better quality and closer to the center of economic activity. The locational rents should have been particularly important for Utah, since transportation was very primitive during this period. Market and other information must also have mattered. What crops were suited to the arid climate? How did one conserve on the scarcest of resources – water? What had been tried and had failed? Duration was one way to accumulate human capital specific to the Utah economy. The effect of such human capital is found in both income and wealth of Utah households.

The rents to duration were an important determinant of inequality. Households similar in all respects except duration had very different wealth and income positions. Moreover, the rise in inequality between 1850 and 1870 was significantly affected by the change in duration. In 1850 no one had been in the economy very long. By 1870 the dispersion in duration had increased; many households had been in Utah over twenty years, and others were just entering the economy. This increase in the dispersion of duration increased inequality even though the rent to each year of duration declined from 1860 to 1870. Duration, an important determinant of the rise in inequality in Utah between 1850 and 1870, is likely to be an important influence on inequality in most frontier societies.[39] If duration matters, then the equalizing effect of the frontier will be short-lived.

[39] Most frontier data sets seem to indicate that duration in the economy has a strong effect on wealth – Curti, *The Making of an American Community*; Donald F. Schaefer, "A Model of Migration and Wealth Accumulation: Farmers at the Antebellum Southern Frontier," *Explorations in Economic History* 24 (April 1987): 130–57; Galenson and Pope, "Economic and Geographic Mobility on the Nineteenth Century Farming Frontier."

172

The constraint of family

One might expect the influence of the family on the distribution of income and wealth to be lessened by the frontier. Family connections might be less important. The infrastructure, especially educational facilities, that families use to pass on advantages to children was less developed on the frontier. Frontier parents probably had less wealth to bequeath to children. Yet, interestingly, the most enduring and pressing constraint for households in Utah was family background. Foreign birth proved to be a temporary barrier that had little long-term effect on the income distribution because of the quality of immigrants. Early entry into Utah gave advantage, but it was an advantage that declined with time. Family background, however, remained a strong factor in determining the wealth and income distributions throughout the nineteenth century. In some ways, family background represents the ultimate Ricardian constraint against which there is little the individual can do to mitigate the effects if he or she happens to receive a poor draw.

The effect of the family comes through a variety of mechanisms – genetics, transmission of good work values, specific knowledge, and economic position of the parent. Here, family background is anything and everything that will make children of a particular family more alike than the general population where their similarity is measured in terms of economic achievement. For Utah, and in all likelihood most samples, family background cannot be measured well by the parents' observed characteristics such as wealth and occupation. These characteristics simply do not capture most of the traits that parents transmit to their children. Consequently, indirect methods of measurement must be used.

To measure the contribution of families to income inequality (Y), one can begin with a typical specification:

$$\ln(Y_{ij}) = X_{ij}B + e_{ij},$$

where i indexes siblings (in this sample, brothers) in the jth family and j indexes families, and

$$e_{ij} = u_j + w_{ij}.$$

The term u_j is the unobserved family component of the residual, and w_{ij} is the individually specific component of the residual. X_{ij} is a vector of observed characteristics that may or may not be determined or influenced by family. For example, occupational class might be one of the variables included in X_{ij} and may be partially determined by family background. To the extent that family-related variables are included in X_{ij}, u_j will decrease in importance.[40]

It is somewhat surprising that Utah families on the American frontier in the nineteenth century accounted for a significant portion of the variance in income and wealth, just as family background accounts for a large part of the variance in economic rewards in contemporary samples.[41] Table 4.6 reports the variance accounted for by observed variables and the variance accounted for by the unobserved common family background. The procedure has been followed for brothers, both full and half, fathers and sons, and brothers where the father's characteristics are included as observed variables. (In all specifications, the dependent variable, either wealth or income, has been observed for the two family members in the same year. All variances are computed in terms of the logarithm of the variable.)

Twenty-one percent of the variance in the income of a sample of brothers is accounted for by common family background, adjusting for age and year of observation. Controlling for all observed variables including age, ethnicity, duration in Utah, urban or rural residence, and occupation reduces the effect of the unobserved family background to 17 percent of the variance in income. It should be noted that much of the variance in a single year's income will be random, owing to the transitory nature of income, and some of the variance in this sample is due to the fact that pairs of brothers may be observed in any of the twelve years in which tithing has been recorded. The variance accounted for by observed characteristics of the individual, including occupation, age, residence, place of birth, and duration in Utah, is 11 percent of the total variance. As noted above, family has some influence on these observed characteristics, since the percentage of variance due to family background fell from 21 percent to 17 percent when occupations, residence, duration, and ethnicity were added to the regression. No doubt all of these observed variables are correlated within families. Nevertheless, residual family background accounts for more of the variance (17 percent) than all of the observed characteris-

---

[40] This specification and the results that follow are discussed in more detail in J. R. Kearl and Clayne L. Pope, "Unobservable Family and Individual Contributions to the Distributions of Income and Wealth," *Journal of Labor Economics* 4 (July 1986): S48–S79.

[41] For examples of the literature on family background and economic achievement, see Taubman, ed., *Kinometrics*; Zvi Griliches, "Sibling Models and Data in Economics: Beginnings of a Survey," *Journal of Political Economy* 87 (October 1979): S37–S64; Jencks et al., *Who Gets Ahead?*; Gary Chamberlain and Zvi Griliches, "Unobservables with a Variance Components Structure: Ability, Schooling and the Economic Success of Brothers," *International Economic Review* 16 (June 1975): 422–49.

Table 4.6. *Impact of family on wealth and income*

Family relationship	Dependent variable	Observed variables	% of variance explained by observed variables	% of variance explained by common family background
All brothers	Income	Age, year dummies	5	21
	Income	All	11	17
	Wealth	Age, year dummies	15	30
	Wealth	All	22	28
Full brothers	Income	Age, year dummies	5	20
	Income	All	10	18
	Wealth	Age, year dummies	15	31
	Wealth	All	21	29
Half-brothers	Income	Age, year dummies	3	20
	Income	All	15	15
	Wealth	Age, year dummies	17	27
	Wealth	All	25	22
Fathers & sons	Income	Age, year dummies	11	18
	Income	All	15	15
	Wealth	Age, year dummies	14	22
	Wealth	All	24	18
Brothers with characteristics of father entered as explanatory variables	Income	Age, year dummies	7	17
	Income	All	15	14
	Income	All, father's	19	10
	Wealth	Age, year dummies	13	27
	Wealth	All	23	23
	Wealth	All, father's	26	19

Notes: The dependent variables are treated in log form. "All" observed variables means that age, age squared, time in Utah, dummies for foreign birth, white-collar, craftsmen, service workers, unskilled laborers, and residence in a rural county are included in an OLS regression. Then the residuals of brothers or other kin are paired and the intraclass correlation coefficient is calculated, which gives an estimate of the percentage of variance explained by the common unobserved family background. "All, father's" for the observed variables means that the "All" variables listed above are included in the regression, as are the same characteristics of the father, and that the father's income or wealth is included.

tics combined. Consequently, we are led to the conclusion that family background is a powerful and pervasive determinant of income and that variance in family background is an important source of income inequality.

When one turns to wealth, the pattern is similar. Family background accounts for 30 percent of the variance in wealth with no controls for observable characteristics other than age and year of observation. Controlling for occupation and so on reduces the effect of common family background to 28 percent. Characteristics observable in the Utah sample account for 22 percent of the variance. Thus, family background accounts for slightly more of the variance than occupation, age, duration, birthplace, and residence combined.

It is clear that family background, whatever is shared by the brothers in this sample, is an important element in the creation of inequality of both wealth and income. One could interpret the family-background coefficient in the following manner. If family background accounts for 30 percent of the variance in wealth and we find one brother who is 10 percent above the mean of the sample, we would on average find that the other brother would be 5.5 percent above the mean.[42]

What is not clear is the means of transmission of this family background. Is it primarily through genetics or through environment? Do the observable characteristics of parents play a central role? This question of transmission is a difficult one, but the Utah data provide some interesting insights into this issue. Though the Utah data do not yield precise estimates of the relative importance of environment and genetics, we have found two results that suggest that both are important means of transmission of family background.

If genetics were all that mattered in family background, the fathers and sons, after controlling for age differences, should be as similar economically as brothers. The genetic similarity (excess homozygosity) of fathers and sons is equal to the expected genetic similarity of brothers, although brothers could, in principle, share all genes (identical twins) or none (brothers with completely different draws of genes from their parents). Since, on average, fathers and sons are genetically as similar as brothers, they should be economically as similar if genetics is the sole determinant of family background. Such is not the case.

---

[42] This calculation is only illustrative. If R^2, or variance explained, is .30, then the correlation would be $.30^{\frac{1}{2}}$, or .55. If we repeatedly drew out brothers who were 10 percent above the mean wealth or income, then on average their brothers would be 5.5 percent above the mean. In fact, the simple correlation between brothers' wealth in the 1860 and 1870 censuses is .43. Evidently, control for age, duration, residence, and so forth raises the correlation.

In several different specifications, the percentage of variance in income and wealth attributable to family is lower for father–son combinations than it is for brothers. In general, the common family background accounts for 10 to 20 percent less income variance and about 20 to 50 percent less variance in wealth for fathers and sons as compared with brothers. This result is strong evidence that genetics is not the sole contributor to the economic similarity of family members. If genetics were all that mattered, fathers and sons would be as alike as brothers.[43]

In the Utah sample, about 25 percent of the brothers are only half-brothers (same fathers). (The large sample of half-brothers is due to the polygynous marriages in Utah at this time.) The percentage of variance in income explained by family background is nearly the same for half-brothers and full brothers, which suggests that environment is playing a rather large role in what we are calling family background. Leaving aside the effects of assortative mating, the expected genetic similarity (excess homozygosity) of half-brothers is 25 percent compared with 50 percent for full brothers.[44] Since the genetic component of family background should be only half as strong for half-brothers, this finding of income similarity for full brothers and half-brothers at near the same level supports a conclusion that environmental and value elements rather than genetics dominate the contribution of common family background to income.

The wealth of half-brothers is not as similar as that of full brothers. Depending on specification, the variance explained by common family background of half-brothers accounts for 75 to 86 percent of the variance explained by the family background of full brothers. Wealth of family members is linked by direct transfers as well as through genetics or environment. In the Utah plural or polygynous marriages, transfers were not equal among the children of different wives. That is, wives had some claim on the assets that they helped to create. If a

---

[43] The argument cannot be turned around easily. The finding that the incomes of fathers and sons are similar does not necessarily imply that genetics is an important factor in family background. Brothers usually share similar environments. Fathers and sons will have environments that are less similar; they grow up in different homes at different times. But there is certainly some similarity in the environments of parents and children because of the intergenerational transmission of values. Therefore, the significant contribution of family background to variance in incomes of a sample of fathers and sons could still be partially or largely due to environmental or value similarities.

[44] A portion of the polygynous marriages involved sisters married to the same man. In this case, the half-brothers would have expected excess homozygosity greater than 25 percent because of the genes shared by their mothers.

particular wife had been instrumental in creating a particular farm or business, her children were more likely to receive these assets at times of transfer. This asymmetry in the treatment of half-brothers in wealth transfers may explain why the income of half-brothers is much more alike than their wealth.

The conclusion most consistent with the evidence concerning half- and full brothers and the evidence from the father–son sample is that genetics plays a role in the transmission of family economic similarity but is by no means the full story. Indeed, the values, educational efforts, and work habits of the family appear to play the major role in the creation of similar economic conditions for family members.

Whether the primary source of family background is genetic or environmental, it is not well measured by the occupation and wealth of the parent. For a subsample of the brothers, we can observe fathers as well as the two brothers. Consequently, we can enter the fathers' characteristics as direct explanatory variables of sons' income or wealth. The characteristics of the father add little explanatory power beyond that of the son's characteristics. One can explain 23 percent of the variance in the wealth of sons by their own occupation, residence, birthplace, duration in Utah, and age. Introducing the father's same characteristics increases the explained variance to only 24 percent; adding the father's wealth to the regression raises the explained variance to 26 percent. Furthermore, the extent of variance in wealth explained by unobserved common family background only falls from 23 percent without any father's characteristics to 19 percent when all his characteristics have been added to the explanatory variables. It is clear, therefore, that families transmit their propensities for economic success or failure through channels that are largely independent of the actual economic success or failure of the parents. Since incomes of fathers and sons are more closely linked than their wealth, fathers' characteristics add more explanatory power to the income regressions. The residual effect of unobserved family background falls more in the case of income than in the case of wealth.

The details of the family economic connections should not be allowed to obscure the basic message of the analysis of the effect of family background. Even on the frontier, family background was a powerful determinant of both income and wealth. A disadvantageous background was not fatal, for there was certainly sharp intergenerational regression toward the mean in both income and wealth. However, families did exert intergenerational influence. The similarities in brothers' incomes and wealth is striking. If families were distributionally important on a frontier where much of the family wealth was dissipated in migration and families were often disrupted and broken by religious differences, families are probably important in nearly every context. Family background may well be the most formidable barrier to economic equality in every society.

The influence of the family does not appear to have changed over time in Utah. Tests of statistical differences between the family effects in early and later periods have not yet produced significant differences between the effect in early and late years, though more work is needed to be sure of this conclusion. Consequently, family background, though important as a determinant of inequality, does not appear to contribute to the rise in inequality, though, again, more work needs to be done on this issue.

Choices and their consequences

There are, of course, a variety of choices that individuals and households make that mitigate or enhance the effects of the fixed characteristics or constraints that they have been given. Given capacity for learning and natural skills, individuals choose their investments in human capital as well as their occupations.[45] Given the location of their parents, individuals choose the location of their households by considering the costs and benefits of migration. Households choose their own size and structure. These choices and others are taken to maximize lifetime consumption, given the constraints discussed above. Rents are associated with the various constraints such as age, intelligence, family background, and birthplace, while returns and costs are associated with each of the choices. Markets influence the rents associated with specific fixed characteristics only by changing the equilibrium or market value associated with that particular characteristic. However, markets, interacting with household choices, can operate quite fully to equate marginal costs and returns of choices. These choices certainly narrow the distributions of economic rewards. Certainly, the scope for choice as a mechanism to change the distributions of earnings, income, and wealth is narrowed when markets are operating efficiently, since returns and costs will equilibrate on the margin. Nevertheless, choices and their consequences are important, for they are the method by which individuals and households can change their economic positions. Here we shall consider two types of choice – occupational and residential change.

---

[45] Gary S. Becker, "Human Capital and the Personal Distribution of Income: An Analytical Approach," Woytinsky Lecture no. 1, Institute of Public Administration, Ann Arbor, Michigan, 1967.

Clayne L. Pope

Occupational choice

As one would expect in a settlement economy with rapid entry of new households, rapid expansion of the economy, and few barriers to entry, occupational change was pervasive in nineteenth-century Utah. Table 4.7 shows that about 40 percent of household heads changed their broad occupational class (farmer, white-collar, service, craftsman, or unskilled laborer) in any decade, as measured by the occupations reported in the manuscript censuses of the nineteenth century. Of course, many more individuals made less dramatic changes in occupation within occupational classes (for example, carpenter to mason). As expected in a settlement economy, much of the occupational change was toward more extensive land ownership and farming. Over half of nonfarmers reported in the 1850 census who were found in the 1860 census had shifted into farming by 1860. The shift toward farming declined dramatically after 1860. Farming was not for everyone, even in nineteenth-century Utah. By 1860 a quarter of the farmers were shifting to other occupations. Unskilled laborers generally found upward occupational mobility rather easy, with fewer than 23 percent of the unskilled remaining in that category over a census decade. However, the decade from 1860 to 1870 appears to have been hard for unskilled laborers; they found it relatively difficult to enter farming in this decade or to shift to skilled craft occupations even though Salt Lake City was growing rapidly.

Nevertheless, the process of frontier settlement appears to have opened up substantial occupational opportunities when one compares the patterns in Salt Lake City with those of more settled areas. Thernstrom found that 68 percent of Boston's unskilled and 62 percent of its semiskilled of 1880 were in the same occupational class ten years later. Indeed, on average fewer than 25 percent of blue-collar workers in various city studies reviewed by Thernstrom were able to move up the occupational ladder.[46] If one considers unskilled laborers and service workers as blue-collar workers in Utah, only 38 percent of such workers were in the same occupation in both 1860 and 1870. Much of the upward movement was into farming. If one excludes from the comparison those blue-collar workers in 1860 who moved into farming, the percentage who stayed in the blue-collar occupations over the decade rises to 70 percent. Thus, it was the movement into farming that made the frontier more open. As in Utah, Curti and his

---

[46] Stephan Thernstrom, *The Other Bostonians: Poverty and Progress in the American Metropolis, 1880–1970* (Cambridge: Harvard University Press, 1973), pp. 53, 234.

Table 4.7. *Patterns of occupational and residential change*

	1850–60	1860–70	1870–80	1850–70	1860–80	1880–1900
Number of households	937	2,933	2,168	793	1,504	1,007
Occupation						
Percentage who change occupation	42	40	37	45	43	39
Percentage of farmers shifting out of farming	18	25	25	25	27	32
Percentage of nonfarmers entering farming	54	35	33	47	41	41
Percentage of unskilled laborers who remain unskilled	16	23	15	18	13	12
Percentage of unskilled laborers who become farmers	65	49	49	58	55	64
Percentage of unskilled laborers who become craftsmen	15	13	17	20	17	9
Percentage of nonlaborers who become laborers	6	9	7	9	6	8
Residence						
Percentage who change county of residence	39	34	17	57	27	20
Percentage moving to an urban area (Salt Lake County)	7	7	5	8	3	3
Percentage moving to a rural area	37	34	9	56	45	13
Combined						
Percentage who change residence and occupation	16	15	8	25	18	8
Percentage who change residence but not occupation	23	18	7	32	21	9
Percentage who change occupation but not residence	25	24	29	20	24	30
Percentage who change neither	36	42	56	24	37	53

Source: J. R. Kearl and C. L. Pope, "Choices, Rents and Luck: Economic Mobility of Utah Households," in Stanley Engerman and Robert Gallman, eds., *Long Term Factors in American Economic Growth* (Chicago: University of Chicago Press, 1986), p. 238.

colleagues found that the unskilled of Trempealeau County generally moved into farming.[47]

The observations here are consistent with a maximizing view of occupational choice and change. Occupational change is costly; the individual must learn new skills and acquire market information. The data clearly reflect those costs. In all categories except unskilled laborer, individuals who moved into an occupation did not enjoy as high an income as those who had been in an occupation longer. In other words, time in an occupation had a positive effect on earnings, holding other characteristics constant.[48]

Those most likely to change occupations are those with the necessary abilities and the least cost in making the change.[49] Age has something of a U-shaped effect on occupational change. The young shift occupations because the higher income associated with the occupational change will be enjoyed for a longer period of time, so that the return from the occupational change is higher. The elderly may also be more likely to shift occupation as they move toward less-vigorous work. Economic success as measured by wealth reduces the probability of changing occupations, as those with higher wealth may be more successful in their current occupations and enjoying higher incomes. If income, age, and other characteristics are held constant, wealth should not and does not have an effect on occupational change, and it did not in nineteenth-century Utah. Indeed, wealth was sufficiently associated with occupational class so that its effect was not significant when initial occupation is included in the regression. Farmers and service workers were least likely to shift occupations; common laborers were most likely to change. Foreign birth had no effect on the likelihood of occupational change when age, wealth, and duration are held constant. Rural households were less likely to change their occupations. How-

---

[47] Curti, *The Making of an American Community*, pp. 198–208, 253–58. The precise extent of upward mobility on the frontier is difficult to gauge because of the shift of large numbers of the unskilled into farming. Undoubtedly this shift is a step up. But the size of the step is not always known, since farming covers a wide range of economic status. The ambiguous economic status of farming as an occupation makes wealth and wealth accumulation more useful measures of economic success on the frontier.

[48] It is, of course, possible that there were complex selection mechanisms at work so that those entering an occupation had on average lower ability than those already in the occupation. This proposition can be tested by examining the convergence in incomes as the individual who changed gained more time within the occupation. Lagged changes do not appear to have had significant effect on earnings, suggesting that the costs of occupational change were borne early.

[49] The results discussed in this paragraph are found in Tables 5.8, 5.10, 5.11, and 5.12 of Kearl and Pope, "Choices, Rents and Luck."

ever, once one controls for initial occupation so that the effect of an initial occupation of farmer is removed, rural households were more likely to change occupations. At any given time, rural counties were in earlier stages of settlement and apparently provided greater opportunities for those seeking change.

Taken as a whole, the picture of occupational change in nineteenth-century Utah is one of impressive opportunity for the households in an economy. With two households out of five making substantial changes in occupation in any decade, it is difficult to argue for substantial rigidity or class in this economy. It would be most interesting to know if this pattern holds true for most societies in the process of settlement.

The consequence of occupational change is heterogeneous and complex. Occupational change represents both expected success and response to failure. The household head's decision to change occupation is presumably made with the expectation of economic gain. Of course, those expectations are not always borne out. Certainly, if these expectations were based on the success of those already in an occupational class, those who changed were disappointed, for they rarely did as well as individuals who were in the occupation initially. But some generalizations can be made, and they illustrate patterns that are consistent with choices that narrowed the distributions as expected. With the exception of unskilled laborers, the household heads doing less well in each occupational class tended to shift to another occupational class. As they shifted occupational class, they did better and therefore narrowed the gap in wealth between them and their initial reference group. The most successful of the unskilled laborers shifted up the occupational ladder to farmers or craftsmen and improved their relative wealth position. In general, occupational change had a positive effect on income and wealth rather quickly after the initial change.[50]

Residential change

Residential change, reported in Table 4.7 and measured by movement across a county line, was common early in the settlement of Utah and declined steadily through time. Over half the households moved to another county between 1850 and 1870, whereas only 27 percent made such a change from 1860 to 1880 and 20 percent from 1880 to 1900.

---

[50] However, the changes in income were less dramatic than the changes in wealth. Many nonfarmers who changed occupation moved into farming and did not improve their incomes substantially even though they accumulated more wealth. It may be that they did not tithe on the time used to develop their farms, so that their income may be understated.

The early moves tended to be urban-to-rural moves, but by 1880 few urban households were moving to the rural counties. There were never very many moves back into the urban county of Salt Lake City even though incomes and wealth were higher there. Early in the settlement process, residence change and occupational change were quite closely associated as nonfarmers pushed out into unsettled areas and made farms. By the 1880–1900 period, the tendency for residential change to accompany occupational change had fallen to less than a third of its previous level. There was initially a strong interaction between occupational and residential change, as seen in this summary of Table 4.7.

1. As settlement progressed, more households were keeping both their occupation and county of residence the same.
2. Occupational change independent of residential change actually rose over time.
3. Residential change (both that associated with occupational change and location change with the same occupation) declined significantly as settlement proceeded.
4. Occupational change in general declined slightly through time.

The young, the poor, the natives, and the nonfarmers were more likely to move than others – not a surprising result.[51] The young, who probably incurred lower costs when moving, could enjoy returns from the change for a longer period of time. The poor also may have incurred lower costs in moving if assets were illiquid and would have been more likely to have higher income if they moved. So the cost–benefit calculation would tend to support a change of residence for the poor. Nonfarmers moved to gain access to land and farming.

The only surprising result is the lower propensity of the foreign-born to move, controlling for other characteristics. There was a noticeable clustering of the foreign-born into ethnic neighborhoods within the larger communities. Evidently, the foreign-born received some benefit in terms of utility or income from living near others who came from the same European area. This gain was sufficient to limit their residential change significantly.

Residential change was extremely costly in terms of wealth. Whereas

---

[51] The results of this paragraph are taken from Table 5.9 of Kearl and Pope, "Choices, Rents and Luck." Utah may have had more young households than some frontier areas. Bogue (*From Prairie to Corn Belt*, p. 22) indicates that most pioneers in Illinois and Iowa were married and between twenty-five and forty-five years of age. The Utah migrants of the early period had a young mean age for household heads in 1847, perhaps thirty-four or thirty-five. Curti (*The Making of an American Community*, p. 56) finds a young median age for all gainfully employed, which would include many young men who were not household heads.

occupational change quickly had a positive effect on wealth, residential change had a pronounced negative effect. Households who moved to a new county between 1860 and 1870 had a wealth trajectory that was 22 percent below the average, controlling for age, ethnicity, duration in Utah, and occupational change. To be sure, the households who changed were about 11 percent poorer, ceteris paribus, in 1860, but by 1870 they were 33 percent poorer. In view of these wealth losses, why did people move? Because they obtained very good growth in their income. Households shifting from Salt Lake County to the rural areas enjoyed income growth 37 percent above the control group – native farmers living in Salt Lake County making no changes. Over time, the effect of the residential change was reflected not only in better income but also in faster wealth accumulation.

Both occupational and residential change had a beneficial effect on the incomes of those households making those choices. Wealth was initially adversely affected by residential change. Occupational change narrowed both distributions of income and wealth. Residential change narrowed the distribution of income but probably exacerbated inequality of wealth near the time of locational change. The cost of residential change was a contributing factor in the rise of inequality between 1860 and 1870, when 34 percent of the households observed in both censuses moved across county lines. Certainly, these choices of location and occupation did little to overcome the inequality generated by the constraints of age, duration, nativity, and family discussed above. Neither occupational change nor locational change within Utah would explain much increase in income inequality. The movement out of Salt Lake County to the outlying counties would help to explain the rise in inequality in the first two decades of settlement.

Luck

Finally, after all the patterns have been squeezed from the data, luck remains a powerful element in the distributional story. In any cross section of income or wealth data, there is a large unexplained residual variance that might be associated with luck.[52] However, this unexplained cross-sectional variance is not a good indicator of the power of luck in the distribution of income or wealth because there are always unobserved variables ranging from education in the Utah data to ambition or risk attitudes in the most complete of data sets. The

---

[52] For example, Arleen Leibowitz ("Family Background and Economic Success") reviews ten studies that have fairly rich assortments of explanatory variables including family background variables. The variance explained averages about 20 percent.

influence of unobserved variables will be combined with stochastic effects in the error term of a cross-sectional regression. Data that contain family connections can be used to reduce the unexplained variance by introducing unobserved family background as an explicit factor in the explanation of the distribution. As shown above, family background was perhaps as important as any factor contributing to inequality. Furthermore, panel data can be exploited to estimate unobserved individual characteristics that are fixed through time. The Utah panel allows us to add both unobserved family effects and unobserved individual effects to the explanation and thereby reduce the unexplained variance to a reasonably accurate estimate of the effect of the truly stochastic element or luck in the distribution of income and wealth. These unobserved family and individual effects are measured through the covariances in the error structure of the equations using the observed variables to explain income or wealth.[53]

This approach implies a particular definition of luck. Here, luck is confined to serially uncorrelated events that either help or hurt the households. Anything that is serially correlated such as settling on a farm with oil underneath it will show up as a family or individual characteristic. Any random event without serial effects such as a particularly good harvest will be included in luck.

Table 4.8 reports the decomposition of the variance of income and wealth for a two-observation procedure on the brother sample described above estimated jointly for all years from 1855 to 1900.[54] For income, 39 percent of the variance in the logarithm of income remains unexplained after introducing age, age squared, duration in Utah, birthplace, urban or rural, occupation, an unobserved family background effect, and an unobserved individual effect. The observable characteristics such as age and occupation explain only 13 percent of variance of income. If education and intelligence were observed, this explained variance would undoubtedly rise and the unobserved individual and family effects would fall. The unobserved individual effect accounts for 32 percent of the total variance, and the unobserved

---

[53] Specify the statistical model as follows:

$$\ln Y_{ij} = X_{ij}B + e_{ij}$$

where $e_{ij} = u_i + v_j + w_{ijk}$, and i indexes the family j indexes the individual, and k indexes the time period. The covariance of the wealth or income of brothers is an estimate of u_i. The covariance of random error terms (w_{ijk} and $w_{ijk + 1}$) is expected to be 0. Consequently, the covariance of e_{ij} and $e_{ij + 1}$ will yield an estimate of v_j when u_i is subtracted from it.

[54] Future work will expand the number of periods beyond two, so that any serial correlation for shorter periods will not be included in the estimated individual effect.

Table 4.8. *Decomposition of variance in income and wealth*

	Income	Wealth
Variance of ln	.68	.95
Percentage of variance accounted for by the observed characteristics	13	18
Percentage of variance accounted for by an unobserved individual effect	32	8
Percentage of variance accounted for by an unobserved family effect	16	19
Stochastic variance of luck	39	55

Note: Observed characteristics are age, occupation, duration in Utah, urban or rural residence, and birthplace.
Source: J. R. Kearl and C. L. Pope, "Unobservable Family and Individual Contributions to the Distributions of Income and Wealth," *Journal of Labor Economics* 4 (July 1986): S73.

family effect accounts for 16 percent. Obviously luck (39 percent of the variance) is a powerful force in the distribution of income, accounting for three times as much of the variance as the observed characteristics. Unobserved individual characteristics are also surprisingly important, but it must be kept in mind that education, IQ, and on-the-job training are part of the unobserved individual component.

The wealth distributions had, of course, more inequality or variance than the income distributions, and less of that variance is explained, with 55 percent of the variance in the log of wealth remaining unexplained. More of the variance of wealth than of income is accounted for by the observed characteristics (18 percent for wealth vs. 13 percent for income) and unobserved family effects (19 percent for wealth vs. 16 percent for income). However, the unobserved individual effect is much less important for wealth than for income (8 percent for wealth vs. 32 percent for income). This is a striking result worthy of more exploration if other panel data sets with wealth, income, and family relationships were available.

What could account for powerful unobserved individual effects on income and much weaker effects on wealth? The omission of human capital from the measurement of wealth is probably part of the story. Human capital, here an unobserved individual and, to a degree, family effect, would have a strong positive influence on income, but would only gradually affect wealth as savings were used to accumulate physical assets. Initially, the accumulation of human capital would probably have an adverse effect on nonhuman wealth.

Another element in the story could be compensating intergenerational transfers within the family. Theorists have hypothesized that families invest in children to maximize family income but that they transfer wealth to ameliorate within-family differences.[55] If this hypothesis is true, family effects would be relatively more important for explanations of wealth differences, whereas individual effects would be more powerful determinants of income differences. The results in Table 4.8 seem to bear out that conclusion.

As yet, we have no evidence on any time trend in the stochastic element of the distributions of income and wealth. Is the frontier more or less risky than a more developed market economy? Further research is needed to establish any connection between the rise in inequality and a rise in luck within the economy.

Conclusion

The frontier retains its position in the American historical imagination not only as a place of romance and adventure, but also as one of equality, opportunity, and at least eventual prosperity. The reality of the Utah experience does not completely invalidate this conception of the frontier. Households were able to find prosperity. Households arriving before 1850 saw the value of their real estate grow rapidly. Incomes were initially high relative to wealth and grew throughout the period. Many households were able to buy land and create productive farms. Still others were able to move up the occupational ladder to better jobs with more income and wealth.

But the dream of equality on the Utah frontier proved to be ephemeral. As settlement proceeded, inequality replaced relative equality. The effects of differences in family background and individual characteristics combined with the playing out of the life cycle of productivity were too strong for whatever equalizing power the frontier possessed. Duration in the economy combined with some initial disadvantage for the foreign-born served to increase inequality as waves of foreign immigrants came to Utah. This disappearance of equality may disappoint but should not surprise. The natural forces toward inequality have proven too strong for governments of all stripes in the twentieth century. In view of the futility of these interventions, it should probably not surprise us that the frontier was insufficient to the task of producing an egalitarian society in the nineteenth century. Furthermore, any disappointment about the inequality on the frontier

[55] Gary Becker and Nigel Tomes, "Human Capital and the Rise and Fall of Families," *Journal of Labor Economics* 4 (July 1986): S1–S39.

should be offset by the enduring economic mobility and success of households on the frontier.[56] The Utah frontier increasingly became an unequal economy, but it remained an economy of substantial opportunity. Such may well be the story of other frontier settlements as well.

[56] Frontier occupational mobility can be contrasted with the mobility in more settled cities – Thernstrom, *The Other Bostonians*; Clyde Griffen and Sally Griffen, *Natives and Newcomers: The Ordering of Opportunity in Mid-Nineteenth Century Poughkeepsie* (Cambridge: Harvard University Press, 1978); Ralph Mann, "Frontier Opportunity and the New Social History," *Pacific Historical Review* 53 (November 1984): 463–91.

5

Businessmen, the raj, and the pattern of government expenditures: the British Empire, 1860–1912

Lance E. Davis and Robert A. Huttenback

Every schoolboy growing up in the 1930s knew that "the sun never sets on the British Empire"; but even in that simpler age, if he did not live between Land's End and John O'Groats, in all probability he could not provide a precise definition of "the British Empire." For those born since World War II, the whole idea of a British Empire that spanned the globe appears somewhat ludicrous – the Falkland Islands, after all, now constitute more than three-quarters of that empire's land mass; however, recent evidence aside, on the eve of World War I the British exercised at least formal hegemony over about one-quarter of all the people in the world.

In the interest of providing a common vocabulary, a short historical digression. Although the Sudan was an exception, the overseas empire can be thought to have been, like Gaul, divided into three parts: India (with a population in 1862 of 139 million and in 1912 of 322 million), the dependent colonies (population 4 million and 52 million), and the colonies with responsible government (5 million and 24 million) (see Table 5.1 and the Appendix). India was administered through the India Office; and, through the bureaucracy at home and on the subcontinent, the British government exercised almost complete political authority. The dependent colonies were administered through the Colonial Office; and though ultimate political authority rested in Whitehall, the colonial governors often took advice from a local (sometimes elected) council. The colonies with responsible government seldom looked toward London for any direction – for all intents and purposes, political authority rested entirely with the local legislative bodies. When the crown had granted responsible government (by 1914 such grants had been made to Canada, Newfoundland, the seven

---

Although the term raj usually only refers to the British in India, we use the term here to capture the political and business power elite anywhere in the empire. We apologize to the pure imperial historians, but we feel that the word has no adequate synonym.

Table 5.1. *Empire population by status*

	Population (000)							Percentages				
Year	UK	RG	DC	India	Dependent empire	Overseas empire	Total	UK	RG	DC	India	Dependent empire
1862	29,245	5,434	3,647	139,360	143,007	148,441	177,686	16.5	3.1	2.1	78.4	80.5
1867	30,409	5,961	4,319	148,674	152,993	188,954	189,363	16.1	3.1	2.3	78.5	80.8
1872	31,874	7,018	5,399	160,788	166,187	173,205	205,079	15.5	3.4	2.6	78.4	81.0
1877	33,576	7,834	6,167	177,702	183,869	191,703	225,279	14.9	3.5	2.7	78.9	81.6
1882	35,206	8,801	13,800	209,017	222,822	231,623	266,824	13.2	3.3	5.2	78.3	83.5
1887	36,598	9,795	15,342	260,741	276,083	285,878	322,476	11.3	3.0	4.8	80.9	85.6
1892	38,134	10,876	18,337	288,683	307,020	317,896	356,030	10.7	3.1	5.2	81.1	86.2
1897	39,937	12,258	25,993	292,207	318,200	330,458	370,395	10.8	3.3	7.0	78.9	85.9
1902	41,483	14,331	39,405	296,453	335,858	350,189	391,672	10.6	3.7	10.1	75.7	85.7
1907	43,737	21,877	46,258	301,795	348,043	369,930	413,667	10.6	5.3	11.2	73.0	84.1
1912	45,436	24,186	51,852	322,441	374,293	398,479	443,915	10.2	5.4	11.7	72.6	84.3

UK: United Kingdom
RG: Responsible government
DC: Dependent colonies
Dependent empire: Dependent colonies + India

Note: The Anglo-Egyptian Sudan is not included. If it were, the 1902 dependent empire figure would be increased by about 2 million, the 1907 figure by about 2.5 million, and the 1912 figure by about 3 million.

Australian colonies joined since 1902 in the Commonwealth, New Zealand, and the four South African colonies that had recently been combined into the Union of South Africa) an attempt was made to retain control of public lands, tariff policy, and foreign relations. The newly "independent" colonies, however, always acted as if they controlled both public lands and tariff policy; and the British were never able to mount a serious challenge to this de facto usurpation of power.

Critics from Vladimir Lenin to George Bernard Shaw have claimed that the British Empire was a political machine designed and built to transfer income from the mouths of third-world natives to the purses of bloated British capitalists. Other commentators, including Karl Marx and Benjamin Disraeli, were not so sure – Disraeli, after all, believed that the "colonies are a millstone around our neck" and Marx wrote that those colonies will "cost more than they will ever be worth."

Any attempt to close this debate by analyzing the "profits of empire" would have to examine at least three facets of the imperial experience: (1) the level and nature of Britain's financial ties to the empire; (2) the private returns to investment in the empire; and (3) the relationship between the empire political structure and those returns. Recent work has examined the first and second facets in some detail, and the remainder of this introduction will briefly summarize those findings. The principal focus of this essay will be on the third aspect of the British–Imperial relation: political manipulation and economic profit.

It is almost universally recognized that the structure of overseas investment (its level and its spatial and geographic composition) was the most distinguishing feature of the British economy in the late nineteenth century. The economist Joseph Schumpeter has argued that in Britain the third Kondratieff (a cycle that in the rest of the world rested on innovations in electricity and electrical equipment) was associated with "a strong increase in capital export," and that investment in "foreign and particularly colonial enterprise was the dominant feature of the period."[1] Schumpeter, in fact, concluded that the late-nineteenth-century explosion of foreign investment had played such a crucial role in British development that he thought it only fitting to christen the third long cycle that encompassed the period the "Neo-Mercantalist Kondratieff."[2]

Recent studies have provided further support for Schumpeter's conjectures. New quantitative work has shown that Britain in general, and the City of London in particular, pumped massive amounts of capital

---

[1] Joseph A. Schumpeter, *Business Cycles: A Theoretical and Statistical Analysis of the Capitalist Process*, (New York: 2 vols. McGraw-Hill, 1939), vol. 1, pp. 430–31.
[2] Ibid., vol. 1, p. 398.

into the world economy in the five decades before the outbreak of World War I. A recent estimate indicates that as late as 1900 the island nation accounted for almost three-fourths of all international capital movements.[3]

For an understanding of the political economy of empire, however, it is not the movements of capital but the movements of finance that are important. A focus on the international movements of capital raises an artificial distinction between some types of home and foreign markets. Although the capital-export figures would deny it, a firm with half its assets committed to a domestic distribution system and the other half invested in colonial suppliers was as concerned with maintaining the empire connection as a firm with all its assets invested in one of the empire's far-flung outposts. There were, in addition, problems raised by the treatment of "rolled over" investments in the capital accounts. Capital initially exported to the foreign sector and later transferred to the empire (or vice versa) or capital initially invested in one overseas industry and then shifted to another is recorded as a capital movement at the time of the initial export or investment, but the subsequent transfers or shifts never appear in those estimates. Those later reallocations may, of course, be a very important part of any study of the political economy of empire.

For such a study – a study focusing on the political-economic nexus – an examination of the financial, rather than the real, transfers, although not without problems, seems more appropriate. Thus, the measure used in this essay to estimate the direction, level, and composition of Britain's economic links to the empire is the flow of new long-term financial issues that passed through the City. Since only a part of all finance is long term, and since only a fraction of all long-term finance (albeit a very large fraction) was handled by the City of London, the flows should be viewed only as an index of British financial activity and, of course, not even as an index of real capital transfers.

Fig. 5.1 displays the long-run trends in the minimum estimates of the identified new-issues series and Fig. 5.2, the proportions of the overseas flows that were directed toward the empire.[4] The total flow

---

[3] The proportions are 80 percent for 1880, 72 for 1900, and 59 for 1914 (P. J. Buckley and B. R. Roberts, *European Direct Investment in the United States before World War I* [New York: St. Martin's, 1982], pp. 12–13).

[4] To make comparisons easier, the values cited in this summary and in the accompanying figures and tables are expressed in constant pounds of 1913. The deflator used is the overall Saurbeck–*Statist* Price Index – 1846–1938. See B. R. Mitchell, *Abstract of British Historical Statistics* (Cambridge: Cambridge University Press, 1962), pp. 474–75.

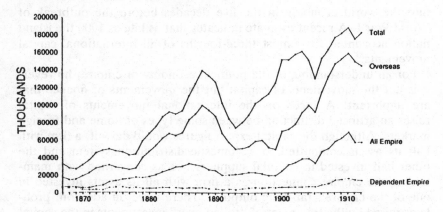

Fig. 5.1. Capital called up: five-year moving average (in 1913 pounds). *Source:* Lance E. Davis and Robert A. Huttenback, *Mammon and the Pursuit of Empire: The Political Economy of British Imperialism, 1860–1912* (Cambridge: Cambridge University Press, 1986), Table 2.1, pp. 40–41.

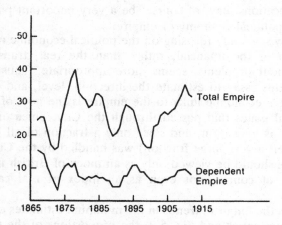

Fig. 5.2. Empire capital called up as a fraction of all overseas capital called (five-year moving average of a five-year moving average). *Source:* Davis and Huttenback, *Mammon*, p. 42.

(domestic plus foreign plus empire) averaged about £35 million a year in the late 1860s but had risen to almost £90 million in the decade between 1875 and 1884. From that latter date through 1900 the total fluctuated between £90 million and £125 million; however, soon after

194

the turn of the century the floodgates opened, and in the last prewar quinquennium the annual average was £175 million.

Some stylized facts to the contrary, the domestic economy does not appear to have been forsaken in the flight of British accumulations to the four corners of the globe. Between 1880 and 1914 more than a third of the total went to firms whose activities were almost entirely domestic; and in the decade that spanned the end of the century (1895–1904) the proportion was more than half. Over the entire five decades that preceded World War I, the domestic economy was the destination of 30 percent of the total; 45 percent was directed abroad but to parts of the world not painted red; and only one pound in four found its way to any part of the overseas empire.

Moreover, the dependent colonies and India (the so-called dependent empire), the only parts of the colonial establishment over which Britain exercised more than a modicum of political control, received only one-third of the *empire*'s share (see Fig. 5.2). That is, the colonies with responsible government were the destination for 17 percent, whereas India received but 5 percent and all of the dependent colonies less than 4 percent of the London financial total.

Even a casual analysis of the geographic distribution of the financial flows tends to further underscore the relatively minor role assigned to the dependent empire in the British financial mosaic. North America was the recipient of one-third of all overseas finance. The United States was the primary beneficiary of that transfer; Canada (and the colonies that joined together to form the Dominion) received about one-fifth, but the dependent colonies were recipients of less than 0.2 percent of the continent-wide total. South America and the Caribbean islands stood second in line at the City's gate. The southern neighbors drew about 20 percent of the overseas total; however, the dependent colonies in the region received only slightly more than one pound in every one hundred of the continent's take. Europe was the destination for 11 percent of the overseas transfers, but the claims of Gibraltar, Malta, Cyprus, and, for a few years, the Ionian islands were hardly noticeable among the panoply of issues that directed capital to every one of what are now the Common Market and the Warsaw Pact countries, Yugoslavia, Switzerland, and the Scandinavian nations. With a claim on 12 percent of the overseas total, Oceania was, on a per capita basis, the greatest beneficiary of the British financial largesse. Aside from a few pounds diverted to Fiji and Tonga, however, all of the British funds went to New Zealand or to the colonies that joined together in 1902 to form the Commonwealth of Australia.

Only in Asia and Africa does the dependent empire appear to have made a significant dent on the City's financial resources. Asia received 14 percent of the funds directed across the seas, and India and the dependent colonies drew three out of every five of those pounds. In Africa, although the picture is muddied by the changing status of the Transvaal and the Orange Free State, the dependent colonies appear to have drawn about two-fifths of the continent's 6 percent share.

Thus of the more than £350 million that were directed toward the dependent empire, Asia received 78 percent (seven-eighths went to India) and Africa, 16 percent. Government issues constituted about one-half of the Indian total, but the crown's share of paper investments in the two continents' dependent colonies was substantially less (about three pounds out of ten in Africa and two-thirds of that proportion in Asia).

Of the private sector's share in the financial flows to the continents' dependent colonies, transportation (almost all railroads) received 12 percent of the Asian and 18 of the African total. Finance (a sector that includes the financial land and development companies) drew more than 45 percent on the southern continent but only 25 on the eastern one. The agricultural and extractive sector claimed 60 percent of the private total in Asia and 25 in Africa. Given the dominant position of financial land and development companies in the African financial sector, it appears that on the two continents in question more than three-quarters of the private total went to industries whose prosperity depended on a system of well-defined and enforced property rights. The remaining few percent that was not invested in land or transport was divided among manufacturing, public utilities, and trade and services. Of that group only public utilities on the Dark Continent were important; they drew 8 percent of the private total.

In marked contrast to the dependent colonies, on the Indian subcontinent transport (railroads) received more than 70 percent of the private total, and the agricultural and extractive sector received less than one pound in eight. The remaining 15 percent was distributed almost evenly among finance, public utilities, and trade and services, although 1 percent did find its way into manufacturing.

In aggregate, overseas finance played a very important part in the British economic drama, and the role of empire finance, although clearly a supporting one, was still important enough to garner a Tony. The role of the dependent empire, the sector of the political mosaic over which Britain held total political sway, however, appears to have been not much larger than that assigned to a walk-on and was certainly no more important than that given to a juvenile lead ("Tennis, anyone?"). Still, £350 million was not a negligible figure; and if the British had been able to exploit their political monopoly, the returns on those

196

paper investments might have been high enough to bloat, or at least swell, the purses of the English and Scottish capitalists.[5]

Attempts to measure those imperial profits, however, raise a series of vexing questions. First, it is necessary to choose the appropriate standard against which a potentially exploitative profit should be judged. Empire profits cannot be examined in isolation if the purpose of the exercise is to determine if a return of 5, 50, or 500 percent is or is not exploitative. Second, in the finance literature it is usual to measure the profits earned on portfolio investments by calculating the market returns (that is, dividends plus capital gains divided by the market price of the security), but in the present context, that choice of measures raises at least as many questions as it answers. To the extent that a capital market is efficient – and no one has ever argued that the London market was not – the market price of a security will adjust to equalize the percentage returns to all securities – automobiles or zoos, domestic, foreign, or empire – in a given risk class.

Although neither solution is perfect, in this analysis empire returns are measured against those that could have been earned from investments in firms operating in the domestic and foreign sectors. The profit measure chosen is not a market rate of return but a measure of accounting profits (a firm's earnings divided by the real value of its assets). In defense of these choices it can be argued that, at minimum, few would conclude that domestic and foreign earnings were the result of imperial exploitation; and whatever problems it may have, the accounting measure does finesse the "efficient market problem."

The basic data are drawn from the records of 476 firms that operated either in the domestic or the foreign or the empire sectors – firms that did not normally operate in more than one of those regions.[6] The evidence suggests that firms in a single industry tended to have similar asset and liability structures but that there were also often significant interindustry differences in those profiles. Thus, comparisons of empire and domestic (or empire and foreign) "profits" (where profits are the accounting measure) within an industry appear to be more reliable than those among firms that are engaged in quite different economic activities (that is, firms from different industries). The results of those comparisons are displayed in Table 5.2. Ratios greater than 1 indicate that, on average and for comparable periods, profits in the

[5] For a more complete discussion of the flows of finance, see Lance E. Davis and Robert A. Huttenback, *Mammon and the Pursuit of Empire: The Political Economy of British Imperialism, 1860–1912* (Cambridge: Cambridge University Press, 1986), ch. 2.
[6] A more complete discussion of the sample and the treatment of the data can be found in Davis and Huttenback, *Mammon*, pp. 81–84.

Lance E. Davis & Robert A. Huttenback

Table 5.2. *Relative rates of return (476 firms)*

Industry	Profit ratios Empire/domestic	Empire/foreign
Commercial banks	1.00	0.87
Financial trusts	2.07	0.88
Brewing and distilling	1.00	1.34
Iron and steel	0.33	0.77
Commercial and industrial	0.72	0.60
Railroads	0.69	0.34
Shipping	0.77	0.78
Trams and omnibuses	0.58	0.76
Gas and electric companies	1.06	1.34
Waterworks	1.19	2.53
Agriculture and extractive	1.20	0.80
Financial land and development	1.15	0.68

Source: Lance E. Davis and Robert A. Huttenback, *Mammon and the Pursuit of Empire: The Political Economy of British Imperialism* (Cambridge: Cambridge University Press, 1986), calculated from Tables 3.3–3.13.

empire were higher than those in the domestic or foreign sector. Figures smaller than 1 indicate relatively lower empire profits.[7]

Two facts stand out. First, the much-maligned domestic economy does not appear to have done too badly. Although earnings in textiles and other traditional industries may not have been as high as they had been in the middle third of the nineteenth century, new industries, particularly those motivated to serve the growing consumer market, demonstrated very substantial earnings. The Maypole Dairy, Huntley and Palmers (the Reading biscuit makers), and the Aerated Bread Company all reported robust profits; and even the Metropolitan Tower Construction Company – a firm launched to build a full-size replica of the Eiffel tower in Wembley Park – proved itself at least marginally profitable until its liquor license was revoked.

Second, empire investors do not appear to have received vast exploitative profits. Returns in the goods-producing and transportation sectors were generally lower than those available at home or in the rest of the world. Financial-sector profits may have been higher than those in Britain, but they were lower than those in overseas regions that did

---

[7] For a more complete discussion, see ibid., ch. 3.

not recognize Victoria, Edward VII, or George V as their titular head of state.

The highest returns were reported by firms in the agricultural and extractive industries, but those profits were not limited to the empire – they accrued to firms in the foreign sector as well. Extractive profits were related to gold in the empire and nitrates in the foreign sector. In the empire (but not in the foreign sector) investments in local waterworks were almost as profitable as funds directed toward the agricultural and extractive industries, and gas and electric companies were only a little less rewarding than those two pacesetters. Thus, to the extent that there were exploitative profits to be earned, they were found in the land-related and public utility sectors. That result is hardly surprising given the close connections between those industries and the political process. The agricultural and extractive and the financial land and development industries depend for their very existence on an ability to enforce a well-defined set of property rights; and the extra profits accruing to waterworks and to gas and electric companies rest not only on the government charter that granted them their monopoly but also upon that government's definition of a reasonable rate of return. In the foreign sector, the local governments appear to have been but little interested in the welfare of English stockholders; and public utility profits were even lower than those earned by firms operating in the tightly regulated domestic market.

Some exploitation there may have been, but there are limits to how far the exploitation argument can be stretched. Returns in land-related industries (agriculture and extractive and financial land and development) – returns that rested on an enforceable set of property rights – were higher in the empire than they were at home, but they were lower than those earned by similar firms in the foreign sector.

Although some industries were profitable, the intraindustry comparisons suggest that, overall, empire profits were not wildly excessive if the standard of comparison is the profits available at home or in the foreign sector. Most of the rhetoric about the profitability of empire, however, has been cast in terms of "the" rate of return; and despite the problems it raises, some such estimate could prove enlightening. There are a myriad of problems raised by any such calculation, and the reader should be aware that they cannot all be solved. Two, however, seem particularly important and must at least be addressed, if not solved, before any calculation is possible. In the first place, the measure of accounting profits is not well suited for interindustry comparisons (it was, after all, designed with a very different purpose in mind). In the second place, it is not clear what set of weights should be used to average the firms into industries and the industries into "econo-

199

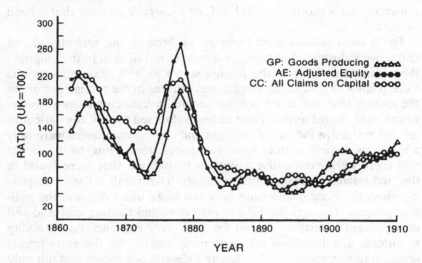

Fig. 5.3. Relative rates of return: three measures (UK = 100): empire to United Kingdom (five-year moving average). *Source:* Davis and Huttenback, *Mammon*, p. 110.

mies" – economies whose firms yield "the" rate of return. Thus, there are two caveats. These estimates are based on variations on the accounting profit measure; and in the rate-of-return calculations, each firm, no matter how large or small and no matter how important or unimportant an industry it represents, is assigned an equal weight. The reader should recognize that for at least these, if for no other, reasons the estimates are highly speculative.[8]

Fig. 5.3 displays the ratio of empire to domestic earnings for three measures of profitability. The goods-producing index is the same measure that was used for the intraindustry calculations, but it aggregates the three "manufacturing industries" – brewing and distilling, iron and steel, and commercial and industrial – into a single superindustry. The usefulness of that aggregation depends on the correctness of the assumption that the three were economically similar; the evidence indicates that the three did have similar asset and liability structures. The adjusted-equity index is produced by dividing a firm's net earnings by its total equity (capital stock plus retained earnings plus loans from owners minus loans to owners). The all-claims-on-capital index is calculated by adding other loans and bonds to the denominator and the interest payments on those instruments to the numerator of the

[8] For details on construction, see ibid., pp. 105–10.

200

adjusted-equity measure. Although none of the three measures are free of criticism, it is somewhat reassuring to note that all display a similar pattern.

Empire returns in the early years were substantially above those earned at home no matter what measure is chosen. From the early 1880s to the turn of the century, however, empire profits were lower than domestic earnings; and in the present century those empire returns may still have been lower, and they were at most only slightly higher, than domestic earnings. The relatively high returns in the early years very likely reflect the payoffs to pioneer enterprises – enterprises that moved into new markets and opened new sources of supply. It would be very useful to compare those empire profit figures with the earnings of similar pioneer enterprises in the foreign sector (American investments in the Rocky Mountain or Pacific region or Russian enterprise in the Caucasus, for example), but unfortunately these data would not support such an analysis. Still, until the early 1880s the empire appears to have been good business, although there is no evidence that the profits were associated with anything more than the transitory monopoly often attained by the first entrants in any new market.

In a similar fashion, the lower relative returns of the 1880s and 1890s are consistent with an erosion of that first-entry monopoly position as new firms entered to exploit the demonstrated profit opportunities. With few exceptions (firms with positions protected by a government monopoly charter or those that were able to convert their early-entry position to a permanent monopoly by acquiring a property right to a valuable piece of land or other resource), the British Empire was competitive. A British businessman found himself in competition not only with his peers from Glasgow, London, and Manchester but also with Americans, Frenchmen, Germans, and Russians as well as profit-oriented natives from any colony in the empire. The success of Indian merchants, not only in India, but in South Africa and the Caribbean as well, underscores the extent of the competitive threat from within the empire.

Expenditures in support of business

Thus, at least at the aggregate level, it appears that if the empire was designed to transfer income from poor to rich, it proved a relatively inefficient mechanism; however, the facts that the Kohinoor diamond is on display in the Tower of London and that a former National Basketball Association star is considered a potential candidate for the American presidency provide some evidence that, though the mechanism may have been inefficient, there may have been those who could make the empire connection work for them. Today, in a world marked by mountains of butter, bloated "Star Wars" contracts, and the SST, it is not surprising that special business interests channel millions of dollars into the political arena. There is no evidence that nineteenth-century businessmen were any less astute than their twentieth-century peers, although the lines between government and the economy were far less pervasive in that simpler age. Even in Victoria's time, however, there were government policies that affected business; and businessmen must have recognized that there were costs that, if not paid by government, devolved on the business community.

A well-designed legal system can make it possible to enforce contracts cheaply, discourage crimes against property, reduce the risks inherent in long-term projects, and in general lower the transaction costs of doing business. A government-funded army or police force reduces the need for private military forces and security services; and if the government builds railroads and highways there is less need for investment by the private sector. The East India Company, for example, had to charge the costs of both the Indian army and navy to its trading revenues; and Goldie's Royal Niger Company was forced to include not only the cost of the military and police forces but also expenditure on highways, railroads, and even the salaries of diplomats against its operating profits. It is hardly surprising that these two enterprises became early examples of "lemon socialism" when their owners successfully unloaded the "not for profit" institution on an unsuspecting public.

The empire was, however, a political structure; and, in principle at least, it should have been possible to manipulate that institution to produce a pattern of government expenditures that underwrote business-supporting services and a revenue structure that charged those costs to someone besides the British businessman. In the foreign sector British businessmen had little influence on government fiscal decisions (in fact, given the experience of British nitrate producers and British-owned public utilities in South America, it might be fair to say that they often appear to have had a negative influence); however, in the empire it might have been possible to increase the level of business support and transfer the resulting costs to the British or colonial taxpayer. To the extent that British businessmen could accomplish such an act of political legerdemain, their profits should have been higher (or their losses lower).

Business (and, more important, the owners of business) benefited from government expenditures on such traditional capital items as roads, railways, bridges, gas and water works, sewage systems, lighthouses, harbor improvements, and, in Australia, even rabbit fences. In addition, business costs were reduced by expenditures of less-traditional capital items: those on institutions that increased the productivity of labor (education, public health, immigration support), maintained and enforced property rights (police, the courts, and often a part of defense expenditures), and socialized business services that would otherwise have been performed at private expense (agricultural marketing boards and business information services, to cite two examples).

If the political structure was manipulated to favor the British businessman, then the patterns of public expenditure in the empire should have been different from those in countries that were economically similar but not under British hegemony. Although no comparison between countries or colonies can ever capture exactly the differences that are under scrutiny (any expenditure pattern reflects a governmental response to a vast number of political, economic, and natural pressures), some contrasts do seem on average reasonable. Thus, in this study the United Kingdom and the responsibly governed colonies are compared with the foreign developed sector, the dependent colonies with the foreign underdeveloped sector, and India alternately with the foreign underdeveloped sector, with the princely states, and with Siam. In addition, if there were political costs to manipulation, one would expect that manipulation would be greatest where potential gains were the highest. This study examines the expenditure patterns in the empire and compares them with those observed in "comparable" countries; and, for the forty-nine dependent colonies and protectorates, it attempts to relate levels of business-supporting expenditure in a colony to the contribution that that colony made to the welfare of British businessmen. Finally the fiscal behavior of the dependent colonies, where the British had a strong voice in policy, is compared with the behavior of the colonies with responsible government, where Whitehall had no voice.

Four expenditure categories – law and justice, public works, science and human capital, and direct business support – and their total are examined in detail.[9] Law and justice reflect the expenses incurred in maintaining property rights and enforcing contracts; public works are the real capital component of social overhead capital; science and

---

[9] In these accounting tables, individual countries, princely states, and colonies (responsibly governed and independent) have been combined using population weights. That choice (as opposed to country or colony weight) has no observable impact on the foreign developed or underdeveloped countries, and little on the dependent colonies. It does, however, *reduce* the contrast between the responsibly governed colonies and the UK or foreign developed sector.

human capital captures the nontraditional components of that infrastructure; and direct support includes administrative institutions like the departments of labor and commerce, production subsidies, and any other funds expended in support of agriculture, manufacturing, commerce, or mining.[10]

The category of science and human capital includes expenditures on education, science, medicine, charity, relief, immigration, and even religion. Total expenditures in support of business are included because a rational policy of budget manipulation might dictate one type of support in the face of one set of relative prices or incomes and a different type in a colony characterized by different economic parameters.

Economists have never been able to agree about the arguments in a politician's objective function; but, for whatever reasons, at home the British government appears to have displayed a taste for government expenditures that provided support for business (see Table 5.3). Parliament authorized no public funds for the nation's railways; but, that category of expenditure aside, British spending on the national level was, on average, about half again as high as the level observed in a typical developed country in the late nineteenth century. Even if railroads are included (some in foreign countries; none in the United Kingdom) the British figure is more than 25 percent higher than the foreign average.

That taste for government appears to have carried over to the empire – particularly to those colonies with responsible government. There, by even the most conservative measures, spending was almost five times the level of an average developed country if railroads are not included, and almost six times if they are. In the dependent colonies such expenditures averaged more than twice the levels that were observed among foreign underdeveloped countries (2.2 if railroads are included; 2.4 if they are not). The British taste for business was, however, less obvious on the Asian subcontinent. In India expenditures in support of business were about equal to those incurred in the princely states if railroads are included, but they amounted to only about 80 percent if that form of transport is excluded.

A similar (but not identical) pattern is displayed for each of the

[10] Expenditures on railroads were also clearly important, but they were sometimes government-owned, sometimes privately owned, and sometimes owned by a government–private partnership and were often, even when private, the recipients of governmental subsidies. Since the structure differed markedly from country to country, inclusion of explicit expenditures tends to distort intercountry comparisons. Still, they were important, and the general comparisons have been drawn both with and without the railroads in the public-works figures.

Table 5.3. Grand total spent for support of business (£s per capita)

	Railroads out								Railroads in							
Years	UKN	UKT	RG	DC	India	PSts	FD	FU	UKN	UKT	RG	DC	India	PSts	FD	FU
1860–64	0.18	ND	0.87	0.34	0.06	0.05	0.12	0.06	0.18	ND	1.00	0.34	0.06	0.05	0.13	0.07
1865–69	0.19	0.40	0.77	0.35	0.06	0.06	0.17	0.05	0.19	0.40	0.82	0.35	0.06	0.06	0.21	0.07
1870–74	0.23	0.74	0.86	0.36	0.07	0.06	0.13	0.05	0.23	0.74	0.98	0.38	0.08	0.06	0.15	0.08
1875–79	0.34	1.10	1.06	0.36	0.09	0.08	0.15	0.08	0.34	1.10	1.40	0.39	0.11	0.08	0.15	0.10
1880–84	0.36	1.24	1.60	0.44	0.08	0.09	0.23	0.10	0.36	1.24	2.24	0.46	0.13	0.10	0.25	0.15
1885–89	0.45	1.54	1.82	0.51	0.06	0.09	0.30	0.15	0.45	1.54	3.00	0.52	0.11	0.09	0.32	0.20
1890–94	0.42	1.61	1.60	0.60	0.05	0.10	0.30	0.13	0.42	1.61	2.46	0.63	0.07	0.10	0.35	0.17
1895–99	0.54	2.25	1.78	0.45	0.05	0.10	0.44	0.17	0.54	2.25	2.27	0.50	0.09	0.11	0.54	0.26
1900–1904	0.56	2.91	2.10	0.29	0.07	0.11	0.41	0.22	0.56	2.91	2.62	0.34	0.10	0.12	0.47	0.24
1905–1909	0.63	3.20	1.54	0.27	0.07	0.11	0.44	0.41	0.63	3.20	1.98	0.30	0.12	0.11	0.52	0.46
1910–12	0.87	3.43	1.66	0.27	0.07	0.11	0.54	0.32	0.87	3.43	2.28	0.39	0.11	0.11	0.60	0.36
Average[c]	0.42	1.78	1.42	0.39	0.07	0.09	0.29	0.16	0.42	1.78	1.90	0.42	0.09	0.09	0.33	0.19

UKN: United Kingdom national[a] PSts: Indian princely states
UKT: United Kingdom total[b]   FD: Foreign developed countries
RG: Responsible government   FU: Foreign underdeveloped countries
DC: Dependent colonies

[a] United Kingdom national excludes expenditures by local government bodies.
[b] United Kingdom total is the sum of expenditures by the national and local governments.
[c] Average of decade averages.
Source: Davis and Huttenback, Mammon, pp. 118–23 and Table 4.3.

Lance E. Davis & Robert A. Huttenback

Table 5.4. *Government expenditure: law and justice (£s per capita)*

Years	UKN	UKT	RG	DC	India	PSts	FD	FU
1860–64	0.10	ND	0.22	0.12	0.03	0.02	0.03	0.02
1865–69	0.11	0.13	0.19	0.12	0.03	0.02	0.05	0.02
1870–74	0.12	0.18	0.13	0.12	0.03	0.02	0.03	0.02
1875–79	0.15	0.23	0.19	0.11	0.03	0.02	0.02	0.03
1880–84	0.18	0.28	0.24	0.14	0.03	0.02	0.03	0.03
1885–89	0.21	0.33	0.30	0.15	0.02	0.02	0.03	0.05
1890–94	0.14	0.29	0.29	0.14	0.02	0.02	0.04	0.04
1895–99	0.13	0.30	0.32	0.11	0.02	0.03	0.05	0.04
1900–1904	0.12	0.29	0.36	0.07	0.02	0.03	0.05	0.05
1905–1909	0.11	0.30	0.27	0.06	0.03	0.03	0.05	0.07
1910–12	0.11	0.29	0.26	0.06	0.03	0.02	0.07	0.05
Average[a]	0.14	0.26	0.25	0.11	0.03	0.02	0.04	0.04

UKN: United Kingdom national   PSts: Indian princely states
UKT: United Kingdom total   FD: Foreign developed countries
RG: Responsible government   FU: Foreign underdeveloped countries
DC: Dependent colonies
[a] Average of decade averages.
Source: Davis and Huttenback, *Mammon*, Table 4.3.

individual categories of business support. The empire was, for example, marked by a relatively high level of expenditure on law and justice – expenditures that provided the set of legal institutions needed to tie a decentralized economy together (see Table 5.4). It is difficult to imagine a free-enterprise economy operating efficiently in the absence of a legal structure that defined and enforced a system of property rights. When a British businessman ventured into parts of the world not painted red, he often found it necessary to incur substantial costs in order to assure himself that the local authorities enforced what the businessman had assumed were his property rights; and there is evidence that even then he often found these payments insufficient to keep local courts and politicians from redefining those rights – sometimes in the middle of an ongoing business transaction. In the empire property rights were well defined and they were enforced; and they were enforced at society's – not the businessman's – expense.

At home the legal system cost about three and a half times as much as the system in a "typical" developed country; however, in the colonies with responsible government the expenditures on law and justice were six and a quarter times that nonempire benchmark. In Australia the ratio of colonial to United Kingdom expenditures was more than four; in New Zealand and South Africa it was almost three; and only

206

in North America (where provincial expenditures are not included in the total) was the ratio less than one. Even there, however, the level in Newfoundland was almost equal to that in the home country.

In the dependent colonies the contrast with foreign countries at a similar stage of development is less marked, but the system of British justice still cost two and three-quarters times as much – even though those "underdeveloped" nations spent almost as much on law and justice as their more developed peers. The average for the dependent colonies was pushed upward by a few colonies that spent as much as their responsibly governed brethren (the Falkland Islands, Gibraltar, and British Honduras), but those weights were more than offset by the very low expenditures in the newly acquired colonies of East and Central Africa where the army provided a partial substitute for the local police. Perhaps a better comparison is provided by the colonies in the Caribbean and West Africa – colonies that had been long a part of the empire. In those two regions per capita expenditures on law and justice fell between a tenth and a quarter of a pound per annum (twenty-five colonies reported average expenditures in that interval); and even the lower figure was higher than the figure in all but three of the twenty-five underdeveloped countries whose budgets were analyzed.

In India the British government spent half again as much on its courts and police as did the rulers of the princely states; however, that figure amounted to only three-quarters of the expenditures of a typical underdeveloped country. In fact, the Indian figure is smaller than the level observed in twenty of the twenty-five nations, including neighboring Siam – probably the best independent yardstick against which to examine the fiscal behavior of the representatives of Her Majesty's Government.

In the case of public works, the empire deviated from the British model, but that deviation is probably only a statistical aberration reflecting the allocation of duties between national and local political units (see Table 5.5). In regard to the rest of the world, the generally observed empire pattern remains largely intact. Although the treatment of railroads makes some difference, Britain (at the national level) spent no more than 40 percent of the figures observed elsewhere in the developed world.[11] Among the colonies with responsible government, however, the expenditure levels ranged from something more than

---

[11] If *local* expenditures are added to those incurred at the *national* level, a comparison with the *national only* figures for a typical developed country indicates that at all levels Britain was spending over three times as much even when railroad expenditures – Britain had none – are included.

Table 5.5. Government expenditure: public works (£s per capita)

	Railroads out								Railroads in							
	UKN	UKT	RG	DC	India	PSts	FD	FU	UKN	UKT	RG	DC	India	PSts	FD	FU
1860–64	0.03	ND	0.38	0.09	0.02	0.02	0.05	0.00	0.03	ND	0.51	0.09	0.03	0.02	0.05	0.01
1865–69	0.04	0.12	0.31	0.10	0.02	0.02	0.06	0.00	0.04	0.12	0.36	0.10	0.03	0.02	0.10	0.03
1870–74	0.06	0.25	0.46	0.11	0.03	0.02	0.05	0.01	0.06	0.25	0.57	0.13	0.04	0.02	0.07	0.04
1875–79	0.11	0.39	0.44	0.11	0.04	0.03	0.06	0.01	0.11	0.39	0.78	0.14	0.06	0.03	0.07	0.03
1880–84	0.06	0.39	0.84	0.15	0.04	0.03	0.13	0.03	0.06	0.39	1.48	0.16	0.10	0.04	0.14	0.07
1885–89	0.07	0.47	0.87	0.18	0.02	0.03	0.14	0.04	0.07	0.47	2.06	0.20	0.07	0.03	0.16	0.09
1890–94	0.05	0.47	0.66	0.26	0.02	0.04	0.14	0.03	0.05	0.47	1.52	0.30	0.05	0.05	0.18	0.07
1895–99	0.06	0.68	0.72	0.18	0.02	0.03	0.22	0.06	0.06	0.68	1.20	0.23	0.05	0.04	0.32	0.14
1900–1904	0.06	1.10	0.84	0.12	0.02	0.04	0.21	0.08	0.06	1.10	1.36	0.17	0.06	0.04	0.28	0.10
1905–1909	0.07	0.93	0.49	0.12	0.03	0.04	0.22	0.14	0.07	0.93	0.93	0.15	0.08	0.04	0.30	0.19
1910–12	0.10	0.94	0.47	0.11	0.03	0.04	0.27	0.11	0.10	0.94	1.08	0.23	0.07	0.04	0.33	0.15
Average[a]	0.06	0.56	0.59	0.14	0.03	0.03	0.14	0.04	0.06	0.06	1.08	0.17	0.06	0.03	0.18	0.08

UKN: United Kingdom national
UKT: United Kingdom total
RG: Responsible government
DC: Dependent colonies
PSts: Indian princely states
FD: Foreign developed countries
FU: Foreign underdeveloped countries
[a] Average of decade averages.
Source: Davis and Huttenback, *Mammon*, Table 4.4A.

four (railroads not included) to six times those observed in Western Europe and the United States. Although spending on public works was highest in Australia and New Zealand, even Canada spent at a rate about twice as high as the typical developed country (the figures are 1.8 with railroads out and 2.1 with railroads included) and half again as high as the level observed in the Pacific region of the United States, a young, rapidly developing region of a highly developed country.

Among the dependent colonies, despite any well-articulated policy emanating from Whitehall, expenditure levels were between two (railroads included) and three and a half times those found in independent underdeveloped countries, and they were about equal to those of the developed ones. Although the African trader John Holt ranted about the government's failure to support railroad development in the western part of the dark continent, it is clear that the failure was not universal. Some governors actively supported expansion of public works; others were less committed. In 1911, for example, the average per capita expenditure on public works in those dependent colonies was about a third of a pound (£0.33), but the standard deviation over those colonies was .20 and the range was from £0.001 to £2.63. Despite the colony-to-colony variation, among the governors, their local advisors, and the Colonial Office the dependent colonies structured their pattern of public expenditures to yield a substantial block of real capital – capital that provided a valuable and productive input into the business process.

In India, despite the near-socialist fervor for government-funded public works expressed by India Office policymakers, the contrast between empire and nonempire expenditure patterns is less marked. In 1865 Sir John Lawrence, then viceroy, wrote:

I am strongly under the opinion that the government should undertake such work [public works] itself. For social, financial, and even political reasons, I consider this to be the right course. With all its shortcomings I believe it can be shown that the Public Works Department can – and does – work cheaper than private companies.[12]

Overall, if railroads are not included, the government of India spent about as much on public works as the princes who ruled the semiindependent Indian states. Since there were few railroads in those states, however, total expenditures ·on public works in British-ruled India were about twice those prevailing in the typical state. When compared with typical underdeveloped countries, however, the Indian picture

[12] Laird Mair papers (India Office Library), NRA 11215, F90, vol. 30, no. 62, Lawrence to Wood, October 19, 1865.

appears less robust. Whether railroads are included or not, the India Office directed only three-quarters of the resources into public works that were spent by an average underdeveloped country.

For most of the empire the average relationship between empire and independent country captures fairly well the pattern that prevailed over the entire sixty-two years (that is, there is little evidence of any trend), but in India such is not the case. Lawrence and his followers did have an influence on policy. In the years from 1860 through 1884, India spent on average between 1.2 and 2.0 times as much as the princely states and between 1.5 and 2.8 times as much as the typical underdeveloped country (in each case the lower figure excludes expenditures on railroads). The threat of famine and an increasingly binding overall budgetary constraint (the product of an overly rigid tax structure), however, forced the government to alter its policies drastically. Between 1885 and 1910, per capita expenditures on public works actually declined. Over that period the government spent only 0.6 times as much as the princely states if railroads are not included, and but 1.7 times as much if they are. The comparable figures for the underdeveloped countries are 0.3 and 0.5.

Investment in human capital represents another source of potential business profits; and the now-familiar story is largely repeated – but again with a slight modification (see Table 5.6). In Britain, expenditure levels, which had originally been about on a par with other developed countries, rose much more rapidly; and over the entire period they averaged more than three and a half times those in a typical developed country.

As high as those figures were, however, they pale in comparison with the expenditure in the responsibly governed colonies. Although because of the exclusion of provincial expenditures the Canadian figure is no higher than the foreign developed average, the other colonies spent much more. With New Zealand leading the way (and the Australian colonies only a step behind), the average for all responsibly governed colonies, despite the fact that Canada was by far the largest and most of its expenditures were made by the provinces, was more than five and a half times as great as that for a typical developed country.

The dependent colonies also invested heavily in human capital. Those colonial governments spent about two and three-quarters times as much as the underdeveloped countries and about 1.8 times as much as the developed ones. Again, however, the pattern was one of wide colony-to-colony variation – an apparent reflection of the preferences of the individual governors and their advisors rather than of any coherent central policy. Although twenty-six colonies spent less than £0.05, twenty-two spent more than £0.20 (the figure for developed

Table 5.6. *Government expenditure: human capital (£s per capita)*

Years	UKN	UKT	RG	DC	India	PSts	FD	FU
1860–64	0.05	ND	0.17	0.11	0.00	0.01	0.03	0.02
1865–69	0.04	0.14	0.15	0.11	0.01	0.02	0.03	0.01
1870–74	0.05	0.29	0.16	0.11	0.01	0.02	0.03	0.01
1875–79	0.08	0.44	0.25	0.12	0.02	0.03	0.03	0.02
1880–84	0.12	0.53	0.34	0.13	0.01	0.02	0.05	0.02
1885–89	0.17	0.68	0.42	0.14	0.01	0.02	0.07	0.04
1890–94	0.23	0.80	0.39	0.15	0.01	0.02	0.07	0.03
1895–99	0.35	1.18	0.42	0.12	0.01	0.02	0.10	0.04
1900–1904	0.37	1.41	0.52	0.07	0.02	0.02	0.09	0.04
1905–1909	0.45	1.84	0.40	0.06	0.01	0.02	0.10	0.10
1910–12	0.66	2.02	0.55	0.06	0.01	0.03	0.12	0.07
Average[a]	0.22	0.89	0.33	0.11	0.01	0.02	0.06	0.04

UKN: United Kingdom national   PSts: Indian princely states
UKT: United Kingdom total   FD: Foreign developed countries
RG: Responsible government   FU: Foreign underdeveloped countries
DC: Dependent colonies
[a] Average of decade averages.
Source: Davis and Huttenback, *Mammon*, Table 4.5.

countries was £0.06 and for underdeveloped ones £0.04). The latter group – those that could be termed high rollers – included Mauritius, Malta, British Guiana, and almost all of the Caribbean islands.

Britain spent a great deal on human capital, and in the empire the colonies, both dependent and "independent," even more; but the Indian story was very different. On the subcontinent the government spent only half as much as the rulers of the princely states and less than one-quarter as much as the governments of the underdeveloped countries. Neighboring Siam, to cite an extreme example, spent eleven times as much; and, among the twenty-five underdeveloped countries included in the study, only one spent less.

It was not that the British government failed to recognize the potential productivity of such expenditures. Randolph Churchill echoed a common thought when he wrote: "Every day brings to our notice fresh objects for which public education is most desirable."[13] But there were potential political costs as well. As Hardinge notes at the close of the period:

[13] Randolph Churchill papers (Churchill College, Cambridge), NRA 13273, no. 1011, memorandum of October 1885.

Lance E. Davis & Robert A. Huttenback

Table 5.7. *Government expenditures on direct business support*
(£s per capita)

Years	UKT	RG	DC	India	PSts	FD	FU
1860–64	ND	0.13	0.05	0.00	0.00	0.02	0.02
1865–69	0.01	0.13	0.05	0.00	0.00	0.03	0.02
1870–74	0.03	0.13	0.05	0.00	0.00	0.02	0.02
1875–79	0.04	0.21	0.05	0.00	0.00	0.02	0.02
1880–84	0.04	0.22	0.05	0.00	0.02	0.03	0.02
1885–89	0.05	0.29	0.06	0.00	0.02	0.06	0.03
1890–94	0.06	0.27	0.06	0.00	0.02	0.06	0.03
1895–99	0.08	0.35	0.05	0.00	0.02	0.07	0.04
1900–1904	0.10	0.46	0.04	0.00	0.02	0.06	0.06
1905–1909	0.13	0.39	0.04	0.00	0.02	0.07	0.11
1910–12	0.18	0.41	0.04	0.00	0.02	0.09	0.10
Average[a]	0.07	0.27	0.05	0.00	0.01	0.05	0.04

UKT: United Kingdom total
RG: Responsible government
DC: Dependent colonies
PSts: Indian princely states
FD: Foreign developed countries
FU: Foreign underdeveloped countries
[a] Average of decade averages.
Source: Davis and Huttenback, *Mammon*, Table 4.6.

At present we are anxious to spend money on technical education at the same time that Gokhale and some of his followers advocate very strongly free primary education. . . . I cannot help but feel, apart from their desire of educational advantages for the people, they have at the back of their heads that education will create unrest among a class without whom they feel that no movement in the country can acquire any serious force.[14]

It is clear that, in the case of human capital, India stands in marked contrast to the usual pattern of relatively high empire expenditures; and whereas the explanation can be debated, it may reflect the government's belief that maintaining the empire was more important than business profits.

Finally, some expenditures were made directly in support of business; and although they were on average smaller than those reported in the other three categories, they were not trivial (see Table 5.7). In the United Kingdom the levels were less than half again as large as those in the rest of the developed world, but in the colonies with representative government they were almost five and a half times as large. Moreover, in New Zealand, and to a somewhat lesser extent in

[14] Crewe papers (Cambridge University Library), Hardinge to Crewe, February 9, 1911.

212

Australia, the governments appear to have discovered the benefits of such expenditures long before the residents of the mother country had become more than dimly aware of the possible advantages. In the 1860s, for example, when New Zealand was spending £0.90 per capita per year; the level in Britain was £0.01.

In the dependent colonies spending was much below that in their more autonomous cohorts; but it still averaged about 25 percent more than the level obtained in a typical underdeveloped country; and it was about equal to the per capita expenditure in a developed one. It should, however, be noted that although expenditure levels in those dependent colonies were increasing, they were rising less rapidly than in the nonempire sector; and by the end of the period the colonies were spending less than a typical underdeveloped country. Despite the evidence of flagging effort as the present century dawned, and despite the fact that there was a great deal of intercolony variation – twenty-eight spent more than £0.06 (the foreign developed average), but thirteen spent less than £0.01 (the average for the princely states) – in some colonies the governors displayed a strong probusiness orientation. Although he was likely more succinct than most, Walter Davidson, the governor of the Seychelles, was not alone when he said:

> The Agricultural Board sent in a series of unanimous resolutions asking that the surplus revenues of the colony be invested in loans to planters. They have my hearty sympathy. . . . I hold that investments locally to develop land bearing interest at 6 percent are better value than 3 percent gilt edged securities at home.[15]

If the Colonial Office felt that government should provide fiscal support to business, the same cannot be said for the India Office. In India few resources except those budgeted for transportation appear to have been committed to the direct support of any kind of commercial activity. In the early years some funds had been spent to subsidize private irrigation projects, but they were never large. In the 1880s the establishment moved briefly and tentatively into the business sector when, in an attempt to aid the development of an iron industry, the government bought the Bengal Iron Works. It was, however, a move from which Her Majesty's representative almost immediately withdrew. In the first decade of the present century, at the same time that Davidson was releasing government funds to support a local agricultural loan program, the Indian viceroy said no to a proposal to establish a government-supported agricultural bank on the subcontinent. At no

---

[15] Davidson papers (Rhode House, Oxford University), Ocean S217, Davidson to Colonial Office, November 3, 1908.

Lance E. Davis & Robert A. Huttenback

time is there evidence that either the India Office or the government of India ever spent any significant amount of money on direct business support.

The comparison of expenditures in the empire with those in the rest of the world leads to some puzzling results both for the critics who believe that the British government manipulated the colonial budgets for the benefit of Her Majesty's businessmen and for the social Darwinians who believed it did not. Clearly in both the dependent colonies and those colonies with responsible government, business-supporting expenditures were high when these colonies are compared with other countries at similar stages of development; and although the evidence is less clear in the case of India, it may have been true there as well. However, it was in the responsibly governed empire, where Britain had no voice in government policy, that the relative level of business-supporting expenditures was highest.

In the dependent colonies, although expenditure levels appear high when compared with those budgeted by independent underdeveloped countries, they were well below those observed in the regions of responsible government; and in those dependent colonies there was often some local political influence. Moreover, at first glance it appears that the highest levels were observed in colonies that must have been potentially the least productive from the point of view of the British businessman and lowest in the colonies that should have been potentially the most productive. Of the fifteen dependent colonies that spent an average of more than £0.90 per capita per year on all business-supporting activities, five were in the Caribbean, seven were other island colonies (the Falklands, St. Helena, Gibraltar, Hong Kong, Malta, Tonga, and Mauritius), and three were on the Malay Peninsula. Only in the Falklands, Hong Kong, Tonga, and the Federated Malay States did the expenditures appear to serve a foreign business community; and in the case of Tonga those businessmen came from Australia and New Zealand, not from the United Kingdom. Conversely, of the twenty colonies that spent on average less than £0.20, thirteen were in Africa – an area of alleged economic imperialism.

Finally, on the Indian subcontinent (where the voice of the British businessman should have been easily heard) the total of business-supporting expenditures was below the level observed in forty-four dependent colonies, equal to the level in one, and greater than the level in only nineteen. Moreover, whereas increasing levels of such support were observed elsewhere in the empire, the Indian level was no higher in 1912 than it had been in 1860.

To the extent that the British business community had any political influence or interest, it does not appear to have used it very effectively;

214

and it seems to have been exerted particularly ineffectively in India. The analysis of expenditure patterns cannot negate the allegation that the British warped the political process to bolster the profits of the business community, but neither does it confirm the charge. A more detailed analysis of the dependent colonies may, however, offer some additional evidence.

Political manipulation, business support, and trade

The dependent colonies provide a reasonable basis for a systematic comparison. All were subject to much the same set of political constraints, there was enough colony-to-colony variation in budgetary behavior to indicate that all did not follow an identical policy, and there is a sufficient historical record to provide the basis for a tentative analysis. This section of the essay focuses on that set of colonies in each of the census years 1871, 1881, 1891, 1901, and 1911.[16] In each of those years the colonies' expenditures on the four classes of business-supporting expenditures (and the total) for the previous decade are related to various measures of the colonies' trade with Great Britain and the rest of the world. The trade measures chosen are the total volume of trade (imports plus exports) per capita between the colonies and (1) the United Kingdom and (2) all other countries.

If British businessmen had been able to pressure the government into manipulating the colonial budgets, since there were real political costs imposed on the colony by such expenditures – even colonists don't like to pay taxes, a fact that the British had discovered in 1776 – one might expect that the levels of business-supporting expenditures would have been highest in those colonies where potential British profits were greatest. Those should have been the colonies with the strongest trade links to the mother country. Of course, if the measures of trade prove positively correlated with past business-supporting expenditures, it is not possible to tell whether trade and expenditures were both correlated with income or whether the potential for trade induced the government to coerce the local citizens into underwriting more business-supporting activities. If, however, they are unrelated, one might conclude that the policy of manipulation for profits did not

---

[16] There were forty-eight colonies in 1911, forty-one in 1901, thirty-one in 1891 and 1881, and twenty-eight in 1871. There are, however, no trade data for Hong Kong, Gibraltar, and Cyprus; and those colonies were eliminated. In addition the Falkland Islands pursued a very idiosyncratic expenditure policy and was also marked by very high levels of per capita trade (in 1871, for example, per capita trade was twice that of the next colony and four times that of the third). The Falklands were therefore also excluded.

exist or, if it did, was hopelessly ineffective. On the other hand, if expenditures are related to British trade but not to trade with other countries, then there is some evidence that the policy did exist and that it was at least partially effective.

We do not report the results, but initial experiments showed that if total (not per capita) trade is taken as the dependent variable, there is no evidence of any significant relationship between trade with Britain, with other countries, or with all countries and any class of per capita expenditures on business-supporting activities.[17] In fact, the coefficient on the expenditure variable has the wrong sign almost as often as it has the predicted one.[18]

If, however, attention is directed at a measure of per capita trade – it can be argued that if political costs are measured in terms of per capita expenditures, then potential revenues should be measured in terms of per capita trade – a somewhat different pattern emerges. These results are shown in Table 5.8. In every year the coefficients have the expected sign, and over time measures of both British and all other trade become increasingly more significant. Although the coefficients on "Other" tend to be larger than on British trade, it is the latter that appear to be the more significant. One caveat: Even with this specification (that is, a regression with per capita foreign trade as the dependent variable and the past-decades accumulated business-supporting expenditures as the independent one) the model contributes only a relatively small part to the explanation of colony-to-colony differences. Between 1871 and 1911 the F statistics rise steadily from 0.97 to 1.52 to 3.07 to 10.48 and to 11.87, but the associated adjusted r^2's are .00, .02, .07, .21, and .21.

In the first year (1871), although the signs are correct, significance levels on the models predicting both British and other trade are low. The pattern is still much the same ten years later, but at that date there appears to have been a somewhat stronger relationship between trade with Britain and past business-supporting expenditures. By 1891 the relationship appears clear; the coefficient is significant at almost the 10 percent level. By 1901 the significance level has reached 3 percent, and in 1911 the t value on the expenditure value is 3.45. At that time the

---

[17] Since the colonies included in the study are an almost complete enumeration of Britain's dependent colonies, it is not clear what significance means, but the measures are included for the benefit of those who like such things.

[18] In the case of total expenditures for business-supporting activities, for example, for both Great Britain and for other countries, the coefficient (never significant at more than the 30 percent level) is positive three times and negative twice. Clearly the most sensible interpretation is that there was no relationship between total trade and the measures of per capita expenditures.

Table 5.8. *Regression results: dependent colonies (per capita trade*
$= \alpha + \beta$ *[sum of ten years' expenditures in total support of business])*

Decade ending	N	Trade with Great Britain			Other trade		
		β	F	r^2	β	F	r^2
1871	26	.282 (0.99)	0.97	−.001	.855 (1.34)	1.06	.002
1881	28	.455 (1.24)	1.52	.019	.986 (0.87)	0.75	−.009
1891	27	.880 (1.75)	3.07	.074	.998 (1.30)	1.68	.026
1901	36	.357 (3.24)	10.48	.213	.347 (0.78)	0.61	−.011
1911	42	.288 (3.45)	11.87	.210	.703 (1.76)	3.09	.046

Note: Hong Kong, Gibraltar, Cyprus, and the Falkland Islands are not included. Numbers in parentheses are *t* values.
Source: Expenditure figures are from Davis and Huttenback, *Mammon*, ch. 4. The original data are drawn from the annual reports of the colonial governors to the Colonial Office. The trade figures are from the Colonial Office's triannual reports *Statistical Tables for the Colonies* (CO 442, appropriate years).

size of the coefficient implies that a £1 per capita increase in business-supporting activities is associated with a £29 increase in per capita trade with Great Britain. One obvious interpretation of these trends suggests that whereas British businessmen may have been slow to get under way, by the turn of the century they had begun to manipulate colonial budgets to their benefit.

On closer inspection, however, the saga of British manipulation does not appear to capture the entire picture. In the first place, progress toward effective manipulation does not seem to have affected all parts of the empire equally. If the three Mediterranean colonies (Gibraltar, Malta, and Cyprus) are excluded (there are no trade data for two), the remainder of the dependent colonies can be divided into three groups: (1) Asia and the Pacific, (2) Africa, and (3) the Caribbean and South America.

When, in 1891, there is some substantial evidence of possible manipulative behavior in the empire aggregate analysis, there is no such evidence in Asia and Africa – all the action is in the Caribbean. The relationship between business-supporting expenditures and trade in the other half of the empire is little different from what it had been a decade earlier. By the turn of the century, however, both Africa and

217

the Caribbean show a significant degree of association; but the relationship is absent in the Asia–Pacific colonies; nor is there any more evidence in the case of those eastern colonies a decade later. Manipulation may have occurred in the Caribbean and African theaters, but there is no evidence of such activity west of the international date line. It should be noted, however, that almost three-fifths of the African colonies' trade was with the United Kingdom, about a third of the trade of the colonies in the Caribbean but less than a fifth of the exports and imports of the colonies on the Pacific rim.

In the second place, it is clear that political manipulation does not tell the whole story; other factors appear to have been at work as well. Although there was a growing relationship between expenditures and British trade, there is also evidence of a growing relationship between those same expenditures and trade to other countries. By 1911 the regression of business-supporting expenditures on per capita trade to other countries displays a coefficient on the expenditures variable that is not only substantially larger than the one on the British trade regression, but, more important, the coefficient for the first time is significant at the 10 percent level. Moreover, in a pattern that is reminiscent of the British case, a regional breakdown shows no particular relationship in the Pacific or African region (in the former case there is no difference between the other trade and the British trade regressions), but it indicates a strong relationship in the Caribbean region. In fact, in that year not only is the region's coefficient larger for other than for British trade, but so is the *t* statistic.

The pattern may suggest nothing but a general relationship between both trade and expenditures and economic development. On the other hand, to the extent that the British trade regressions suggest manipulation, the observed pattern may indicate that local businessmen, observing the success of the British manipulations, discovered that two could play the game. That is, the traders, merchants, and manufacturers in Trinidad and Bulawayo came to recognize that the same set of expenditures can support all, not just British, trade.

As appealing as that alternative hypothetical scenario may be, the ability to employ it usefully to help explain events in the late nineteenth and early twentieth centuries rests on one crucial assumption: that British-owned businesses in the empire were at most only indirectly affected by foreign trade. (In this context "foreign" refers not only to trade with foreign countries but also to trade with other parts of the empire.) Certainly the profits accruing to a railroad or to a gas and light company might well increase if an expansion in such trade led to an increase in demand for the services of the British-owned public utility, but the effect is indirect. If, on the other hand, British-owned

218

empire businesses were as heavily involved with "foreign" as they were with domestic colonial and with British trade, then their owners would have been interested in providing taxpayer-funded fiscal support for all arteries of commerce. If such were the case, an observed positive correlation between business-supporting expenditures and *any* measure of trade would provide equally compelling support for the original hypothesis of political manipulation.

The evidence, however, indicates that British Empire investment was much more likely to be directed toward businesses whose activities were focused either in the local colonial economy or in the nexus between the local and the British economy. Most of the empire industries in which Britons invested their resources (commercial banking, financial land and development companies, railroads, trams and omnibuses, gas and electric companies, mines, waterworks, and agricultural enterprises) were location-specific; and although they might have benefited indirectly from foreign commerce, it is all but impossible to measure those gains. For one class of empire firms – firms that the directors of the London stock exchange classified as "commercial and industrial" (a classification that included most manufacturing, services, and trade) – it is possible to determine with considerable accuracy each firm's major geographic focus and to distinguish among those firms that were primarily involved in the local colonial economy, those that directed their attention toward Anglo-colonial trade, and those that manufactured for, serviced, or traded with markets that were located in another part of the empire or in some foreign country. The firms listed on the exchange were, of course, almost entirely British-owned. Recent work indicates that about nine out of ten stockholders resided in England, Scotland, Ireland, or Wales, with the remaining 10 percent distributed between foreigners and colonial residents in a ratio of about one to four.[19]

Table 5.9 classifies the 118 *empire* commercial and industrial firms that were listed on the exchange in 1905 into those three categories – categories based on the primary geographic base of their business. The domestic firms served the local colonial market, those in the UK and those classified as "UK plus domestic" earned their profits by some mix of local business and trade with the home country, and those grouped as "others" found at least part of their opportunities spread over the rest of the world.

It should be noted that the most generous definition of "other" was employed to maximize the potential role of the British investor in those "foreign" trading patterns. Thus, because of the proximity to the

[19] See Davis and Huttenback, *Mammon*, ch. 7 and particularly Table 7.5.

Table 5.9. *Principal trading partners of 118 empire commercial and industrial firms listed on the London stock exchange in 1905 (percentage of total)*

Colony	Principal trading partners			
	Domestic	UK and (UK + domestic)	Other[a]	Total
Responsible government				
Australia & New Zealand	11.0	17.8	2.5	31.4
Canada	6.8	0.8	7.6	15.3
South Africa	10.2	7.6	0.8	18.6
Total responsible government	28.0	26.3	11.0	65.3
Dependent colonies				
Asia	0.0	1.7	1.7	3.4
Africa	10.2	5.9	0.8	16.9
Europe	0.0	0.8	0.0	0.8
North America	0.0	0.8	0.0	0.8
South America & Caribbean	0.0	0.8	2.5	3.4
Total dependent colonies	10.2	10.2	5.1	25.4
India	3.4	4.2	0.0	7.6
Empire, general	0.0	0.8	0.8	1.7
All-empire total	41.6	41.5	16.9	100.0

[a] Includes domestic + UK + foreign, domestic + UK + empire, and domestic + UK + foreign + empire. There are no examples of firms in a colony dealing exclusively with the foreign sector or with the foreign + empire sector.
Source: London Stock Exchange, *Stock Exchange Annual Yearbook*, 1905.

U.S. market, all Canadian manufacturing, processing, and extractive firms have been classified as "other" unless there was an explicit note to the effect that the firm traded only with Great Britain. To a similar end, firms that were obviously British but that listed a colonial city among their overseas branches were classified both as "UK" and as "Other." That treatment was, for example, afforded the London publishing firm of Cassell and Company Ltd. – a firm with branches in New York, Paris, and Melbourne. There were no examples of firms that dealt solely with foreign countries or solely with other colonies (that is, had no local business) and only one (the South African and Australasian Supply and Cold Storage Company) that, in addition to its local business, traded only with other parts of the overseas empire and not with the mother country.

Table 5.10. *Regression results: colonies with responsible government*

Decade ending	N	Trade with Great Britain			Trade with rest of the world		
		β	F	r^2	β	F	r^2
1871	11	.270	9.28	.453	.370	8.24	.420
		(3.05)			(2.87)		
1881	11	.367	22.88	.686	.525	6.24	.344
		(4.78)			(2.50)		
1891	12	.246	10.80	.471	.513	108.47	.907
		(3.29)			(10.41)		
1901	12	.266	7.70	.379	.224	13.59	.534
		(2.78)			(3.69)		

Note: Numbers in parentheses are *t* values.
Source: See Table 5.8.

More than two out of five of the exchange-listed and predominantly British-owned firms serviced the local colonial economies, and a similar number devoted at least a part of their resources to trading with the United Kingdom. Only one in six, however, conducted any business with other empire members or with political units that were not a part of that august body. Moreover, of that relatively small total, three in five were either Canadian or were engaged in extracting and marketing asphalt in Trinidad. It appears that ownership followed the flag even if trade sometimes did not.

An examination of the behavior of the responsibly governed colonies provides some additional information but unfortunately does not settle the question. There were, of course, far fewer such colonies; and any interpretations of the data should be made with that fact in mind. There were, however, eleven colonies with responsible government in 1871 and 1881 and twelve in 1891 and 1901 (by 1911 consolidation had reduced the number to five). Thus, for the first four decades at least, there is a body of evidence, although perhaps a smaller body than one might like (see Table 5.10).

In the case of those colonies that set their own political agendas, there is no lack of association between the expenditures in support of business and various measures of per capita trade – both with Britain and with the rest of the world. In fact the association is so strong in all years and for all measures that there is no way to deny the possibility that all that is captured by the model is the joint relations between both expenditures and trade and economic development. In no year, for example, is the F statistic on the regression less than 6.24 (probability .03), nor the adjusted r^2 less than .34 (see Table 5.10).

On the other hand, the regressions do appear to provide some clues. Over time there is little change in the relationship between the expenditures in support of business incurred over the previous decade and the measure of per capita trade with Great Britain. The t value on the measure of aggregate expenditure, for example, rises from 3.05 in 1871 to 4.78 in 1881 but then declines to 3.29 in 1891 and to 2.78 in 1901. In the case of trade with the rest of the world, however, there is some suggestion of a continuing movement toward a stronger relationship. In both 1871 and 1881 the relationship between expenditures and other trade is weaker than that between expenditures and British trade. In 1891 and 1901, however, the reverse is true.

The cross-sectional studies of both the dependent and the "independent" colonies, then, offer a possible alternative to the scenario of expenditure manipulation. Although it is possible that the observed regularities may reflect nothing but either a collinearity between development, expenditures, and trade or the consequences of the "villainous" behavior of British businessmen, a third scenario – one that is consistent with the earlier observations on empire and nonempire expenditures – seems more consistent with the evidence. Expenditures may well have been manipulated, but who were the manipulators and who were the beneficiaries of those manipulations? Although the evidence is still not sufficient to confirm the argument, local colonial businessmen could have played the role attributed by Lenin and Shaw to the rapacious capitalists in the home country. Consider the following scenario: Trade was important to the local businessmen; and they recognized that their profits could be increased if some of the costs of doing business were transferred to society (either theirs or British) at large. In the early stages of development it was the merchants with ties to the mother country who enjoyed the greatest political influence – they were, after all, usually the first merchants on the scene. As time passed, other trade networks began to develop, and a second group of businessmen gained political influence. Such ex-empire developments were more rapid in the colonies of white settlement, but by the turn of the century non-British trade was becoming important (and its practitioners politically influential) in the dependent colonies as well, especially in the Caribbean, where the United States was a rapidly expanding alternative market. In short, all businessmen were becoming equally influential in the local governmental councils; and the colonial governments responded to the concerns of all businessmen, not just the subset who dealt with Britain.

Conclusions and speculations

Anyone who has read Ed McBain or Erle Stanley Gardner or who has stared at the tube while "The Streets of San Francisco" or "Hill Street Blues" unfolded on the screen knows that the key to a successful criminal prosecution is MOM – the police and the prosecuting attorney must show motive, opportunity, and means. The historian faces the same task, although the evidence on which he depends may be somewhat different from that gathered by Hamilton Burger or Mike Stone. In this instance, if the Lenin–Shaw indictment is to be substantiated, it is necessary to convict the British business community of deliberate political manipulation for profit, and to prove that British politicians and bureaucrats were, at minimum, accessories before the fact.

Certainly there was sufficient motive. British business did invest in the empire. On the question of whether the owners and managers of imperial firms recognized that their profits would be enhanced if they could induce the Colonial and India offices to shoulder some of the costs of doing business, the evidence is overwhelming. The West African trader John Holt, for example, irritated with the slow progress of government-financed railroad development in the region of his primary economic interest, in 1902 ranted against "those vampires of our colonies who are in Downing Street."[20] Nor was his the only voice. The business community, speaking through local and national chambers of commerce, continually berated the government for not spending enough to develop the empire's commercial infrastructure. As early as 1877 (almost a decade before Upper Burma was formally annexed to the empire) the Associated Chambers of Commerce had urged the completion of a "land route for commerce between Rangoon . . . [and] the southwest frontier of China"; and twenty years later, urged on by the local chambers in Manchester and London, the delegates had anticipated Holt's call for speedier construction of railroads in West Africa. In that instance, however, the association's goals were not as limited as those of the African trader. The interests of its members were not restricted to West Africa, and the chambers demanded that the government finance a railroad in Uganda as well.[21]

Motive, yes; but opportunity is more difficult to prove. The evidence, however, although far from conclusive, suggests that opportun-

---

[20] John Holt and Company papers (Rhodes House, Oxford), NRA 19042, Ms.Afr. s.1525, December 18, 1902.
[21] Minutes of the meeting, Associated Chambers of Commerce of the United Kingdom, February 21, 1877, and June 12, 1896.

Lance E. Davis & Robert A. Huttenback

ity *may* have been present. Laissez-faire was the state religion; and most government bureaucrats were recruited from a social class that looked down on commerce as not altogether respectable. Perhaps for these reasons, or perhaps for others, the government often did resist the business community's attempts to exploit the political process.

In India, for example, as early as 1865 Sir John Lawrence, then viceroy, argued that the government, rather than private enterprise, should be charged with railway construction because "I consider that with all precaution, private companies by the pressure they can bring to bear on government, both at home and in India, will force us into an arrangement and engagement injurious to the state and the people."[22] In a similar vein, although it ultimately acceded to political reality, the entire Indian establishment fought long and hard to retain the Indian cotton duties; and in the final analysis the viceroy in India and the ministers in Whitehall surrendered only when it became obvious that the government would fall if those duties were not repealed.[23]

---

[22] Laird Mair papers (India Office Library), NRA 11215, F90, vol. 30, no. 62, Lawrence to Wood, October 19, 1865.

[23] Lytton papers (India Office Library), E218/517/1, Gathorn Hardy to Lytton, February 23, 1879; Hardinge of Penhurst papers (Kent County Record Office, Maidstone), V927/Vcs, no. 291, Hardinge to Chirol, February 16, 1911. The Indian cotton duties (tariffs on imported cotton cloth – at the time almost all produced in Great Britain) were originally levied as a revenue measure at 10 percent in the early 1860s. Although this figure was reduced in 1864 and again in 1875, the Midlands textile interests remained outraged. Morley wrote Lytton in 1876: "At this moment . . . not a seat in Lancashire can beget a man who did not go for total and immediate repeal of the import duty on cotton." At a time when the government majority was fifty-two and the Lancashire and Yorkshire seats totaled seventy-one, Gathorn-Hardy wrote Lytton in a similar vein: "A great deputation from Lancashire on the cotton duties has just left me and they are backed by a formidable force. The question occupies the minds of manufacturers and operatives and the import duties are looked upon as the main cause of their distress. The subject may materially influence the Lancashire elections at present so much in our favour." Increasingly alarmed, Gathorn-Hardy again wrote the viceroy: "I continue to be picked upon about the cotton duties. Mr. Chancellor of the Exchequer has just sent over four Lancashire letters which speak of the loss of fourteen seats as inevitable unless remission is commenced." Lytton Papers (India Office Library), E.218/S17/1, no. 201(a), Morley to Lytton, April 20, 1876; E.218/S16/4, no. 8, Gathorn-Hardy to Lytton, February 4, 1879; E.218/S16/4, no. 14, Gathorn-Hardy to Lytton, February 23, 1879.

"Responding to the determination of the chambers, the manufacturers, and the Lancashire members, the House of Commons denounced the Indian duties on cotton as protective and demanded their abolition. Succumbing to the pressure, the government of India removed the duty on the coarser grades of cotton (the most common import) and later abolished virtually all tariffs. As has been previously noted, revenue

In the case of foreign, as opposed to empire, trade, the political establishment was even more obdurate. Nowhere is the official position more clearly enunciated than in Sir Robert Morier's response to the Earl of Rosebery, then Secretary of State for Foreign Affairs. Morier wrote, "No rule has been more absolutely insisted upon in the dealing of Her Majesty's Missions abroad than this one, that, unless there is a denial of justice or treatment of British subjects engaged in mercantile transactions contrary to Treaties or the spirit of Treaties, no assistance shall be rendered to further private interests."[24] A careful review of the government's behavior indicates that, with very few exceptions, de jure and de facto policy were nearly identical. Or, as an unidentified Treasury official phrased it: "It is My Lord's conviction that it is unsound commercial policy to seek to assist British enterprise in its struggle with foreign rivals out of the pocket of the general taxpayer."[25]

Perhaps, however, the establishment protested too much. In those parts of the world not formally attached to the empire, the evidence is clear. There were at most only a handful of examples of overt interference for purely commercial gain in the half-century before World War I. Yet in the case of the empire, and particularly India, there were more than a few. The political turmoil surrounding both the cotton duties and the Indian Factory Acts elicited a response in parliament. Furthermore, there is evidence that early in the present century the Indian government moved to protect British business in Burma by thwarting a competitive challenge from the American-based Standard Oil Company.

Moreover, an examination of a quite different body of evidence suggests that the owners of colonial enterprises may have been particularly well placed to ameliorate the bureaucrats' traditional distaste for business and their alleged unswerving support for a policy of laissez-faire. An analysis of the men and women who owned British incorporated businesses indicates that, merchants aside, the middle classes (the butchers, the bakers, and the candlestick makers) were far less

---

shortfalls prompted by these 'reforms' forced the Indian authorities to reinstitute a general 5-percent duty in 1894; but to mollify the critics, an equivalent excise tax was levied on all cotton goods manufactured in India. Even that compromise proved politically unacceptable, and in 1896 both the import and the excise taxes were reduced" (quoted from Davis and Huttenback, *Mammon*, p. 258).

[24] Cited in Winifred Baumgart, *Imperialism* (New York: Oxford University Press, 1982), p. 130.

[25] Cited in John S. Galbraith, *Mackinnon and East Africa, 1878–1895* (Cambridge: Cambridge University Press, 1972), p. 161.

Table 5.11. *Shareholders' relative holdings in home and empire firms, by occupation (businessmen and elites only)*

	Location of firms	
Occupation	UK	Empire
Merchants	100	76
Manufacturers	100	13
Professional & management	100	64
Miscellaneous business	100	41
All businessmen	100	45
Financiers	100	97
Military officers	100	76
Miscellaneous elites	100	260
Peers & gentlemen	100	166
All elites	100	153

Source: Davis and Huttenback, *Mammon*, Table 7.6, p. 212.

likely to invest in the empire than they were to direct their financial resources toward the domestic economy. The elites (the financiers, military officers, government officials, peers, and gentlemen), on the other hand, the very groups to whose sons the Treasury and the India, the Colonial, and the Foreign offices turned for their recruits, were half again as likely to choose empire as domestic investment (see Table 5.11). In addition, although elites throughout the kingdom displayed a somewhat similar affinity for empire investment, it was the businessmen of London, in contrast to those who plied their trades in Birmingham, Manchester, and Glasgow – businessmen particularly well placed to lobby, both formally in the halls of parliament and informally in the smoking rooms of their London clubs – who were the most likely to hold the shares of empire firms (see Table 5.12).

Finally, not only did the elites display a strong preference for empire investment in general, but they also displayed an even stronger preference for those particular activities that were the most likely beneficiaries of any successful political manipulation. Of the fifteen imperial industries in which Englishmen invested their funds, the eight show elites appearing in substantially greater than proportionate numbers. Of those eight, seven (railroads; financial land and development companies; trams and omnibuses; telephones and telegraphs; gas, light, and electric companies; iron, coal, and steel firms; and waterworks)

Table 5.12. *Relative attractiveness to shareholders of home and empire firms, by occupation and location (businessmen and elites only; ratio is London to non-London)*

	Location of firms	
Occupation	UK	Empire
Merchants	19	110
Manufacturers	44	162
Professional & management	22	126
Miscellaneous business	2	635
All businessmen	17	142
Financiers	61	103
Military officers	132	94
Miscellaneous elites	152	90
Peers & gentlemen	49	105
All elites	62	102

Source: Davis and Huttenback, *Mammon*, Table 7.10, p. 216.

were either land-related or depended on a government grant or charter (see Fig. 5.4).[26]

Motive, certainly; opportunity, perhaps; but means is quite a different matter. Lobbying must have occurred, but there is little evidence that it was effective except in those rare instances (the cotton duties, for example) where intensity of feelings went hand in hand with a geographic concentration of the affected voters. Moreover, an analysis of the voting patterns of individual members of the House of Commons produces no evidence that House members drawn from the ranks of elites voted any differently on measures that would either strengthen the empire or make empire-based businesses more profitable than did members with middle-class backgrounds. It is certainly possible that the mechanism of manipulation operated on the members of parliament indirectly through the discipline imposed by the political parties; or perhaps it might have worked directly on government policy through the permanent undersecretaries, bypassing parliament completely; or perhaps the MPs successfully managed to hide the evidence of their manipulation; but in any case there is no compelling evidence

[26] The smaller the number, the higher the proportion of elite relative to business investors. For a more complete analysis of the shareholdings in imperial enterprise, see Davis and Huttenback, *Mammon*, Table 7.7.

Lance E. Davis & Robert A. Huttenback

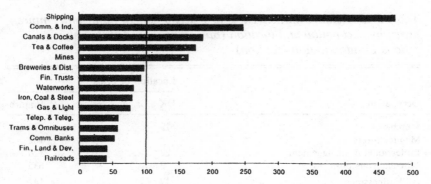

Fig. 5.4. Relative attractiveness of empire investments (business/elites): occupation's holdings in all locations (industry total = 100). *Source:* Davis and Huttenback, *Mammon*, Table 7.7, p. 213.

to support any of those hypotheticals. In short, there is no smoking gun.

The analysis of the expenditure patterns (both the colonial–noncolonial comparisons and the cross-sectional examination of dependent and responsibly governed colonies) cannot disprove the allegation that the British government at the urging of the domestic business community deliberately warped the pattern of colonial expenditures to bolster British profits. On the other hand, the evidence does not confirm the charge and, perhaps more important, may even provide some support to an alternative hypothesis.

If the British government had set out to effect such a policy, the political mechanism should have produced quite different results. Political control was greatest in India and least in the colonies with responsible government. Therefore, the evidence of manipulation (the level of business-supporting expenditures) should have been strongest on the subcontinent and weakest in the colonies of white settlement. The facts are just the reverse. The evidence of a policy of business-supporting activities is weakest in India, where political control was almost absolute. Next, in order of expenditures, were the dependent colonies, where there was frequently at least a modicum of local consultation. Finally, government involvement was most intense in those colonies with little or no British political control.

Similarly, one would not have expected the British government to waste its time and effort manipulating budgets in those colonies that traded with the Americans, the Australians, or the Chinese. But there is evidence that, over time, expenditures came to be as closely associa-

228

ted with profits earned on those non-British trade routes as they did on the monies squeezed from the "sinews of empire."

Thus, an alternative explanation appears to be at least as appealing as the manipulation hypothesis. Yes, government may well have warped the political process to aid business, but it was local, not British, business that was the primary recipient. British businessmen did, of course, benefit; but Whitehall may have been, at most, only marginally involved; and although the process could not have been carried out without the support of the colonial governors, it appears they may have listened to the business leaders in Kingston and Montreal at least as closely as to those in Manchester and Birmingham.

Appendix

Colony name	Date added	Colony name	Date added
Responsible government			
Australia	1901	Pacific	
New South Wales		Fiji	1874
Queensland		British New Guinea	1884
South Australia		British Solomon Islands	1893
South Australia		Gilbert & Ellice Islands	1896–99
(Northern Territory)		Tonga	1900
Tasmania		Africa	
Victoria		Ascension & St. Helena	
Western Australia		Gambia	
Canada	1867	Sierra Leone	
Nova Scotia		Gold Coast	
New Brunswick		Lagos	1861
Ontario		Basutoland	1868
Quebec		Egypt	1882
Manitoba		Somali Coast Protectorate	1884
British Columbia		Bechuanaland	1885
Prince Edward Island		Niger Coast & Southern Nigeria	1885
Alberta		Northern Nigeria	1885
Saskatchewan		Zanzibar	1890
Yukon		Southern Rhodesia	1890
Northwest Territories		Nyasaland	1891
Newfoundland		Northern Rhodesia	1893
Newfoundland		Uganda	1893
Labrador		Kenya (Br. East Africa)	1895
New Zealand		Sudan	1898
Union of South Africa	1910	Swaziland	1903
Cape Colony		Indian Ocean	
Natal		Aden (incl. Perim & Socotra)	

229

Colony name	Date added	Colony name	Date added
Orange River	1900	Mauritius	
Transvaal	1902	Seychelles	
		Europe	
India		Gibraltar	
British India		Malta	
Burma	1885	Ionian islands	
Princely states		Cyprus	1878
		Caribbean and South America	
Dependent colonies		Antigua	
Asia		Bahamas	
Ceylon		Barbados	
Straights Settlements		Bermuda	
Labuan		British Guiana	
Hong Kong		British Honduras	
Federated Malay States	1896	British Virgin Islands	
Perak	1874	Dominica	
Selangor	1874	Falkland Islands	
Sugei–Ujong	1875–76	Grenada	
Pahang	1887	Jamaica	
Negri Sembilan	1874–89	Montserrat	
North Borneo	1881	St. Kitts–Nevis–Anguilla	
Brunei	1888	St. Lucia	
Sarawak	1888	St. Vincent	
Unfederated Malay States	1909	Tobago	
Kelantan	1909	Trinidad	
Trenggam	1909	Turks Island	
Kedah	1909	Virgin Islands	
Perlis	1909		
Johore	1885		
Weihei	1898		

Note: Undated areas were in the empire by 1860.

6

The impact of the economy and the state on the economic status of blacks: a study of South Carolina

Richard J. Butler, James J. Heckman, and Brook Payner

1. Introduction

Two decades of research have failed to produce professional consensus on the contribution of federal government civil rights activity to the economic progress of black Americans. There are several reasons why this is so. In part it is due to the lack of convincing measures of federal civil rights activity. In part it is due to the reliance of much of the literature on notoriously fragile macro time series in which numerous plausible explanations compete for scarce degrees of freedom. Highly aggregated time series or cross-section studies do not isolate well-defined labor markets in which supply and demand factors can be meaningfully separated, although it is the separation of these factors that is essential to the resolution of the debate on federal impact. Much valuable institutional detail may be lost in the process of data aggregation or in the fitting of "general purpose" wage equations that constrain equality in coefficient estimates across diverse sectors.

This essay takes a new look at this old – but still highly relevant – question using a unique body of data on employment and wages by race and sex for the manufacturing sector of South Carolina. Some of

This research was supported by NSF grants SES-77-11231, SES-81-4225, DAR-792594, SES-84-11246, and SES-87-39151. The research was originated at the University of Wisconsin in the fall of 1977 and has been assisted at various stages by Chris Flinn, Jon Moen, and Guilherme Sedlacek. Steve Cameron provided first-class research assistance for the work reported here. Margaret Watson, formerly of the South Carolina Department of Labor, provided valuable advice on the South Carolina data used here. We have benefited from comments received from 0. Ashenfelter, Steve Cameron, David Galenson, J. Hotz, T. Mroz, T. W. Schultz, T. N. Srinivasan, David Weir, Glynn Williams, Gavin Wright, and participants in seminars at Stanford, the Hoover Institution, Sloan School – MIT, the University of South Carolina, NBER-Cambridge, the University of Pennsylvania, the Economic History Workshop at the University of Chicago, and Yale University. Portions of this paper appear in abbreviated form in Heckman and Payner (1989).

Richard J. Butler, James J. Heckman, & Brook Payner

the data are available at the disaggregated county level, affording useful cross-sectional variation. By focusing attention on well-defined labor markets, it is easier to separate out supply- and demand-side impacts on black status. Unlike most previous studies that focus exclusively on black wages, our study analyzes both black wages and black employment.

Trends in black economic progress in South Carolina are typical of trends for the South as a whole. As noted by Vroman (1974), Butler (1985), Smith and Welch (1986), and the U.S. Commission on Civil Rights (1986), a sizable component of the post-1960 U.S. aggregate relative wage and occupational improvement for blacks is due to relative wage improvement in the South.

Table 6.1 breaks down the percentage increase in the relative mean earnings of black men compared with white men between 1960 and 1970 into its five component parts.[1] These are: northern and southern relative wage changes within occupations, northern and southern changes in the relative occupational distribution, and North–South migration changes. The least important empirically is the shift of the black population from the lower-paying South to the North. This has a small, but insignificant, impact on relative wages, accounting for an

---

[1] For a given race, mean earnings (E) is simply

$$E = P_N(\sum_i P_i^N E_i^N) + P_S(\sum_i P_i^S E_i^S)$$

where P_j = Proportion in region j

P_i^j = Proportion of that race group in region j that have earnings in occupation i

E_i^j = Average earnings in region j and occupation i.

The percentage change in earnings can be approximated by

$$d\ln E = (\frac{P_N \sum_i P_i^N E_i^N}{E} \, d\ln P_N + \frac{P_S \sum_i P_i^S E_i^S}{E} \, d\ln P_S) \quad \text{Regional migration}$$

$$+ (\sum_i \frac{P_i^N E_i^N P_N}{E} \, d\ln P_i^N) \quad \text{Occupational shift in the North}$$

$$+ (\sum_i \frac{P_i^S E_i^S P_S}{E} \, d\ln P_i^S) \quad \text{Occupational shift in the South}$$

$$+ (\sum_i \frac{P_i^N E_i^N P_N}{E} \, d\ln E_i^N) \quad \text{Wage changes in the North}$$

$$+ (\sum_i \frac{P_i^S E_i^S P_S}{E} \, d\ln E_i^S) \quad \text{Wage changes in the South}$$

Since $d\ln (E_{\text{black}}/E_{\text{white}}) = d\ln E_{\text{black}} - d\ln E_{\text{white}}$, we can decompose relative wage growth into the component parts above by subtracting the white change from the respective black change. This is how we arrive at the calculations in Table 6.1. Note that all the weights for the changes (i.e., the $P_i^j E_i^j p_j$) were averaged over the 1960 and 1970 censuses. All pecuniary variables are in 1967 dollars.

232

Table 6.1. *Real relative wage gains of black vis-à-vis white males in the sixties*

	Percentage growth in relative mean wage income due to				
	Northern wage changes	Northern occupational changes	Southern wage changes	Southern occupational changes	North–south migration
Total	0.82	3.36	8.97	4.13	0.55
By occupation					
Professional	-0.97	-2.99	0.39	-0.43	—
Managers	-0.73	-0.83	0.07	0.55	—
Sales	-1.01	0.05	-0.34	0.10	—
Clerical	0.15	1.29	0.29	1.34	—
Craftsmen	-0.76	2.68	1.24	2.55	—
Operatives	2.03	4.91	3.16	2.46	—
Laborers	1.54	-1.76	2.14	-1.79	—
Farmers	-0.95	0.65	0.09	-0.36	—
Farm laborers	-0.08	-0.41	0.55	-0.45	—
Service	1.59	-0.23	1.37	0.17	—

Sources: The date are for males in the experienced labor force, 25 to 64 years old, who reported earnings. The 1960 data are for nonwhites and come from the U.S. *Census of Population: 1960*, subject report *Occupation by Earnings and Education*, Tables 2 and 3. The 1970 data are for black and white males and come from the 1970 subject report *Earnings by Education*, Tables 3 and 4. We could not find similar data for females.

increase of less than one percentage point.[2] Both occupational shifts and wage growth within each of the regions appear to be more important than interregional migration, with the intraregional growth of the South accounting for most of the change in U.S. aggregate wages. The relative wage increase between 1960 and 1970 *within occupations in the South* accounts for nearly nine percentage points – over half of the growth of the aggregate relative wages of black males. As we break down the increase by occupations, over three percentage points are due to the growth in wages and over two percentage points are due to the growth of relative wages in the nonfarm labor category. Most relative wage growth in the South attributable to occupational changes is due to the shifting of blacks into the relatively higher-paying "production" jobs associated with the operative and craftsman occupational groupings. Indeed, though the North accounts for less than a fourth of the growth in relative wages, the pattern of changes there is similar. Except for the wage and occupational changes associated with operative positions, relative black wages would actually have decreased in the northern states. That they increased at all is due to shifts in the craftsman, operative, and nonfarm labor occupations. Trends in relative wages and employment trends of southern production workers provide the key to understanding the dynamic changes in the U.S. aggregate trends.[3] This is the first empirical analysis to look at this essential, but hitherto missing, piece in the puzzle of the black labor market experience during the 1960s.

Three major – and not necessarily mutually exclusive – explanations have been advanced to explain the growth in black male relative (to white male) earnings of the sort recorded in Table 6.1. (1) Some authors, seizing on the coincidence in timing between the passage of Title VII and other related federal antidiscrimination activity and the relative improvement in black wages, assign a central role to federal antidiscrimination activity (Freeman 1973, 1981; Vroman 1974; and Brown 1984). More conservative scholars tend to deny this claim (see, e.g., Smith 1984 and Smith and Welch 1986). (2) Welch (1973), Smith

---

[2] This may appear surprising in light of the large influx of blacks especially to the northeastern and north-central regions of the United States, but it is not inconsistent with those trends. Two factors are at work. (1) There has been a drastic increase in the number of blacks employed in southern industry, so that the number of blacks in the experienced labor force (measured in thousands) rose from 2,019 to 2,126, an increase comparable with the northern change of 1,876 to 2,037, and (2) not all migrants end up in the experienced labor force (hence, the northern migration flows are greater than the flow of experienced labor).

[3] The importance of these southern trends for interpreting the U.S. aggregate changes was first noted in Butler and Heckman (1977).

(1984), and Smith and Welch (1986) assign a central, but not necessarily exclusive, role to human-capital formation and the importance of previous state-government discrimination in the provision of schooling. (3) Still others (Tobin 1965; Wilson 1986; Friedman 1962) assign an important role to the rising cost of discrimination in tight labor markets associated with industrialization, the emergence of competitive markets, or demand management policies.

Few scholars dispute the importance of schooling in raising black incomes. Most acknowledge that tight labor markets favor employment of blacks, although there is considerable controversy surrounding the effect of tight labor markets on racial wage differentials (Butler 1985). Most of the disagreement in the literature centers on the role of federal antidiscrimination activity. For this reason we focus on that question.

We address the question by using a form of empirical proof by elimination. Using a variety of data sources and measures of federal activity and eliminating other plausible explanations, we conclude that federal policy benefited black economic status in South Carolina.

Ours is a tale of two sectors. The strongest evidence of federal impact is found in the traditional manufacturing sectors of the state that were already thriving when Jim Crow laws formalized racial separation in employment in 1915. Human-capital stories or nonautological tight-labor-market stories cannot explain the timing of black improvement there.

There is little evidence of federal impact on black status in the more modern sectors of the state that emerged after 1945. Somewhat surprisingly, we also find no evidence of employment discrimination in state, local, or federal government hiring once qualifications are accounted for. The growth in black employment and wages in these sectors appears to be driven by market or supply-side factors. Our analysis establishes the value of more disaggregated industrial and institutional analyses in assessing the contribution of federal activity to black status. We demonstrate the importance of accounting for the relevant economic and institutional histories of industries in understanding black economic progress. Our evidence confirms the wisdom of Wright's (1986) emphasis on the role of institutions in explaining the economic history of the South. Our analysis provides evidence against the widely held belief espoused by Murray (1984) and other conservatives that federal government policy has not contributed to the elevation of black economic status.

The plan of this essay is as follows. In Section 2, we present salient features of the South Carolina labor market experience of blacks. Five rather striking graphs may convince the committed reader that the federal government played an important role in improving black status. Although we shall demonstrate that such first impressions are, in fact, correct, we sound cautionary notes against accepting the first impression without further argument. The rest of the essay executes the argument.

Section 3 summarizes previous analyses of the South Carolina black breakthrough. There we demonstrate that competent social scientists have reached conflicting conclusions about the role of government policy in elevating black status in the South Carolina labor market. Section 4 evaluates the basic quality of the data, which – since they are self-reported by firms being targeted by federal activity – may be suspect. We establish the validity of the basic sources of data. We also establish that trends in South Carolina are like those in the rest of the South. Thus our analysis of South Carolina data may contain important lessons for understanding the progress of blacks in the South and hence their progress in the United States as a whole.

Section 5 states and Sections 6 and 7 evaluate competing arguments using detailed analyses of the data. The essay concludes with a summary of the evidence.

2. Salient features of the South Carolina data

Figs. 6.1 and 6.2 plot the South Carolina industrial data on employment and wages by race and sex for the period 1940–80. The data are from the South Carolina *Annual Report of the Department of Labor*. In Section 3 we establish the validity of these self-reported data collected from firms.

Black employment is a stable fraction of total employment between 1940 and 1965 (Fig. 6.1). Suddenly in 1965 the proportion of black employment begins to grow at a time when total manufacturing employment is growing. The relative wage series for black workers shows an upturn at the same time, although it is less dramatic (Fig. 6.2).

Textiles are the major industry in the state, accounting for 80 percent of all manufacturing employment in 1940 and a still sizable 40 percent in 1980. Most of the breakthrough in black employment occurs in this industry and the related apparel industry. There is much less evidence of any dramatic breakthrough in the non-textile non-apparel sector of the manufacturing sector, although there is visible growth in the share of black *female* employment after 1965 (see Fig. 6.3) and little evidence of improvement in relative wages for black males, and there is a steady improvement in black male wages beginning before 1965 (see Fig. 6.4). The decline in the black male share in this sector and the rise in the female share for both races is primarily due to the

236

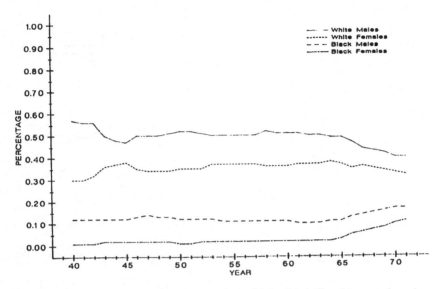

Fig. 6.1. Aggregate employment shares in the South Carolina manufacturing industries.

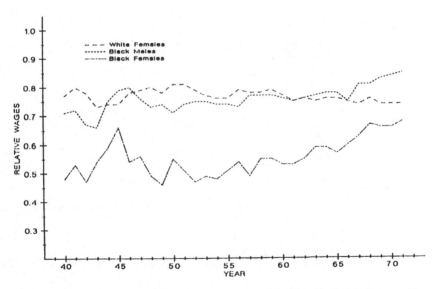

Fig. 6.2. South Carolina manufacturing industries: wages relative to white males.

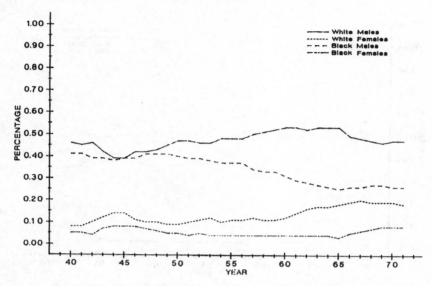

Fig. 6.3. Aggregate employment shares in South Carolina non-textile non-apparel manufacturing.

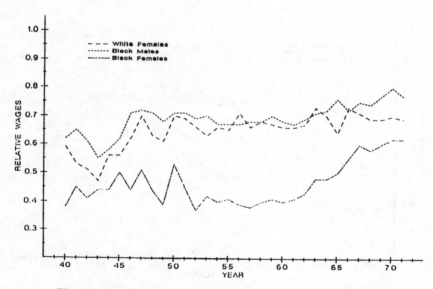

Fig. 6.4. South Carolina non-textile non-apparel manufacturing wages relative to white males.

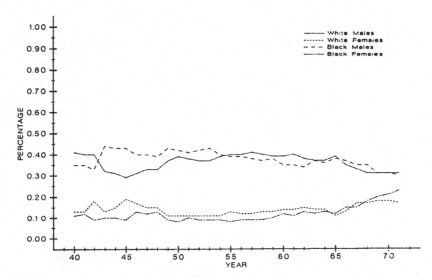

Fig. 6.5. Aggregate employment shares in the South Carolina food products manufacturing industry.

entry into the food industry of new firms employing women of both races in equal proportions after 1965 (see Fig. 6.5).

Fig. 6.6 presents employment shares by race and sex in textiles between 1910 and 1980.[4] It confirms the impression conveyed by Fig. 6.1. Through two world wars, the Great Depression, and the booms of the 1920s and 1950s the share of blacks in textile employment remains constant at a low level despite growth in the quality and quantity of black schooling and despite economic scarcity resulting from tight labor markets. Suddenly in 1965 the black share in employment begins to improve when Title VII legislation becomes effective and the Equal Employment Opportunity Commission begins to press textile firms to employ blacks and when Executive Order 11246 forbids discrimination by government contractors at the risk of forfeiture of government business. The textile industry sold a significant proportion of its output to the federal government in 1965.[5] The improvement in black employment and wages occurs at a time and in an industry that suggests a major role for government activity.

---

[4] Data on wages were not collected before 1940. There are consistent time-series data on employment in non-textile industries before that date.
[5] About 5% or $120 million in 1965 dollars.

239

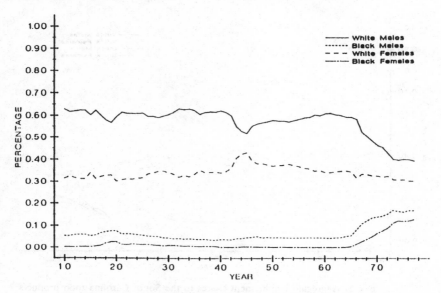

Fig. 6.6. Aggregate employment shares in the South Carolina textile industries.

This evidence of government impact is reinforced by some additional background information on South Carolina textiles. That industry may well have been an ideal textbook example of Arrow's (1972) model of discrimination. Initial racial exclusion ratified by a 1915 Jim Crow law may have been perpetuated by fixed costs of employment coupled with a taste for discrimination on the part of fellow employees. The costs of marginal experimentation in hiring blacks may well have been raised by the geographical isolation of mills from existing supplies of black labor: Residential integration was required to effect industrial integration. Southern textiles was one of the few industries found by Bunting (1962) to have monopsony power because of its geographical isolation from other employers.

Title VII and related antidiscrimination activity seem likely to have had their most visible effect in industries like South Carolina textiles in which exclusion of blacks was so blatant. The Equal Employment Opportunity Commission targeted southern textiles and conducted hearings on employment discrimination in that industry in late 1966 and early 1967. These hearings were widely publicized (see Rowan 1970). About 120 charges of wage and employment discrimination were filed against textile firms in North and South Carolina in 1965 (see Kidder, Evans, Simons, and Smith 1972). Any rational theory of

240

government bureaucracy would make South Carolina textiles an inviting target for equal rights intervention. The Defense Department, which was in charge of monitoring textile affirmative action programs, was known to be relatively vigorous in pursuit of equal opportunity. Three large textile companies in North and South Carolina had government contracts withdrawn for a brief period in 1968 because of noncompliance with the order (see Kidder et al. 1972).

Before any conclusion about the efficacy of federal policy is embraced, however, it is important to raise some cautionary questions, the answers to which constitute the remainder of this essay.

The first argument against the obvious is that the data are suspect. Since textile and apparel firms report the basic data underlying Figs. 6.1–6, they may have lied about the growth in black employment after 1965 to avoid federal intervention, and they may have lied about the level of black employment before 1965 to avoid state intervention on behalf of Jim Crow laws. In Section 4 we document the accuracy of the data, so this claim can be dismissed.

The second argument against the obvious is harder to refute. The South Carolina labor market was unusually tight after 1964. Tightness arose from the 1960s national boom coupled with the growth in real manufacturing output (Fig. 6.7, in 1967 constant dollars) and entry of firms and investment (Fig. 6.8). There were historically low layoff rates and high quit rates and new-hire rates in textiles (Fig. 6.9). Textile output was expanding during the period of the black breakthrough (Fig. 6.10). The growth in demand for textile labor coupled with a dramatic contraction in the traditional sources of supply associated with the secular decline in South Carolina agriculture may have created unusual pressure for integration of the industry as a means of keeping down labor costs. Federal antidiscrimination activity may simply have facilitated the inevitable by giving employers an excuse for doing what they wanted to do anyway.

As documented in Section 3, many economists who have analyzed the desegregation of southern textiles claim that the primary source of black improvement was the tight labor market. For this reason alone the argument should be taken seriously. Some versions of it are irrefutably true – for example, the argument that 1965 was a "uniquely tight" labor market and that once the fixed costs of desegregation of mills and mill communities were incurred, black employment gains were not easily erased. The argument is irrefutable because it assumes that the year 1965 was unique.

Other more easily answered arguments can also be advanced against the obvious explanation. The first is a supply-shift argument that focuses on the decline in South Carolina (and southern) agriculture as a

241

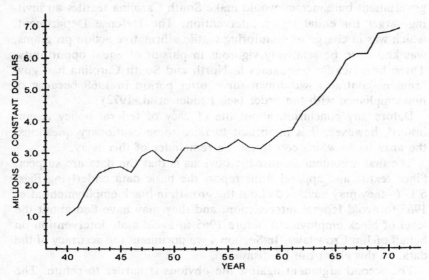

Fig. 6.7. South Carolina manufacturing industries: total real manufacturing output.

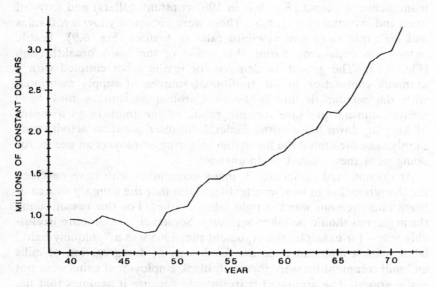

Fig. 6.8. South Carolina aggregate manufacturing industries: real capital stock.

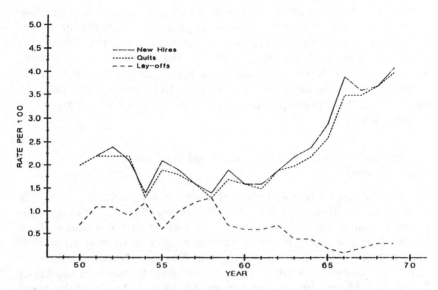

Fig. 6.9. Average turnover rates in the textile industry: cotton-weaving mills (per 100 employees).

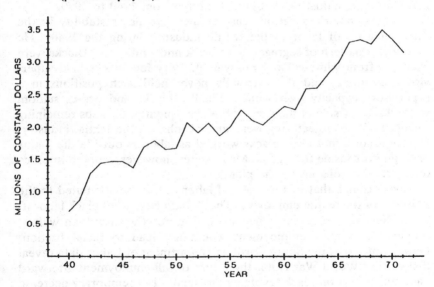

Fig. 6.10. The South Carolina textile industry: real textile output.

source of growth in black industrial employment. The second argument is the "human-capital" argument. One version of this argument mirrors Smith's (1984) explanation of black progress and claims that growth in the quality and quantity of black schooling may have accounted for the black breakthrough in textiles and related industries.

We address these questions in this paper. Before presenting our own analysis, we first review previous studies of the black breakthrough in South Carolina.

3. Previous studies of blacks in textiles and blacks in South Carolina

There have been several studies of racial employment in the textile industry and in South Carolina. Donald Dewey (1955) examines trends of black employment in the South and factors that influenced those trends. Dewey's study is based on interviews and surveys from 1950 and 1951 covering black employment in Durham, North Carolina, as well as employment in tobacco and textile manufacturing in the upper South. In addition, he uses data from the *Annual Report of the South Carolina Department of Labor* for analysis of black employment in the manufacturing industries of South Carolina from 1940 to 1950.

Dewey summarizes various case studies. He notes stability in the racial division of labor in the textile industry during the 1940s. He describes a pattern of segregation in black and white jobs. Blacks were excluded from white-collar employment. Very few blacks held supervisory positions, and they virtually never held such positions in a supervisory capacity over whites. Finally, blacks and whites seldom worked side by side at the same job. Consequently, the jobs remaining for blacks in manufacturing were menial jobs. In the textile industry, Dewey reports that most blacks worked as laborers outside the plants or as janitors inside the plants. Most whites, however, worked in office or production jobs inside the plants.

Dewey claims that this division of labor cannot be attributed to the attitudes of the textile employers. They would have used black labor if, given the wage rate, blacks had worked more efficiently than whites, provided that their employment would not lead to racial friction. Dewey notes that the South Carolina Department of Labor data reveal that neither World War II nor the return of full employment afterward had much effect on black textile employment. The temporary decrease in white male textile employment during the war was partially offset by an increase in white female employment but produced very little change in black employment. If Dewey's survey of employer attitudes is to be believed, the fear of racial friction must have been quite significant.

Dewey points to four main reasons for the racial status quo in the textile industry. First, the textile industry was considered a high-wage industry by the standards of the communities in which the firms were located. Consequently textile jobs were more desirable than most other opportunities. Second, most textile tasks could be performed by women. Any shortage of white male labor could thus be made up by white female labor, as, in fact, occurred during World War II. Third, new mills were discouraged from hiring blacks for the more skilled positions because of the lack of trained blacks for knitting, weaving, and spinning operations. Finally, the mill community was not an environment that encouraged the acceptance of blacks into the work group. According to Dewey, the company-owned town that was characteristic of the industry was on the way out, but a large fraction of the white workers lived together in the same neighborhoods and formed socially cohesive groups. These whites neither lived nor worked with blacks, so textile employers were wary of racial friction that might result from the integration of work groups.

Two studies were prepared in the mid-sixties for the Equal Employment Opportunity Commission (EEOC) regarding black employment patterns and opportunities in the textile industry of the Carolinas. The first of these, by Wallace and Beckles (1966), analyzes 1964 and 1965 EEO reports prepared from firm responses to questionnaires prepared by the Equal Employment Opportunity Commission. They describe racial employment patterns very similar to those observed by Dewey but with one important exception. Between 1964 and 1965 blacks made significant gains in employment for the first time. Wallace and Beckles indicate that between 1964 and 1965 black textile employment increased by 59 percent in South Carolina and by 73 percent in North Carolina. However, blacks were still largely underrepresented in the industry when compared with their proportion in the population at large.

A second study, by Osburn (1966), is more extensive. Osburn characterizes the textile industry in the mid-sixties as having: (1) wages that were at the lower end of the range in manufacturing, (2) mostly blue-collar jobs, (3) under 10 percent of workers unionized, and (4) historically a record of near-total exclusion of black employees.

After 1960 the industry's employment patterns and wage scales changed. The labor market tightened by the mid-sixties as higher-paying industries such as chemicals and machinery moved into the South. Osburn maintains that the textile industry had three alternatives: (1) raising wages, (2) employing blacks, or (3) making technological advances. Since the domestic textile industry operated in a highly competitive world market and had low value added per worker, the most practical choice was to turn to the black labor market. Osburn argues that it was primarily labor market conditions in concert with governmental regulations prohibiting racial discrimination that led to increased utilization of blacks in the textile industry by 1966. However, he presents no quantitative evidence on the relative importance of these factors.

Richard Rowan (1970) also reports the exclusion of blacks from textiles from 1880 to 1960 and notes that during the 1960s they became employed in almost every aspect of textile manufacturing. Rowan's study examines the past practices of textile employers in dealing with racial employment and the fundamental changes that occurred during the 1960s.

Rowan's report is based largely on surveys of southern textile plants. The surveys included 46 companies and 444 plants covering 41 percent of southern textile employees in 1968. The surveys track the same companies in 1964, 1966, and 1968. Rowan claims that employers were very cooperative and responses were generally complete. In addition, Rowan uses the *Annual Report of the South Carolina Department of Labor* as well as employment data obtained from the EEOC and the Office of Federal Contract Compliance (OFCC).

Rowan's account of racial employment in the southern textile industry is very similar to Dewey's. Prior to 1965, blacks made up a very small proportion of the textile workforce. Employed blacks were usually given the most menial jobs. There were also many white women employed in the industry but virtually no black women.

Rowan describes the textile production process as having four main characteristics. First, most jobs could be learned in six months or less. Second, there were few skilled jobs. Third, technology had not altered job classifications in the preceding decade. Finally, many operations could be and were performed by women. Rowan claims that these characteristics were responsible for blacks' being able to make fast gains in textiles once the industry opened up to them.

Rowan's analysis includes comparisons of the changes in the distributions of demographic employment by occupation from 1964 to 1968. He stresses the differences between 1966 and 1968 owing to the larger and more representative data sets covering those years. Like Osburn, he mainly attributes the change in black status to the growth of southern industry and the subsequent tight labor market of the late 1960s but gives no evidence on either the timing of the change or the magnitudes of the change.

Another factor considered by Rowan is the effect of the civil rights movement and the government's influence on black employment. In the textile industry, Executive Order 11246 was enforced by the Department of Defense. Companies desiring defense contracts had to develop equal employment opportunity programs and have them reviewed before a contract would be awarded. Rowan confirms Kidder's account that large contracts were awarded in February 1969 to three large mills even though EEO plans were not yet in effect in those mills. The three mills did, however, agree to complete EEO programs and did so within the next year. Rowan reports that the majority of the smaller to medium-size firms did not have written EEO programs in mid-1969, although they may have been employing blacks at that time.

The timing of government action in the textile industry described above suggests that blacks may have been hired before significant government pressure was exerted. However, this could have been because of employer expectations of future government pressure. Rowan contends that government pressure was not necessary for increasing black employment in textiles, because "the labor market brought the major change" (1970, p. 135). He does claim, however, that government influence made it easier for employers to integrate the mills without racial friction. Little quantitative evidence is presented in support of these claims.

Kidder et al. (1972) studied the growth of black employment in the textile industry during the 1960s using a more quantitative approach. They sought to determine the causes of the sudden growth in black textile employment in North Carolina and South Carolina. See also Kidder (1972).

Three explanations are given. The first is the tight-labor-market hypothesis – the hypothesis most strongly supported by Rowan and Osburn. The second explanation, the government-activity hypothesis, attributes the observed changes to federal intervention. The final, "community mores," hypothesis asserts that changes in community values, independent of economic or legal forces, are responsible for the change. Kidder et al. endorse the final hypothesis as the primary cause of change.

For their study, Kidder et al. use data from EEOC reports on racial employment obtained from all textile establishments with more than one hundred employees. Using Carolina reports for 1966 and 1969, they found 715 establishments that could be matched for the two years. These matched records reveal the extent of the change in black participation in textiles between 1966 and 1969. In addition, Kidder et al. compiled interviews from 41 companies in 1971. Most of these companies declined to give complete interviews, so the company surveys

247

were not as useful as they might have been. Interviews were also taken from 233 textile employees as well as from industry personnel, government agency personnel, and community leaders. These data were used to test the three hypotheses stated above.

Kidder et al.'s version of the tight-labor-market hypothesis asserts that whites left the textile industry for higher-paying industries. Owing to increased competition from imports, the textile industry could not raise wages and thus had no choice other than to hire black labor. Kidder et al. note that the 1960s were years of tight labor markets that coincided with black gains, but that earlier periods of tightness such as the early 1950s produced no black gains whatsoever. They also claim that white laborers moved into many industries besides textiles, some of which were higher-paying and some of which were lower-paying industries. Finally, they estimate the available white "labor reserve" in North Carolina in 1966 and find a substantial pool of available white labor that could have filled the needs for employment in textiles during the sixties. Kidder et al. conclude that labor market tightness likely contributed to the degree of change in black participation in textiles but that it was not a sufficient condition for change. In their regression analyses, they find no statistically significant tight-labor-market effect on black employment using two different measures of labor market tightness. The first measure is the county unemployment rate in 1966 and the second is the ratio of employment to population.

As for the government-activity hypothesis, they argue that the 1964 Civil Rights Act that created the EEOC might have been responsible for the change by guaranteeing equal employment opportunity regardless of race, color, religion, sex, or national origin. The EEOC collected data on minority employment from employers of one hundred or more persons in 1966. During the period 1966–69, coverage was increased to establishments with twenty-five or more employees. Kidder et al. assert that in 1966 about half the textile firms in the Carolinas had fewer than a hundred employees, so half were not required to report. In addition, they found that about 30 percent of those firms required by law to report failed to do so in either 1966 or 1969, or both. These factors suggest that the Kidder et al. regression results based on these data might be subject to sample-selection bias.

Three channels of government impact examined by Kidder et al. were occurrence of technical assistance program visits, OFCC and Department of Defense reviews for government contracts, and specific charges of discrimination brought against individual companies. They claim none of these channels were particularly effective in increasing black textile employment.

The State of South Carolina Technical Assistance Program was designed to encourage the development of voluntary compliance with the objectives of EEO and to promote the training of workers for new tasks. Firms were selected for visits on the basis of size and proximity to large numbers of textile plants. Kidder et al. claim that firms visited by the Technical Assistance Program were more likely on average to show increases in black employment than firms not visited. However, their regression results show no statistically significant effect of the program.

The Department of Defense had authority to develop affirmative action programs with textile contractors. Affirmative action programs were required of firms with $50,000 or more in contract work. In 1967, the OFCC investigated the employment practices of the ten largest Carolina companies. In 1968, contracts were held up for three companies for several months. The contracts were finally awarded in 1969, however, and minority employment increased dramatically in the affected firms between 1968 and 1970.

Kidder et al. observe higher than average increases in minority employment following government contract reviews in selected firms. However, their regression analysis shows no statistically significant effects of government contracts on improvement in minority employment. It should be noted, however, that Kidder et al. use contracts in 1971 as an explanatory variable for changes in minority employment from 1966 to 1969. Use of this asynchronous variable might explain their poor empirical results with this variable.

The compliance system of the EEOC was established to deal with allegations of discrimination against employers, unions, and employment agencies. The first step in this system involved the filing of complaints with the EEOC. A complaint was investigated in the field and a report was submitted to the commission. If probable cause was found, the case was sent to conciliation. If conciliation failed, the case was submitted by the commission to the federal courts or, as in most cases, the charging parties were told they could take the case to court at their own risk and if they lost they would pay the costs. Very few cases actually went to court even when they were not settled in conciliation. As late as 1969, no important cases concerning textile plants had been through the courts. Kidder et al. find no specific impact of the conciliation process on subsequent changes in black employment in either their firm-by-firm analysis or in their regression analysis. They attribute this finding to the ineffectiveness of the EEOC process because of difficulties in finding probable cause, which resulted in few cases ending with successful conciliation.

The final hypothesis examined by Kidder et al. is the community-mores hypothesis. They note that the subtle pressure of interested groups, informal contacts between members of the black and white communities, and the like are almost impossible to document. Nonetheless, they conclude that "examination of the history of employment change in the textile industry reveals that this community effect must be considered a major causal factor" (p. 86).

Kidder et al. point to successful integration in many areas of community life in the early and mid-1960s and claim that the "growing sense of the inevitability of change made integration of textile plants an easier task for managers" (p. 86). They claim that a change in "community mores probably has interacted with the passage of equal employment opportunity legislation to promote textile employment for minorities. . . . Had the white community decided to ignore the law, the significant changes in black participation would not have been so smoothly accomplished" (p. 92).

Kidder et al. make the important point that the effectiveness of government policy depends on community values and attitudes. The authors base their argument in support of the community-mores hypothesis on their findings that neither economic factors nor government-policy variables were statistically significant determinants of the observed changes in their analysis of black economic status in the Carolinas.

Evidence presented below suggests that government activity was more effective than Kidder et al. believed was the case. Although we do not claim that government policies are established or act independently of the social environment, we claim that government policy played a significant role in improving black economic status in South Carolina rather than merely reflecting changes that were already taking place.

Hoffman (1975) presents a radical economics analysis of the relationship between racial discrimination and economic development in South Carolina. Drawing primarily on U.S. Census Bureau and state data sources, she presents an extensive regression analysis of the 1960–70 change in development (as measured by an index of growth of heavy manufacturing and modern industry) and discrimination (as measured by an index of occupational similarity between blacks and whites).

She reports that: (1) occupational discrimination slows down development, (2) development promotes the employment of blacks in low-skill industries but *decreases* it in other industries, (3) nationally based firms tend to contribute to the reduction in discrimination more than locally based firms, and (4) state training programs (Technical

Assistance Programs) contribute to *enhanced* occupational discrimination. She presents a hierarchical view of the South Carolina labor market in which whites escape low-skill jobs and leave them for blacks. Evidence against this hypothesis is presented in Section 7. Hoffman claims that development (industrialization) reduces occupational discrimination only weakly if at all. She interprets the positive effect of nationally based firms on black status as being a consequence of federal antidiscrimination activity.

Frederickson (1982) presents a historical analysis of the status of blacks in the textile industry. She claims that the seeds of the 1960s black breakthrough were sown in the emerging tight labor markets of the forties and fifties. Although she presents no quantitative evidence on the matter, she claims that the tight labor market of the sixties made compliance with EEOC and OFCC rules attractive to textile employers who had difficulty recruiting workers to the industry.

In his insightful discussion of the politics of race in South Carolina in the fifties and sixties, Sproat (1986) notes that leading figures in the state urged accommodation with the 1954 U.S. Supreme Court school desegregation ruling even in the late fifties. Community leaders urged changes in schooling and employment policies. Leading industrialists integrated their workforces in the early sixties – before the federal laws mandating integration of firms were on the books. His presentation of the growing awareness in South Carolina of the need to integrate blacks into the society lends support to Kidder et al.'s emphasis on the importance of changes in community mores in facilitating the integration of blacks. Federal legislation was imposed on a South Carolina that had already become receptive to change.

In a *New York Times Magazine* article, Cleghorn (1969) reports the black breakthrough in textiles in Erwin, North Carolina. In interviews with local businessmen about the causes of the breakthrough, he records a prototypical account by a local bank manager of the employment of blacks in Burlington Mills, a leading textile firm: "Burlington is just like everybody else, bending over backwards for the Negro . . . it's the Government contracts, pure and simple" (p. 147).

Together, these studies suggest that tight labor markets, government pressure, community mores, and changing educational quality may each have played a role in the increase in black employment in the South Carolina textile industry during the mid-1960s. However, different writers attribute the increase to different factors. This study utilizes much of the same data used by previous authors. We supplement it with additional data to reexamine the impact of these factors on black economic status in South Carolina textiles.

Richard J. Butler, James J. Heckman, & Brook Payner

4. Data quality and South Carolina in context

We have combined data from U.S. government sources with data from published reports of the South Carolina Department of Labor and the State Superintendent of Education to assemble an unusually detailed body of time-series cross-section data on manufacturing workers in South Carolina. A complete listing and description of the variables are given in Appendix A. Because the South Carolina Department of Labor (SCDOL) data are a nonstandard self-reported data source collected from firms that are the object of regulation, it may be fruitful to examine its quality before too much is made of Figs. 6.1–6 and inferences drawn from them; firms may have an incentive to misrepresent their employment and wages by race.

The SCDOL collected data from schedules mailed to every manufacturing establishment in the state in June of each year.[6] All plants were required by law to supply the requested information covering the past fiscal year. Failure to file or late filing was a misdemeanor. As of 1971, the maximum penalty for these offenses was a hundred-dollar fine and a thirty-day jail sentence. Clearly these penalties are not severe. Therefore the threat of legal enforcement does not seem sufficient to ensure accurate reporting. In what follows, we describe our analysis of the reliability of the SCDOL data based mainly on comparisons with data from U.S. government sources.

We examine the time series of each variable for internal consistency. With the exceptions noted below, we found the data to be consistent. The exceptions apparently resulted from typographical errors occurring in certain years for certain variables. Neither updates nor corrections were issued by the South Carolina authorities, so we could not obtain help from the original source. The first outliers appeared in 1966, when values for white male textile employment, white female textile employment, male textile wages, and female textile wages in Chester and Oconee counties seemed out of line with the corresponding values in the preceding and following years. These variables also seemed out of line with other variables in 1966. As a fix-up, we replaced these values with the average of the corresponding values in 1965 and 1967. The other inconsistency occurred in 1969. In Laurens County, the value for total manufacturing output in that year appeared to be out of line. We replaced the reported value with the average of the 1968 and 1970 values for total manufacturing output. These data adjustments have virtually no effect on the results of our analyses, all of which were checked for sensitivity to these substitutions.

---

[6] All manufacturing industries except lumber, timber, and turpentine are covered.

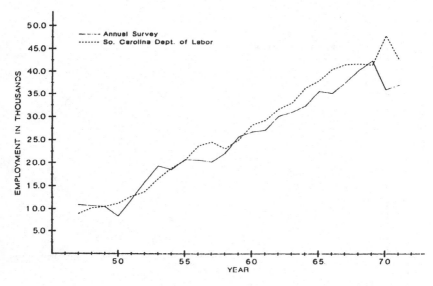

Fig. 6.11. A comparison of South Carolina and *Annual Survey of Manufactures* data: the apparel industry (production workers).

We next compared aggregate statewide data on production-worker employment and man-hours for various manufacturing industries with the same measures reported in the U.S. Census Bureau's *Annual Survey of Manufactures* and *Census of Manufactures* (*ASM*).[7] The state and federal series are not strictly comparable, because the scdol uses a fiscal-year basis and the *ASM* uses a calendar-year basis. In addition, the *ASM* reports average figures from mid-month employment in March, May, August, and November, whereas the scdol data report daily averages over the entire fiscal year. Moreover, the scdol data cover all manufacturing establishments, whereas the *ASM* samples those manufacturing establishments with 100 or more employees (250 or more in apparel, printing, and publishing). Finally, the *ASM* uses the Standard Industrial Classification (sic) definitions of industries, and the scdol uses its own classifications. Despite these differences, the data from these sources follow each other closely. Plots of production-worker employment for apparel, non-electrical machinery, electrical machinery, fabricated metals, paper and pulp, and chemicals are shown in Figs. 6.11–16. With the exception of the chemical industry, which is considered in more detail below, the graphs are reassuring.

[7] The exact sources for the *ASM* data used in this chapter are given in Appendix A.

253

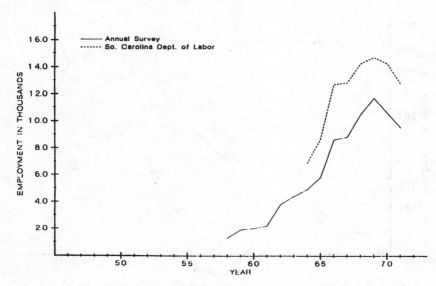

Fig. 6.12. A comparison of South Carolina and *Annual Survey of Manufactures* data: the electrical machinery industry (production workers).

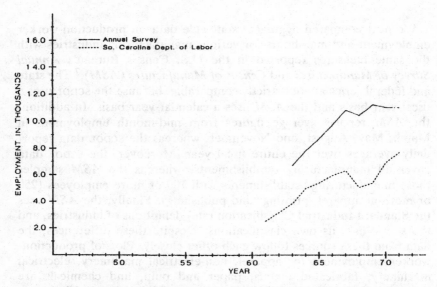

Fig. 6.13. A comparison of South Carolina and *Annual Survey of Manufactures* data: the non-electrical machinery industry (production workers).

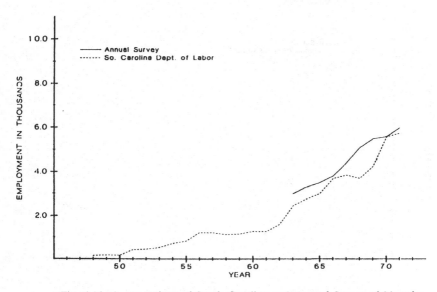

Fig. 6.14. A comparison of South Carolina and *Annual Survey of Manufactures* data: the fabricated metals industry (production workers).

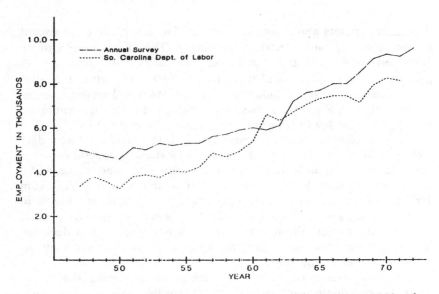

Fig. 6.15. A comparison of South Carolina and *Annual Survey of Manufactures* data: the paper and pulp industry (production workers).

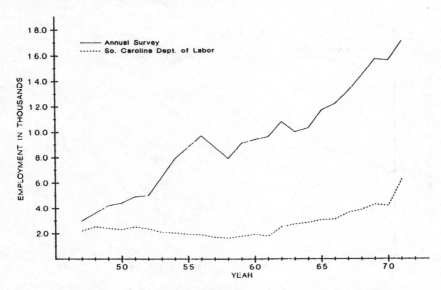

Fig. 6.16. A comparison of South Carolina and *Annual Survey of Manufactures* data: the chemical industry (production workers).

The turning points and timing are similar. The levels are close except for non-electrical and electrical machinery. This discrepancy can be explained by the fact that the SCDOL data do not use SIC codes. A portion of the non-electrical machinery industry (SIC codes) is allocated, according to SCDOL industry definitions, to the electrical machinery industry. As Fig. 6.17 shows, when these industries are combined the employment levels from the two sources are quite close.

A more extensive analysis is performed on the textile industry data collected by the SCDOL. Figs. 6.18 and 6.19 show production-worker employment and man-hours as reported by the SCDOL and by the *ASM*. The series follow each other closely from 1947 to the early 1960s. From 1965 to 1969, SCDOL data show approximately a 10 percent increase in production-worker employment. *ASM* data, however, show only about a 4 percent increase. From 1969 to 1972, SCDOL data show a decrease in employment of about 8 percent, whereas *ASM* data show an increase of about 1.5 percent.

The divergence between the two textile series during the sixties creates a potentially serious problem. According to the SCDOL data, blacks made significant gains in textile industry employment from 1965 to 1972, during a period of substantial growth in total employment. The *ASM* data, however, indicate that textile employment was not

256

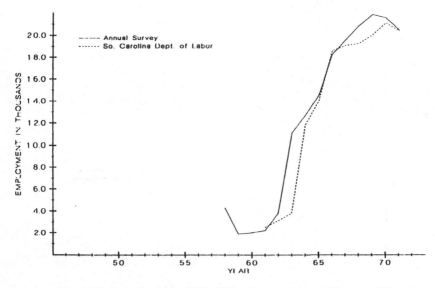

Fig. 6.17. A comparison of South Carolina and *Annual Survey of Manufactures* data: electrical and non-electrical combined (production workers).

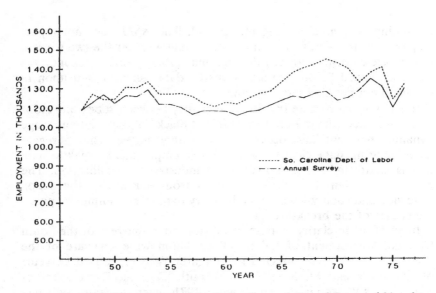

Fig. 6.18. A comparison of South Carolina and *Annual Survey of Manufactures* data: textiles (production workers).

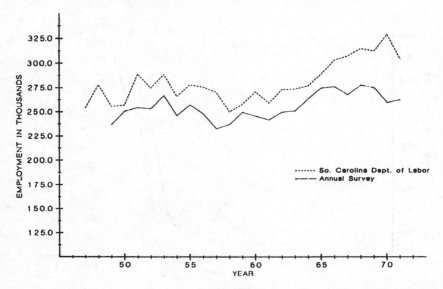

Fig. 6.19. A comparison of South Carolina and *Annual Survey of Manufactures* data: textiles (production-worker man-hours).

expanding very much during this period. The *ASM* does not report employment by race, so we cannot determine whether the two sources of data are consistent for any demographic group. The discrepancy has to be explained before the scdol textile data can be relied upon in conducting a detailed industry study.

It is important to note that the discrepancy between scdol and *ASM* textile industry data does not suggest that black employment and wage dynamics may not have occurred as described above. The aggregate manufacturing data clearly show a black employment breakthrough that is unaffected by the possibility of industry misclassification. The potential problem for this study arises from our use of the scdol statewide and county-level textile industry data in examining the possible causes of the breakthrough.

In an effort to clarify matters, we contacted employees of the South Carolina Department of Labor, all of whom were unaware of the discrepancy. We were directed to Margaret Watson, retired Director of Standards and Statistics for the South Carolina Department of Labor. Miss Watson informed us that in 1971, when the scdol switched industry classification systems from its own codes to sic codes, certain plants that had been counted in the textile totals before 1971 were reclassified into other industries. In particular, some chemical

258

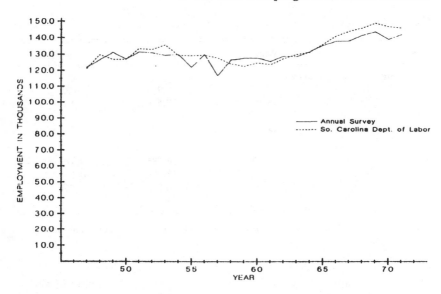

Fig. 6.20. A comparison of South Carolina and *Annual Survey of Manufactures* data: textiles and chemicals combined (production workers).

plants and glass industry plants, fiberglass for example, had been counted as textile plants before 1971. This information is consistent with the underreporting in the chemical industry by the SCDOL relative to the *ASM*, as shown in Fig. 6.16 for the chemical industry. These plots reveal a difference between *ASM* and SCDOL chemical industry employment starting in the early fifties and increasing throughout the period. Inspection of the textile plots, however, indicates that the chemical misclassification problem is really severe only in the sixties. One explanation is that the SCDOL does not include the turpentine industry in its chemical industry data, whereas turpentine is included in the *ASM* data. We therefore expect SCDOL chemicals employment to be low throughout the period.

The glass industry is not very large in South Carolina, so data problems in that sector do not have much effect on the reported textile totals. The chemical industry is much larger. Fig. 6.20 displays production-worker employment in textiles and chemicals combined from the SCDOL and the *ASM*. The plots confirm that the chemical industry misclassification accounts for much of the discrepancy between SCDOL and *ASM* textile industry figures.

If the chemical industry and the textile industry were similar enough, the chemicals misclassification would not be important. For instance, if

Richard J. Butler, James J. Heckman, & Brook Payner

Table 6.2. *Chemicals and textiles employment*

Year	White males	White females	Black males	Black females
Chemicals and allied products				
1970	13,753	4,227	2,715	835
	63.9%	19.6%	12.5%	3.9%
1960	9,043	1,717	1,777	34
	71.9%	13.7%	14.1%	0.3%
Textile mill products				
1970	69,036	48,670	16,585	9,575
	48.0%	33.8%	11.5%	6.7%
1960	78,651	46,601	6,513	34
	59.5%	35.3%	4.9%	0.3%

Source: 1960: U.S. Bureau of the Census (1964, p. 346); 1970: U.S. Bureau of the Census (1973b, p. 680).

the chemical and textile industries hired employees with similar skills, employed blacks in similar proportions, and had similar capital–labor ratios, then our study based on the county textile data would not be affected by the misclassification of certain chemical plants as textile plants. Unfortunately, the two industries are rather different.

According to the U.S. census bureau, the chemical industry employed more males in 1970 and more blacks in 1960 than the textile industry (see Table 6.2). In addition, the chemical industry employs relatively more skilled workers and is a higher valued-added industry than the textile industry.[8] The problem is not insoluble, however, because prior to 1971 the SCDOL reports the name of each textile establishment. Although it does not report data by establishment, it does report the city and county in which each establishment is located, the kind of goods manufactured, and an index of approximate employment of the firm. We cannot create corrected series from this information, but we can delete the counties in which non-textile firms appear to be counted as textile firms. There are fifteen counties for which consistent time series for all relevant variables can be constructed for the entire sample period. Of those, we use eleven counties that, based on the listing of establishment, are unaffected by the "chemical

[8] From the 1970 Public Use Sample for South Carolina, the average number of school years completed for white males is greater than 12 in the chemical industry in 1970. In the textile industry, the average number of years of school completed is 9 for white males in 1970. In 1970, value added per worker is $7.63 in the textile industry and $19.61 in the chemical industry (Marr and Williams 1973, p. 30).

260

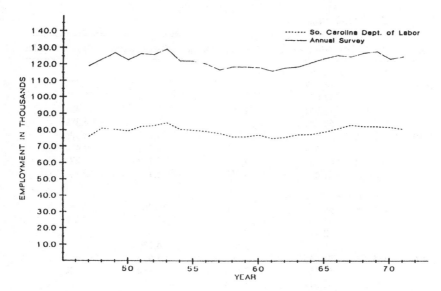

Fig. 6.21. A comparison of South Carolina aggregate eleven-county and statewide aggregate *Annual Survey of Manufactures* employment data for textile production workers.

problem." These counties, Abbeville, Anderson, Cherokee, Chester, Greenville, Lancaster, Laurens, Oconee, Orangeburg, Pickens, and Spartanburg, range from large textile counties (Spartanburg with sixty plants in 1969) to small textile counties (Orangeburg with three plants in 1969). Fig. 6.21 shows textile industry production-worker employment for the eleven-county aggregate and for the *ASM*. Although the levels are different, the trends are quite similar.

As an additional check, we compare SCDOL data on demographic employment in textiles to those reported in the U.S. *Census of Population* for 1940, 1950, 1960, and 1970. The SCDOL data and the census data are not expected to be the same in any year, since the census includes all employees, whereas the SCDOL includes only production workers. In addition, the census interviews workers and the SCDOL interviews firms. Finally, the census includes part-time workers. For these reasons, we expect the census figures to be larger, except perhaps in 1970 when the chemical problem might inflate the SCDOL numbers. Table 6.3 confirms these expectations and documents the black breakthrough observed in the South Carolina data. Similar checks for other industries confirm a close match between the *Census of Population* and SCDOL figures.

261

Richard J. Butler, James J. Heckman, & Brook Payner

Table 6.3. *Textile employment*

Year	Total	White males	White females	Black males	Black females
Total textile employment from U.S. census					
1970	143,779	68,977	48,642	16,585	9,575
		47.8%	33.8%	11.5%	6.5%
1960	132,166	78,951	44,601	6,513	401
		59.5%	35.3%	5.0%	0.3%
1950	131,558	75,613	49,326	6,113	506
		57.5%	37.5%	4.7%	0.4%
1940	100,461	61,701	34,355	5,128	277
		61.4%	34.2%	4.1%	0.3%
Production-worker textile employment from SCDOL					
1970	145,108	68,992	48,548	19,488	8,080
		47.6%	33.5%	13.4%	5.6%
1960	120,665	72,122	42,903	5,448	192
		59.8%	35.6%	4.5%	0.2%
1950	124,379	71,065	42,903	5,987	311
		57.1%	37.8%	4.8%	0.3%
1940	92,725	57,517	31,484	3,555	168
		62.2%	34.0%	3.8%	0.2%

Source: 1940 census data from U.S. Bureau of the Census (1943, p. 370); 1950 census data from U.S. Bureau of the Census (1953, p. 183); 1960 census data from U.S. Bureau of the Census (1964, p. 346); 1970 census data from U.S. Bureau of the Census (1973b, p. 680); SCDOL data from the Department of Labor of the State of South Carolina as described in Appendix A.

South Carolina and the South

For the period 1960–70 two-thirds of the growth in the aggregate occupational index of black males relative to white males is due to improvement in relative wages or occupational standing in the South. Much of this improvement comes in the operative and craftsman categories that are concentrated in manufacturing. Scholars at the U.S. Commission on Civil Rights (1986, Table 8.1) document that the rate of convergence of black male wages to white male wages in percentage terms was almost twice as fast in the South as elsewhere over the period 1960–80 for males aged 25–54. Since roughly half of the black population lives in the South, their estimates imply that two-thirds of the growth in relative black status over the period is attributable to developments in the South.[9] If it can be established that trends in

[9] Smith and Welch (1986) estimate that a sizable component (4–10%) of black male wage improvement in the period 1960–80 occurs in the South. The Smith and Welch

262

Table 6.4. *Employment of blacks and whites in textiles in other southern textile states*

	1950	1960	1970	1980
North Carolina				
Whites	206,383	213,161	282,935	267,207
Blacks	8,746	8,565	46,910	76,620
Georgia				
Whites	95,254	88,659	143,175	145,015
Blacks	7,029	5,955	27,361	46,778
Virginia				
Whites	38,249	34,804	68,702	68,195
Blacks	2,189	1,783	11,969	18,188

Source: U.S. Census Bureau, *Employment by Industry*, 1950, 1960, 1970, and 1980.

black relative status in South Carolina resemble those in the rest of the South, our study of that state acquires a more general character.

The dramatic breakthrough in black employment in South Carolina textiles was also experienced in other major southern textile states. Table 6.4 documents this claim using census data. Annual data are not available for these contiguous states, so it is not possible to compare the timing of the black breakthrough. But we can be sure that the breakthrough in all states occurred in the same decade. It is likely that lessons learned about South Carolina textiles apply to these states as well.

South Carolina is not a microcosm of the South, but the state and the region share many trends. The proportion black in 1940 is higher in South Carolina (44%) than for the South as a whole (26%). The proportion of the population that is black declines in both geographic entities until 1970. Table 6.5 reveals that both South Carolina and the South experienced a substantial decline in agricultural employment between 1940 and 1980 and a substantial growth in manufacturing employment. Owing to the presence of the textile industry in the state, the fraction of the workforce employed in manufacturing is higher in South Carolina than in the South as a whole. The breakout of blacks from traditional sectors was similar in the South and in South Carolina. Tables 6.6 and 6.7 reveal that trends in employment by race and sex

estimate is *net* of educational improvement in the South; the U.S. Commission on Civil Rights estimate includes the effect of educational improvement. Much of the educational improvement of blacks occurred in the South, so there is no necessary inconsistency between the two estimates reported in the text.

Table 6.5. *Industrial distribution of employed persons: all workers (21-65) (percentages)*

Industry	1980	1970	1960	1950	1940
South Carolina					
Agriculture	3.0	4.9	11.7	28.9	34.6
Business services	7.1	5.3	4.5	3.0	1.7
Government	4.4	4.3	3.3	3.0	2.6
Manufacturing	32.3	34.9	33.7	29.3	24.4
Mining/construction	7.6	7.5	6.3	6.1	8.0
Personal services	3.9	7.5	10.2	8.1	11.2
Professional services	18.6	14.5	10.3	5.6	5.0
Trade	16.8	16.0	15.2	11.6	8.6
Other	6.4	5.1	4.8	4.5	4.0
The census South					
Agriculture	3.1	4.3	9.5	20.7	27.3
Business services	9.8	7.4	6.3	4.5	3.8
Government	6.5	6.5	5.7	6.0	4.3
Manufacturing	20.2	21.6	22.3	19.6	16.2
Mining/construction	9.1	8.5	8.9	10.7	11.6
Personal services	3.8	6.6	8.7	7.5	10.1
Professional services	20.1	17.4	11.8	6.5	6.0
Trade	18.9	20.2	19.4	16.6	13.8
Other	8.4	7.4	7.5	8.0	6.9

Source: Computed from 1940, 1950, 1960, 1970, and 1980 Public Use Samples.

are also similar. The convergence of the industrial distribution of black employment to white employment is similar in both regions. Employment in domestic service (personal services) and agriculture declines for black women, and employment in manufacturing and professional services increases in South Carolina and in the South. Trends in government employment are similar for all demographic groups. The time-series pattern of relative wages is similar in South Carolina and the South. See Table 6.8 for wage rates of workers aged 21-65. (The recorded jump in relative black male wages in the South in the 1950 census and its subsequent decline is not a typographical error and constitutes an exception to the basic pattern of similarity between southern and South Carolina data.) The pattern of educational improvement is the same in the South as in South Carolina (see Table 6.9).

There are differences between South Carolina and the South in terms of labor market characteristics. South Carolina has a higher percentage black, more manufacturing employment, and lower wages,

Table 6.6. *Industrial distribution of employed persons: (21–65) in South Carolina (percentages)*

Industry	1980	1970	1960	1950	1940
Black females					
Agriculture	2.6	8.7	24.2	39.2	39.2
Business services	3.5	1.0	0.2	0.5	0.0
Government	3.5	0.9	0.2	0.2	0.2
Manufacturing	32.5	19.9	4.1	2.4	2.0
Mining/construction	0.6	0.3	0.2	0.1	0.0
Personal services	13.9	36.9	51.2	43.8	51.4
Professional services	29.7	22.7	14.5	9.3	5.7
Trade	11.3	8.3	4.6	4.0	1.4
Other	2.3	1.2	0.7	0.6	0.1
Black males					
Agriculture	6.4	12.6	27.2	50.6	58.3
Business services	3.8	2.6	1.7	1.6	1.0
Government	4.5	3.7	1.8	1.3	0.7
Manufacturing	38.2	33.0	24.2	19.7	14.5
Mining/construction	15.6	16.1	14.7	8.6	10.5
Personal services	1.9	3.7	4.6	2.9	4.1
Professional services	8.9	8.3	6.3	3.2	2.3
Trade	12.0	11.9	12.2	6.5	4.4
Other	8.8	8.1	7.2	5.6	4.3
White females					
Agriculture	1.1	1.0	2.8	7.6	9.6
Business services	8.9	6.3	5.8	2.7	1.0
Government	3.9	3.6	3.7	2.6	3.3
Manufacturing	28.8	39.3	43.3	51.9	48.2
Mining/construction	1.7	1.3	0.6	0.9	0.9
Personal services	3.8	4.8	4.7	4.9	7.9
Professional services	27.8	21.8	17.1	12.9	14.7
Trade	20.3	18.8	18.5	14.4	12.4
Other	3.8	3.2	3.6	2.0	1.9
White males					
Agriculture	3.6	4.5	8.2	20.8	26.4
Business services	7.9	6.6	6.1	4.6	2.9
Government	5.0	6.2	4.8	5.0	4.3
Manufacturing	33.5	36.6	40.5	34.7	30.5
Mining/construction	12.5	12.4	9.8	8.5	11.6
Personal services	1.3	1.6	1.7	1.5	2.5
Professional services	9.8	7.5	4.9	3.0	3.3
Trade	17.1	17.4	17.5	15.9	12.5
Other	9.2	7.1	6.4	5.9	6.0

Source: Computed from 1940, 1950, 1960, 1970, and 1980 Public Use Samples.

Table 6.7. *Industrial distribution of employed persons: (21–65) in the census South (percentages)*

Industry	1980	1970	1960	1950	1940
Black females					
Agriculture	1.6	3.8	15.6	16.5	17.7
Business services	7.0	3.0	2.4	1.4	0.9
Government	8.1	4.4	2.3	1.9	0.7
Manufacturing	17.2	12.0	4.4	5.1	3.5
Mining/construction	0.9	0.4	0.0	0.2	0.3
Personal services	13.7	34.7	48.9	53.1	65.8
Professional services	33.0	27.3	15.0	10.4	6.6
Trade	14.3	12.3	10.0	10.4	4.0
Other	4.2	2.1	1.3	1.0	0.5
Black males					
Agriculture	4.9	10.1	18.8	33.2	43.6
Business services	5.9	3.8	2.7	2.8	2.5
Government	6.4	7.5	5.4	3.6	1.5
Manufacturing	26.9	27.1	23.4	20.9	14.2
Mining/construction	13.6	12.6	12.5	10.8	12.6
Personal services	2.5	4.5	6.3	5.3	7.5
Professional services	12.9	10.3	7.3	3.6	2.8
Trade	14.5	12.9	14.1	10.8	8.2
Other	12.4	11.3	9.5	9.0	7.1
White females					
Agriculture	1.5	1.5	3.0	6.3	5.0
Business services	12.0	8.6	7.9	5.0	4.1
Government	5.7	5.2	5.7	6.7	6.3
Manufacturing	16.7	19.7	21.6	23.0	22.9
Mining/construction	2.2	1.7	1.4	1.1	0.9
Personal services	4.9	6.9	8.6	9.3	16.1
Professional services	30.0	27.0	20.7	17.0	18.8
Trade	22.2	25.0	25.9	26.7	21.7
Other	4.8	4.4	5.3	5.0	4.3
White males					
Agriculture	4.4	5.8	11.2	22.2	30.0
Business services	9.1	7.9	6.5	5.1	4.4
Government	7.0	7.8	6.3	6.8	5.0
Manufacturing	22.6	23.9	25.8	20.0	16.7
Mining/construction	15.6	14.7	15.0	14.7	15.5
Personal services	1.3	1.9	2.2	2.0	2.3
Professional services	10.7	9.1	5.9	3.8	3.6
Trade	17.7	18.9	17.4	15.9	14.4
Other	11.6	10.0	9.7	9.4	8.3

Source: Computed from 1940, 1950, 1960, 1970, and 1980 Public Use Samples.

Table 6.8. *Average wages (in 1967 dollars) of employed persons with earnings (ages 21–65)*

	Average hourly wage				Black/white wages	
Year	White males	White females	Black males	Black females	Males	Females
South Carolina						
1940	1.49	1.33	0.48	0.54	0.32	0.41
1950	1.47	1.22	0.68	0.53	0.46	0.43
1960	2.49	1.76	1.42	1.07	0.57	0.61
1970	3.16	2.26	1.89	1.52	0.60	0.67
1980	3.13	2.16	2.34	2.07	0.75	0.96
Census South						
1940	1.61	1.23	0.76	0.51	0.47	0.41
1950	1.53	1.39	1.10	0.87	0.72	0.63
1960	2.85	2.02	1.79	1.33	0.63	0.66
1970	3.58	2.40	2.45	2.20	0.68	0.92
1980	3.48	2.27	2.76	2.26	0.79	1.00
South Carolina relative to the United States						
1940	0.75	0.95	0.52	0.90		
1950	0.81	0.80	0.49	0.50		
1960	0.77	0.77	0.67	0.68		
1970	0.79	0.83	0.65	0.65		
1980	0.83	0.89	0.85	0.83		
Census South relative to the United States						
1940	0.81	0.88	0.83	0.85		
1950	0.84	0.91	0.80	0.82		
1960	0.89	0.88	0.84	0.84		
1970	0.90	0.88	0.84	0.94		
1980	0.93	0.93	0.89	0.83		

Source: Computed from 1940, 1950, 1960, 1970, and 1980 Public Use Samples.

and its workers are less educated than those in the rest of the South. Nonetheless, the trends in southern labor markets are undeniably reflected in the labor market of South Carolina. Lessons learned about black progress in South Carolina seem likely to apply to the South as a whole.

5. The causes of the improvement in black economic status in South Carolina manufacturing

Various demand-side and supply-side explanations have been offered as the cause of the black breakthrough in manufacturing in South

Richard J. Butler, James J. Heckman, & Brook Payner

Table 6.9. *Highest grade completed (employed persons with earnings)*

	Average grade				Black/white average	
Year	White males	White females	Black males	Black females	Males	Females
South Carolina						
1940	8.6	9.1	4.2	5.4	49%	59%
1950	9.1	9.8	5.1	6.3	56%	64%
1960	9.8	10.6	6.2	7.7	63%	73%
1970	10.9	11.3	7.7	9.4	71%	83%
1980	12.3	12.3	10.3	11.4	84%	93%
Census South						
1940	8.8	10.5	5.3	6.6	60%	63%
1950	9.2	10.8	5.8	7.3	63%	68%
1960	10.1	11.1	7.3	8.7	72%	78%
1970	11.3	11.6	8.9	9.9	79%	85%
1980	12.7	12.6	11.1	11.9	87%	94%
South Carolina relative to the United States						
1940	93%	87%	75%	78%		
1950	93%	91%	78%	81%		
1960	92%	95%	78%	85%		
1970	93%	96%	80%	90%		
1980	95%	96%	90%	93%		
Census South relative to the United States						
1940	96%	101%	95%	96%		
1950	94%	100%	89%	94%		
1960	94%	99%	91%	96%		
1970	97%	98%	93%	95%		
1980	98%	98%	97%	98%		

Source: Computed from 1940, 1950, 1960, 1970, and 1980 Public Use Samples.

Carolina. On the supply side, one explanation relates to the decline of agricultural employment in the South, which was a consequence of technology and government policy and which led to shifts in the supply of blacks available to manufacturing as blacks migrated from the rural areas to the cities. In South Carolina, black employment in agriculture declined by about 98,000 workers between 1950 and 1970. Over the same two decades, black employment in manufacturing increased by about 40,000 workers. The timing of these changes suggests a possible causal role, with the decline of agriculture releasing supplies of black labor to the manufacturing sector.

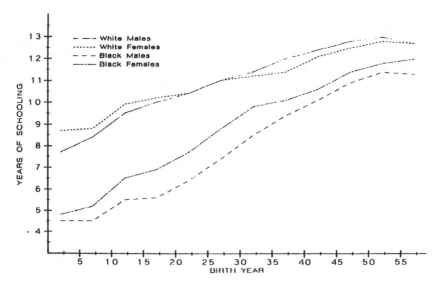

Fig. 6.22. Average highest grade completed in South Carolina, by year of birth.

A second supply-side explanation relates to the increasing quantity and quality of black education during the 1940s and 50s that made blacks better qualified to compete with whites in the labor market. In South Carolina, there is considerable evidence of black educational gains relative to whites during the years leading up to 1965. Fig. 6.22 shows the average highest grade completed by five-year birth cohort from 1900 to 1954.[10] The figure shows steady convergence over the period. It is well known, however, that one year of schooling for a black student was not equivalent to one year of schooling for a white student in the system of segregated schools that existed in South Carolina prior to 1960. The convergence demonstrated in Fig. 6.22 understates the true convergence measured in terms of quality-adjusted years of schooling completed, because the quality of black schooling was increasing over time.

The fact that blacks were making gains relative to whites in terms of education can be seen in Figs. 6.23 and 6.24. These figures show total current expenditure per student from 1931 to 1957 by race in South

[10] These figures were calculated using the 1950 Public Use Sample for the cohorts born between 1900 and 1924 and the 1980 Public Use Sample for the cohorts born between 1925 and 1954.

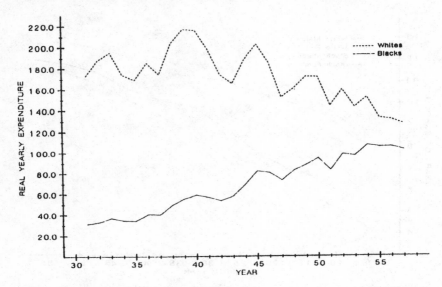

Fig. 6.23. Real education expenditure per student in South Carolina: elementary students.

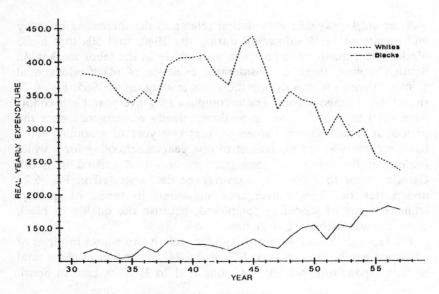

Fig. 6.24. Real education expenditure per student in South Carolina: high school students.

Carolina.[11] Elementary school expenditure per student began to converge in the 1940s (Fig. 6.23). High school expenditure per student began to converge in the mid to late 1940s, though there was a much larger expenditure gap for high school students in 1931 than for elementary school students (Fig. 6.24).[12] Black students educated in the latter part of the period clearly received better education relative to whites than students educated in the earlier years.

On the demand side, one explanation relates to labor market conditions in the South during the 1960s. The argument goes that as labor markets tightened and the demand for labor increased, the costs of discrimination increased as white workers' wages rose relative to those of black workers. If the costs of discrimination were high enough, opportunities would increase for blacks in the industries that had been discriminating. As previously noted, evidence of tight labor markets during the mid-sixties was strong. The period of the mid to late sixties was characterized by strong economic growth and low unemployment. South Carolina was an active participant in the growth of the South and actively recruited firms to the state (Cobb 1982, 1984).

On the demand side, the most obvious explanation assigns a central role to federal government affirmative action and civil rights activity.

6. Macro time-series evidence on the impact of government policy

The conventional econometric approach to the analysis of the impact of public policy specifies an economic model in which policy variables are explicitly parameterized and estimates the model on aggregate time-series data. In an influential study of this kind, Freeman (1973) analyzed the aggregate U.S. relative wage data and concluded that government civil rights and affirmative action policy raised black relative wages. Subsequent analyses by Butler and Heckman (1977) and Brown (1984) refine Freeman's analysis in various ways and demonstrate the fragility of the macro time-series evidence on the impact of government policy.

Butler (1985) estimates a model like Freeman's using data for the South Carolina manufacturing sector for the period 1940–71. He also estimates a structural model of the demand for labor by race for South

---

[11] Since black and white schools were completely segregated during the 1940s and 50s, differences in schooling quality can be proxied by differences in total current expenditure per student in black versus white schools.

[12] Data are from the *Annual Report of the State Superintendent of Education to the State of South Carolina*, Tables XXIV and XXV, various years 1931–57.

Carolina. The demand for labor is specified to depend on wages, a post-1965 dummy variable proxying federal affirmative action activity and deviations of real manufacturing output in South Carolina from a linear trend interpreted as a measure of business-cycle impact. Supply is postulated to depend on wages, a quality-adjusted measure of schooling (schooling expenditure by race), measures of social welfare program benefits (Aid to Families with Dependent Children and unemployment insurance payments as well as the maximum weeks of unemployment insurance eligibility), opportunities outside the state (the average South Carolina wage relative to the U.S. average wage), and opportunities in agriculture (the number of acres of cotton harvested). See Table 6.10 for more precise definitions of the variables. Butler concludes that there is strong evidence that measured policy variables raise black employment both in levels and in ratios (relative to whites). He finds weaker evidence that measured policy variables raise black relative wages.

In light of the notoriously fragile nature of aggregate time-series regression models fitted on short time series, his evidence is intrinsically unconvincing. The serially correlated nature of time-series data coupled with the instability of fitted models to the inclusion or exclusion of regressors that are only weakly motivated by behavioral theory causes most economists to view aggregative time-series evidence with skepticism. Compounding this disbelief is the lack of any convincing measure of policy variables – a common problem that plagues many policy evaluations. In this section of the essay, we summarize our exploration of the fragility of the time-series evidence and our reanalysis of the Butler model using an approach to robust model evaluation developed by Edward Leamer. A more complete analysis is presented in Appendix B.

In his book (Leamer 1978) and in a later paper (Leamer and Leonard 1983), Leamer suggests classifying potential explanatory variables into two groups: "important" variables, which are thought to belong in any specification, and "doubtful" variables, which are thought to be controversial. Regressions are fitted including and excluding all possible combinations of doubtful variables for a variety of specifications of the "important" variables. The robustness of a model is measured by the range of values assumed by the coefficients of the "important" variables when models with all possible linear combinations of the "doubtful" variables are fitted, including all possible exclusions of those variables.

Leamer has developed a computer program called SEARCH that implements his methodology. It computes the upper value and lower value of each "important" coefficient for all possible linear combina-

Table 6.10. *Definitions of explanatory variables used in aggregative analysis*

Variable	Definition
Cycle	Deviation of annual industrial sales in South Carolina from trend[a]
Relative wage	Wages of white males in South Carolina relative to wages of male production workers in the USA as a whole
Gov't policy (1) ("Dum")	Dummy variable = 1 after 1965; = 0 otherwise.
Gov't policy (2) ("Dum·Time")	Gov't policy multiplied by time (last two digits of calendar year)
Gov't policy 3 ("EEO Trend")	A variable = 0 before 1966, 1 in 1966, 2 in 1967, 3 in 1968, etc.
AFDC	South Carolina per capita expenditures for the AFDC program
Max benefit	Maximum weekly unemployment insurance benefits in South Carolina
Max weeks	Maximum number of weeks one can receive unemployment benefits
Cotton	Log of the number of acres of cotton harvested each year in South Carolina
Human capital	See Appendix C

[a] Residuals from the regression (t statistics in parentheses)

$$RVLA = 14.134 - .058 \,(\text{Time}) \quad R^2 = 0.71$$
$$(376.2) \quad (25.58)$$

where time is a linear time trend taking a value of 1 in 1940 and *RVLA* is the real value of annual product. The regression is fitted over the sample period 1940–71. The source of *RVLA* is the *Annual Report of the Department of Labor of the State of South Carolina*. *RVLA* is closely related to value added by manufactures as reported in the *Annual Survey of Manufactures*, which is only available after 1947. For the period 1948–71, the regression of value added (*RVA*) on *RVLA* is

$$RVA = -215.96 + 0.00055 \, RVALA$$
$$(3.13) \quad (35.3)$$
$$R^2 = 0.983$$

tions of the "doubtful" variables. We use SEARCH to estimate the impact of policy on the reduced forms of Butler's model for South Carolina.

Three alternative measures of government policy are used: (1) a dummy variable that assumes the value of 1 after 1965; (2) a dummy variable as in (1) plus a time trend interacted with the dummy (time is measured by the last two digits of the calendar year); and (3) a pure time trend that equals 1 in 1965, 2 in 1966, and so on. No single measure is especially cogent.

We apply Leamer's extreme-bounds analysis to aggregate manufacturing data for the state. There are thirty-two observations over the period 1940–71. To see how robust the estimated "policy-shift" effect is in Butler's model, we look at the variability in the estimated shift (a post-65 dummy) coefficient given linear combinations of other variables that might plausibly be included in the analysis. The "doubtful" variables are listed in the notes at the foot of Table 6.11. The estimated upper and lower bounds given for each of the three possible policy measures by race and gender are given in the main body of the table. For example, the "0.713" in the right-hand column of the first row is the least-squares coefficient of the dummy shift variable in the black female employment equation. If we adopt a two-standard deviation rule for the measure of the stochastic variability of the estimated structural shift, the width of the stochastic uncertainty for this coefficient is 0.872 (four times the standard error of 0.218). We want to contrast the stochastic uncertainty of the parameter estimate with the uncertainty due to lack of knowledge of the correct regression model specification. This latter type of uncertainty we call "specification error," or coefficient "fragility." That is measured by the difference between the largest (2.018 for our example) and smallest (0.505) estimated values of the coefficient, given all possible linear combinations of the doubtful variables. For black females we find that the specification uncertainty is twice as great as the stochastic uncertainty. Indeed, for all race/gender groups and for all specifications of the structural shift, the stochastic uncertainty for the policy measures in the employment equations is less than half the size of the specification uncertainty, and often it is only about a tenth of the size. However, there is more fragility in the estimated structural shift for wages than for employment, and more specification uncertainty (with respect to structural shift) for whites than there is for blacks.

In Appendix B we report the results of an extensive SEARCH analysis using additional samples and specifications. A parallel analysis is performed for the textile industry data isolated from the aggregate manufacturing data. Disaggregation sharpens our empirical results: Specification uncertainty declines relative to estimation error. There are positive upper and lower bounds of estimated policy effects on employment for both black groups for all measures of policy except "EEO Trend" – a post-1965 linear trend indicating a positive effect of measured policy variables on black employment. Our results for aggregate manufacturing and for the textile sample are generally robust to

Table 6.11. *South Carolina aggregate manufacturing*

	White male	White female	Black male	Black female
Race/gender-specific employment as the dependent variable				
Specification 1[a]				
Dum (Std. error)	−0.027 (0.052)	−0.094 (0.035)	0.396 (0.074)	0.713 (0.218)
Upper	0.448	0.637	0.833	2.018
Lower	−0.244	−0.367	0.253	0.505
Specification 2[b,c]				
Dum (Std. error)	1.126 (2.73)	0.381 (0.242)	−1.604 (0.314)	−4.856 (0.996)
Upper	2.294	2.249	−0.649	0.7615
Lower	−0.531	−1.836	−2.726	−8.944
Dum·Time (Std. error)	−0.039 (0.009)	−0.016 (0.008)	0.069 (0.011)	0.194 (0.034)
Upper	0.021	0.065	0.110	0.349
Lower	−0.073	−0.070	0.042	0.018
Specification 3[b]				
EEO Trend (Std. error)	−0.024 (0.008)	−0.020 (0.006)	0.093 (0.009)	0.217 (0.025)
Upper	0.077	0.124	0.188	0.479
Lower	−0.053	−0.061	−0.076	0.185
Race/gender-specific wages as the dependent variable				
Specification 1[a]				
Dum (Std. error)	−0.039 (0.029)	−0.032 (0.027)	0.064 (0.048)	−0.094 (0.112)
Upper	0.682	0.649	0.898	1.166
Lower	−0.376	−0.375	−0.472	−0.587

Table 6.11. (cont.)

	White male	White female	Black male	Black female
Specification 2[b]				
Dum (Std. error)	0.178 (0.207)	0.219 (0.196)	−0.503 (0.299)	−0.929 (0.775)
Upper	2.211	2.229	2.178	2.412
Lower	−1.995	−1.927	−3.153	−4.068
Dum·Time (Std. error)	−0.007 (0.007)	−0.008 (0.007)	0.016 (0.010)	0.031 (0.026)
Upper	0.071	0.068	0.112	0.146
Lower	−0.068	−0.069	−0.064	−0.068
Specification 3[b]				
EEO trend (Std. error)	−0.007 (0.005)	−0.007 (0.005)	0.003 (0.008)	0.013 (0.019)
Upper	0.130	0.123	0.179	0.232
Lower	−0.059	−0.062	−0.060	−0.060

Note: In all specifications, the logarithms of the following variables were also included as "doubtful" variables: per capita AFDC expenditures, unemployment benefits and maximum number of weeks of eligibility, acres of cotton harvested each year, and the logarithmic difference between S.C. and U.S. wage rates. The "important" or "free" variables in all specifications included the intercept, deviations of industrial output from S.C. trend, and the "structural shift" variables listed above.

[a] The log of aggregate capital was included.

[b] A linear time trend was included.

[c] Note in specification 2 that the effect of policy is the coefficient on Dum + the coefficient of Dum·Time multiplied by the last two digits of the calendar year. This coefficient is positive for all black male models and all except the extreme-lower-bound model for black females.

Table 6.12. *Manufacturing and agricultural employment*

Year	White males	White females	Black males	Black females
Manufacturing				
1950	110,182	63,883	34,020	2,663
1960	137,357	82,251	34,097	3,798
1970	162,652	106,437	50,515	25,819
Agriculture				
1950	72,773	7,730	89,882	27,794
1960	33,318	4,304	43,724	14,290
1970	18,305	2,333	15,403	3,737

Source: 1950: U.S. Bureau of the Census (1953, p. 183); 1960: U.S. Bureau of the Census (1964, p. 346); 1970: U.S. Bureau of the Census (1973b, p. 680).

the inclusion of cubic time trends and lagged variables to control for serial correlation.

These results corroborate what may be obvious from Figs. 6.1–6: that there is an upward structural shift in the employment time series for blacks in aggregate manufacturing and textiles after 1965. This shift does not go away when a variety of plausible demand-side and supply-side variables are used as control variables and when time trends are introduced and account is taken of serial correlation. Macro time-series evidence of policy effects on wages for any demographic group is much weaker.

7. The micro evidence

Supply shifts

In this section, we examine in detail the micro evidence in support of the major hypotheses beginning with the supply-shift hypothesis. Table 6.12 shows agricultural and manufacturing employment in South Carolina in 1950, 1960, and 1970 by race and sex. The numbers indicate that although black agricultural employment declined by 60,000 during the fifties, black manufacturing employment increased by only 1,200, suggesting virtually no effect of the decline in agriculture during the fifties on manufacturing employment. During the sixties, black agricultural employment decreased by about 38,000 and black manufacturing employment increased by a similar amount. However, the changes by sex demonstrate that black males accounted for most of the decline in agricultural employment (28,000) but for less than half of the in-

Richard J. Butler, James J. Heckman, & Brook Payner

Table 6.13. *Industry in 1965 of manufacturing employees in 1970: workers aged 26–65 in 1970 (percentages)*

Industry in 1965	Black females	Black males	White females	White males
Agriculture	1.74	3.63	0.00	1.17
Manufacturing	42.61	64.35	70.54	77.91
Government	0.00	0.66	0.52	1.17
Mining/construction	0.00	3.63	0.00	1.92
Services	9.57	2.97	1.68	2.09
Trade	2.61	4.29	2.33	2.42
Other	0.00	2.97	0.26	1.00
Industry not reported	6.09	9.57	4.78	6.75
Unemployed or out of labor force	37.39	7.92	19.90	5.58

Source: Computed from 1970 Public Use Sample.

crease in black manufacturing employment (10,000). Most of the increase in black manufacturing employment was accounted for by females (22,000), whereas black female agricultural employment declined by only 10,000. A simple supply-shift argument cannot account for the growth in black manufacturing employment during the sixties or the fifties.

We also have a direct method of determining whether new entrants into manufacturing previously worked in agriculture.[13] The data come from the 1970 Public Use Sample of the U.S. Census Bureau. Table 6.13 gives the distribution of employment in 1965 of all workers employed in manufacturing in 1970. For black females, under 2 percent of manufacturing employees in 1970 were employed in agriculture in 1965. For black males, under 4 percent were in agriculture in 1965. The corresponding percentages for white females and white males are 0 and 1 respectively. Although only 42 percent of black females in manufacturing in 1970 were in the same industry in 1965, compared with 70 percent for white females, very few black females came from agriculture. Most black females came from the prior status unemployed or out of the labor force. Most of the rest of the black females came from the service sector.

For black males, 64 percent were in manufacturing in 1965 as well as in 1970, compared with 78 percent for white males. Again, relatively few black males came from agriculture. In fact, black males came from

[13] In this analysis agriculture is defined as including forestry and fisheries.

278

Table 6.14. *Average and adjusted years of school completed: textiles, 1960*

Cohort	White males		White females	
	Average	Adjusted	Average	Adjusted
21–25	9.3	11	10.6	12
26–30	8.7	11	9.6	12
31–35	8.6	11	9.6	12
36–40	8.1	10	9.0	11
41–45	8.1	10	8.0	10
46–50	7.3	9	7.7	10
51–55	6.8	9	6.7	9
56–60	6.0	8	6.4	8

Source: Computed from 1960 Public Use Sample.

several industries in fairly equal proportions, including services, mining and construction, and trade.

Schooling quality and quantity

We next consider the hypothesis that assigns a control role to schooling quality and quantity. Table 6.14 gives the average education, by five-year cohort, of white males and white females employed in the textile industry in 1960. These averages are indicative of the education required for employment in the textile industry in 1960.[14] Since the quality of black schooling is lower than that of whites, Table 6.14 also reports quality-corrected or -adjusted years of education. The adjusted figures are formed by adding two years to the white average and rounding to the nearest complete year, or to twelve, whichever is smaller. The purpose of this admittedly ad hoc adjustment is to correct for the difference in schooling quality by race to see if blacks are qualified to work in textiles on the basis of their educational attainment.

In Table 6.15, we show the percentage of black males and females in South Carolina with years of schooling completed greater than or equal to the white male and female adjusted averages given in Table 6.14. By comparison, Table 6.16 shows the percentage of black males and females with twelve or more years of schooling completed.

Table 6.15 reveals that by 1960 over 25 percent of all blacks in South

[14] Since Table 6.14 reports average education of whites currently employed in textiles, the actual required education must be less than these figures.

Table 6.15. *Percentage of blacks with average education level of whites: textiles, 1960*

Cohort	Black males	Black females
21–25	25.9	31.7
26–30	25.4	22.4
31–35	17.7	18.2
36–40	15.3	20.9
41–45	8.4	21.6
46–50	14.2	20.4
51–55	10.2	11.4
56–60	16.2	18.8

Source: Computed from 1960 Public Use Sample.

Carolina between the ages of 21 and 30 had sufficient education to be employed in textiles. In the older cohorts, about 20 percent of black females and 15 percent of black males had sufficient education. Table 6.16 tells a similar story even if we assume that a black would require twelve years of schooling to be qualified to work in the textile industry. Yet fewer than 1 percent of employed black females and fewer than 5 percent of employed black males between the ages of 21 and 65 worked in the textile industry in 1960. About 25 percent of all employed whites in the same age range worked in textiles in 1960. As early as 1960, lack of education was not keeping blacks out of textiles.

One implication of a pure form of the educational-improvements hypothesis is that, controlling for education, age, and other individual characteristics, blacks should not be underrepresented in the textile industry in 1960 relative to 1970. Tables 6.17 and 6.18 give the coefficients on a race dummy variable from a series of linear-probability regression models for males and females respectively. The sample of all employed persons is broken down by gender and five-year cohort.[15] The left-hand-side variable is equal to 1 if the individual is employed in a given industry and is 0 otherwise. The right-hand-side variables include an intercept, years of schooling, years of schooling squared, and a race dummy equal to 1 for blacks and 0 for whites.[16] The

[15] The regressions were also run using civilian labor force and total population as the sample instead of employed persons. The qualitative results described in the text are the same as those obtained for the additional samples.

[16] Selected regressions were repeated using a probit specification to correct for heteroskedasticity. The results are qualitatively similar to those reported here.

Separate regressions are run for each sex group. Thus the dummy variable measures the employment probability for blacks of a given sex relative to whites of the same sex group.

Table 6.16. *Percentage of blacks completing twelve or more years of schooling in 1960*

Cohort	Black males	Black females
21–25	19.9	31.7
26–30	20.4	22.4
31–35	12.7	18.2
36–40	9.8	14.9
41–45	4.4	11.6
46–50	7.1	10.4
51–55	6.3	4.0
56–60	6.1	6.0

Source: Computed from 1960 Public Use Sample.

Table 6.17. *Race coefficients from male employment: linear-probability models (t-statistics in parentheses)*

Age	1940	1950	1960	1970	1980
Agriculture, forestry, and fisheries					
21–25	0.19	0.08	0.16	0.03	0.02
	(4.73)	(1.16)	(5.74)	(2.69)	(2.55)
26–30	0.22	0.28	0.11	0.06	0.01
	(5.66)	(4.26)	(3.95)	(4.03)	(0.88)
31–35	0.19	0.18	0.08	0.04	0.01
	(3.98)	(2.47)	(3.06)	(2.83)	(2.06)
36–40	0.31	0.17	0.16	0.03	0.01
	(6.63)	(2.33)	(4.92)	(1.59)	(1.7)
41–45	0.24	−0.11	0.16	0.04	0.03
	(4.33)	(1.09)	(4.27)	(2.34)	(3.14)
46–50	0.22	0.26	0.12	0.03	0.02
	(4.04)	(2.56)	(3.14)	(1.61)	(2.49)
51–55	0.23	0.45	0.12	0.06	0.03
	(3.7)	(4.26)	(2.4)	(2.46)	(2.85)
56–60	0.12	0.24	0.21	0.06	0.02
	(1.73)	(1.68)	(3.83)	(2.4)	(1.69)
61–65	0.20	0.25	0.24	0.00	0.01
	(2.53)	(1.66)	(2.5)	(0.04)	(0.71)
Mining and construction					
21–25	−0.03	0.02	0.07	−0.04	−0.03
	(1.23)	(0.47)	(2.5)	(1.99)	(2.3)
26–30	−0.02	−0.05	0.09	0.02	−0.04
	(0.59)	(0.99)	(2.54)	(0.7)	(3.39)
31–35	−0.06	0.07	0.03	−0.04	−0.02
	(1.59)	(1.15)	(0.94)	(1.41)	(1.32)
36–40	0.01	0.03	−0.04	−0.04	−0.01

281

Table 6.17. *(cont.)*

Age	1940	1950	1960	1970	1980
	(0.24)	(0.54)	(1.25)	(1.36)	(0.37)
41–45	−0.04	0.06	0.02	0.06	0.01
	(1.01)	(1)	(0.61)	(2.29)	(0.93)
46–50	−0.01	0.09	0.06	0.07	0.01
	(0.24)	(1.26)	(1.9)	(2.5)	(0.87)
51–55	−0.05	−0.08	0.07	0.02	0.02
	(1.15)	(1.42)	(1.55)	(0.62)	(1.51)
56–60	−0.01	−0.05	−0.05	−0.04	0.05
	(0.38)	(1.05)	(1.1)	(1.41)	(2.64)
61–65	−0.08	0.08	−0.04	0.01	0.04
	(1.45)	(0.66)	(0.69)	(0.29)	(1.71)
Transportation, communication, and utilities					
21–25	0.01	0.01	0.01	−0.02	−0.02
	(0.68)	(0.16)	(0.25)	(1.07)	(2.7)
26–30	−0.02	−0.02	0.02	0.00	−0.02
	(0.8)	(0.5)	(0.76)	(0.19)	(2.27)
31–35	—[a]	0.01	0.01	0.02	−0.01
	—	(0.14)	(0.47)	(1.05)	(1.05)
36–40	0.00	0.10	0.04	−0.02	−0.00
	(0.39)	(2.04)	(1.4)	(0.69)	(0.25)
41–45	−0.03	0.14	0.04	−0.00	−0.00
	(1.17)	(2.03)	(1.48)	(0.17)	(0.22)
46–50	0.04	−0.04	−0.00	0.02	0.00
	(1.46)	(0.71)	(0.04)	(1.02)	(0.07)
51–55	−0.03	−0.03	0.03	0.06	0.01
	(1.1)	(1.31)	(0.83)	(2.79)	(0.81)
56–60	−0.04	−0.04	0.00	0.02	0.02
	(1.21)	(1.21)	(0.01)	(1.21)	(1.38)
61–65	0.01	−0.04	−0.02	−0.00	0.03
	(0.59)	(0.48)	(0.52)	(0.04)	(1.4)
Wholesale and retail trade					
21–25	0.04	−0.08	−0.01	−0.05	−0.05
	(1.31)	(1.39)	(0.23)	(2.11)	(3.85)
26–30	−0.03	−0.13	0.02	−0.05	−0.07
	(1.43)	(2.24)	(0.47)	(2)	(5.81)
31–35	0.03	−0.09	−0.03	0.00	−0.06
	(1.03)	(1.4)	(0.73)	(0.03)	(4.9)
36–40	−0.05	−0.06	−0.03	0.04	−0.05
	(1.56)	(1.02)	(0.84)	(1.32)	(3.42)
41–45	−0.03	−0.02	0.02	−0.01	−0.05
	(0.75)	(0.3)	(0.42)	(0.27)	(3.09)
46–50	−0.10	−0.01	−0.03	−0.04	−0.05
	(2.9)	(0.16)	(0.97)	(1.54)	(2.83)
51–55	−0.04	−0.11	0.02	−0.06	−0.04
	(0.93)	(1.12)	(0.33)	(1.91)	(2.31)

Table 6.17. *(cont.)*

Age	1940	1950	1960	1970	1980
56–60	−0.06	−0.14	−0.07	−0.05	−0.05
	(1.8)	(1.52)	(1.48)	(1.64)	(2.24)
61–65	−0.02	−0.14	−0.07	−0.05	−0.11
	(0.5)	(0.95)	(0.8)	(1.2)	(3.61)
Federal government					
21–25	−0.04	—	0.00	0.00	0.00
	(2.86)	—	(0.01)	(0.04)	(0.88)
26–30	−0.01	−0.01	−0.00	0.00	0.00
	(0.90)	(0.44)	(0.10)	(0.16)	(0.30)
31–35	0.01	−0.00	0.02	−0.00	−0.00
	(0.52)	(0.24)	(1.00)	(0.27)	(0.56)
36–40	−0.01	0.03	−0.01	0.00	−0.00
	(0.88)	(1.90)	(0.54)	(0.20)	(0.58)
41–45	0.00	−0.01	−0.01	−0.01	0.00
	(0.05)	(0.19)	(0.66)	(0.67)	(0.24)
46–50	0.01	−0.00	−0.01	−0.01	0.00
	(0.31)	(0.06)	(0.65)	(0.67)	(0.55)
51–55	0.01	−0.03	−0.01	0.00	0.01
	(0.76)	(0.57)	(0.41)	(0.15)	(0.82)
56–60	−0.01	—	0.01	0.03	0.01
	(0.73)	—	(0.26)	(1.45)	(0.57)
61–65	0.01	—	−0.03	0.01	0.01
	(0.35)	—	(0.82)	(0.52)	(0.63)
State government (excluding schoolteachers)					
21–25	−0.00	—	—	−0.00	0.01
	(0.63)	—	—	(0.18)	(2.20)
26–30	−0.00	−0.00	−0.00	−0.01	0.01
	(0.25)	(0.38)	(0.42)	(0.19)	(1.13)
31–35	−0.01	—	−0.00	−0.00	0.00
	(0.61)	—	(0.52)	(0.48)	(0.36)
36–40	−0.01	—	−0.00	−0.00	0.00
	(0.50)	—	(0.25)	(0.61)	(0.89)
41–45	−0.01	—	0.00	−0.00	0.00
	(0.61)	—	(0.04)	(0.65)	(0.45)
46–50	−0.01	—	−0.00	0.00	0.02
	(0.90)	—	(0.42)	(0.75)	(2.75)
51–55	−0.03	−0.02	−0.00	−0.00	−0.01
	(1.33)	(0.54)	(0.21)	(0.42)	(1.19)
56–60	−0.02	—	−0.00	−0.01	0.01
	(1.01)	—	(0.17)	(0.98)	(1.00)
61–65	−0.01	—	−0.01	−0.00	−0.00
	(0.59)	—	(0.41)	(0.35)	(0.32)
Local government (excluding schoolteachers)					
21–25	—	−0.00	0.01	−0.01	−0.00
	—	(0.13)	(0.81)	(1.08)	(0.59)

Table 6.17. *(cont.)*

Age	1940	1950	1960	1970	1980
26–30	—	—	−0.01	−0.01	−0.00
	—	—	(0.60)	(0.76)	(0.23)
31–35	—	0.07	−0.00	−0.00	0.00
	—	(3.29)	(0.35)	(0.10)	(0.40)
36–40	—	−0.01	0.00	0.01	0.00
	—	(0.46)	(0.08)	(1.30)	(0.24)
41–45	—	−0.04	0.01	0.01	−0.00
	—	(1.05)	(0.48)	(1.43)	(0.12)
46–50	—	−0.04	−0.03	−0.01	−0.01
	—	(1.96)	(1.92)	(1.28)	(1.41)
51–55	—	−0.02	0.01	−0.03	0.01
	—	(0.65)	(0.82)	(2.28)	(1.84)
56–60	—	—	−0.04	−0.01	−0.01
	—	—	(1.61)	(0.76)	(0.52)
61–65	—	−0.03	−0.03	−0.03	−0.01
	—	(0.48)	(1.03)	(1.80)	(0.50)
Personal services					
21–25	0.02	0.04	0.02	0.01	−0.00
	(1.41)	(1.42)	(1.87)	(1.4)	(0.53)
26–30	0.03	−0.01	0.02	0.01	−0.00
	(1.58)	(0.54)	(1.15)	(0.84)	(1.41)
31–35	0.07	0.08	0.04	0.00	0.00
	(3.08)	(2.68)	(2.29)	(0.32)	(0.76)
36–40	0.04	0.02	0.01	0.02	0.01
	(2.02)	(1.11)	(0.69)	(2.02)	(2.01)
41–45	0.01	0.07	0.04	0.01	0.00
	(0.38)	(2.05)	(2.99)	(1.12)	(0.96)
46–50	0.01	0.05	0.05	0.04	0.02
	(0.81)	(0.95)	(3.17)	(3.21)	(3.14)
51–55	0.07	—	−0.02	0.02	0.00
	(3.04)	—	(0.9)	(1.24)	(0.07)
56–60	0.06	0.03	0.10	0.05	0.02
	(2.2)	(0.46)	(3.06)	(2.73)	(2.28)
61–65	0.02	—	0.01	0.05	0.04
	(1.67)	—	(0.34)	(2.24)	(3.72)
Professional services					
21–25	0.01	0.04	0.08	0.03	0.02
	(0.49)	(1.82)	(3.97)	(2)	(2.63)
26–30	0.04	0.02	0.07	0.04	0.04
	(2.87)	(1.2)	(3.18)	(2.55)	(4.01)
31–35	0.04	0.01	0.08	0.05	0.04
	(2.19)	(0.22)	(3.81)	(3.07)	(4.09)
36–40	0.03	0.07	0.05	0.07	0.03
	(1.62)	(2.16)	(2.3)	(3.92)	(2.72)

Table 6.17. *(cont.)*

Age	1940	1950	1960	1970	1980
41–45	0.05	0.02	0.02	0.04	0.06
	(2.39)	(0.55)	(0.9)	(2.13)	(4.58)
46–50	0.03	0.04	0.05	0.06	0.06
	(1.65)	(0.88)	(2.22)	(3.04)	(4.63)
51–55	0.05	0.09	0.10	0.08	0.06
	(2.25)	(1.64)	(3.26)	(3.9)	(4.7)
56–60	0.04	0.00	0.02	0.10	0.05
	(2)	(0.05)	(0.7)	(4.26)	(3.27)
61–65	0.00	−0.01	0.12	0.16	0.11
	(0.12)	(0.25)	(2.13)	(4.18)	(4.95)
Recreational services					
21–25	0.01	−0.02	−0.01	0.01	−0.00
	(1.03)	(0.94)	(1.13)	(2.28)	(1.54)
26–30	0.00	0.01	0.01	−0.00	−0.00
	(0.11)	(0.54)	(1.97)	(0.54)	(0.6)
31–35	0.02	—	−0.00	0.00	0.00
	(2.24)	—	(0.25)	(0.76)	(1.46)
36–40	0.00	—	0.00	0.00	0.00
	(0.03)	—	(0.55)	(0.44)	(0.01)
41–45	−0.00	—	—	0.00	0.00
	(0.42)	—	—	(0.01)	(1.27)
46–50	−0.01	−0.00	0.01	0.01	0.01
	(0.77)	(0.23)	(1.27)	(2.02)	(1.77)
51–55	0.01	−0.01	−0.00	0.00	0.00
	(1.23)	(0.33)	(0.51)	(0.41)	(0.99)
56–60	−0.01	—	0.03	0.01	0.00
	(0.63)	—	(2.54)	(1.16)	(0.48)
61–65	−0.00	—	−0.01	−0.00	0.01
	(0.2)	—	(0.55)	(0.44)	(0.82)
Financial and business services					
21–25	−0.00	0.01	−0.04	−0.03	−0.02
	(0.37)	(0.24)	(2.34)	(2.18)	(2.45)
26–30	0.01	−0.01	−0.04	−0.02	−0.02
	(0.39)	(0.28)	(1.49)	(1.2)	(2.66)
31–35	−0.01	−0.04	−0.04	−0.01	−0.04
	(0.76)	(1.14)	(1.8)	(0.38)	(4.38)
36–40	−0.01	−0.05	−0.04	−0.05	−0.04
	(0.44)	(1.11)	(1.54)	(2.7)	(3.28)
41–45	0.02	0.01	−0.01	−0.05	−0.02
	(1.39)	(0.26)	(0.27)	(2.64)	(2.03)
46–50	0.00	0.03	−0.03	−0.05	−0.04
	(0.25)	(0.53)	(1.57)	(2.37)	(3.08)
51–55	−0.00	−0.05	0.01	−0.01	−0.04
	(0.34)	(0.83)	(0.21)	(0.67)	(2.76)

Table 6.17. *(cont.)*

Age	1940	1950	1960	1970	1980
56–60	0.05	0.03	−0.01	0.01	−0.04
	(1.95)	(0.85)	(0.21)	(0.33)	(2.46)
61–65	−0.01	−0.02	0.05	−0.01	−0.05
	(0.31)	(0.24)	(0.94)	(0.32)	(2.34)
Non-traditional manufacturing (non-textile)					
21–25	−0.00	−0.01	−0.02	0.03	0.01
	(0.10)	(0.72)	(1.00)	(1.58)	(1.42)
26–30	−0.01	−0.01	−0.03	−0.03	0.01
	(0.99)	(0.40)	(1.20)	(1.43)	(1.15)
31–35	−0.02	−0.03	−0.02	−0.04	0.01
	(1.46)	(0.98)	(0.80)	(1.76)	(0.89)
36–40	−0.02	0.01	−0.01	−0.02	−0.00
	(1.68)	(0.43)	(0.30)	(1.01)	(0.15)
41–45	0.02	0.02	−0.01	−0.03	−0.01
	(1.41)	(0.39)	(0.59)	(1.50)	(0.62)
46–50	0.00	−0.05	0.02	−0.03	−0.01
	(0.26)	(1.57)	(0.79)	(1.53)	(0.78)
51–55	—	−0.05	−0.01	0.02	−0.01
	—	(1.05)	(0.44)	(0.77)	(0.59)
56–60	−0.01	−0.04	−0.03	0.02	0.01
	(0.74)	(0.74)	(1.07)	(0.94)	(0.94)
61–65	−0.01	—	−0.03	0.01	−0.01
	(0.43)	—	(0.57)	(0.28)	(0.26)
Traditional manufacturing (non-textile)					
21–25	0.04	0.14	0.06	0.05	0.02
	(1.47)	(2.30)	(1.79)	(2.91)	(1.78)
26–30	0.03	0.14	0.02	−0.00	0.03
	(0.93)	(2.79)	(0.53)	(0.17)	(4.07)
31–35	0.09	−0.00	0.03	0.02	0.03
	(2.85)	(0.02)	(1.06)	(1.05)	(3.68)
36–40	0.03	0.08	0.14	0.06	0.01
	(0.86)	(1.51)	(4.16)	(2.70)	(1.26)
41–45	0.01	0.03	−0.01	0.06	0.02
	(0.18)	(0.36)	(0.29)	(2.58)	(1.48)
46–50	−0.00	0.03	0.01	0.06	0.04
	(0.04)	(0.40)	(0.35)	(2.78)	(3.11)
51–55	0.01	0.02	0.02	0.07	0.05
	(0.28)	(0.33)	(0.36)	(2.63)	(3.51)
56–60	0.02	0.20	0.08	0.02	0.03
	(0.50)	(2.42)	(2.02)	(0.92)	(1.96)
61–65	−0.00	0.06	−0.03	0.07	0.06
	(0.16)	(0.66)	(0.52)	(2.35)	(2.93)

Table 6.17. *(cont.)*

Age	1940	1950	1960	1970	1980
Chemicals					
21–25	0.03	0.00	−0.01	−0.02	−0.01
	(3.11)	(0.08)	(0.76)	(1.60)	(1.81)
26–30	0.03	0.00	−0.00	−0.02	0.00
	(2.58)	(0.18)	(0.08)	(1.28)	(0.12)
31–35	0.02	0.05	−0.01	−0.01	0.00
	(1.68)	(1.92)	(0.36)	(0.69)	(0.10)
36–40	0.01	−0.01	−0.03	0.01	0.01
	(1.76)	(0.36)	(1.78)	(0.52)	(1.08)
41–45	−0.00	0.03	0.02	−0.02	0.01
	(0.25)	(0.87)	(0.98)	(1.43)	(0.80)
46–50	0.00	−0.00	0.01	0.01	−0.01
	(0.75)	(0.11)	(0.56)	(0.53)	(0.82)
51–55	0.00	0.00	−0.03	0.01	−0.02
	(0.48)	—	(1.35)	(0.49)	(2.35)
56–60	0.01	0.04	0.02	0.01	−0.00
	(0.60)	(1.18)	(0.94)	(0.63)	(0.41)
61–65	0.01	—	−0.00	−0.00	0.01
	(0.57)	—	(0.08)	(0.24)	(0.43)
Apparel					
21–25	−0.00	—	−0.01	−0.01	0.01
	(0.29)	—	(0.90)	(1.21)	(2.83)
26–30	—	—	−0.02	0.01	0.00
	—	—	(1.45)	(2.34)	(1.24)
31–35	—	—	0.00	0.01	0.00
	—	—	(0.99)	(0.53)	(0.24)
36–40	−0.00	−0.01	−0.00	−0.01	0.00
	(0.53)	(0.74)	(0.31)	(0.93)	(0.09)
41–45	−0.00	−0.02	−0.01	−0.01	−0.00
	(0.11)	(0.91)	(0.80)	(1.05)	(0.28)
46–50	—	—	−0.00	−0.01	−0.01
	—	—	(0.20)	(0.73)	(1.04)
51–55	—	—	0.00	−0.01	−0.01
	—	—	(0.15)	(0.71)	(0.99)
56–60	—	—	−0.02	−0.00	−0.01
	—	—	(1.10)	(0.38)	(1.38)
61–65	—	—	−0.00	−0.00	0.00
	—	—	(0.08)	(0.09)	(0.11)
Textiles					
21–25	−0.26	−0.23	−0.31	0.02	0.05
	(8.89)	(4.04)	(8.49)	(0.63)	(4.95)
26–30	−0.30	−0.22	−0.24	−0.02	0.05
	(9.14)	(3.75)	(5.87)	(0.95)	(5.39)
31–35	−0.35	−0.29	−0.20	−0.06	0.02
	(8.76)	(4.28)	(5.78)	(2.16)	(1.49)

287

Table 6.17. *(cont.)*

Age	1940	1950	1960	1970	1980
36–40	−0.34	−0.38	−0.23	−0.11	0.01
	(9.73)	(5.68)	(6.13)	(4.03)	(0.78)
41–45	−0.22	−0.18	−0.27	−0.07	−0.03
	(5.93)	(2.64)	(5.93)	(2.75)	(1.89)
46–50	−0.18	−0.34	−0.22	−0.14	−0.07
	(5.24)	(3.93)	(5.88)	(4.80)	(4.17)
51–55	−0.22	−0.18	−0.29	−0.21	−0.08
	(5.34)	(2.17)	(5.04)	(6.97)	(4.53)
56–60	−0.13	−0.26	−0.25	−0.20	−0.11
	(3.41)	(2.89)	(5.01)	(5.92)	(5.16)
61–65	−0.14	−0.15	−0.16	−0.20	−0.13
	(2.93)	(1.52)	(2.30)	(5.21)	(4.87)

[a]Dash denotes not computed owing to insufficient observations.

Table 6.18. *Linear-probability models for females*

Age	1940	1950	1960	1970	1980
Agriculture, forestry, fisheries					
21–25	0.22	0.30	0.08	0.03	0.00
	(5.41)	(4.2)	(3.9)	(3.99)	(0.33)
26–30	0.16	0.16	0.12	0.01	0.00
	(3.42)	(2.04)	(3.99)	(1.7)	(1.36)
31–35	0.21	0.11	0.05	0.02	0.01
	(4.16)	(1.68)	(1.76)	(2.04)	(1.76)
36–40	0.28	0.08	0.06	0.02	0.00
	(4.8)	(1.31)	(2.05)	(3.02)	(0.45)
41–45	0.07	0.22	0.01	0.01	−0.00
	(0.86)	(2.44)	(0.19)	(0.71)	(0.83)
46–50	0.34	0.23	0.11	0.03	—[a]
	(4.39)	(2.3)	(3.26)	(2.61)	—
51–55	0.21	0.22	0.02	0.05	−0.00
	(1.98)	(1.67)	(0.52)	(2.67)	(0.57)
56–60	0.42	0.45	0.14	0.00	0.01
	(3.8)	(3.05)	(3.07)	(0.17)	(1.82)
61–65	0.21	1.00	0.03	−0.02	0.01
	(0.94)	(6.41)	(0.39)	(0.91)	(1.29)
Mining and construction					
21–25	−0.02	−0.01	−0.00	−0.01	−0.01
	(1.79)	(0.48)	(0.48)	(1.97)	(2.27)
26–30	−0.01	−0.01	−0.02	−0.01	−0.01
	(1.65)	(0.35)	(2.46)	(1.37)	(3.02)

Table 6.18. *(cont.)*

Age	1940	1950	1960	1970	1980
31–35	—	—	−0.01	−0.02	−0.02
	—	—	(0.75)	(1.85)	(3.61)
36–40	−0.00	−0.01	0.01	−0.00	−0.01
	(0.28)	(0.4)	(2.07)	(0.18)	(1.99)
41–45	—	—	0.01	−0.01	−0.01
	—	—	(0.72)	(0.58)	(2.35)
46–50	—	−0.00	−0.00	0.00	−0.01
	—	(0.06)	(0.42)	(0.16)	(0.89)
51–55	−0.04	—	—	−0.01	−0.01
	(1.49)	—	—	(1.12)	(1.52)
56–60	—	—	—	−0.00	−0.01
	—	—	—	(0.38)	(1.51)
61–65	0.01	−0.02	—	−0.01	0.01
	(0.01)	(0.08)	—	(0.58)	(1.49)

Transportation, communication, and utilities

Age	1940	1950	1960	1970	1980
21–25	−0.01	−0.04	−0.05	−0.03	−0.01
	(1.01)	(1.11)	(1.97)	(1.84)	(1.39)
26–30	−0.01	−0.02	−0.02	−0.02	−0.00
	(0.67)	(0.68)	(1.5)	(1.7)	(0.71)
31–35	−0.01	−0.01	−0.02	−0.02	−0.01
	(0.81)	(0.31)	(0.82)	(1.55)	(2.15)
36–40	−0.00	—	0.00	−0.01	−0.02
	(0.44)	—	(0.15)	(1.24)	(3.17)
41–45	—	−0.01	−0.01	−0.02	−0.02
	—	(0.15)	(0.8)	(1.47)	(2.43)
46–50	−0.02	—	−0.02	−0.00	−0.03
	(0.95)	—	(1.34)	(0.48)	(3.45)
51–55	−0.02	—	−0.02	−0.01	−0.02
	(0.49)	—	(0.74)	(0.86)	(2.21)
56–60	−0.02	−0.08	—	0.02	−0.01
	(0.58)	(0.65)	—	(1.32)	(1.43)
61–65	—	—	—	−0.02	−0.01
	—	—	—	(0.94)	(0.79)

Wholesale and retail trade

Age	1940	1950	1960	1970	1980
21–25	−0.08	−0.11	−0.04	−0.08	−0.09
	(3)	(1.57)	(1.03)	(3.22)	(7.42)
26–30	−0.08	−0.01	−0.07	−0.09	−0.08
	(2.78)	(0.13)	(1.92)	(3.44)	(7.32)
31–35	−0.07	−0.07	−0.10	−0.05	−0.08
	(1.83)	(0.84)	(2.23)	(1.79)	(6.77)
36–40	−0.07	−0.14	−0.11	−0.13	−0.09
	(1.63)	(1.7)	(2.35)	(4.47)	(6.08)
41–45	−0.09	−0.07	−0.03	−0.06	−0.07
	(1.88)	(0.87)	(0.63)	(2.03)	(4.23)
46–50	0.01	−0.08	−0.09	−0.04	−0.10

Table 6.18. *(cont.)*

Age	1940	1950	1960	1970	1980
	(0.27)	(1.08)	(2.24)	(1.19)	(5.81)
51–55	−0.06	—	−0.10	−0.13	−0.09
	(1.02)	—	(1.95)	(3.32)	(4.59)
56–60	−0.12	−0.33	−0.17	−0.12	−0.11
	(1.68)	(1.9)	(2.53)	(2.83)	(4.55)
61–65	0.05	−0.18	−0.17	−0.20	−0.11
	(0.44)	(0.86)	(1.6)	(3.54)	(3.27)
Federal government					
21–25	−0.00	−0.01	−0.00	−0.01	0.00
	(0.07)	(0.48)	(0.45)	(0.82)	(1.3)
26–30	−0.01	0.02	−0.01	0.01	0.00
	(0.91)	(0.97)	(0.79)	(1)	(1)
31–35	−0.01	−0.01	−0.01	−0.02	−0.00
	(0.85)	(0.43)	(0.86)	(1.81)	(0.58)
36–40	—	−0.02	−0.00	−0.01	0.00
	—	(0.57)	(0.18)	(1.11)	(0.19)
41–45	−0.02	—	−0.02	−0.02	−0.01
	(0.81)	—	(0.91)	(1.37)	(0.95)
46–50	−0.03	−0.05	−0.00	−0.02	0.00
	(1.39)	(1.75)	(0.42)	(1.1)	(0.01)
51–55	−0.01	−0.09	−0.01	−0.01	−0.00
	(0.39)	(1.01)	(0.65)	(0.52)	(0.44)
56–60	−0.02	0.02	−0.02	0.00	−0.01
	(0.48)	(0.21)	(0.73)	(0.14)	(0.99)
61–65	—	—	−0.01	−0.02	−0.00
	—	—	(0.17)	(1.07)	(0.65)
State government (excluding schoolteachers)					
21–25	−0.02	—	−0.01	−0.00	0.01
	(1.28)	—	(0.64)	(0.27)	(3.05)
26–30	−0.01	0.024	−0.01	0.00	0.00
	(0.6)	(0.97)	(1.14)	(0.85)	(1)
31–35	−0.01	0.000	−0.00	−0.00	0.00
	(0.69)	—	(0.42)	(0.71)	(0.09)
36–40	0.00	−0.009	−0.00	−0.00	0.00
	(0.03)	(0.4)	(0.38)	(0.15)	(0.1)
41–45	—	—	—	—	0.01
	—	—	—	—	(2.2)
46–50	—	−0.049	—	−0.01	−0.01
	—	(1.75)	—	(0.93)	(1.08)
51–55	—	−0.045	−0.00	−0.00	−0.00
	—	(0.67)	(0.33)	(0.4)	(0.86)
56–60	—	0.022	−0.01	−0.00	−0.01
	—	(0.33)	(0.48)	(0.38)	(1.7)
61–65	—	—	—	—	−0.01
	—	—	—	—	(1.08)

Table 6.18. *(cont.)*

Age	1940	1950	1960	1970	1980
Local government (excluding schoolteachers)					
21–25	—	−0.01	0.01	−0.00	0.01
	—	(0.6)	(1.85)	(1.16)	(2.89)
26–30	—	—	−0.02	−0.00	−0.01
	—	—	(1.13)	(0.130)	(1.6)
31–35	—	—	−0.01	−0.02	−0.00
	—	—	(0.86)	(1.8)	(1.16)
36–40	—	—	−0.01	−0.01	−0.01
	—	—	(0.66)	(0.7)	(1.76)
41–45	—	—	−0.03	−0.00	−0.00
	—	—	(1.27)	(0.77)	(0.37)
46–50	—	—	−0.01	−0.01	−0.00
	—	—	(0.62)	(0.96)	(0.45)
51–55	—	−0.06	−0.01	−0.00	0.00
	—	(0.77)	(0.49)	(0.43)	(0.76)
56–60	—	—	−0.02	−0.01	−0.01
	—	—	(0.57)	(0.90)	(1.45)
61–65	—	—	−0.06	−0.01	−0.00
	—	—	(0.95)	(0.56)	(0.28)
Personal services					
21–25	0.47	0.34	0.49	0.11	0.02
	(10.4)	(5.35)	(13.01)	(5.74)	(2.83)
26–30	0.47	0.43	0.46	0.20	0.00
	(9.52)	(4.9)	(10.96)	(9.57)	(0.21)
31–35	0.49	0.38	0.47	0.24	0.02
	(8.97)	(3.93)	(11.83)	(10.76)	(2.13)
36–40	0.48	0.42	0.49	0.30	0.05
	(7.81)	(5.39)	(12.58)	(11.8)	(5.28)
41–45	0.50	0.59	0.48	0.24	0.08
	(6.91)	(7.44)	(11.53)	(9.63)	(7.92)
46–50	0.23	0.48	0.44	0.31	0.13
	(3.45)	(4.75)	(8.82)	(11.37)	(11.23)
51–55	0.32	0.49	0.64	0.40	0.17
	(3.08)	(2.69)	(13.43)	(13.5)	(12.19)
56–60	0.15	0.23	0.41	0.43	0.26
	(1.36)	(1.28)	(5.66)	(11.5)	(15.35)
61–65	0.31	−0.21	0.37	0.52	0.32
	(1.57)	(0.77)	(3.9)	(10.24)	(11.71)
Professional services					
21–25	0.07	0.107	0.06	0.05	0.00
	(2.39)	(1.67)	(1.51)	(2.17)	(0.11)
26–30	0.07	0.04	0.09	−0.11	0.03
	(2.27)	(0.73)	(2.32)	(3.61)	(2.21)
31–35	0.02	0.01	0.15	0.10	0.05
	(0.68)	(0.19)	(3.72)	(3.45)	(3.1)

Table 6.18. *(cont.)*

Age	1940	1950	1960	1970	1980
36–40	0.00	0.25	0.09	0.14	0.08
	(0.02)	(4.19)	(2.59)	(4.68)	(4.93)
41–45	0.05	−0.03	0.09	0.15	0.09
	(1.04)	(0.3)	(2.11)	(4.57)	(4.82)
46–50	0.03	−0.02	0.08	0.15	0.19
	(0.74)	(0.32)	(1.73)	(4.69)	(9.63)
51–55	0.11	0.06	0.03	0.14	0.17
	(1.95)	(0.72)	(0.69)	(3.75)	(7.87)
56–60	0.08	−0.02	0.01	0.10	0.19
	(1.49)	(0.2)	(1.55)	(2.37)	(7.73)
61–65	−0.06	0.01	0.08	0.12	0.12
	(0.74)	(0.04)	(0.54)	(1.95)	(3.41)
Recreational services					
21–25	—	0.06	−0.01	−0.00	0.00
	—	(2.11)	(0.73)	(0.72)	(0.13)
26–30	−0.01	—	—	0.00	−0.00
	(1.65)	—	—	(0.07)	(1.33)
31–35	—	—	0.02	0.00	−0.00
	—	—	(2.28)	(0.25)	(0.94)
36–40	—	−0.01	−0.00	−0.00	0.00
	—	(0.35)	(0.38)	(0.43)	(0.85)
41–45	−0.01	—	−0.00	0.01	0.00
	(0.61)	—	(0.33)	(1.7)	(0.87)
46–50	0.02	0.02	−0.00	0.00	−0.00
	(1.57)	(0.73)	(0.42)	(0.34)	(1.3)
51–55	—	—	—	−0.01	−0.00
	—	—	—	(0.89)	(0.87)
56–60	—	—	−0.01	0.01	0.01
	—	—	(0.76)	(1.77)	(1.82)
61–65	—	—	—	0.00	−0.00
	—	—	—	(0.01)	(0.49)
Financial and business services					
21–25	−0.00	−0.02	−0.09	−0.07	−0.08
	(0.86)	(0.55)	(2.62)	(4.12)	(8.21)
26–30	−0.00	−0.06	−0.03	−0.07	−0.06
	(0.54)	(1.18)	(1.73)	(3.08)	(6.8)
31–35	−0.00	0.04	−0.03	−0.05	−0.06
	(0.48)	(0.7)	(1.54)	(3.03)	(6.5)
36–40	—	−0.02	−0.02	−0.05	−0.06
	—	(0.54)	(0.66)	(2.58)	(5.44)
41–45	−0.02	−0.02	−0.03	−0.05	−0.05
	(0.91)	(0.31)	(1.16)	(2.94)	(4.02)
46–50	−0.00	—	−0.01	−0.02	−0.05
	(0.37)	—	(0.58)	(1.41)	(4.2)

Table 6.18. *(cont.)*

Age	1940	1950	1960	1970	1980
51–55	—	—	−0.05	−0.01	−0.03
	—	—	(1.69)	(0.76)	(2.51)
56–60	—	—	−0.02	−0.02	−0.01
	—	—	(0.71)	(1.33)	(1.05)
61–65	−0.01	—	−0.06	−0.03	0.00
	(0.1)	—	(0.77)	(1.56)	(0.02)

Traditional manufacturing (non-textile)

Age	1940	1950	1960	1970	1980
21–25	−0.02	−0.04	−0.01	0.00	0.01
	(1.37)	(0.74)	(0.41)	(0.17)	(1.64)
26–30	−0.02	0.02	−0.01	−0.02	0.02
	(0.85)	(0.46)	(0.38)	(1.34)	(2.7)
31–35	−0.02	0.03	−0.05	0.01	−0.00
	(1.09)	(1.11)	(1.92)	(0.83)	(0.37)
36–40	−0.01	0.01	0.02	−0.02	0.01
	(0.61)	(0.21)	(0.77)	(1.52)	(1.25)
41–45	−0.06	0.04	−0.01	−0.02	−0.00
	(2.28)	(0.75)	(0.69)	(1.69)	(0.25)
46–50	−0.02	−0.02	−0.01	−0.04	−0.00
	(1.19)	(0.82)	(0.53)	(2.97)	(0.29)
51–55	−0.00	—	−0.02	−0.02	−0.00
	(0.1)	—	(1.04)	(1.03)	(0.49)
56–60	−0.00	—	0.01	−0.02	0.00
	(0.1)	—	(0.15)	(0.88)	(0.36)
61–65	—	−0.28	0.04	−0.00	−0.02
	—	(1.42)	(0.5)	(0.28)	(1.18)

Non-traditional manufacturing (non-textile)

Age	1940	1950	1960	1970	1980
21–25	−0.01	−0.01	−0.03	0.01	0.03
	(0.8)	(0.41)	(1.58)	(0.34)	(3.75)
26–30	−0.01	—	−0.01	−0.01	0.01
	(1.0)	—	(1.18)	(0.75)	(0.71)
31–35	—	−0.02	−0.04	−0.04	0.02
	—	(0.54)	(2)	(2.12)	(2.01)
36–40	−0.02	—	−0.01	−0.04	0.02
	(1.91)	—	(1.1)	(2.01)	(1.58)
41–45	—	−0.00	−0.00	0.01	−0.01
	—	(0.1)	(0.51)	(0.37)	(0.82)
46–50	—	—	−0.00	−0.03	−0.01
	—	—	(0.54)	(1.55)	(1.4)
51–55	—	—	−0.01	−0.02	−0.02
	—	—	(0.59)	(1.5)	(2.21)
56–60	—	—	—	−0.01	−0.02
	—	—	—	(1.05)	(1.78)
61–65	—	—	—	−0.01	−0.04
	—	—	—	(0.68)	(2.7)

Table 6.18. *(cont.)*

Age	1940	1950	1960	1970	1980
Chemicals					
21–25	—	—	−0.01	−0.01	−0.00
	—	—	(0.84)	(0.73)	(1.19)
26–30	—	−0.03	−0.02	−0.00	0.00
	—	(1.32)	(1.2)	(0.37)	(0.97)
31–35	—	—	−0.02	−0.00	0.00
	—	—	(1.62)	(0.35)	(0.45)
36–40	—	−0.03	−0.01	−0.01	−0.00
	—	(1.02)	(0.66)	(1.44)	(0.39)
41–45	−0.01	—	—	−0.01	−0.01
	(0.61)	—	—	(1.39)	(0.73)
46–50	−0.01	—	—	−0.01	−0.02
	(0.41)	—	—	(1.35)	(2.41)
51–55	—	—	—	—	−0.01
	—	—	—	—	(1.62)
56–60	—	—	—	−0.01	−0.01
	—	—	—	(1.07)	(1.47)
61–65	—	—	—	−0.01	−0.01
	—	—	—	(0.71)	(1.23)
Apparel					
21–25	−0.06	0.06	−0.19	0.05	0.05
	(3.29)	(1.16)	(4.23)	(2.61)	(5.79)
26–30	−0.02	−0.23	−0.15	−0.01	0.03
	(1.25)	(3.49)	(3.85)	(0.53)	(4.31)
31–35	−0.08	−0.09	−0.11	−0.03	0.05
	(2.68)	(1.53)	(3.11)	(1.42)	(5.18)
36–40	−0.05	−0.04	−0.14	−0.02	0.02 ·
	(2.39)	(1.08)	(3.47)	(0.87)	(1.62)
41–45	−0.08	−0.11	−0.07	−0.04	0.01
	(2.63)	(1.11)	(1.97)	(1.84)	(0.79)
46–50	−0.09	−0.04	−0.08	−0.07	−0.00
	(2.54)	(1.23)	(2.76)	(2.71)	(0.13)
51–55	−0.25	−0.11	−0.09	−0.08	−0.03
	(3.84)	(1.53)	(2.47)	(3.61)	(2.03)
56–60	−0.17	−0.03	−0.05	−0.08	−0.09
	(2.89)	(0.41)	(1.5)	(2.78)	(5.68)
61–65	−0.43	—	—	−0.07	−0.09
	(3.94)	—	—	(2.75)	(4.07)
Textiles					
21–25	−0.54	−0.48	−0.21	−0.05	0.05
	(14.47)	(5.92)	(4.93)	(1.84)	(5.46)
26–30	−0.52	−0.32	−0.29	−0.09	0.05
	(13.3)	(4.24)	(6.38)	(3.03)	(5.26)
31–35	−0.51	−0.37	−0.27	−0.13	0.05
	(11.03)	(4.65)	(6.13)	(4.02)	(4.02)

294

Table 6.18. *(cont.)*

Age	1940	1950	1960	1970	1980
36–40	−0.61	−0.50	−0.36	−0.17	−0.01
	(13.17)	(5.36)	(7.71)	(5.95)	(0.57)
41–45	−0.33	−0.60	−0.39	−0.17	−0.02
	(6.24)	(5.05)	(8.21)	(5.52)	(1.19)
46–50	−0.47	−0.52	−0.39	−0.26	−0.09
	(8.14)	(5.64)	(8.31)	(8.66)	(5.49)
51–55	−0.28	−0.51	−0.38	−0.30	−0.11
	(4.32)	(4)	(7.43)	(8.45)	(6.18)
56–60	−0.34	−0.24	−0.37	−0.27	−0.18
	(4.35)	(1.44)	(5.83)	(6.85)	(8.38)
61–65	−0.08	−0.32	−0.21	−0.24	−0.19
	(0.9)	(1.66)	(2.9)	(5.67)	(7.1)

[a]Dash denotes not computed owing to insufficient observations.

regressions are repeated each census year from 1940 to 1980. The industry categories, based on SIC codes, are:

1. Agriculture, forestry, and fisheries
2. Mining and construction
3. Transportation, communication, and utilities
4. Wholesale and retail trade
5. Federal government
6. State government
7. Local government
8. Personal services
9. Professional services
10. Recreational services
11. Financial and business services
12. Traditional manufacturing – paper, printing, publishing, food products, stone, clay, miscellaneous manufactures, lumber, and furniture
13. Non-traditional manufacturing – transportation equipment, electrical and non-electrical machinery and metal industries, i.e., industries that enter the state on a large scale after 1945
14. Chemicals
15. Apparel
16. Textiles

The race dummy coefficient may be interpreted as arising from discrimination on the demand side. Controlling for individual characteristics, the coefficient on the dummy variable indicates whether blacks are more or less likely than whites to be employed in a given industry. Alternatively, and less plausibly, the coefficient on the dummy may be interpreted as the outcome of racial sectoral preferences on the supply side. In either case, the coefficient tells the relative likelihood of finding a black worker in a given industry, controlling for individual characteristics.

The race dummy coefficients are reported for selected industries with the least-squares *t* statistic in parentheses in the tables above. Prior to 1960, we find that, adjusting for qualifications, blacks are not underrepresented in *any* industry except textiles and apparel. Blacks are overrepresented in agriculture and professional services as of 1960. It is important to note that in 1960 blacks are underrepresented in the non-traditional manufacturing industries in relation to their share in the population and the labor force. However, controlling for individual characteristics, Table 6.17 shows that black males are not underrepresented in these industries.

For black females, the story in Table 6.18 is quite similar. For this group the coefficient on the dummy is taken relative to white females. In addition to textiles, however, black females are underrepresented in the closely allied apparel industry. In 1960 black females are overrepresented in most industries, including non-traditional manufacturing, chemicals, government, services, and trade.

The 1970 regressions show little change from 1960 for black males except in textiles. In the younger cohorts of textile workers, blacks are no longer underrepresented, and in the older cohorts they are much less so than in 1960. For black females, the 1960-to-1970 comparison yields similar results. The younger cohorts are no longer underrepresented in textiles by 1970, and the older cohorts are less underrepresented. A similar story also holds for female apparel workers. The improvement in the status of young workers is consistent with theories that stress the incentives of making firm specific investments in younger workers with longer expected working lives than older workers.

These regressions show that, controlling for education and other individual characteristics, blacks are significantly underrepresented in the textile industry in 1960 and before. In 1970, however, the underrepresentation disappears for the younger cohorts and diminishes considerably for the older cohorts. If educational improvement led to the black gains in textile employment, the regressions controlling for education would have shown no underrepresentation of blacks in 1960 and no change in underrepresentation from 1960 to 1970.

In order to examine the effect of improvements in black schooling quality on our analysis, we ran regressions using quality-corrected education variables formed by using educational expenditure by race as described in Appendix A. The results for manufacturing are shown in Table 6.19. Owing to the data limitations discussed in Appendix A, these regressions can be run only for the younger cohorts of workers. For this group, the qualitative results are the same as those obtained without adjusting for quality of education.

As a final test of the importance of education to the breakthrough in black status, we ask the question, What would happen to the probability of finding a black employed in a given industry if we increased the average level of black education from its 1960 to its 1970 level? The results for blacks are shown in Table 6.20 using the 1970 linear-probability-model regression coefficients.[17] For blacks in most industries, including non-traditional manufacturing, chemicals, government, services, and trade, the effect of increasing education is to increase the probability of employment. In textiles, as well as in traditional manufacturing, agriculture, and mining and construction, the effect is to actually *decrease* the probability of employment. Textiles is a low-skill industry. Increasing education has the effect of decreasing the probability of employment in low-skill industries.

Although blacks had already made gains in education relative to whites in the years leading up to 1965, the evidence presented here does not support the claim that educational improvements led to increased black employment and wages in the textile industry. First, the gains, as measured by years of schooling completed and expenditure per student per year, came gradually. Second, by 1960, between one-fifth and one-fourth of the adult blacks in South Carolina had sufficient education to work in the textile industry. However, black females were practically excluded and black males were employed in very small numbers in textiles. Third, even controlling for education, blacks were found to be severely underrepresented in textiles in 1960, but much less so in 1970. Also, in all other industries with the exception of apparel, blacks were not found to be underrepresented when educational levels are taken into account. Finally, if years of schooling of blacks are increased in the textile industry, the probability of blacks being employed in textiles actually decreases.

The evidence presented here confirms the powerful role of education in elevating black employment in other sectors of the economy, especially government and the emerging new industrial sector of the state

---

[17] This analysis was repeated using the 1960 regression coefficients, with qualitatively similar results.

Table 6.19. *Race coefficients from education, quality-adjusted:
employment linear-probability models* (t *statistics in parentheses*)

Males				Females			
Age	1950	1960	1970	Age	1950	1960	1970
Textiles							
21–25	−0.32	−0.37	0.08	21–25	−0.50	−0.29	0.15
	(5.04)	(7.62)	(1.30)		(5.61)	(4.33)	(2.28)
26–30	—	−0.38	−0.18	26–30	—	−0.42	−0.17
		(6.17)	(4.20)			(5.37)	(2.49)
31–35	—	−0.22	−0.11	31–35	—	−0.36	−0.33
		(5.94)	(2.96)			(7.36)	(6.96)
36–40	—	—	−0.21	36–40	—	—	−0.31
			(2.83)				(5.99)
41–45	—	—	−0.08	41–45	—	—	−0.23
			(2.83)				(6.66)
Traditional manufacturing (non-textile)							
21–25	0.19	0.05	0.14	21–25	−0.02	0.02	−0.00
	(2.88)	(1.07)	(2.95)		(0.32)	(0.58)	(0.07)
26–30	—	0.00	−0.04	26–30	—	0.00	−0.06
		(0.09)	(1.19)			(0.02)	(1.72)
31–35	—	0.05	−0.00	31–35	—	−0.05	0.06
		(1.32)	(0.14)			(1.80)	(2.22)
36–40	—	—	0.02	36–40	—	—	−0.04
			(0.66)				(1.38)
41–45	—	—	0.06	41–45	—	—	−0.04
			(2.49)				(2.36)
Non-traditional manufacturing (non-textile)							
21–25	−0.00	−0.02	0.01	21–25	−0.00	−0.03	−0.04
	(0.23)	(0.56)	(0.27)		(0.15)	(0.93)	(1.04)
26–30	—	−0.02	0.01	26–30	—	−0.02	0.03
		(0.68)	(0.18)			(0.08)	(0.75)
31–35	—	−0.03	−0.02	31–35	—	−0.03	−0.01
		(1.20)	(0.80)			(1.24)	(0.44)
36–40	—	—	0.01	36–40	—	—	−0.00
			(0.39)				(0.14)
41–45	—	—	−0.04	41–45	—	—	0.01
			(1.82)				(0.68)
Chemicals							
21–25	0.00	−0.01	−0.01	21–25	0.00	0.01	−0.03
	(0.22)	(0.46)	(0.37)		—	(0.49)	(1.07)
26–30	—	0.03	−0.00	26–30	—	−0.01	0.02
		(1.13)	(0.10)			(0.47)	(0.87)
31–35	—	−0.01	0.00	31–35	—	−0.02	−0.01
		(0.67)	(0.25)			(1.14)	(0.44)
36–40	—	—	0.02	36–40	—	—	0.00
			(0.96)				(0.14)

Table 6.19. (*cont.*)

Males				Females			
Age	1950	1960	1970	Age	1950	1960	1970
41–45	—	—	−0.03	41–45	—	—	0.00
			(1.65)				(0.17)
Apparel							
21–25	0.00	−0.00	−0.00	21–25	−0.05	−0.32	0.13
	—	(0.30)	(0.02)		(0.84)	(4.73)	(2.50)
26–30	—	−0.01	0.02	26–30	—	−0.23	−0.06
		(0.68)	(1.79)			(3.43)	(0.97)
31–35	—	0.01	0.00	31–35	—	−0.12	−0.12
		(1.26)	(0.37)			(3.14)	(3.44)
36–40	—	—	−0.02	36–40	—	—	−0.00
			(1.17)				(0.04)
41–45	—	—	−0.00	41–45	—	—	−0.05
			(0.62)				(1.81)

Table 6.20. *The effect on the probability of employment of increasing black education from its 1960 level to its 1970 level (percentage)*

Age	Male	Female
Industry (1): agriculture, forestry, and fisheries		
21–25	−3.15	−0.68
26–30	−2.60	−0.24
31–35	−2.26	−1.39
36–40	−2.19	−0.65
41–45	−6.89	−1.80
46–50	−1.91	−1.24
51–55	−0.62	−0.36
56–60	−1.52	−1.13
61–65	−1.21	−1.61
Industry (2): Mining and construction		
21–25	−2.25	—
26–30	−0.83	−0.17
31–35	−2.68	0.24
36–40	−1.38	0.34
41–45	−2.28	0.25
46–50	−0.53	−0.02
51–55	−0.22	0.13
56–60	−0.75	0.14
61–65	−0.01	0.36

299

Table 6.20. *(cont.)*

Age	Male	Female
Industry (3): Transportation, communication, and utilities		
21–25	−0.08	0.35
26–30	1.28	0.44
31–35	1.25	0.60
36–40	1.47	0.41
41–45	2.49	0.23
46–50	0.85	−0.18
51–55	0.29	0.37
56–60	0.60	1.03
61–65	0.17	0.84
Industry (4): Wholesale and retail trade		
21–25	1.80	−1.70
26–30	1.43	−0.86
31–35	2.68	0.48
36–40	2.15	1.35
41–45	4.71	2.09
46–50	2.28	2.04
51–55	1.24	3.30
56–60	1.08	4.69
61–65	—	2.94
Industry (5): Federal government		
21–25	0.51	0.34
26–30	0.42	0.27
31–35	0.54	0.43
36–40	1.08	0.87
41–45	1.93	0.87
46–50	1.26	0.80
51–55	0.61	0.70
56–60	0.78	1.83
61–65	0.35	1.29
Industry (6): State government		
21–25	0.32	0.24
26–30	0.18	0.04
31–35	0.06	0.08
36–40	0.14	0.14
41–45	−0.43	—
46–50	0.17	0.16
51–55	0.03	0.06
56–60	−0.02	0.14
61–65	0.03	—
Industry (7): Local government		
21–25	−0.05	0.04
26–30	0.19	0.14
31–35	−0.06	0.19

Table 6.20. *(cont.)*

Age	Male	Female
36–40	0.22	0.38
41–45	0.63	0.12
46–50	−0.29	0.10
51–55	0.01	0.12
56–60	0.25	0.54
61–65	0.05	0.25
Industry (8): Personal services		
21–25	0.07	−2.34
26–30	−0.30	−1.65
31–35	0.31	−2.65
36–40	0.25	−7.15
41–45	0.34	−4.77
46–50	0.16	−2.73
51–55	−0.13	−2.27
56–60	0.13	−6.99
61–65	0.46	−0.18
Industry (9): Professional services		
21–25	2.66	9.31
26–30	1.35	6.53
31–35	0.32	5.83
36–40	0.27	5.78
41–45	−3.71	5.83
46–50	−0.78	3.57
51–55	−0.38	1.16
56–60	0.01	4.90
61–65	−0.33	3.31
Industry (10): Recreational services		
21–25	0.26	0.06
26–30	−0.14	0.08
31–35	0.01	0.05
36–40	−0.17	0.02
41–45	−0.45	−0.23
46–50	0.06	0.06
51–55	0.04	0.07
56–60	0.19	0.23
61–65	0.09	−0.19
Industry (11): Financial and business services		
21–25	−0.33	0.60
26–30	0.53	0.92
31–35	1.19	0.89
36–40	0.20	1.93
41–45	1.45	1.17
46–50	0.65	0.47
51–55	0.29	0.52

Table 6.20. *(cont.)*

Age	Male	Female
56–60	0.41	1.17
61–65	0.03	−0.36
Industry (12): Food and tobacco		
21–25	−0.62	−0.05
26–30	0.05	−0.07
31–35	−0.21	0.32
36–40	0.15	−0.01
41–45	0.48	0.02
46–50	0.09	−0.47
51–55	0.06	−0.32
56–60	0.09	−0.33
61–65	−0.05	—
Industry (12): Lumber and furniture		
21–25	−0.80	−0.06
26–30	−1.42	−0.03
31–35	−1.36	0.28
36–40	−1.31	−0.29
41–45	−1.98	−0.04
46–50	−0.99	0.07
51–55	−0.39	−0.06
56–60	−0.24	−0.77
61–65	−0.26	—
Industry (12): Paper		
21–25	0.11	0.05
26–30	0.16	−0.11
31–35	0.08	0.18
36–40	−0.12	0.04
41–45	0.47	−0.16
46–50	−0.01	0.03
51–55	−0.09	0.02
56–60	−0.08	−0.18
61–65	−0.03	—
Industry (12): Printing, publishing, and engraving		
21–25	0.09	0.06
26–30	0.13	0.07
31–35	0.14	0.14
36–40	0.19	0.09
41–45	0.38	0.13
46–50	0.11	0.13
51–55	0.02	0.20
56–60	0.14	0.08
61–65	0.03	0.13
Industry (12): Photography and equipment		
21–25	0.03	0.01

Table 6.20. *(cont.)*

Age	Male	Female
26–30	0.07	−0.02
31–35	0.11	0.04
36–40	0.11	0.05
41–45	0.10	0.01
46–50	−0.02	0.03
51–55	—	0.01
56–60	—	0.11
61–65	—	—
Industry (12): Stone, clay, and glass		
21–25	0.18	−0.04
26–30	−0.14	0.04
31–35	−0.45	0.04
36–40	0.22	−0.34
41–45	0.50	−0.16
46–50	−0.16	−0.02
51–55	−0.28	—
56–60	—	0.14
61–65	0.09	—
Industry (13): Electrical machinery		
21–25	0.41	−0.40
26–30	0.29	−0.10
31–35	−0.12	0.29
36–40	−0.04	0.61
41–45	0.60	0.45
46–50	0.09	0.10
51–55	−0.01	0.08
56–60	0.10	−0.08
61–65	0.07	—
Industry (13): Metal industries		
21–25	0.35	−0.01
26–30	0.05	0.00
31–35	−0.20	−0.06
36–40	0.13	0.35
41–45	−0.18	−0.17
46–50	−0.02	0.12
51–55	0.05	0.02
56–60	−0.35	—
61–65	−0.16	—
Industry (13): Non-electrical machinery		
21–25	0.52	−0.02
26–30	0.29	0.09
31–35	0.29	−0.03
36–40	0.39	0.14
41–45	0.83	−0.32

303

Table 6.20. *(cont.)*

Age	Male	Female
46–50	0.39	0.09
51–55	−0.01	0.02
56–60	0.13	—
61–65	0.03	0.26
Industry (13): Transportation equipment		
21–25	0.38	0.03
26–30	0.37	0.03
31–35	0.71	0.11
36–40	0.56	−0.54
41–45	−0.59	0.24
46–50	0.16	−0.02
51–55	0.25	0.05
56–60	0.29	0.14
61–65	0.12	0.42
Industry (14): Chemicals		
21–25	0.76	−0.08
26–30	0.74	−0.03
31–35	0.47	0.04
36–40	0.53	0.23
41–45	0.99	0.31
46–50	0.22	0.01
51–55	0.10	—
56–60	−0.12	0.09
61–65	−0.14	0.47
Industry (15): Apparel		
21–25	0.35	−1.85
26–30	0.10	−2.04
31–35	0.13	−1.81
36–40	−0.26	0.33
41–45	−0.01	−0.17
46–50	0.01	−0.44
51–55	0.05	0.46
56–60	—	0.62
61–65	0.04	−1.90
Industry (16): Textiles		
21–25	−1.64	−3.91
26–30	−2.25	−3.17
31–35	−1.45	−4.18
36–40	−2.61	−3.96
41–45	0.81	−3.95
46–50	−1.96	−2.82
51–55	−0.72	−4.37
56–60	−1.15	−6.51
61–65	−0.59	−6.04

Table 6.20. *(cont.)*

Age	Male	Female
Industry: All government		
21–25	0.57	0.62
26–30	0.67	0.45
31–35	0.67	0.67
36–40	1.44	1.38
41–45	2.17	1.02
46–50	1.19	1.10
51–55	0.52	0.88
56–60	1.01	2.65
61–65	0.43	1.54
Industry: Professional services: teachers		
21–25	1.49	6.52
26–30	0.60	4.85
31–35	0.06	3.04
36–40	0.04	1.58
41–45	−0.51	3.05
46–50	0.08	1.80
51–55	−0.29	0.39
56–60	−0.15	0.13
61–65	−0.05	−1.19
Industry: Professional services: nonteachers		
21–25	1.16	2.79
26–30	0.75	1.68
31–35	0.26	2.80
36–40	0.23	4.21
41–45	−3.20	2.77
46–50	−0.86	1.78
51–55	−0.09	0.77
56–60	0.16	4.77
61–65	−0.27	4.50

that apparently never discriminated against blacks (or at least black qualifications) on a statistically or numerically significant scale. As black skills improved, so did their representation in these sectors.

The tight-labor-market hypothesis

With statewide aggregate data, the tight-labor-market hypothesis is not testable. The black breakthrough in textiles is an event that occurs only once. Many other events that occur contemporaneously with the breakthrough are equally plausible candidates for being the cause.

305

Table 6.21. *South Carolina population shares in selected counties in 1960 (percentages)*

County	White males	White females	Black males	Black females	White	Black
Abbeville	33	35	15	17	68	32
Anderson	39	41	9	10	80	20
Cherokee	38	40	10	11	79	21
Chester	29	31	19	21	60	40
Greenville	40	42	8	9	82	18
Lancaster	36	37	13	14	73	27
Laurens	35	36	14	15	70	30
Oconee	47	42	5	6	89	11
Orangeburg	20	20	29	31	40	60
Pickens	44	46	5	5	90	10
Spartanburg	38	40	11	12	78	22

Source: U.S. Bureau of the Census (1964, p. 42).

Without more variation in the data, one cannot differentiate among the possibilities. Many hypotheses are consistent with the aggregate data. Although we do not have evidence from comparably tight-labor-market episodes in South Carolina, we do have a time series of cross sections on the black breakthrough as it occurs in different counties of South Carolina. Even with these data, the labor market hypothesis is not testable if one believes that South Carolina is a single labor market or that the counties are homogeneous economic units. In that case, a tight labor market could cause simultaneous effects across counties just as uniformly applied government policy could. However, if the counties of South Carolina do not form a single labor market, the two hypotheses can be differentiated. A tight labor market would affect the various counties differently, whereas uniformly applied government policy plausibly would affect all counties simultaneously. We argue that the counties of South Carolina are different labor markets and that the simultaneous breakthrough of blacks in textiles across those counties is evidence against the labor market hypothesis and in favor of the government-activity hypothesis. We begin by examining the eleven "clean" South Carolina counties for which we can form a consistent time series over most of the entire sample period. Most but not all of the eleven counties are in the Piedmont region in the northwest portion of the state.

Tables 6.21 and 6.22 show population levels and shares respectively by race and sex for these eleven counties in 1960. They vary in racial

Table 6.22. *South Carolina population in selected counties in 1960 (thousands)*

County	White males	White females	Black males	Black females	White	Black	Total
Abbeville	7.1	7.5	3.2	3.7	14.6	6.9	21.4
Anderson	38.5	40.8	9.2	10.0	79.2	19.2	98.5
Cherokee	13.5	14.2	3.5	4.0	27.7	7.5	35.2
Chester	9.0	9.6	5.9	6.4	18.6	12.3	30.9
Greenville	84.4	88.5	17.5	19.4	172.8	37.0	209.8
Lancaster	14.1	14.6	5.1	5.6	28.7	10.6	39.4
Laurens	16.5	17.0	6.7	7.3	33.5	14.1	47.6
Oconee	19.0	16.9	2.1	2.2	35.9	4.3	40.2
Orangeburg	13.4	14.0	19.8	21.4	27.4	41.2	68.6
Pickens	20.4	21.0	2.2	2.4	41.4	4.6	46.0
Spartanburg	59.5	62.7	16.5	18.2	122.1	34.7	156.8

Source: U.S. Bureau of the Census (1964, p. 42).

composition from Orangeburg with 60 percent of the population black to Pickens with 10 percent of the population black. They vary in size from Greenville with a population of about 209,000 to Abbeville with a population of about 21,000.

Table 6.23 shows total employment and employment in selected industries in 1960. The counties vary from Anderson with 41 percent of the population employed to Orangeburg with 34 percent employed. The industrial composition varies from Lancaster with 55 percent of those employed working in manufacturing to Orangeburg with 20 percent in manufacturing. In terms of size of the manufacturing work-force, the counties vary from Orangeburg with 4,765 employees to Greenville with over 31,000 manufacturing employees. In Lancaster, over 46 percent of all employed persons work in textiles, whereas in Orangeburg about 2 percent work in textiles. In terms of size, Spartanburg employs almost 18,000 textile workers, whereas Orangeburg employs under 500 textile workers. Finally, over 80 percent of all manufacturing workers in Lancaster work in textiles compared with under 10 percent in Orangeburg.

These counties differ greatly in industrial composition, racial demographics, and the level of employment. To the extent that regional labor markets exist, we expect the effect of changing labor market conditions to be different across counties. Tang (1958) documents sharp differences among contiguous Piedmont counties in South Carolina in many leading indicators of economic development.

307

Table 6.23. South Carolina county-level employment by industry in 1960

County	Total	Manufacturing	Textiles	Agriculture	% of population employed	% of employed in Manufacturing	% of employed in Textiles	% of employed in Agriculture	% of manufacturing employees in textiles
Abbeville	7,763	3,521	2,074	708	36	45	27	9	59
Anderson	40,401	19,141	13,196	2,499	41	47	33	6	69
Cherokee	12,980	5,967	3,393	941	37	46	26	7	57
Chester	11,232	4,955	3,913	1,155	36	44	35	10	79
Greenville	80,944	31,404	15,972	1,947	39	39	20	2	51
Lancaster	14,898	8,229	6,875	625	38	55	46	4	84
Laurens	17,647	8,354	4,520	1,346	37	47	26	8	54
Oconee	15,199	7,178	5,094	1,270	38	47	34	8	71
Orangeburg	23,427	4,765	474	5,879	34	20	2	25	10
Pickens	18,313	9,787	3,892	678	40	53	21	4	40
Spartanburg	61,762	27,097	17,707	2,886	39	44	29	5	65

Note: South Carolina Department of Labor data are average annual employment during the fiscal year July 1959 to June 1960. Census data are at a point in time during the census survey.

Sources: All variables except textile employment from U.S. Bureau of the Census (1964, p. 42); textile employment data from Department of Labor of the State of South Carolina as described in Appendix A.

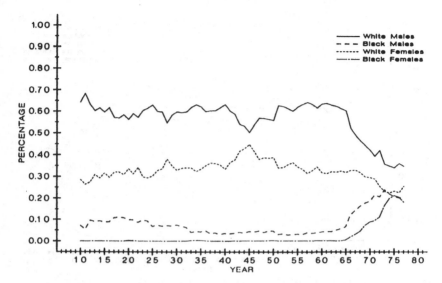

Fig. 6.25. Employment shares in the South Carolina textile industry: Abbeville County.

Figs. 6.25–35 show employment shares by race and sex in the textile industry for our eleven counties from 1910 to 1977. In seven of the eleven, the textile breakthrough for black females occurs in the fiscal year 1965. Recall that the textile industry data are collected on a fiscal-year basis. Therefore fiscal 1966 covers July 1965 through June 1966.[18] In the other four counties, the black female breakthrough in textiles occurs in fiscal year 1966. Since these are fiscal years, we cannot rule out the possibility that the breakthrough occurs in the calendar year 1965 in all counties.

After fifty-five years of near-total exclusion from the industry, black females become employed in significant numbers for the first time in the mid-sixties in each county. Similarly, after constant but low utilization in the industry prior to the mid-sixties, black males significantly increase their employment in textiles at the same time in each county. If the state of South Carolina is a single homogeneous labor market with no mobility costs for workers, a tight labor market might produce a simultaneous breakthrough in black employment of the type exhi-

[18] Since black male textile employment varied somewhat over the sixty-five years, the exact year of the black male breakthrough is difficult to pinpoint. However, since black female employment was near zero prior to the mid-sixties, the breakthrough for black females is easy to pinpoint.

309

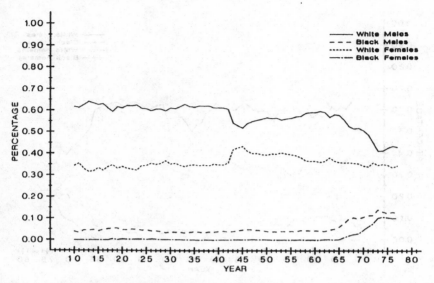

Fig. 6.26. Employment shares in the South Carolina textile industry: Anderson County.

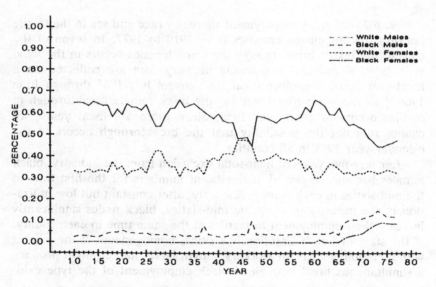

Fig. 6.27. Employment shares in the South Carolina textile industry: Cherokee County.

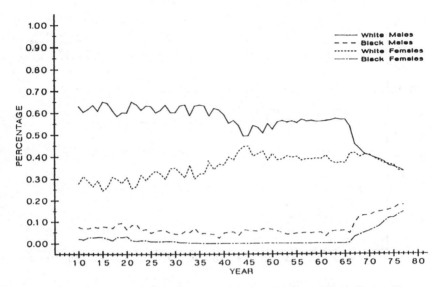

Fig. 6.28. Employment shares in the South Carolina textile industry: Chester County.

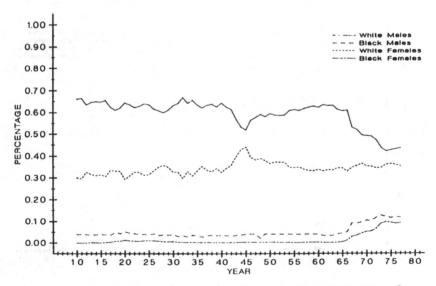

Fig. 6.29. Employment shares in the South Carolina textile industry: Greenville County.

311

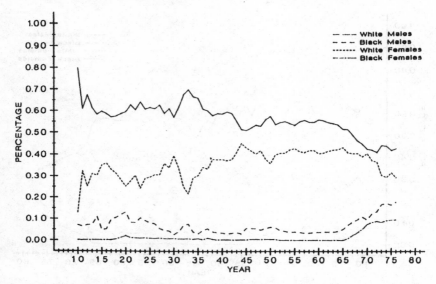

Fig. 6.30. Employment shares in the South Carolina textile industry: Lancaster County.

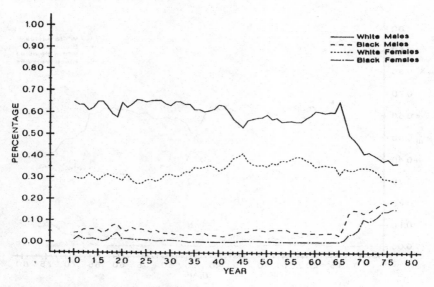

Fig. 6.31. Employment shares in the South Carolina textile industry: Laurens County.

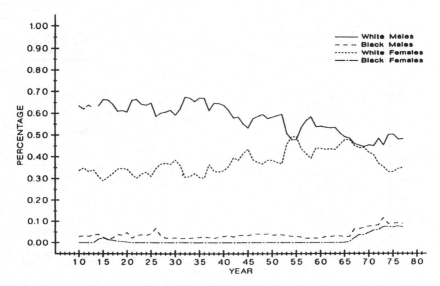

Fig. 6.32. Employment shares in the South Carolina textile industry: Oconee County.

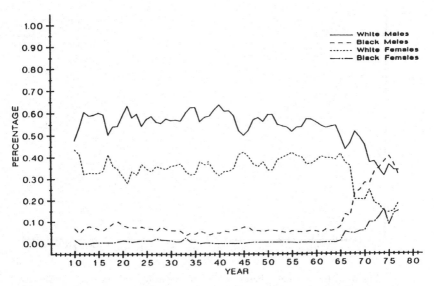

Fig. 6.33. Employment shares in the South Carolina textile industry: Orangeburg County.

313

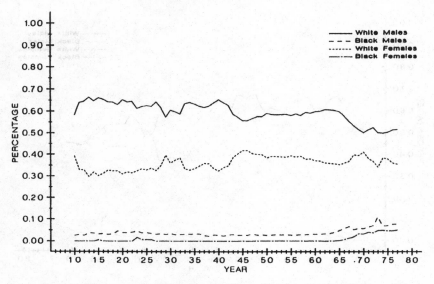

Fig. 6.34. Employment shares in the South Carolina textile industry: Pickens County.

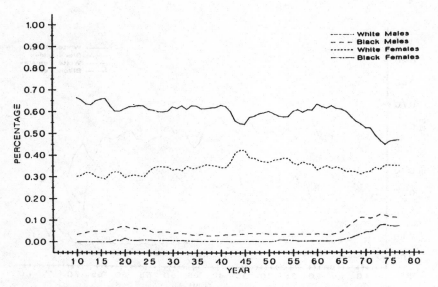

Fig. 6.35. Employment shares in the South Carolina textile industry: Spartanburg County.

Table 6.24. *Industry in 1965 of high-growth manufacturing employees in 1970 (percentages)*

Industry in 1965	Black females	Black males	White females	White males	All workers
Textiles	1.72	1.27	7.44	5.08	5.36
Low-growth manufacturing	1.72	2.53	0.65	3.30	2.14
High-growth manufacturing	39.66	58.23	56.63	58.38	56.43
Unspecified manufacturing	1.72	0.00	0.65	1.52	1.07
Mining and construction	0.00	2.53	0.00	2.54	1.43
Government	0.00	1.27	0.97	2.54	1.67
Agriculture	5.17	3.80	0.00	1.02	1.19
Service industries	6.90	2.53	1.94	3.81	3.21
Wholesale and retail trade	1.72	8.86	2.91	3.55	3.69
Other: Transportation/communication/ utilities/ordnance	0.00	1.27	0.00	2.03	1.07
Industry not reported	1.72	8.86	2.91	6.85	5.24
Out of the labor force	39.66	8.86	25.89	9.39	17.50

Source: U.S. Bureau of the Census, Public Use Sample, 1970. The sample includes all workers aged 26 to 65 in 1970.

bited here. However, given significant differences in employment, in-dustrialization, and racial demographics across counties, we conclude that South Carolina is not a single labor market. Therefore we do not expect changing labor market conditions alone to have the same impact on black textile employment simultaneously across all counties.

As noted in Section 3, Hoffman (1975) advocates a radical economics version of the tight-labor-market hypothesis. She characterizes the black breakthrough in textiles in terms of a job hierarchy model in which whites leave textiles to go to higher-paying industries and blacks take their place at the bottom of the industrial barrel. The linear-probability-model estimates reveal that the newer higher-skill sectors were nondiscriminatory in their hiring, refuting a simple racial hierarchy model of industrial employment. Table 6.24 presents a breakdown by race and sex of the industrial origin (in 1965) of workers in the new or high-growth sector in 1970. New entrants are predominantly from out of the labor force. White entry from the textile industry by no means dominates the white origin-of-entry statistics.

Table 6.25 presents a breakdown by age and sex for employed workers in 1970 who were out of the labor force or unemployed in 1965. There is a high entry rate into textiles for all demographic groups as well as a sizable entry rate into high-growth manufacturing and

315

Table 6.25. *Industry in 1970 of workers unemployed or out of the labor force in 1965, by age cohort (percentages)*

Industry in 1970	Black females				White females				Black males				White males			
	21–25	26–35	36–45	46–65	21–25	26–35	36–45	46–65	21–25	26–35	36–45	46–65	21–25	26–35	36–45	46–65
Textiles	17.48	8.79	10.45	1.52	13.14	14.95	9.15	4.85	16.16	9.26	12.12	2.33	12.29	7.45	3.61	2.30
Low-growth manufacturing	3.88	3.30	1.49	0.00	2.92	4.64	3.66	1.21	7.07	3.70	9.09	6.98	6.64	6.83	3.61	1.15
High-growth manufacturing	20.39	10.99	11.94	4.55	11.68	17.01	15.85	11.52	16.16	7.41	3.03	0.00	11.96	13.04	6.02	6.90
Unspecified manufacturing	0.00	1.10	0.00	0.00	0.36	0.52	1.22	0.00	0.00	0.00	0.00	0.00	0.66	0.62	0.00	0.00
Mining and construction	0.00	0.00	0.00	0.00	1.46	1.03	1.22	0.00	8.08	9.26	21.21	13.95	12.62	16.15	18.07	10.34
Government	0.00	0.00	0.00	0.00	4.01	2.06	3.66	4.24	2.02	0.00	3.03	2.33	4.65	3.73	12.05	6.90
Agriculture	2.91	0.00	5.97	3.03	0.00	0.00	0.61	2.42	5.05	9.26	15.15	13.95	2.66	2.48	7.23	12.64
Service industries	48.54	59.34	59.70	72.73	42.34	34.02	34.76	49.61	18.18	25.93	9.09	32.56	19.60	23.60	19.28	20.69
Wholesale and retail trade	3.88	10.99	10.45	13.64	16.79	19.07	24.39	26.67	12.12	9.26	18.18	16.28	20.60	14.91	6.02	18.39
Other: Transportation/communication																
Utilities/ordnance	0.97	1.10	0.00	1.52	4.38	3.09	1.22	1.82	9.09	12.96	0.00	4.65	6.31	3.73	8.43	5.75
Industry not reported	1.94	4.40	0.00	3.03	2.92	3.61	4.27	6.67	6.06	12.96	9.09	6.98	1.99	7.45	15.66	14.94

Source: U.S. Bureau of the Census. Public Use Sample, 1970. The sample includes all workers aged 21 to 65 in 1970.

services. There is no evidence of any hierarchy in entry rates by race in high-growth manufacturing.

The government-activity hypothesis

Evidence supporting the government-activity hypothesis comes from the time series on statewide textile employment and wages by demographic group presented above. Black textile employment was virtually unaffected by events that occurred from 1910 to 1965. This is especially true for black female employment. Under the tight-labor-market hypothesis, we might expect some black employment changes in the upswings of the numerous business cycles that occur prior to 1965. The government-activity hypothesis predicts that significant changes in black employment and wages will occur after the 1964 Civil Rights Act but has no prediction about black improvement in previous periods. The simultaneous breakthrough of blacks in counties varying in size, racial composition, and industrial composition is consistent with a government policy uniformly applied.

The fact that white male employment begins decreasing at about the same time as black employment increases is also consistent with the government-activity hypothesis[19] (see Fig. 6.36). On the demand side, firms complying with government policy would likely employ fewer whites per unit output expansion as their demand for blacks increased. Evidence documenting that this occurred is given below. Examination of the wage data gives a supply-side explanation for the decrease in white male textile employment that occurred after 1965. After increasing from 1959 through 1965, white male real wages were practically unchanged from 1966 to 1971 despite growth in employment and output in the industry (see Fig. 6.37).[20] Real wages for blacks increased through the end of the sixties. If textile firms were discriminating against blacks before 1965 but not in later years, under the government-activity hypothesis white wages would stop rising as the black labor pool became available to textiles for the first time. Black wages would continue to rise over time as blacks become employed in higher-paying occupations.[21]

---

[19] This decline occurs in the eleven "clean" counties and for the state as a whole.

[20] Wage data are available only for the state as a whole. However, chemical wages are higher than textile wages and were increasing over the period 1960–70. Thus the "chemical problem" biases the data against the inference reported in the text.

[21] Recall that Table 6.1 demonstrates that most of the black relative wage growth in the South attributable to occupational changes is due to a shift of blacks into the operative and craftsman occupations. These are the higher-paying production jobs in textiles that became open to blacks only in the 1960s.

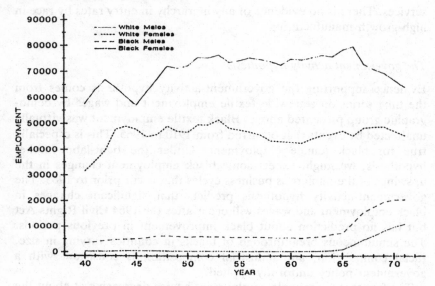

Fig. 6.36. Aggregate employment in the South Carolina textile manufacturing industries.

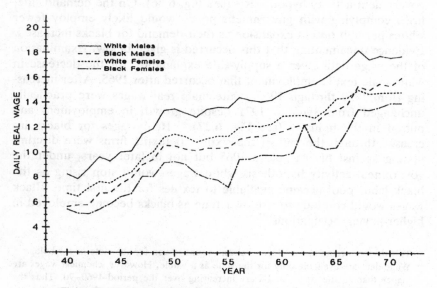

Fig. 6.37. The South Carolina textile industry: average real daily wages.

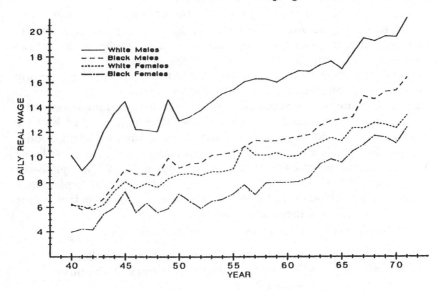

Fig. 6.38. The South Carolina non-textile manufacturing industries: average real daily wages.

White male real wages stop growing in textiles after 1966. As their wages in textiles declined relative to those in other industries, white males left textiles for other industries. The slowing of wage growth for white males does not occur in all industries. Fig. 6.38 shows real wages in non-textile manufacturing. For white males, real wages continue to grow after 1965 at a rate similar to that experienced prior to 1965. Wages for other demographic groups in these industries also grow throughout most of the sixties. These arguments establish that there are plausible demand- and supply-side explanations consistent with the government-activity hypothesis that account for the white male departure from textiles.

In an effort to assess the contributions of government and the tight labor market to the breakthrough in black employment, we estimate reduced-form employment-by-race equations for textiles using the county-level data. Wage data by race and sex are not available at the county level. For the eleven "clean" South Carolina counties, we fit pooled time-series cross-section equations for the years 1947–71.[22]

The regression equations are of the form

$$(1) \qquad Y_{ijt} = \mathbf{X}_{it}\mathbf{a}_j + f_{ij} + g_{jt} + \eta_{ijt}$$

[22] See Section 4 for a discussion of the "clean" counties.

where i refers to the county, j refers to the demographic group, and t refers to time. The fixed effects f_{ij} and g_{jt} are, respectively, county-specific and year-specific intercepts for each demographic group. These estimated fixed effects control for a variety of omitted variables that are likely to affect demographic employment. Absorbed in g_{jt} are any time-varying uniform (across counties) statewide race- and sex-specific factors, like uniform government policy, human-capital improvements, or outmigration of blacks, that plausibly affect employment by race and sex. Absorbed in f_{ij} are any idiosyncratic time-invariant county factors, like the location of the county in relation to product or labor markets or the percentage of the county that is black, that plausibly affect demographic employment. X_{it} is a row vector of explanatory variables, not including an intercept, with associated coefficient vector a_j. *The term* η_{ijt} is a mean zero-error term.

The explanatory variables used in our analysis are:

Textile output	= Real textile output in millions of dollars
New plants	= Number of plants that entered the county after 1957
Old plants	= Number of plants that entered the county before 1958
Non-textile output	= Real non-textile manufacturing output in millions of dollars
Defense contracts	= Real cumulative defense contracts in millions of dollars[23]

Industry demand is proxied by county textile output. Higher levels of output would be expected to lead to greater employment of workers. The number of new plants and the number of old plants are introduced as separate variables to test a version of the industrialization hypothesis that suggests that new entrants into South Carolina are less likely to discriminate against blacks than are older entrants. This might be so because new plants are not encumbered by the restrictive racial legislation that regulated old plants. Initial discrimination in employment might persist because of fixed costs of employment hiring and discrimination by fellow employees. Many new plants were

---

[23] See Appendix A for more discussion of the variables.

Data for defense contracts by establishment were available after 1965. Cumulative contracts were used because a contract award received in one year was not necessarily for that year alone. A similar variable, cumulative EEOC expenditures, was used in Freeman (1973).

The regressions reported below were repeated using the sum of current defense contracts and one or two lags. The results were qualitatively similar to those reported here.

northern-owned, and it is possible that their owners were less discriminatory in their treatment of blacks than more established owners. Hoffman (1975) reports evidence favoring this hypothesis. Even in the absence of an old-plant/new-plant differential, the total number of plants is a plausible regressor that (since output is being held fixed in the regression) measures the effect of plant size on demographic employment.

Non-textile manufacturing output in the county is the best available proxy for the tightness of the non-textile labor market. Manufacturing employed over one-third of all workers in South Carolina between 1960 and 1970. Textile workers have more mobility into non-textile manufacturing than out of manufacturing altogether.[24] Also from the 1970 Public Use Sample we calculate that 43 percent of white males and 49 percent of white females who left textiles between 1965 and 1970 were employed in non-textile manufacturing in 1970.

County-level defense contract expenditure provides a good measure of government activity for the textile industry, because the Office of Federal Contract Compliance and the Defense Department monitored the compliance of textile firms with the affirmative action and nondiscrimination provisions of Executive Order 11246. Cumulative rather than current expenditure is used to measure the long-term impact of contracts. Estimation with a distributed-lag version of this variable does not affect any inference. The effects of uniform government antidiscrimination policies that cannot be directly measured are absorbed into the estimated year effects.

We also estimate an interactive version of the model that permits the a_j coefficients to assume different values after 1964. This interactive specification enables us to test for the presence of structural shift in demographic employment equations that would result from effective government antidiscrimination and affirmative action measures.

Table 6.26 summarizes the slope coefficients from least-squares estimates of equation (1) and from an interactive specification of the model. Since the defense variable is available only after 1965, it is already specified in interactive form. Durbin–Watson statistics for each county (reported in Appendix D) reveal that there is little evidence of serial correlation in the county residuals. Corrections for heteroscedasticity using White's (1980) procedure (not shown) do not affect the basic inferences drawn from the data.

In both specifications, higher levels of defense expenditure are estimated to expand employment for black workers. There is a less statis-

---

[24] From the 1970 Public Use Sample we calculate that of all textile workers in 1965, about 90% were employed in a manufacturing industry in 1970.

321

Table 6.26. *Demographic employment equations (t ratios in parentheses)*

	Black males	Black females	White females	White males
Textile output	1.06 (3.43)	0.30 (1.58)	8.17 (8.49)	7.49 (8.23)
New plants	31.87 (7.99)	15.21 (6.15)	−64.89 (−5.25)	−63.38 (−5.42)
Old plants	11.03 (2.66)	1.87 (0.73)	−13.29 (−1.03)	31.96 (2.63)
Non-textile output	−0.13 (−0.54)	0.29 (1.90)	−5.53 (−7.30)	−4.87 (−6.79)
Defense contracts	4.06 (4.00)	4.17 (6.63)	6.08 (1.93)	−14.97 (−5.04)
R^2	.9732	.9054	.9934	.9975

Interactive specification (Δ refers to coefficient of variable interacted with a post-64 dummy)

	Black males	Black females	White females	White males
Textile output	−0.427 (−1.328)	−0.5810 (−2.68)	10.743 (10.6)	11.423 (12.36)
New plants	7.858 (1.215)	2.550 (0.586)	−33.455 (−1.64)	−20.349 (−1.09)
Old plants	11.238 (2.960)	4.819 (1.8885)	7.857 (6.56)	41.96 (3.85)
Non-textile output	−0.508 (−1.638)	0.0582 (0.278)	−8.232 (−8.41)	−6.38 (0.891)
Defense contracts	3.260 (3.414)	3.136 (4.876)	3.016 (1.002)	−14.77 (−5.389)
Δ Textile output	1.496 (4.4342)	1.257 (5.53)	−3.475 (−3.266)	−5.59 (−5.77)
Δ New plants	10.174 (1.4451)	8.708 (1.83)	19.348 (0.872)	6.28 (0.311)
Δ Old plants	1.271 (0.5063)	−4.765 (2.818)	−17.291 (−2.18)	−1.614 (−0.22)
Δ Non-textile output	−0.347 (−1.23)	−0.0383 (0.202)	5.401 (6.08)	4.138 (5.13)
R^2	.9817	.9238	.9953	.9984

Black economic progress in South Carolina

tically precisely determined positive effect of this variable on white female employment, and there is a statistically significant negative effect of the variable on white male employment. In the noninteractive model, increasing textile output expands the employment of all workers, although the effect is not statistically significant for black female employment. There is clear evidence of a post-1964 interaction in the output variable favoring black employment at the expense of white employment. This is consistent with the installation of affirmative action programs. The sum of the coefficient on the textile output variable and the coefficient on the interacted textile output variable is positive for all demographic groups.

For whites, growth in county non-textile output reduces employment in textiles, although this effect weakens (but remains negative) after 1964. For black workers, there is little evidence of an alternative opportunities effect, especially in the estimates from the interactive models. Evidence on new-plant and old-plant effects is mixed. In the model without interactions there is evidence that new plants hire more blacks than do old plants, which tend to hire more whites. The positive old-plant effect on white employment remains in the interactive specification, but the effects on black employment are less clearly interpretable.

In order to check the robustness of the linear-model results to alternative specifications of the functional form of estimating equation (1), we estimate a variety of models. Use of log X variables in place of X variables does not affect our empirical results. In order to determine the appropriate transformation of the dependent variable, we follow Amemiya and Powell as described in Amemiya (1985) and estimate a nonnormal Box–Cox model that uses

$$\frac{Y_{ijt}^{\lambda_j} - 1}{\lambda_j}$$

rather than Y_{ijt} as the dependent variable. λ_j is estimated along with the other coefficients of the model using nonlinear least squares. Both log and linear versions of X produce the same inference. To simplify the presentation of these results, we report only the linear X version of these estimates in Table 6.27. The slope coefficients are for the stated dependent variable. The sign of the estimated effect on Y_{ijt} is the same as the sign of the coefficient reported in the table. Both interactive and noninteractive specifications were fitted. The interactive models allow the slope coefficients to assume different values after 1964. Durbin–Watson statistics for each county (reported in Appendix D) indicate few problems with serial correlation in the estimated county residuals.

323

Table 6.27. Box–Cox demographic employment equations fitted using the Amemiya–Powell procedure[a] (t statistics shown in parentheses)

	Black males		Black females		White females		White males	
λ_j	0.4	(35.46)	0.45	(25.5)	0.50	(7.79)	0.60	(11.15)
Textile output	0.0018	(16.0)	0.00304	(5.98)	0.0025	(15.2)	0.0018	(16.89)
New plants	0.0217	(12.4)	0.0857	(12.64)	−0.0180	(−8.22)	−0.0108	(−7.51)
Old plants	0.0208	(13.8)	0.0422	(6.16)	−0.0038	(−1.74)	0.0040	(2.70)
Non-textile output	−0.0008	(−9.28)	−0.0011	(−2.742)	−0.0015	(−10.70)	−0.0009	(−10.65)
Defense contracts	0.0013	(3.21)	0.0159	(8.808)	0.0007	(1.23)	−0.0035	(−10.23)

Model with interactions

	Black males		Black females		White females		White males	
λ_j	0.45	(24.14)	0.45	(39.73)	0.775	(13.3)	0.80	(20.56)
Textile output	0.0008	(5.51)	−0.0007	(−1.58)	0.0036	(18.97)	0.0027	(35.3)
New plants	0.0154	(6.18)	0.0631	(7.78)	−0.0014	(−3.31)	−0.0035	(−2.25)
Old plants	0.0231	(15.67)	0.0566	(11.94)	0.0027	(1.32)	0.0080	(8.415)
Non-textile output	−0.0010	(−8.61)	−0.0003	(−0.654)	−0.0024	(−11.57)	−0.0014	(−17.82)
Defense contracts	0.0010	(2.32)	0.0107	(8.67)	0.0006	(1.15)	−0.0034	(−15.2)
Δ Textile output	0.0014	(9.21)	0.0081	(18.1)	−0.0010	(−5.33)	−0.0013	(−16.5)
Δ New plants	0.0025	(0.912)	0.0103	(1.16)	0.0078	(2.07)	0.0018	(1.09)
Δ Old plants	−0.0034	(−3.43)	−0.0429	(−13.69)	−0.0066	(−4.92)	−3.04 × 10^{-6}	(−0.005)
Δ Non-textile output	−0.0002	(−1.69)	−0.0019	(−5.46)	0.0016	(8.83)	0.0009	(13.72)

[a]The instruments used to fit these models are X, squares of X, and all interactions. The Y_{jit} are divided by the grand mean employment (over time and county) for each demographic group. These are 4,082 for white males, 2,687 for white females, 396 for black males, and 78 for black females. Thus the slope coefficients are not directly comparable across demographic groups or with the coefficients presented in Table 6.26.

Corrections for heteroscedasticity using White's method do not over-turn any inference obtained using least-squares standard errors. For the sake of brevity, we report only the results of tests based on the conventional least-squares standard errors.

The empirical results obtained from the Box–Cox models are consis-tent with the main conclusions obtained from the linear specification. There is evidence of statistically significant positive effects of defense contracts on black employment and statistically significant negative effects on white male employment. Increased textile output raises employment for all demographic groups. The interacted output vari-ables reveal a post-1964 shift in favor of black workers. For black females, there is little evidence of any effect from textile output expan-sion before 1965 – a result that should be obvious from inspecting Figs. 6.25–35. The Box–Cox models show a clearer alternative-opportunities effect than do the linear models. In the noninteractive specification, higher non-textile output in a county is associated with less employment in textiles for each demographic group. The pattern is preserved in the interactive model, but the effect strengthens for blacks and weakens for whites.

In the Box–Cox model without interactions there is a clear effect of plant size on employment by race. Smaller plants (measured by output per plant) tend to hire more blacks. Larger firms tend to hire more white females; the estimated scale effect for white males is ambiguous. The only pronounced new-plant/old-plant effect is for black females. There is evidence that new plants hire more black women and fewer whites than do old plants. The interactive specifications reveal that new plants tend to hire more blacks and fewer white males.

Both the linear and the Box–Cox models with and without interac-tion show a steady increase in estimated year effects for black workers in the post-1964 period. The estimates of year effects from the models without interactions are given in Table 6.28. Further evidence of structural shift is revealed by simulating the best-fitting Box–Cox mod-els over the crucial period 1965–70. Such simulations allow examina-tion of the change in employment attributable to changes in each X variable and the change not explained by the regression. The results of such a simulation are presented in Table 6.29, which shows results for both the interactive and the noninteractive models. The simulations for the linear models are comparable.

The most striking feature of Table 6.29 is the failure of each fitted model to account for most of the observed employment change. Much of the improvement in black status is accounted for by unexplained post-1964 year effects. Such year effects are consistent with the opera-tion of unmeasured government antidiscrimination policy. Although

325

Table 6.28. *Estimated year effects (dummies with 1947 set to zero)*
(t *ratios in parentheses*)

Linear model without interactions

Year	Black males	Black females	White males	White females
1960	−129 (2.9)	−45 (1.6)	322 (2.48)	−102 (0.74)
1961	−147 (3.3)	−44 (1.6)	315 (2.4)	−58 (0.42)
1962	−175 (3.9)	−61 (2.2)	135 (2.4)	−26 (0.19)
1963	−173 (3.8)	−72 (2.6)	436 (3.2)	109 (0.8)
1964	−168 (3.7)	−88 (3.1)	438 (3.2)	157 (1.1)
1965	−136 (2.9)	−82 (2.8)	493 (3.6)	163 (1.1)
1966	−72 (1.5)	−65 (2.2)	537 (3.8)	118 (0.8)
1967	115 (2.4)	12 (0.4)	413 (2.9)	279 (1.9)
1968	160 (3.4)	60 (2.1)	370 (2.7)	312 (2.1)
1969	155 (3.4)	102 (3.4)	285 (2.0)	273 (1.8)
1970	136 (2.8)	182 (6.1)	218 (1.54)	260 (1.7)
1971	184 (3.8)	225 (7.5)	413 (2.9)	483 (3.2)

Box-Cox model without interactions[a]

Year	Black males	Black females	White males	White females
1960	−0.22 (11.7)	−0.52 (7.2)	0.10 (6.75)	−0.01 (−.21)
1961	−0.21 (14.3)	−0.39 (5.3)	0.10 (6.51)	0.01 (0.24)
1962	−0.26 (13)	−0.49 (6.7)	0.09 (6.04)	0.01 (0.46)
1963	−0.25 (10.2)	−0.54 (7.3)	0.11 (7.44)	0.05 (2.1)
1964	−0.11 (5.5)	−0.56 (7.4)	0.12 (7.73)	0.07 (3.2)
1965	−0.05 (2.2)	−0.27 (3.5)	0.13 (8.22)	0.07 (3.1)
1966	−0.23 (11)	−0.55 (6.2)	0.13 (8.04)	0.07 (2.7)
1967	0.63 (29)	1.41 (15.6)	0.09 (6.07)	0.12 (4.7)
1968	0.77 (36)	1.80 (20.5)	0.09 (5.96)	0.13 (5.2)
1969	0.82 (36)	2.10 (23.9)	0.07 (4.50)	0.12 (4.7)
1970	0.83 (36)	2.50 (29.5)	0.06 (3.33)	0.12 (4.7)
1971	0.95 (41)	2.83 (33.6)	0.09 (5.49)	0.19 (7.2)

[a]The table shows the year effects for the transformed dependent variable using the scaling given at the base of Table 6.27.

the estimated defense coefficient is statistically significant, the contribution of defense contracts to black employment is numerically weak.[25] If all post-1964 interaction effects are attributed to government policy, between 70 and 80 percent of the predicted change is attribut-

[25] There are conditions under which we underestimate the contribution of defense contracts to the increase in black employment. The contract data refer to work done in the county, but firms were required to comply with Executive Order 11246 in all

Table 6.29. *Effects of changing variables on textile employment, 1965–1970[a]*

	Black males	Black females	White females	White males
From model without interactions				
Actual change	5,041	4,215	565	−6,778
Change from all sources	747	823	−319	−3,045
From output	307	116	2,179	2,131
From new establishments	489	448	−2,256	−2,045
From old establishments	−64	−29	61	−103
From non-textile output	−75	−21	−651	−608
Defense contracts	90	310	347	−2,420
From model with interactions				
Change from all sources	1,241	820	1,412	−1,399
Change from defense contracts and structural shift	903	562	1,151	−2,743
From output	126	−26	2,590	2,946
From new establishments	365	329	−1,292	−601
From old establishments	−68	−40	−38	−174
From non-textile output	−85	−5	−994	−827
Defense contracts	100	208	257	−2,177
From interaction output	223	306	−720	−1,418
From interaction new establishments	588	54	884	309
From interaction old establishments	9	30	94	0
From interaction non-textile output	−17	−36	636	543

[a] For county i and demographic group j the effect of changing the lth component of $\mathbf{X}_{it}$ at time t, $\mathbf{X}_{itl}$ to $\mathbf{X}_{i,t+k,l}$ is estimated by

$$\Delta Y_{jt} = Y_{j,t+k} - Y_{j,t} = \lambda_j a_{jl} \sum_{i=1}^{I} (Y_{ijt})^{(1-\lambda_j)} \left\{ \left[\frac{Y_{ij,t+k}}{Y_{ijt}} - 1 \right] \middle/ \left[\left(\frac{Y_{ij,tk}}{Y_{ijt}} \right)^{\lambda_j} - 1 \right] \right\} \Delta \mathbf{X}_{itl}$$

where I is the number of counties, $t = 1965$, $t + k = 1970$. The coefficients from Table 6.27 are used.

plants, even those not producing goods for sale to the government. There are many textile firms with plants in different counties and different states. County textile defense expenditure is thus an error-ridden measure of the appropriate variable. In a simple demographic model of demand that regresses employment solely on the measured contract variable, the estimated contract effect is downward biased if the variable indicating whether the *plant* has a contract is independent of the disturbance term in the equation. If the demographic demand equation contains additional explanatory variables that are correlated with the indicator variable, the sign of the bias is ambiguous.

327

able to this source. Nonetheless, unmeasured components account for most of the observed change. Such dramatic structural shift seems inconsistent with pure forms of the tight-labor-market or industrialization hypotheses. Government activity – residually defined – seems to be the most plausible source of this change.

8. Summary and conclusions

This essay examines the sources of black economic progress in South Carolina. Lessons from that state are of general interest because trends in black progress in South Carolina resemble trends in the South as a whole, and black improvement in the South accounts for a substantial component of aggregate U.S. black improvement over the period 1960–80. Most of our attention is focused on the manufacturing sector. Much of the southern black progress comes through entry of black workers into craftsman and operative occupations and improvement in relative black wages in those occupations.

Using a unique body of time-series cross-section data on employment and wages by race and sex supplemented by a variety of U.S. government sources, we examine a number of competing explanations for the breakthrough in black employment and wages in the manufacturing sector that occurred after 1964. We demonstrate the value of disaggregating the data and establish that different factors account for black progress in different sectors.

The principal manufacturing employer in the state is the textile industry. This industry was already a substantial employer by 1915 when Jim Crow laws formalized a preexisting exclusion of blacks from the main operative and craftsman occupations of that industry. We document that over the period 1910–64 the share of black employment is low and stable despite a variety of economic circumstances in the state. Suddenly in 1965 blacks of both sexes become employed on a large scale. That year witnessed the implementation of Title VII of the 1964 Civil Rights Act, which forbade employment discrimination. Executive Order 11246 was also issued in that year. The order forbade discrimination by government contractors and required the establishment of affirmative action programs. The South Carolina textile industry sold 5 percent of its output to the U.S. government in 1965. The Equal Employment Opportunity Commission targeted southern textiles and held hearings on the industry in 1966. The improvement in black status after 1964 is uniform across geographically diverse local labor markets. Regression analyses of black employment reveal a structural shift in employment equations that cannot be accounted for by conventional measures of output or the growth in alternative oppor-

328

tunities. There is some evidence of greater black employment in counties that sold more goods to the U.S. government. Both the timing evidence and the regression evidence suggest that government activity played an important role in integrating textiles. As a large new supply of black workers became available to the industry, the real wages of white workers – which had been rising for six consecutive years before 1965 – suddenly flattened. A similar but less well-documented story can be told for black female progress in the closely related apparel industry.

Alternative explanations of this event appear to be much less cogent. A supply-shift story attributing the black improvement to the decline in agriculture cannot account for the timing of the black breakthrough in textiles. Neither can the human-capital story of improvement in black textiles account for the timing. We document that increases in black human capital between 1960 and 1970 would have made black employment *less likely* to occur than otherwise, because textiles is a low-skill industry. By 1960 there were plenty of blacks with skill levels adequate to perform textile jobs.

The only viable alternative to the story of government as the agent of change in textiles is the story that assigns a central role to the tightness of the labor market. By the mid-1960s South Carolina had a booming economy. New industries entered the state, and the traditional reservoir of farm labor had disappeared. Real wages in textiles increased, making competition with low-wage foreign firms more difficult. The incentives to draw on a new source of low-wage labor were great.[26]

What cannot be dismissed and indeed seems quite plausible is that in 1965 entrepreneurs seized on the new federal legislation and decrees to do what they wanted to do anyway. One could argue that the federal antidiscrimination and affirmative action laws came into existence in 1964 precisely because the U.S. labor market was tight to an unprecedented degree and discrimination was becoming costly. This study cannot reject the hypothesis that it was the confluence of tight labor markets and new laws that made integration in textiles occur so rapidly. Separating these factors requires information from another episode in which comparable laws are put in place in a slack labor market.

We do not claim that federal activity accounts for black progress in other sectors of the state. A major finding of our analysis is that, once skill levels are accounted for, blacks were not excluded from other

---

[26] It should be noted, however, that many employers feared that blacks were more likely to join unions (Rowan 1970). In the nonunionized textile labor market this would be a serious negative consideration.

Richard J. Butler, James J. Heckman, & Brook Payner

sectors even in 1960. New industries entering the state after 1945 tended to be color-blind in their employment practices. Surprisingly, so were state and local governments by 1960. Blacks were underrepresented in these sectors only because they lacked skills. As their skill levels expanded, so did their employment and wages.

Appendix A
Data

We have combined data from U.S. government sources with data published by the state of South Carolina. Three types of data were combined to form the South Carolina data base: annual county-level data, annual state-level data, and census year data. For the period 1910–35, the data come from *Reports and Resolutions of South Carolina to the General Assembly of the State of South Carolina.* For the period 1936–71, the data come from the *Annual Report of the Department of Labor to the State of South Carolina.* In addition to the South Carolina data we collected U.S. *Census of Population* data for the census South and selected southern states.

We obtain the following data by county for each fiscal year (July 1 to June 30). For the textile industry, the variables are:

> Value of annual product (dollars)
> Average number of days plants operated
> Total wages of production workers (dollars) by sex
> Average employment of production workers by race and sex
> Number of establishments

Total man-hours are calculated by multiplying (annual) average days plants operated by average annual production-worker employment by eight hours per day. From a listing of all textile plants by name in each county are formed:

> Number of establishments started after 1957
> Number of establishments started before 1958

Establishments are counted at the plant level, although different plants may belong to the same firm. For total manufacturing, we collect annual data on value of annual product (dollars). Total manufacturing excludes lumber, timber, and turpentine. Non-textile output (annual product) by county is formed by subtracting textile output from total manufacturing output. The county textile data exclude totals for knitting mills and synthetics mills for the period 1910–69. In 1970 and 1971 the totals include knitting mills and synthetics. Unlike the county-level data, statewide aggregate data for the textile industry include the knitting and synthetics mills over the entire sample period.

From the U.S. *Census of Population* for 1960 for South Carolina, we obtain population, total employment, manufacturing employment, textile employment, and agriculture employment for selected counties.

The data on new-hire rates, quits, and layoffs displayed in Fig. 6.9 come from reports of the U.S. Department of Labor as summarized in the American

Textile Manufactures Institute journal *Textiles Hi-Light*, Spring 1971, p. 25, and Spring 1969, p. 24.

We obtained defense contract data from *Prime Contract Awards over $10,000 by State, County, Contractor and Place* for South Carolina from 1966 to 1971. Total defense contracts for textile establishments by county by year are formed by matching firm or plant names listed in this data source with firm or plant names listed in the *Annual Report of the South Carolina Department of Labor*.

In addition to the county data, we use aggregate statewide industry data from the South Carolina Department of Labor reports. These data are for every manufacturing industry except lumber, timber, and turpentine. The available data include:

> Value of annual product (dollars)
> Average number of days plants operated
> Average number of production workers by race and sex
> Total wages by race and sex (dollars)

Total capital invested is the reported depreciated value of fixed assets including plant, real estate, machinery and equipment, and other assets. Average daily wages by race and sex are computed by dividing total wages (deflated by the CPI) for each race and sex group by the product of the number of production workers in that group and the number of days plants operated.

Statewide data on employment in textiles, total manufacturing, and agriculture by race and sex were obtained from the U.S. Bureau of the Census, *Census of Population* for 1940, 1950, 1960, and 1970. Statewide textile industry employment by race and sex was collected for 1950, 1960, 1970, and 1980 for the states of North Carolina, Georgia, and Virginia from U.S. Bureau of the Census, *Census of Population*, vol. 2, for those states.

U.S. Census Bureau Public Use Microdata Sample computer tables are another source of data. The 1940, 1950, and 1960 tapes each contain a 1 percent sample, the 1970 tape contains a 2 percent sample, and the 1980 tape contains a 5 percent sample. We use the following variables from each census tape for South Carolina:

> Occupation
> Industry
> Race
> Sex
> Age
> Annual wage income (dollars) last year
> Hours worked last week
> Weeks worked last year
> Highest grade completed
> Labor force status (civilian, employed, unemployed, out of labor force)

From the U.S. Bureau of the Census Public Use Samples we also obtain data for the census South. We use 1 percent samples for 1940 and 1950, 0.1 percent

331

samples for 1960 and 1970, and a 0.5 percent sample for 1980. Data on race, sex, age, industry, and labor force status were obtained for each census year.

From the *Annual Survey of Manufactures* for 1949–53, 1955–57, 1959–62, 1964–66, and 1968–71 and the *Census of Manufactures* for 1947, 1954, 1958, 1963, and 1967, we collected statewide data on production-worker employment by industry for South Carolina. Data for 1948 are unavailable. The following industries are included: textiles, apparel, non-electrical machinery, electrical machinery, fabricated metals, paper and pulp, chemicals, and total manufacturing. For the textile industry, we also obtained production-worker employment for selected counties from the *Census of Manufactures*.

For certain analyses, we form the following five categories of manufacturing industries: textiles, chemicals, apparel, non-traditional manufacturing, and traditional manufacturing. Chemicals and apparel were isolated because of their similarity to textiles. The other two categories were formed on the basis of a ranking of the percentage change in employment from 1960 to 1970 in the remaining manufacturing industries. The five non-traditional high-growth industries are: transportation equipment, electrical machinery, non-electrical machinery, metalworking, and foundries and machine shops. The six traditional low-growth industries are: food products, paper and pulp, stone and clay, lumber and furniture, printing and publishing, and miscellaneous manufacturing.

We also use data from the *Annual Report of the State Superintendent of Education* 1931–57 for South Carolina. The variables are:

> White elementary school current expenditures (district funds)
> White high school current expenditures (district funds)
> Black elementary school current expenditures (district funds)
> Black high school current expenditures (district funds)
> Number of white students in each grade
> Number of black students in each grade

These variables are used to form per student elementary and high school expenditures.

Because some districts count the seventh and eighth grades as elementary school and others count them as high school, we adopt the following convention in constructing a quality-adjusted education variable. We count seventh grade as elementary school and eighth grade as high school. Quality-adjusted education is formed by summing, for each student, real per student expenditures for each year the student is enrolled in school. For example, if an individual started school in 1944 and completed ten years of school, his or her quality-adjusted education is defined as the sum of real per student expenditures for the appropriate race group from 1944 through 1953.

This procedure is used to form quality-adjusted education for 21- to 25-year-olds in 1950, 21- to 35-year-olds in 1960, and 31- to 45-year-olds in 1970. Since schooling expenditure data by race were not collected after 1957, we cannot construct this variable for 21- to 30-year-olds in 1970. For example, a 21-year-old high school graduate in 1970 would have completed high school in 1967. However, we would not have schooling expenditure data for this individual's last ten years of school. Consequently, we construct a slightly different measure for this group in 1970.

For 21- to 25-year-olds with over three years of school in 1970, we compute average educational expenditure for the first three years of school and multiply this figure by the total number of years of schooling. Similarly, for 26- to 30-year-olds with over eight years of school in 1970, we take the average of per student expenditure for the first eight years of school and multiply by the total years of schooling. For comparison purposes, we construct the same measure of quality-adjusted education for 21- to 25-year-olds and 26- to 30-year-olds in 1960.

Data from the South Carolina reports are available for the fiscal year beginning July 1. The U.S. Census Bureau and Department of Defense data are available for the calendar year. We chose the following convention for matching data from the various sources: The fiscal year is defined as corresponding to the calendar year in which the fiscal year ends.

Appendix B

Additional results with SEARCH

Table 6.B.1 records the outcome of a SEARCH analysis for an eleven-county textile sample using the "clean" sample of counties discussed in Section 4. We aggregate over these counties to form yearly aggregates. Hence the eleven-county sample, consisting of time-series data from 1947 to 1971, is less aggregated than the general manufacturing sample discussed in the text in that it is for one industry. A disaggregated analysis of the textile data is presented in Section 7 of the text. There are no wages by race and sex at the county level.

The black employment series exhibits more specification stability than the white series, as is the case for aggregate manufacturing employment equations. A number of interesting contrasts are apparent in the data: Relative to stochastic uncertainty, specification uncertainty is much smaller in the more disaggregated textile sample even though the standard error still tends to be small relative to the size of the coefficient. For most entries of Table 6.B.1, the ratio of stochastic to specification uncertainty is greater than 1, whereas in the aggregate manufacturing results it is always less than 0.5. Moreover, in the textile sample there is no change in sign in the bounds of the coefficients for blacks.

Tables 6.B.2 and 6.B.3 examine the robustness of the aggregate manufacturing and textile results when linear, quadratic, and cubic time trends are included among the doubtful regressors. Extending the list of doubtful regressors in this fashion is seen to increase the specification uncertainty enormously for either sample and for all race/gender groups. The specification reported in the top line in each table is the most robust. This is a consequence of the fact that Specification 1 in neither table measures structural shift as a shift in the linear time trend – unlike the other specifications. Typically the specification bounds increase by a factor of three for specifications that include a dummy interaction with trend (Dum·Time) or that allow for a separate trend (EEO

333

Table 6.B.1. *South Carolina eleven-county textile sample: race/gender-specific employment as the dependent variable*

	White male	White female	Black male	Black female
Specification 1				
Acc Def[a] (Std. error)	-0.022 (0.007)	0.055 (0.007)	0.169 (0.021)	0.556 (0.062)
Upper	-0.020	0.021	0.203	0.659
Lower	-0.032	-0.004	0.168	0.556
Specification 2[b]				
Dum (Std. error)	0.374 (0.170)	-0.495 (0.240)	-1.692 (0.747)	-6.069 (2.022)
Upper	0.747	0.546	-0.564	-2.583
Lower	0.329	-0.793	-2.317	-7.637
Dum·Time (Std. error)	-0.020 (0.008)	0.026 (0.011)	0.112 (0.036)	0.397 (0.097)
Upper	-.017	0.043	0.147	0.485
Lower	-.038	-0.026	0.057	0.225
Specification 3[b]				
EEO Trend (Std. error)	-0.019 (.007)	0.025 (0.010)	0.178 (0.041)	0.617 (0.123)
Upper	-0.016	0.050	0.241	0.792
Lower	-0.037	-0.020	0.110	0.398

[a] Acc Def is accumulated defense contracts in dollars for the eleven-county sample. Federal contractors were required to implement affirmative action programs. See the discussion of this variable in Section 7. In all specifications, the logarithms of the following variables were also included as "doubtful" variables: number of new plants, number of old plants, and non-textile manufacturing output. The "important" variables in all specifications included the intercept, textile output, and the "structural shift" variables listed above.

[b] A time trend was also included in the list of doubtful variables.

Table 6.B.2. South Carolina aggregate manufacturing

	White male	White female	Black male	Black female
Race/gender-specific employment as the dependent variable, allowing for linear, quadratic, and cubic time trends				
Specification 1[a]				
Dum (Std. error)	0.049 (0.049)	−0.011 (0.045)	0.290 (0.067)	0.476 (0.174)
Upper	0.467	0.913	0.941	2.311
Lower	−0.388	−0.560	0.040	−0.023
Specification 2[b]				
Dum (Std. error)	0.313 (0.797)	0.684 (0.696)	−2.187 (0.920)	−1.177 (2.783)
Upper	8.631	12.121	4.048	12.565
Lower	−7.699	−11.417	−8.011	−18.104
Dum·Time (Std. error)	−0.009 (0.030)	−0.026 (0.026)	0.092 (0.034)	0.060 (0.104)
Upper	0.295	0.435	0.314	0.710
Lower	−0.318	−0.449	−0.139	−0.441
Specification 3[b]				
EEO Trend (Std. error)	0.009 (0.027)	−0.024 (0.023)	0.142 (0.037)	0.152 (0.100)
Upper	0.333	0.459	0.417	0.986
Lower	−0.276	−0.399	−0.104	−0.387
Race/gender specific wages as the dependent variable				
Specification 1[a]				
Dum (Std. error)	−0.007 (0.041)	0.010 (0.037)	−0.035 (0.046)	−0.104 (0.141)
Upper	0.949	0.908	1.206	1.488
Lower	−0.611	−0.591	−0.752	−0.920

Table 6.B.2. (cont.)

	White male	White female	Black male	Black female
Specification 2[b]				
Dum (Std. error)	0.921 (0.612)	1.144 (0.541)	1.304 (0.658)	4.370 (1.983)
Upper	12.605	12.603	15.840	20.712
Lower	−11.643	11.374	−15.007	−17.067
Dum·Time (Std. error)	−0.035 (0.023)	−0.042 (0.020)	−0.050 (0.025)	−0.167 (0.074)
Upper	0.443	0.433	0.570	0.649
Lower	−0.467	−0.467	−0.588	−0.769
Specification 3[b]				
EEO Trend (Std. error)	−0.031 (0.020)	−0.032 (0.018)	−0.049 (0.021)	−0.158 (0.065)
Upper	0.463	0.450	0.590	0.688
Lower	−0.415	−0.413	−0.523	−0.687

Note: In all specifications, the logarithms of the following variables were also included as "doubtful" variables: per capita AFDC expenditures, unemployment benefits and maximum number of weeks, and acres of cotton harvested each year, and the logarithmic difference between SC and US wage rates. The "important" variables in all specifications included the intercept, deviations of industrial output from SC trend, and the "structural shift" variables listed in the table.

[a] The log of aggregate capital was included.

[b] A linear time trend was included.

Table 6.B.3. *South Carolina eleven-county textile sample: race/gender-specific employment as the dependent variable, allowing for arbitrary cubic time trends*

	White male	White female	Black male	Black female
Specification 1				
Acc Def[a] (Std. error)	-0.0003 (0.005)	0.003 (0.008)	0.113 (0.024)	0.373 (0.059)
Upper	-0.005	0.035	0.207	0.673
Lower	-0.033	-0.020	0.108	0.355
Specification 2[b]				
Dum (Std. error)	1.175 (0.294)	0.801 (0.615)	1.873 (1.947)	6.980 (4.651)
Upper	2.034	2.995	4.053	13.003
Lower	-0.178	-1.981	-3.449	-10.283
Dum·Time (Std. error)	-0.0620 (0.015)	-0.041 (0.03)	-0.073 (0.100)	-0.280 (0.238)
Upper	0.009	0.105	0.205	0.620
Lower	-0.105	-0.152	-0.182	-0.581
Specification 3[b]				
EEO Trend (Std. error)	-0.047 (0.015)	-0.030 (0.028)	0.114 (0.127)	0.358 (0.378)
Upper	0.010	0.109	0.381	1.184
Lower	-0.090	-0.133	0.092	-0.250

Note: In all specifications, the logarithms of the following variables were also included as "doubtful" variables: number of new plants, number of old plants, and non-textile manufacturing output. The "important" variables in all specifications included the intercept, textile output, and the "structural shift" variables listed above. See the text discussion in Section 7.

[a] Acc Def is as defined in Table 6.B.1.

[b] A linear time trend was also included in the list of doubtful variables.

Table 6.B.4. *South Carolina eleven-county textile sample: race/gender-specific employment as the dependent variable with generalized autocorrelation correction*

	White male	White female	Black male	Black female
Specification 1				
Acc Def[a] *(Std. error)*	−0.007 *(0.005)*	−0.006 *(0.010)*	0.059 *(0.025)*	0.271 *(0.080)*
Upper	−0.008	0.044	0.213	0.731
Lower	−0.041	−0.037	0.044	0.185
Specification 2[b]				
Dum *(Std. error)*	NA	NA	NA	NA
Upper				
Lower				
Dum·Time *(Std. error)*	NA	NA	NA	NA
Upper				
Lower				
Specification 3[b]				
EEO Trend *(Std. error)*	−0.015 *(0.019)*	−0.012 *(0.026)*	0.238 *(0.111)*	1.218 *(0.376)*
Upper	0.032	0.188	0.708	2.645
Lower	−0.079	−0.195	−0.297	−0.862

Note: The generalized autocorrelation correction was accomplished by including the lag of the dependent variable and all of the independent variables as regressors. All variables (except time trends) were entered in logarithmic form. The "important" variables (those which were kept in all SEARCH specifications) were the intercept, textile output, and the structural shift variable (either the log of accumulated defense contracts or a post-1965 time trend). The "doubtful" variables included number of new plants, number of old plants, non-textile output, and their lags. Also included as "doubtful" variables were the lag of the dependent variable and lag of accumulated defense contracts (or the post-1965 trend variable).

[a] Acc Def is accumulated defense contracts as defined in the text.

[b] Time and the lagged dependent variable were also included as "doubtful" variables in its specification.

Trend) that starts up when government policies began. For the specifications in which the policy shift is measured as a dummy variable or by accumulated defense contracts, there is relatively little change in the specification bounds when additional polynomials in time are added to the model.

In a further attempt to measure the robustness of the estimates of policy effects, we include lagged values of the dependent variable and all of the independent variables in the model as doubtful variables in Table 6.B.4. This allows for generalized first-order autocorrelation error processes. The implied first-order "autocorrelation parameter" is not forced to be less than 1 in absolute value and is not constrained to be equal across variables. Unfortunately, space limitations on the version of SEARCH we used preclude all but two of the specifications for the textile sample. These results are recorded in Table 6.B.4. This table, like Tables 6.B.2 and 6.B.3 for the analysis including cubic time trends, indicates relatively more specification instability for the models using a change in trend as a measure of structural shift compared to Specification 1 or the one using accumulated defense contracts. Although the specification bounds are largest when lags and time trends are introduced, the positive sign of the accumulated defense contract variable remains positive in the equations for black males and females.

This analysis suggests several conclusions. The more aggregated the data the more fragile is the estimate. In the general manufacturing sample, the specification error for our various measures of structural shift is larger (relative to the stochastic error of the estimate) than it is in the textile sample. (This remains true even when we drop regressors from the models fitted on the manufacturing sample so that both the textile and manufacturing models have the same number of independent variables. Although the ratio of stochastic to specification error increases slightly for the manufacturing data, its value still remains at about 0.5 or smaller, whereas the ratio for textiles is greater than 1.) Besides the difference due to the degree of aggregation, sample estimates of structural shift are more sensitive to specification when they are measured as changes in linear time trends – either as a new linear trend or as a change in the old one.

More specific demographic conclusions are that estimated shifts in employment are less sensitive to specification error than are estimated shifts in wage equations. For black females we find that the specification uncertainty is twice as great as the stochastic uncertainty. Indeed for all race/gender groups and for all specifications of the structural shift variables the stochastic uncertainty for the policy measures in the employment equations is less than half the size of the specification uncertainty, and often it is only about a tenth of the size. There is more fragility in the estimated structural shift for wages than for employment for all demographic groups and more specification uncertainty (with respect to structural shift) for whites than there is for blacks.

Appendix C

Constructing a measure of human capital using Butler's (1985) method

The research of Welch (1973) and Smith (1984) illustrates the importance of changes in schooling in explaining relative wage growth. Both demonstrate that the qualitative changes (teacher–student ratios, per capita expenditures, proportion of one-room schools) are at least as significant as the quantitative (years of educational attainment) changes. Unfortunately, owing to the aggregate nature of their data sets, they could not construct an index capturing both the qualitative and quantitative dimensions. The South Carolina data allowed Butler (1985) to do that for the first time. Here we describe his method, since we use his variable in the macro analysis of Section 6.

The human-capital variable measures the accumulated effect of formal years of education. It is the total per capita expenditure that an individual receives while in school, $\sum_{i=1}^{T} exp_i$ – where i indexes the years a person is in school and T is the total number of years of formal education. The expenditure data ("*exp*" is measured by the race-specific real per capita teaching expenditures) are taken from the annual reports filed by South Carolina's Superintendent of Education. These data are merged with interpolated data on educational attainment, age distribution, and proportion of immigrants from the decennial census to generate human-capital variables for the representative worker.

Specifically, the mean age for each of eight age-group intervals (16–19, 20–24, 25–29, etc.) is taken as the representative age for that race/sex cohort. This establishes a starting date for the first grade, from which time per capita real expenditures are accumulated for the (median) number of years of formal schooling our representative worker would have obtained (leftover fractions of a year of schooling were multiplied by the following year's expenditures and added to the total). For each year, we now have eight human-capital variables constructed – one each for all eight age groups. The weighted average (by the number of South Carolina employees in blue-collar occupations) of human capital for our eight age groups represents the human capital for that race/sex group. Data on the proportion of workers and the educational attainment for each race/sex/age group are obtained from census data and interpolated between census years. Adjustments are made on the basis of race/sex/age/region-specific data using migration information from the censuses – each age group's human capital now being the weighted average of human capital from South Carolina and the nonsouthern regions. There was virtually no black immigration from other regions of the country during the sample period, so no adjustment was necessary for black immigration. White human-capital proxies, however, were adjusted for immigration from the north-central and northeastern regions of the United States.

For some census years, data on racial educational expenditure and attainment figures in the other regions are lacking, so that total teaching expenditures (not race-specific) from the *Biennial Survey of Education* and total educational attainment of all males (from the census) are used in constructing the nonsouthern human-capital variables. Another problem is that after 1960 South Carolina no longer broke down educational data (except for the enrollment distribution) by race. Two separate adjustments for the post-1960 period were tried, both yielding virtually the same result, principally because of the relatively small proportion of the industrial labor force educated after 1960.

The first is to extrapolate white and black educational expenditures based on the predicted values from regressions including a time trend and total teaching expenditures. The second simply assumes that after 1960 blacks and whites had equivalent per capita expenditures. Here we employ results using only the extrapolated values.

Although the comparability of data (both over time and between South Carolina and other regions) causes us to focus exclusively on teaching expenditures rather than other categories of expenditures as a measure of school quality, we recognize that there may be severe measurement problems if there has been wage discrimination against black schoolteachers. In this case, teaching expenditures will tend to understate the level of black schooling relative to that of whites at any point in time, and may seriously distort the trend of school quality over time if the level of discrimination is changing secularly. Butler (1983) calculates the level of "Becker"-type wage discrimination for white female and for black male and female South Carolina schoolteachers using white males as the benchmark group. In brief, these estimates are constructed by regressing relative wages on the relative marginal product of schoolteaching where the marginal product was calculated from an estimated schooling production function. Since white male teachers are the benchmark group, such adjusted expenditures will be higher than the unadjusted teaching expenditures if schoolteachers are discriminated against on the basis of race and sex. Using these adjusted human-capital variables does not appreciably affect our empirical results with this variable. We present only the results employing the unadjusted human-capital variable in our analysis in Section 6.

These human-capital variables exhibit strong secular trends. The correlation between the human-capital variables and the linear time trend variable is .970 for white males, .989 for white females, .892 for black males, and .869 for black females.

Appendix D

County Durbin–Watson statistics

Table 6.D.1. *Linear model*

County	White male	White female	Black male	Black female
Without interactions				
1	2.88	2.04	2.48	2.59
2	2.11	1.83	1.63	2.52
3	2.55	2.35	2.55	1.60
4	2.11	2.38	2.76	1.87
5	2.33	1.74	2.33	1.89
6	1.84	2.19	2.12	1.79
7	1.74	1.78	2.53	2.46
8	2.84	1.93	2.29	2.28
9	1.75	2.20	1.99	1.89

Table 6.D.1. (*cont.*)

County	White male	White female	Black male	Black female
10	2.35	2.03	2.29	2.27
11	2.10	2.21	2.36	1.89
With interactions				
1	3.02	2.13	2.59	2.08
2	2.48	1.89	1.31	2.16
3	2.34	2.21	2.40	1.70
4	1.92	2.17	2.56	1.34
5	2.12	1.69	2.43	1.95
6	1.69	2.22	2.28	2.10
7	2.29	1.80	2.53	2.37
8	2.38	1.67	2.99	2.48
9	1.76	3.06	2.40	2.04
10	2.24	2.13	2.16	2.00
11	2.56	2.83	2.42	1.88

Table 6.D.2. *Box–Cox model*

County	White male	White female	Black male	Black female
Without interactions				
1	3.09	2.11	2.71	1.83
2	2.35	2.07	1.94	2.84
3	2.43	2.22	1.50	2.25
4	2.13	2.13	2.00	2.02
5	2.37	1.82	2.19	2.31
6	1.73	1.75	2.02	1.42
7	1.97	1.34	2.20	2.36
8	2.89	2.57	2.68	2.73
9	1.97	2.79	1.79	2.25
10	2.25	2.29	1.91	1.46
11	1.83	2.43	1.49	2.09
With interactions				
1	3.14	2.17	2.75	1.89
2	2.60	2.06	1.81	2.86
3	2.34	2.19	1.61	2.09
4	1.96	2.09	2.05	1.88
5	2.11	1.65	2.31	2.27
6	1.65	2.05	2.02	1.38
7	2.41	1.57	2.32	2.14
8	2.48	1.90	2.72	2.34
9	1.70	3.13	1.93	2.43
10	2.32	2.31	1.96	1.60
11	2.32	2.80	2.46	1.51

References

Amemiya, T. (1985), *Advanced Econometrics*, Harvard University Press, Cambridge, Mass.

American Textile Institute (1969), *Textile Hi-Lights* (Spring): 24.

(1971), *Textile Hi-Lights* (Spring): 25.

Arrow, K. J. (1972), "Models of Job Discrimination," in A. H. Pascal, ed., *Racial Discrimination in Economic Life*, Heath-Lexington, Lexington, . Mass.

Brown, C. (1984), "Black–White Earnings Ratios since the Civil Rights Act of 1964: The Importance of Labor Market Dropouts," *Quarterly Journal of Economics* 99, no. 1: 31–44.

Bunting, Robert L. (1962), *Employer Concentration in Local Labor Markets*, University of North Carolina Press, Chapel Hill.

Butler, R. J. (1983), "Direct Estimates of the Demand for Race and Sex Discrimination," *Southern Economic Journal* 49, no. 4: 975–90.

(1985), "Demand Side Changes and Relative Black Wage Growth in the 1960's," unpublished manuscript, Brigham Young University.

Butler, R. J., and J. J. Heckman (1977), "The Government's Impact on the Labor Market Status of Black Americans: A Critical Review," in L. J. Hausman, ed., *Equal Rights and Industrial Relations*, Industrial Relations Research Association, Madison, Wis.

Cleghorn, R. (1969), "The Mill: A Giant Step Forward for the Southern Negro," *New York Times Magazine*, November 9, 1969, pp. 34–156.

Cobb, J. C. (1982), *The Selling of the South: The Southern Crusade for Industrial Development 1936–1980*, Louisiana State University Press, Baton Rouge.

(1984), *Industrialization and Southern Society: 1877–1984*, University Press of Kentucky, Lexington.

Dewey, D. (1955), "4 Studies of Negro Employment in the Upper South," in C. Hoover and E. Palmer, eds., *Selected Studies of Negro Employment in the South*, National Planning Association, Washington, D.C., pp. 145–212.

Frederickson, M. (1982), "Four Decades of Change: Black Workers in Southern Textiles, 1941–1981," *Radical America* 16, no. 6 (November–December): 62–82.

Freeman, R. B. (1973), "Changes in the Labor Market for Black Americans," *Brookings Papers on Economic Activity* 1: 67–120.

(1981), "Black Economic Progress after 1964: Who Has Gained and Why?" in S. Rosen, ed., *Studies in Labor Markets*, University of Chicago Press, Chicago, pp. 247–94.

Friedman, M. (1962), *Capitalism and Freedom*, University of Chicago Press, Chicago.

Heckman, J., and B. Payner (1989), "Determining the impact of Federal Antidiscrimination Policy on the Economic Status of Blacks: A Study of South Carolina," *American Economic Review* 79 (March).

Hoffman, J. (1975), *Racial Discrimination and Economic Development*, Heath, Lexington, Mass.

Kidder, A. (1972), "Federal Compliance Efforts in the Carolina Textile Industry: A Summary Report," *Proceedings of the 25th Annual Meeting of the Industrial Relations Research Association*, pp. 353–61.

Kidder, A., Sidney Evans, Michael Simons, and DuPont Smith (1972), "Changes in Minority Participation in the Textile Industry of North Carolina and South Carolina 1966 to 1969," Department of Economics, North Carolina A & T, Greensboro.

Leamer, E. (1978), *Specification Searches: Ad Hoc Inference with Non-Experimental Data*, Wiley, New York.

Leamer, E., and H. B. Leonard (1983), "Reporting the Fragility of Regression Estimates," *Review of Economics and Statistics* 65 (May): 306–17.

Marr, J., and G. Williams (1973), *An Analysis of Civilian Labor Force and Civilian Employment Changes in South Carolina during the 1960's*, Occasional Studies no. 4, Bureau of Business and Economic Research, College of Business Administration, University of South Carolina, Columbia.

Murray, C. (1984), *Losing Ground*, Basic, New York.

Osburn, D. (1966), *Negro Employment in the Textile Industries of North and South Carolina*, Research Report, 1966–70 (November 21), Equal Employment Opportunity Commission, Washington, D.C.

Rowan, R. L. (1970), "The Negro in the Textile Industry," Part Five of H. Northrup, R. Rowan, D. Barnum, and J. Howard, eds., *Negro Employment in Southern Industry*, University of Pennsylvania Press, Philadelphia, pp. 1–172.

Smith, J. (1984), "Race and Human Capital," *American Economic Review* 74 (September): 685–98.

Smith, J., and F. Welch (1986), *Closing the Gap: Forty Years of Economic Progress for Blacks*, Rand Corporation, Santa Monica, Calif.

South Carolina, Department of Education (1931–57), *Annual Report of the State Superintendent of Education of the State of South Carolina*, Printed under the Direction of the State Budget and Control Board, Columbia.

South Carolina, Department of Labor (1910–36), *Reports and Resolutions of South Carolina to the General Assembly of the State of South Carolina*, Printed under the Direction of the State Budget and Control Board, Columbia.

(1936–77), *South Carolina Department of Labor Annual Report*, Printed under the Direction of the State Budget and Control Board, Columbia.

Sproat, J. (1986), " 'Firm Flexibility': Perspectives on Desegregation in South Carolina," in R. Abzug and S. Maizlish, eds., *New Perspectives on Race and Slavery in America*, Associated Presses of Kentucky, Lexington, pp. 164–84.

Tang, A. M. (1958), *Economic Development in the Southern Piedmont*, University of North Carolina Press, Chapel Hill.

Tobin, J. (1965), "On Improving the Economic Status of the Negro," *Daedalus* 94 (Fall): 878–98.

United States, Bureau of the Census (1943), *Census of Population: 1940*, vol. 2, *Characteristics of the Population*, part 6, U.S. Government Printing Office, Washington, D.C.

(1950), *Census of Manufactures: 1947*, vol. 3, *Statistics by the State*, U.S. Government Printing Office, Washington, D.C.

(1953), *Census of Population: 1950*, vol. 2, *Characteristics of the Population*, part 40, U.S. Government Printing Office, Washington, D.C.

(1961), *Census of Manufactures: 1954*, vol. 3, *Area Statistics*, U.S. Government Printing Office, Washington, D.C.

(1964), *Census of Population: 1960*, vol. 2, *Characteristics of the Population*, part 42, "South Carolina," U.S. Government Printing Office, Washington, D.C.

(1966), *Census of Manufactures: 1963*, vol. 3, *Area Statistics*, U.S. Government Printing Office, Washington, D.C.

(1971), *Census of Manufactures: 1967*, vol. 3, *Area Statistics*, part 2, U.S. Government Printing Office, Washington, D.C.

(1973a), *Census of Population: 1970*, vol. 1, *Characteristics of the Population*, part 1, "United States Summary – Section 1," U.S. Government Printing Office, Washington, D.C.

(1973b), *Census of Population: 1970*, vol. 1, *Characteristics of the Population*, part 42, "South Carolina," U.S. Government Printing Office, Washington, D.C.

(1973c), *Census of Population: 1960*, Public Use Microdata Sample [machine-readable data file], The Bureau [producer and distributor], Washington, D.C.

(1973d), *Census of Population: 1970*, Public Use Microdata Sample [machine-readable data file], The Bureau [producer and distributor], Washington, D.C.

(1973e), *Annual Survey of Manufactures: 1970 and 1971*. U.S. Government Printing Office, Washington, D.C.

(1983a), *1980 Census of Population*, vol. 1, chap. C, "General Social and Economic Characteristics," part 1, "U.S. Summary," U.S. Government Printing Office, Washington, D.C.

(1983b), *1980 Census of Population*, vol. 1, chap. C, "General Social and Economic Characteristics," part 42, "South Carolina," U.S. Government Printing Office, Washington, D.C.

(1983c), *Census of Population and Housing: 1980*, Public Use Microdata Sample (A and B Samples) [machine-readable data file], The Bureau [producer and distributor], Washington, D.C.

(1984a), *Census of Population: 1940*, Public Use Microdata Sample [machine-readable data file], The Bureau [producer and distributor], Washington, D.C.

(1984b), *Census of Population: 1950*, Public Use Microdata Sample [machine-readable data file], The Bureau [producer and distributor], Washington, D.C.

Commission on Civil Rights (1986), *The Economic Progress of Black Men*

Richard J. Butler, James J. Heckman, & Brook Payner

in America, U.S. Government Clearinghouse Publication 91, Washington, D.C.

Department of Defense, Directorate for Information, Operations and Reports (DIOR) (1980), *DOD Prime Contract Awards over $10,000 by State, County, Contractor and Place: Fiscal Years 1966 through 1980*, Department of Defense, Washington, D.C.

Vroman, W. (1974), "Changes in Black Workers' Relative Earnings: Evidence for the 1960's," in G. Von Furstenberg, ed., *Patterns of Racial Discrimination*, vol. 2, chap. 11, Heath–Lexington, Lexington, Mass.

Wallace, P., and M. Beckles (1966), *1966 Employment Survey in the Textile Industry of the Carolinas*, Research Report, 1966–11 (December 11), Equal Employment Opportunity Commission, Washington, D.C.

Welch, F. (1973), "Black–White Differences in the Return to Schooling," *American Economic Review*, 63 (December): 893–907.

White, H. (1980), "A Heteroskedasticity-Consistent Covariance Matrix Estimator and a Direct Test for Heteroskedasticity," *Econometrica* 48: 817–38.

Wilson, W. (1986), *The Truly Disadvantaged: Inner City, the Under Class and Public Policy*, University of Chicago Press, Chicago.

Wright, G. (1986), *Old South, New South*, Basic, New York.

346

Contributors

RICHARD J. BUTLER is Associate Professor of Economics at Brigham Young University.

LANCE E. DAVIS is Mary Stillman Harkness Professor of Social Science at California Institute of Technology and a Research Associate of the National Bureau of Economic Research. He has served as President of the Economic History Association. His publications include *The Savings Bank of Baltimore*, with Peter Payne (1956), *American Economic History: The Development of a National Economy*, with J. R. T. Hughes and D. McDougall (1961), *The Growth of Industrial Enterprise* (1964), *Institutional Change and American Economic Growth*, with Douglass North (1971), *American Economic Growth: An Economist's History of the United States*, with others (1971), and *Mammon and the Pursuit of Empire: The Political Economy of British Imperialism, 1860–1912*, with Robert Huttenback (1986).

DAVID W. GALENSON is Professor of Economics at the University of Chicago and a Research Associate of the National Bureau of Economic Research. His publications include *White Servitude in Colonial America: An Economic Analysis* (1981), and *Traders, Planters, and Slaves: Market Behavior in Early English America* (1986).

ROBERT E. GALLMAN is Kenan Professor of Economics and History at the University of North Carolina and a Research Associate of the National Bureau of Economic Research. He has served as President of the Economic History Association and the Southern Economic Association, and as editor of the *Southern Economic Journal* and the *Journal of Economic History*. His publications include *American Economic Growth: An Economist's History of the United States*, with others (1971), and *Long-Term Factors in American Economic Growth*, with others (1986).

JAMES J. HECKMAN is Henry Schultz Professor of Economics at the University of Chicago, A. Whitney Griswold Professor of Economics at Yale University, and a Research Associate of NORC. He received the John Bates Clark Medal from the American Economic Association in 1983. He is a fellow of the Econometric Society, and has served as editor of the *Journal of Political Economy*. His publications include *Longitudinal Analysis of Labor Market Data*, with Burton Singer (1985), and *Lecture Notes on Longitudinal Data*, with others (forthcoming).

TERESA D. HUTCHINS is a doctoral candidate in economics at the University of North Carolina.

ROBERT A. HUTTENBACK is Professor of History at the University of California, Santa Barbara, where he has also served as Chancellor. His publications include *The British Imperial Experience* (1966), *Gandhi in South Africa: British Imperialism and the Indian Question, 1860–1914* (1971), *Racism and Empire: White Colonists and Colored Immigrants in the British Empire of Settlement, 1830–1910* (1976), and *Mammon and the Pursuit of Empire: The Political Economy of British Imperialism, 1860–1912*, with Lance E. Davis (1986).

DONALD N. MCCLOSKEY is John F. Murray Professor of Economics and History at the University of Iowa. He has served as President of the Social Science History Association and as editor of the *Journal of Economic History*. His publications include *Economic Maturity and Entrepreneurial Decline: British Iron and Steel, 1870–1913* (1973), *Enterprise and Trade in Victorian Britain: Essays in Historical Economics* (1981), *The Applied Theory of Price* (1985), *The Rhetoric of Economics* (1986), *The Writing of Economics* (1986), and *Econometric History* (1987).

BROOK PAYNER is Vice-President of Citicorp, New York.

CLAYNE L. POPE is Karl Maeser Professor of General Education and Economics at Brigham Young University and a Research Associate of the National Bureau of Economic Research. His publications include *The Impact of the Ante-Bellum Tariff on Income Distribution* (1975) and *American Heritage: An Interdisciplinary Approach*, with others (1986).

THEODORE W. SCHULTZ is Charles L. Hutchinson Distinguished Service Professor Emeritus at the University of Chicago. He received the Francis A. Walker Medal from the American Economic Association in 1972 and the Nobel Prize for Economic Science in 1979. He has served as President of the American Economic Association. His publications include *Agriculture in an Unstable Economy* (1945), *The Economic Organization of Agriculture* (1953), *The Economic Value of Education* (1963), *Transforming Traditional Agriculture* (1964), *Economic Growth and Agriculture* (1968), *Investment in Human Capital: The Role of Education and of Research* (1971), and *Investing in People: The Economics of Population Quality* (1981).

Index

Africa, 195, 196, 217–18
age, income and wealth distribution
    (Utah in mid-1800s) and, 164–70, 182
*Agrarian History of England and Wales,
    The* (Bowden), 23
agricultural sector: black employment in
    South Carolina and, 241–42, 263, 264,
    268, 277, 278, 296; *see also* farming in
    strips
Allen, Robert, 20, 21–22
Asia, 195–96, 204, 217–18
Australia, 192, 203, 206, 209, 212

Baack, B. D., 30
Bayldon, J. S., 24
Beckles, M., 245
black economic status analysis (South
    Carolina): agricultural employment and,
    241–42, 263, 264, 268, 277, 278, 296;
    chemical industry and, 253, 259–60,
    296, 297, 332; civil rights and defense
    contracts and, 321, 326, 331; civil rights
    and employment and, 231, 234, 239,
    240, 247, 248, 249, 251, 317–28, 329;
    civil rights impact on, 271–77; data and,
    231–32, 235, 252–56, 330–39; data
    concerning education and, 279–305;
    data concerning industry and, 236, 307;
    data concerning manufacturing and,
    236, 262, 307; data concerning textile
    sector and, 236, 237–43, 244, 246, 247,
    256–61, 309; data concerning tight-
    labor-market hypothesis and, 305;
    discrimination and, 235, 240, 249, 250,
    271, 320; education and, 264, 269–71;
    education and black employment and,
    239, 244, 251, 267; education and data
    quality and quantity and, 279–305;
    education and wages and, 235; electrical
    and non-electrical machinery sector
    and, 253, 256; employment (1960–70)

and, 262–67, 269–71; employment and
community mores and, 247, 251–52;
employment and human capital
argument and, 244, 339–41;
employment and tight-labor-market
hypothesis and, 241, 247, 248, 305–17,
319; employment data and, 236–43,
244–51, 252–67; Equal Employment
Opportunity Commission and, 239, 240,
245, 249, 328; glass industry and, 259;
government employment and, 264, 296;
manufacturing and, 236, 262, 269–71,
278, 321; occupational shifts and, 234;
textile industry and, 263, 277; textile
industry and civil rights activity and,
236, 237–43, 244, 246, 247, 256–61, 309;
textile industry and schooling and, 279–
80, 296, 297; textile industry and tight-
labor-market hypothesis and, 305, 309,
315, 319; textile industry employment
and, 236, 237–43, 244, 246, 247, 256–
61, 309, 331–32; textile industry wages
and, 236–43, 245–46, 317, 319; training
programs and, 250–51; wages and, 232–
35, 236–43, 245–46, 252, 262, 271, 272,
317, 319; women and, 236, 239, 240,
246, 252, 274, 279, 280, 296, 297, 309,
317, 323
blacks, 154; *see also* slavery
Bloch, Marc, 35
Book of Husbandry (Fitzherbert), 13
bound servants, 53, 87; *see also* servants
    (indentured)
Bowden, Peter, 23
Brady, Dorothy, 3
British Guiana, 211
British Honduras, 207
Broad, John, 17
Brown, C., 271
budgets: family, 3; British Empire
    colonial, 215–22
Burma, 223, 225
Butler, R. J., 232, 271, 272

349

Canada, 190, 209, 210, 220, 221
capital: British Empire and movement of, 193–96; farming in strips and, 13, 48
Capital and Growth (Hicks), 2
Cassell and Company, Ltd., 220
Chambers, J. D., 9
chemical industry (South Carolina), 253, 259–60, 296, 297, 332
Churchill, Randolph, 211
civil rights activity (South Carolina): black employment and, 231, 234, 239, 240, 247, 248, 249, 251, 317–28, 329; defense contracts and, 321, 326, 331; impact of, 271–77
Clark, Gregory, 21, 27, 28, 43
Cleghorn, R., 251
Coase, Ronald, 26
Cohen, J. S., 30
commercial policy of British Empire, *see* government expenditures (British Empire during 1860–1912 period)
Company of Royal Adventurers (slave trade), 69
Connecticut, 94
consumption, 152, 153, 155, 169
convict labor, 64–65
corporal punishment (indentured servants), 56–57
Curti, Merle, 180
Cyprus, 217
Czechoslovakia, 11

Dahlman, Carl, 28
Davidson, W., 213
Davis, Thomas, 16
Delaware, 76
Design of Experiments, The (Fisher), 39
Dewey, Donald, 244–45
Dias, Joseph, 111–12, 122, 125, 139
diets (medieval), 29–30
discrimination: employment and, 235, 240, 249, 250, 320; wages and, 271; *see also* black economic status analysis (South Carolina)
disease in colonial America, 55
dissavings, 169, 170
Dovring, Folke, 11

Earl of Rosebery, 225
earnings, *see* wages
East India Company, 202
economic status analysis of blacks in South Carolina, *see* black economic status analysis (South Carolina)
education: black economic status and, 235, 239, 244, 251, 267, 279–305; British Empire and, 204, 211–12; income

distribution (Utah in mid-1800s) and, 166, 186; training program (government) and, 250–51
electrical and non-electrical machinery sector (South Carolina), 253, 256
Ellis, John R., 16, 18
employment (black economic status analysis): agricultural sector and, 241–42, 263, 264, 268, 277, 278, 296; black economic status improvement and, 269–71; black occupational and wage improvement (1960–70) and, 262–67; civil rights activity and, 231, 234, 239, 240, 247, 248, 249, 251, 271–77, 317–28, 329; community mores and black, 247, 251–52; data on textile industry and, 236–43, 244–51; data quality and, 252–67; human capital argument and, 244, 339–41; tight-labor-market hypothesis and, 241, 247, 248, 305–17, 319
enclosure, *see* farming in strips
Engel, Ernst, 3
Engerman, Stanley, 165
Equal Employment Opportunity Commission, 239, 240, 245, 249, 328

Faith, Rosamund, 32
Falkland Islands, 207, 214
family: budgets of, 3; income and wealth distribution (Utah in mid-1800s) and, 154, 173–79, 186–87, 188
farming in strips: average holdings in, 8; common fields and, 30–34; enclosure and, 9–10, 12–13, 13–21, 49–50, 51; features of, 5–12; field drainage and, 49; fragmentations of land into strip holdings and, 5–6; grazing land and, 10, 28–29, 30–31; inefficiency and, 12–13, 22–25; joint plowing and, 26–27; land consolidation and, 10–11; land market and, 30–34; legal strips and, 7–8; livestock and, 28–29; missing market as explanation of, 25–34; open fields and, 10, 20, 21, 26, 30–34, 48–51; origin of system of, 8–9; present-day conditions and, 11–12; rents and, 13–21, 50; risk aversion and, 34–46, 49; storage of grain and, 46–48; tenents and, 6, 7, 13–14, 27; virgates (land measures) and, 6–7; yields and, 12–13, 22–25, 37–38
federal civil rights activity, *see* civil rights activity (South Carolina)
Fellows, John, 16
felons as scrvants (colonial America), 64–65; *see also* servants (indentured)
Fenoaltea, Stefano, 27
Fisher, R. A., 39

Fitzherbert, Master, 13
Fogel, Robert, 165
Forde, C. Daryll, 35–36
Fowler, George, 33
France, 10, 11
Frederickson, M., 251
Freeman, R. B., 271

Georgia, 66, 76
General View of the County X, A (Board of Agriculture, England), 15
Germany, 9, 10, 11
Gibraltar, 207, 214, 217
glass industry (South Carolina), 259
Gonner, E. C. K., 9
government employment (South Carolina), 264, 296
government expenditures (British Empire during 1860–1912 period): business and, 201–15; capital movement and, 193–96; commercial policy analysis conclusions and, 223–29; defining empire and, 190–92; dependent colonies and, 190, 203, 204, 207, 213, 214, 215, 222; direct support of business and, 203, 212–15; domestic economy and, 195, 198, 200; East India Company and, 202; exploitation and, 199; financial ties to empire and, 192; human capital and, 203–04, 210–12; independent colonies and, 190–91, 214, 222; investment and elites and, 226–27; investment rate of return and, 192, 197–201; investment structure overseas and, 192, 219; legal system and, 202, 203, 206–07; political economy of empire and, 192–93; political manipulation of colonial budgets and, 202, 203, 204, 215–22; public works and, 203, 207–10; Royal Niger Company and, 202; science and, 203–04
grain, analysis of farming in strips and, 19, 28–29, 46–48, 49
Gray, H. L., 7
Greece, 11

Hardin, Garrett, 30
Hatcher, J., 29
Heckman, J. J., 271
Hegarty, Reginald B., 111
Herlihy, David, 51
Hicks, John, 2
historical economics: defining, 1–2; doctoral instruction and, 2; main task of, 2–3; theory and, 3–4
Hoben, Alan, 36
Hoffman, J., 250–51, 315, 321

Holland, 11
Holt, John, 209, 223
Homer, Henry, 14
Hong Kong, 214
Hueckel, Glenn, 23
human capital, 3; black economic status analysis and, 244, 339–41; British Empire and, 203–04, 210–12; India and, 211, 212; productivity peak and schooling and, 166

income: family budgets and, 3; farming in strips and, 13, 25–26, 37, 38, 49
income distribution (Utah in mid-1800s): age and, 164–70, 182; birthplace and, 154, 170–71, 173; church records (Mormon) and, 150, 156–58; data and, 150, 152, 155–58; duration of stay in Utah and, 172; economic structure of early Utah and, 158–60; estimates of early settler, 148–49, 150; family and, 154, 173–79, 186–87, 188; income analysis and, 152–53; inequality trends and, 152, 160–64; luck and, 155, 185–88; occupational choice and, 169, 179, 180–83, 184, 185; occupations and, 158–59; residential choice and, 154–55, 169, 183–85; settlement process and, 150–52, 158; *see also* wealth distribution (Utah in mid-1800s)
indentured servants, *see* servants (indentured)
India, 190, 195, 224, 226; capital flows to, 196; direct commercial support (lack of) and, 213–14; human capital expenditures and, 211, 212; legal system and, 207; public works in, 209–10; strip farming and, 12; transport in, 196
Indonesia, 12
inefficiency, analysis of farming in strips and, 12–13, 22–25
interest rates, 48
investment (British Empire analysis): elites and, 226–27; rate of return and, 192, 197–201; structure of overseas, 192, 219
Ireland, 12

Jamestown (Virginia), 52–54
Japan, 12
Jencks, Christopher, 153

Kidder, A., 247–48, 249–50, 251
King, Gregory, 28, 93
Korea, 12
Kosminsky, E. A., 7

labor: farming in strips and, 13, 27, 29;
  tight-labor-market hypothesis (black
  economic status analysis) and, 241, 247,
  248, 305–17, 319; whaling and, 113,
  116, 123
labor–leisure choices, 152
labor market (colonial America): bound
  servants and, 53, 87; convict labor and,
  64–65; free labor, 56, 84–95;
  Jamestown and, 52–54; service in
  husbandry and, 87–92; *see also* servants
  (indentured); slavery
land: as fixed asset, 153; held by early
  Utah settlers, 149, 160–61, 180; *see also*
  farming in strips
Latter-day Saints (LDS); *see* Mormons
  (Latter-day Saints, LDS)
Lawrence, John, 209, 210, 224
Leamer, Edward, 272, 274
leases (agricultural land), 19, 22
legal system (British Empire), 202, 203,
  206–07
Leicestershire (Pitt), 19
Loder, Robert, 40
luck, 155, 185–88

Maitland, F. W., 33, 50
Malay, 214
Malta, 211, 214, 217
manufacturing sector (South Carolina),
  236, 262, 269–71, 278, 321
marriage (indentured servants), 67
Marshall, William, 14
Maryland: indentured servants in, 60, 62–
  63, 65; slavery and, 76, 78, 79, 81, 83
Mauritius, 211, 214
Melville, Herman, 98–99
Miller, E., 29
Modigliani, Franco, 3
monopoly, 201
Morier, Robert, 225
Mormons (Latter-day Saints, LDS), 164;
  church records and, 150, 156–58, 161–
  63; economic structure of Utah (mid-
  1800s) and, 158; income inequality and,
  161; settlement of Utah and, 148, 149–
  50, 151; tithing and, 156–57, 161–63;
mortality rates: colonial, 59, 85; of slaves
  on ships, 71–72, 73; Utah in mid-1800s
  and, 164
Murray, C., 235

nativity (birthplace), income and wealth
  distribution and, 154, 170–71, 173
New Bedford whalers, *see* whaling
  productivity analysis

Newfoundland, 190
New Jersey, 76
New York, 76
New Zealand, 192, 195, 206, 210, 211, 214
Nordhoff, Charles, 137
North Carolina, 76

occupational choices (Utah in mid-1800s),
  169, 179, 180–83, 184, 185
occupational shifts (South Carolina),
  234
occupations (Utah in mid-1800s), 158–59
open fields, *see* farming in strips
Osburn, D., 245–46, 247
output, farming in strips and, 12–13, 22–
  25, 37–38

Pakistan, 12
Parain, Charles, 27
Pennsylvania, 63, 66, 76, 86, 94,
Pitt, W., 15, 19
planters (colonial America): indentured
  servants and, 55–56, 66; slavery and,
  75–76, 78, 79, 80–83
Poland, 11
politics (British Empire analysis), 192–93,
  202, 203, 204, 215–22
polygyny, 149, 158, 177
Portugal, 11
Postan, M. M., 31
productivity, *see* slavery, productivity and;
  whaling productivity analysis; yields,
  farming in strips and
property values (Utah in mid-1800s), 148–
  49
public works (British Empire), 203, 207–
  10

railroads, 207, 209, 210, 223, 224
rate of return to investment in Empire, *see*
  investment (British Empire analysis)
Reid, Margaret, 3
rent, 179; economic growth and
  agricultural land, 3; farming in strips
  and, 13–21, 22, 23, 24, 50; income and
  age and, 169–70; income and duration
  of stay in Utah and, 158–59; income
  and earning variances and, 153–54
residential choice (Utah in mid-1800s),
  154–55, 169, 183–85
risk aversion, farming in strips and, 34–46,
  49
Rogers, J. E. Thorold, 47
Rowan, Richard, 246–47
Royal African Company (slave trade), 69–
  75
Royal Niger Company, 202

Russia, 9, 11, 201
Rutland (Parkinson), 20

St. Helena, 214
Scammon, Charles M., 122
Schumpeter, Joseph, 3, 192
science, 203–04
SEARCH computer program (black economic status analysis), 272–74, 333–39
Seebohm, Frederic, 26
servants (indentured): accomplishments of freed, 62–63; contracts and, 58–61, 87, 88; corporal punishment and, 56–57; cost (debt) for passage and, 56, 58, 61, 67–68; felons as, 64–65; hired labor in preindustrial England and, 56; as landowners, 62; length of servitude and, 58–60, 61, 62; marriage and, 67; in New England colonies, 86–87; number of, 60, 64, 78, 79, 81; planters and, 55–56, 66; private merchants and, 57–58; replacement of (by slaves), 79–83; sale price of, 61–62; stages of use of, 65–68; wages and, 57, 59; work incentives and, 57
ships: passage of indentured servants and, 56, 58, 61, 67–68; slavery and, 71–73, 74; whaling and, 106–07, 119–20, 120–21, 124, 128, 129, 130, 136, 138; whaling crews and, 107–09, 113, 123, 133–34, 136, 137; whaling voyage length and distances and, 104–05, 137; whaling voyage transhipment points and, 123–24, 129, 136
Siam, 207, 211
Slater, Gilbert, 9
slavery, 65, 66, 92; auctions and, 75; background on transatlantic trade and, 68–69; children as slaves and, 74; competition in trade and, 71; English American colonies and, 76, 77–84, 85, 86; number of slaves and, 78, 79–80; planters and, 75–76, 78, 79, 80–83; prices of slaves and, 74, 75; productivity and, 165; replacement of indentured servant labor system by, 79–83; Royal African Company and, 69–75; seasonality of trade in, 73; selection of slaves (in Africa) and, 74–75; transportation conditions (slaving ships) and, 71–73; transportation costs and, 74; Utah and, 166; in West Indies, 74–77, 83
Smith, J., 232, 234–35
South Carolina, 66, 76, 77; *see also* black economic status analysis (South Carolina)

Sproat, J., 251
Staffordshire (Pitt), 15
Starbuck, Alexander, 111, 113
sugar industry, 76, 86
Swann, Brenda, 17–18
Sweden, 10

Taiwan, 12
Tang, A. M., 307
Tanzania, 12
tenants (strip farm), 6, 7, 13–14
textile industry (South Carolina), 263, 277; civil rights activity and, 236, 237–43, 244, 246, 247, 256–61, 309; employment data and, 236, 237–43, 244, 246, 247, 309, 331–32; employment data quality and, 256–61; schooling and, 279–80, 296, 297; tight-labor-market hypothesis and, 305, 309, 315, 319; wages in, 236–43, 245–46, 317, 319; women and, 236, 239, 240, 246, 309, 317
Thailand, 12
Thernstrom, Stephan, 180
Thirsk, Joan, 8
Thomas, John W., 34
Thomas, R. P., 30
tight-labor-market hypothesis, *see* labor
tithing (Mormons), 156–57, 161–63
tobacco growing: indentured servants and, 55, 60, 63; slavery and, 77–78
Tonga, 214
Tower, Walter S., 113
Trow-Smith, Robert, 28–29
Turner, Michael, 9, 16

Union of South Africa, 192
United States, 195, 201, 209, 220, 222
Utah, *see* income distribution (Utah in mid-1800s); wealth distribution (Utah in mid-1800s)

villages, historical account of English, 6
Vinogradoff, Paul, 26, 33
Virginia: indentured servants in, 60, 65, 86; slavery, in, 76, 77, 78
Virginia Company, 52–54, 55, 56, 57
Voelcker, J. A., 39
Vroman, W., 232

wages: black economic status analysis and, 232–35, 236–43, 245–46, 252, 262, 271, 272, 317, 319; colonial free labor and, 88, 89, 92–93; indentured servants and 57, 59; whaling vessel crews and, 109, 123, 133–34, 136

Wallace, P., 245
Walton, J. R., 18
water, income distribution in Utah
 (mid-1800s) and, 150
Watson, Margaret, 258
wealth distribution (Utah in mid-1800s),
 155; age pattern and, 169–70; birthplace
 and, 154, 171, 173; church records
 (Mormon) and, 150, 156–58; duration
 of stay in Utah and, 172; family and,
 176–78, 186–87, 188; inequality and,
 152, 160–64; initial levels of, 148–49;
 mean normal, 159; occupational choice
 and, 182–83; residential choice and,
 184–85; settlement and, 148–49, 151–
 52; *see also* income distribution
 (Utah in mid-1800s)
Wealth of Nations, The (Smith), 70
Wedge, John, 16
Weitzman, M. L., 30
Welch, F., 232, 234–35
West Indies, 59, 60, 63, 66, 85, 86; slavery
 in, 74–77, 83
whaling productivity analysis: data sample
 representativeness and, 124–25;
 equations and variables and interaction
 terms (industry statistical results) and,
 124–34; historical background on
 whaling and, 98–111; hunting grounds
 for whales and, 118–19; industry
 analysis conclusions and, 134–37; labor
 competition and, 123; labor data and,
 113, 116; overhunting and, 128–29;
 price data and, 113; productivity data
 sources and, 111–13; productivity
 indexes and, 113–16; productivity
 influences analysis and, 116–24;

productivity time variable and, 124, 130,
 134; profits and, 109–11; resupply and
 transshipment points and, 123–24, 129,
 136; spermaceti and, 101; sperm oil and,
 101, 109, 114, 116, 135; technical
 innovation and, 97, 99, 121–22, 130–32;
 vessel age and, 121; vessel crews and,
 107–09, 113, 123, 133, 137; vessel
 design advances and, 122; vessel rigs
 and, 119–20; vessels transferred to
 whaling fleet and, 120–21, 129; vessel
 tonnage and, 124; vessel types and,
 106–07, 119–20, 130, 136, 138; voyage
 distances and, 115; voyage length and,
 104–05, 137; wages of crews and, 109,
 123, 133–34, 136; whalebone (baleen)
 and, 102, 103, 109, 114, 116, 118, 134;
 "whalecraft" (whaling implements) and,
 122, 131, 142–47; whale oil and,
 101–02, 102–03, 109, 114, 116, 118, 135;
 whale stocks and, 101, 103–04, 114,
 115, 117, 128–29, 137–42; whale types
 and, 101, 114, 118, 130, 137; whaling
 agents and, 98, 107, 125, 136, 137;
 whaling ports and, 105–06
Winthrop, John, 92
women, 274, 323; civil rights activities
 and, 309, 317; data and, 252; education
 and, 279, 280, 296, 297; textile sector
 and, 236, 239, 240, 246, 309, 317
Wright, G., 235

yields, farming in strips and, 12–13,
 22–25, 37–38
Young, Arthur, 15, 20

Printed in the United States
By Bookmasters